Dr. Hergenröther

Anti-Janus

An historico-theological criticism of the work entitled ``The Pope and the Council``

Dr. Hergenröther

Anti-Janus

An historico-theological criticism of the work entitled ``The Pope and the Council``

ISBN/EAN: 9783742893987

Manufactured in Europe, USA, Canada, Australia, Japa

Cover: Foto ©ninafisch / pixelio.de

Manufactured and distributed by brebook publishing software
(www.brebook.com)

Dr. Hergenröther

Anti-Janus

ANTI-JANUS:

AN HISTORICO-THEOLOGICAL CRITICISM OF THE WORK,

ENTITLED

"THE POPE AND THE COUNCIL,"

By JANUS.

BY

Dr HERGENRÖTHER,

PROFESSOR OF CANON LAW AND OF ECCLESIASTICAL HISTORY AT THE
UNIVERSITY OF WÜRZBURG.

Author of the "Life, Writings, and Times of the Patriarch Photius."

TRANSLATED FROM THE GERMAN
BY

J. B. ROBERTSON, Esq.,

PROFESSOR OF MODERN HISTORY AND ENGLISH LITERATURE AT THE
CATHOLIC UNIVERSITY, DUBLIN,

*Author of "Lectures on Modern History and Secret Societies,"
Life and Times of Edmund Burke," Translator of Möhler's "Symbolism,"
and of Schlegel's "Lectures on the Philosophy of History."*

WITH AN INTRODUCTION BY HIM,
GIVING A HISTORY OF GALLICANISM FROM THE REIGN OF LOUIS XIV.
DOWN TO THE PRESENT TIME.

DUBLIN:
W. B. KELLY, 8 GRAFTON STREET.
LONDON: BURNS, OATES, & COMPANY;
AND SIMPKIN, MARSHALL, & CO.
NEW YORK: THE CATHOLIC PUBLISHING SOCIETY,
9 WARREN STREET.
1870.

To

The Very Rev. Dr Russell,

President of St Patrick's College, Maynooth,

This Translation

Is inscribed,

As a mark of personal regard,

As a

Slight token of admiration for his virtues and talents, and of

thankfulness for many acts of kindness received,

by his obliged Friend,

THE TRANSLATOR.

CONTENTS.

CHAP.		PAGE
	TRANSLATOR'S INTRODUCTION,	v
	NOTES TO INTRODUCTION,	xlv
I.	THE FIVE ARTICLES IN THE "ALLGEMEINE ZEITUNG,"	1
II.	THE FIVE ARTICLES IN THE "AUGSBURG GAZETTE," AND THEIR NEW EDITION,	15
III.	MAKING THE SYLLABUS DOGMATIC,	27
IV.	THE DOCTRINE OF PAPAL INFALLIBILITY,	50
V.	ALLEGED ERRORS AND CONTRADICTIONS OF THE POPES,	74
VI.	THE PRIMACY AND THE PAPACY,	94
VII.	THE PRIMACY AND ITS DEVELOPMENT,	108
VIII.	ROMAN FORGERIES,	144
IX.	A GLANCE AT COUNCILS,	186
X.	THE POPEDOM IN HISTORY,	217
XI.	THE CHURCH, THE DOGMA, AND THE NEW COUNCIL,	240
XII.	THE RESULTS OF JANUS,	263
	APPENDIX,	287

INTRODUCTION.

BY THE TRANSLATOR.

THE German work, of which an English translation is here offered to the public, appeared about six months ago. Its author is Professor of Ecclesiastical History and Canon Law at the University of Würzburg, in Bavaria, and has earned a great reputation by a most learned and elaborate history of the life, writings, and times of the founder of the Greek schism, the Patriarch Photius. Dr Hergenröther was one of the German divines who, at the invitation of his Holiness Pope Pius IX., took part in the preparatory labours of one of the theological Commissions, that preceded the assembling of the present Œcumenical Council. The work now presented to the British public, I leave to the appreciation of the reader. But I think the Catholics of these countries will agree that, with the exception, perhaps, of some writings of Father Bottalla, no treatise in our language contains such a mass of patristic evidence for the prerogatives of the Papacy. The doctrine of Papal Infallibility, which, at the time the author wrote this Reply to Janus, was not yet defined as a dogma, is here rather defended against the captious objections of that book, than put forward in its full objective truth. It is, however, more or less implied throughout his work. But his main concern, besides a defence of the rights and prerogatives of the Holy See, is the refutation of the many historical misrepresentations and calumnies, which his adversary has poured forth against the Papacy. He tracks him through his long labyrinth of falsehood and sophistry, exposes his many inconsistencies, places in a true light the facts he has misrepresented, and shows how his fanatical attacks on Papal Infallibility recoil on the doctrine of Papal Supremacy, which he professes to believe, and even on the authority of the Church herself.

In the Latin, French, German, and Italian languages, there are classical works in defence of the dogma of Papal Infallibility. But such a mass of historical objections, supported by such an array of learning as Janus, however confusedly, has brought to bear upon this doctrine, required a special refutation. And such it has found in the present work; and as this is its peculiar feature, so it will impart to this production, I think, a permanent interest. In the execution of his task, the author has displayed a rare acuteness of mind, as well as an extraordinary acquaintance with the fathers, the schoolmen, the canon law, and the records of civil and ecclesiastical history.

Of Janus it is needless to speak. Severely censured by all the German prelates assembled last year at Fulda, and placed on the Roman Index, it has called forth the reprobation, and excited the disgust, of all true Catholics. It is not only a schismatical, but an heretical, and, in some respects, even an impious book. It has nothing, indeed, so shockingly outrageous as the declaration of the old Protestant Book of Homilies, "That for

Introduction.

eight hundred years Christendom was plunged in damnable idolatry." But is it much less impious to say with Janus, that though Christ our Lord founded a Church, and instituted a visible Head, and promised, "That the Holy Spirit should abide with that Church for ever, and lead her into all truth;" yet that, in despite of that solemn promise, "the action of the head had paralysed the body, that that head had become a choking excrescence," and thus the designs of the Divine Founder of the Church had been frustrated? In despite of the promise of the perpetual indwelling of the Holy Spirit, the old Jansenistic theory of an obscuration prevalent in the Church for many centuries, has been revived by this writer.

It would be too painful to believe that a celebrated scholar and divine, who has rendered such eminent services to religion, should, in his old age, have taken part in a work so scandalous and afflicting to all Catholics. Strong as the circumstantial evidence is said to be as to his share in the authorship of this odious book, and blamable as are some of his acknowledged recent writings, savouring too much of the spirit of Janus; yet, as long as it is possible, I would fain acquit him of the charge. His culpable silence under the grave imputation has been censured by one of the most eminent prelates of Germany, Dr Ketteler, Bishop of Mayence; and the Archbishop of Cologne has declared that not a single German bishop approves of his late proceedings. How different a position did he occupy in 1848, when, with the sanction of the whole German prelacy, he defended, in the Parliament assembled at Frankfort, the interests of religion and of social order!

During my abode in Germany I had the honour of his acquaintance; and, like others, I found him a most kind-hearted man and an excellent clergyman. He was then one of an illustrious group of writers, such as Görres, Möhler (too soon, alas! carried off), Phillips, Jarcke, Windischmann, Moy, Höfler, Arndts, Hermann Müller, the younger Görres, and others, carrying on a great historical and political periodical, the noblest in Germany, and which our *Protestant Quarterly Review* once called "a most powerful journal"—I mean the *Historisch-Politische Blätter* of Munich. Most of its then contributors are now no more; but all their survivors, except himself, have remained faithful to their religious and political principles; while the journal itself, as I am informed, retains its pure Catholic spirit, as well as high literary reputation. The clergyman I speak of, is not, and never was, what his flatterers call him, "the first theologian of the age;" for he has not the philosophic cast of mind necessary to constitute a theologian of the highest order. But he is, nevertheless, a writer of great sagacity, wonderful critical acumen, and vast and varied learning. Let us hope and pray that he will remain true to the Church, and to the principles he for so many years professed, and that he will not be of the number of those who, in the evening of life, forfeit, alas! the hard-earned wages of their morning and their noonday toil!

It did not enter into the plan of the author of the present work to treat the doctrine of Papal Infallibility in its practical bearings. Nor in the many letters and pamphlets which this question has recently called forth, or which at least have fallen under my notice, does this part of the subject seem to have been discussed. And as many Protestants believe, that by the recent Definition of the Vatican Council, the liberty of particular Churches will be seriously restricted; and as some

Introduction.

ill-informed Catholics have a vague apprehension on that head; it will be my object, in the first part of this Introduction, to show the freedom which what is called the Ultramontane system insures to all Churches, and, on the contrary, the heavy servitude which the Gallican error imposes on those ecclesiastical communities which have accepted it. This fact I will illustrate by a rapid sketch of the state of the French Church in the eighteenth century.

In the second part, I will endeavour to trace the various causes that produced, in the early part of this century, the anti-Gallican reaction, the gradual renovation of opinion which then ensued in the Church of France, and which, under the direction of the Holy Spirit, has been so instrumental in bringing about that Definition of Papal inerrancy, that has carried consolation and gladness from the centre to the remotest parts of the Church.

I. The Papacy is a central, but not a centralizing institution. It tolerates a variety of customs, usages, and privileges in local churches; and even where there is an imperious necessity, or there has been a long prescription, it admits a diversity of rites and languages in the celebration of the liturgy itself. Its object is to give to national churches as much freedom as is compatible with the preservation of religious unity. Hence the Holy See encourages the annual meeting of diocesan synods, and the periodical celebration of provincial councils. It is the vigilant guardian of all ecclesiastical rights, whether of the bishops, or of the inferior clergy, secular and regular. It ever strenuously resists the encroachments of the civil power on the spiritual rights and jurisdiction of the bishops, as well as on their temporal privileges and property. The religious liberties of the sovereign Pontiff, of the bishops, the inferior clergy, and of the laity, are all indissolubly bound up together.

"The Catholic Church," as Cardinal Bellarmine observes, "is not an absolute monarchy, but one tempered by aristocracy and democracy." "The Papal power," says the eminent German canonist, Professor Walter, whose work on ecclesiastical jurisprudence is much approved of at Rome—"the Papal power is by no means absolute and arbitrary in its exercise, but on all sides bound and attempered by the spirit and the practice of the Church, by the consciousness of the duties annexed to Pontifical rights, by respect for Œcumenical Councils, by regard for ancient observances and customs, by the mild forms of the ecclesiastical government, by the recognized rights of the Episcopate, by the consequent distribution of functions, by the relations with the secular powers; lastly, by the spirit of nations.*" So the constitution of the Catholic Church leaves no room for the exercise of arbitrary power. Where the canons are in force, and except in cases of extreme emergency, the Pope cannot deprive a bishop of his see, nor the bishop a rector of his cure, without a regular canonical trial. Thus not only does the Church in regard to the State preserve her spiritual autonomy; but all the orders of her hierarchy freely move in their respective spheres, and guided by a central power, act in harmonious co-operation. When heresy strives to disturb that harmony, the Holy Spirit, that watches over the Church, soon banishes discord from her bosom.

But let that great central authority, here spoken of, be once weakened; then immediately disorder and perturbation arise in the Church. If the doctrinal Infallibility of the Holy See be once denied

---

* Manuel du Droit ecclesiastique, Trad. Française, p. 170.

in any portion of the Church, there its action becomes enfeebled, and the whole framework of that local church becomes more or less disjointed. If the prelates and the clergy of the second order take up an attitude of critical distrust towards the bishop of bishops, then the laity gradually lose much of their reverence for the Apostolic See, and for the Episcopate itself; and civil governments assail the spiritual rights of both. For there is a close inter-communion between the mother and the daughters—between the Roman and the subject churches.

The truth of the remarks here made received a sad illustration in the history of the Gallican Church during the eighteenth century. The French Episcopate of that age displayed, on the whole, a loyal devotion to the Holy See; and this is the main reason, as the distinguished Archbishop of Malines well observes, why the Gallican error was so long tolerated, or at least remained without express censure. The real representatives of Gallicanism were the magistrates, or the members of the French Parliaments. These, imbued with the despotic principles of the Roman jurisprudence, and partially tainted with Jansenism, sought by every means, whether by chicanery or by violence, to domineer over the Church of France. In the Articles of the Assembly of 1682, subscribed by a minority of French bishops, they found a weapon ready-made to their hands. Even in the reign of Louis XIV., who kept this corporation in check, Bossuet had occasion to say, "That the magistrates understood the maxims of the Church of France in a sense very different from her bishops." * Fleury, a still more ardent stickler for

* Vie de Bossuet par Cardinal Bausset, vol. iv. Lettre au Cardinal d'Estrées, Decembre 1681.

those opinions, and who long survived the Bishop of Meaux, lived to confess, "That the liberties of the Gallican Church had better be called its servitudes."* And Fénélon, ever strongly opposed to the Gallican system, ventured even to say, "That, in his time, the King of France was nearly as much master of the Church in that kingdom, as the King of England of the Anglican communion." † And though this expression is doubtless hyperbolical; yet it shows to what fearful lengths the civil power had already carried its encroachments!

The recent work of M. Gérin ‡ has thrown great light on all the transactions which preceded, accompanied, and followed the Ecclesiastical Assembly of 1682. We there see what artifices and intimidation the French Government resorted to in order to bring about a declaration, designed to humble the Sovereign Pontiff, and to insure to the State a certain domination over the Church. The great Bossuet, who took a prominent part in this Assembly, was, in the course he pursued, influenced by motives of a twofold kind. On the one hand, he feared to incur the displeasure of Louis XIV. ; for this great man, with all his virtues and genius, had (as the Abbé de la Mennais once said), a certain courtly weakness,—"une certaine faiblesse de cour;" § and, on the other hand, he dreaded to see the Church of France, through the violence of some prelates, like the Bishop of Tournai, precipitated into a schism. Under the

---

* Les Opuscules de Fleury.
† Lettre de Fénélon, cited by the Abbé de la Mennais in his work entitled, "De la Religion considerée dans ses rapports avec l'ordre civil et politique." Elsewhere he says, "In France the King is practically more head of the Church than the Pope," Œuvres, t. xxii., p. 586.
‡ L'Assemblée de 1682. Par M. Charles Gérin. Paris, 1869.
§ See Note A.

influence of these diverse motives, he steered a middle course between the doctrine of Papal inerrancy on the one hand, and the danger of a schismatical rupture with the Holy See on the other.

Since the times of the Council of Constance, the opinion as to the superiority of the Council over the Pope had been occasionally ventilated in the schools of the Sorbonne. This opinion was not shared by the majority of the Episcopate, and by the great body of the clergy. This is proved by the numerous assemblies of the French clergy in 1626, 1653, and 1654, where the inerrancy of the dogmatic decisions of the Holy See was solemnly proclaimed. Cardinal Duperron defended Papal Infallibility against a doctor of the Sorbonne, Edmund Richer, who went so far as to say, that the Pope was a mere ministerial head of the Church, and that to the whole Church, and even to the laity, was committed, by the ordinance of Christ, the power of the keys. When Richer himself expressed his willingness to retract his heterodox opinions, he was required by Cardinal Richelieu to acknowledge not only the supremacy, but the infallibility of the Holy See in matters of faith.

The Declaration of 1682 was not passed unanimously by the twenty-six bishops assembled on the occasion.* It was opposed, too, by many of the bishops and of the dignified clergy throughout the kingdom, as well as by the various theological Faculties, including the far greater part of the doctors of the Sorbonne, and the most pious and learned divines. From all the bishops and priests, who had taken part in this assembly, and who were

* The great Fénélon and the learned oratorian Thomassin, by their writings, opposed the Declaration.

afterwards nominated or promoted to episcopal sees, Pope Innocent XI. before he would give them institution, required a retractation of their acts. Pope Alexander VIII., in his last illness, summoned the cardinals around him, called Heaven to witness that he protested against the Declaration of 1682, and pronounced its articles null and void. At the same time the Churches of Spain and of Hungary put forth most energetic protests against the same Declaration.

After the lapse of ten years, Louis XIV. made his peace with the Holy See, and suspended the execution of the obnoxious edict, whereby he had made it incumbent on all Professors of Theology in his kingdom to subscribe the Four Articles. Bossuet, in the meantime, was constantly engaged in retouching his defence of the Declaration of 1682, entitled "Defensio Declarationis Cleri Gallicani," and in making the work approximate more to the Roman doctrines. In his last illness, he enjoined his executors never to let the book be published. But this injunction was violated by his Jansenist nephew, the Abbé Bossuet, who, twenty-six years after his uncle's death, brought out the work; and, as Dr Döllinger thinks highly probable,* suppressed the various emendations which his great relative had from time to time made.

On the death of Louis XIV., however, the above-named edict, whose execution had been suspended by that monarch, was revived by the Government of the Regent Philip, and strictly enforced by the Parliaments. Henceforth the Four Gallican Articles became a terrible engine of oppression against the Church of France. We have heard the complaints, which, even in the reign of Louis XIV., Bossuet, and Fleury, and

* See Kirchen-Lexicon, art. Bossuet, Freiburg, 1850.

Fénélon had made of those articles, as most subversive of the freedom of the Gallican Church. If such had been the language of those great men even at that time, what words would have expressed their sorrow and indignation, could they have beheld the workings of the Gallican system, and the evils it entailed on the Church of France during the eighteenth century! What a sense of grief and shame would have overpowered them, could they have beheld Episcopal charges and Papal bulls burned in the name of the Gallican liberties by the hands of the public executioner, and at the bidding of the Paris Parliament! Nay, more, the orthodox clergy forced by the mandates of that body to carry amid a guard of soldiers the last Sacraments to the dying Jansenists! What, too, would have been their feelings, could they have beheld the facility with which, entrenched behind these Four Articles, Jansenism so long eluded the censures of the Holy See, and defied the authority of the bishops! In the course of the last century, the Jansenists, while they kept more out of view their peculiar doctrines on Grace, were distinguished for the craftiness, as well as violence, wherewith they resisted the ecclesiastical authorities. And in this warfare they found a weapon ready furnished to their hands in the Gallican maxims. Hence an eminent prelate, Mgr. Gerbet, in his early days, once observed to me, "That it is very difficult to know where Gallicanism ends, and where Jansenism begins;" and this was particularly true of the more violent Gallicans, whose hierarchical views were so akin to those of the Jansenists. The sympathy, too, which the infidel party of the last century, as well as of the present, has ever evinced for the too famous maxims of

1682, is a circumstance calculated to make the deepest impression on the mind of a reflecting Catholic.

When the Revolution of 1789 broke out, the Jansenists, who had so long hampered and distracted the Catholic clergy in their conflict with unbelief, and thus had helped to prepare the way for that catastrophe, became the authors of that schismatical Constitution, called "The Civil Constitution of the Clergy." And this schismatical Constitution they attempted to uphold by an appeal to the Four Articles. In that destructive Assembly, mis-named the Constituent, which was consigning to the tomb all ecclesiastical liberty, as well as all civil order, freedom, and prosperity, those words, "liberties of the Gallican Church" echoed from the Jansenist benches, must have sounded like bitter irony.

But the dreadful conflagration which now ensued, opened the eyes of many a sleeper. By its lurid light many truths were discerned, which had hitherto escaped observation, or had been but dimly perceived. In the awful persecution which now desolated the Church of France from 1791 to 1800, the bishops, the priests, the religious orders of both sexes, and the devout laity, displayed a patience, resignation, zeal, and courage, worthy of the first ages of Christianity. Spoliation, poverty, imprisonment, exile, and death were the portion of the faithful children of the Church, as well as of the devoted adherents of their king and country. Since the days of the Emperor Diocletian, a more fearful persecution had never visited the Church. A thing unique in the history of the world! For ten years all exercise of religion of whatever kind was proscribed. Blood flowed in torrents, in all the cities

Introduction. xiii

of France; but as of old, the blood of martyrs became again the seed of Christians. Multitudes of each sex, and of every age, rank, and calling, flocked to the newly-opened churches; and faith revived in many a heart, where it had been long a stranger.

To repair the ruins of the Sanctuary, the newly-elected Pontiff, Pius VII., in the year 1800, entered into a Concordat with the First Consul of the French Republic, Napoleon Buonaparte. For the organization of the Church of France, a new circumscription of dioceses was under the circumstances needed. The sovereign Pontiff solicited the French bishops, most of whom were living in exile, to tender the resignation of their sees, giving them withal to understand, that that resignation was a matter of absolute necessity. The greater part of the French prelates immediately complied with the Papal demands; while a minority presented a respectful remonstrance against the very comprehensive measure proposed. On the Pope's reiterating his demand, and pointing out its necessity, that minority, with one or two exceptions, ultimately withdrew their remonstrance. These one or two prelates, followed by a certain number of ecclesiastics, founded the schism of the Petite Eglise, or the schism of the Blanchardists, so called from an Abbé Blanchard, who was its most prominent member.* This schism was the direct fruit of the Four Gallican Articles. For by the Third Article, as its partisans alleged, the Pope could never rise above the canons of the Church; whereas in the Concordat just concluded with the First Consul, the Pontiff, they said, had trampled these canons underfoot. It was in vain Catholic writers, and among others Mr

* See Note B.

Charles Butler, pointed out how Bossuet in his
"Defensio Declarationis Cleri Gallicani," had asserted that the Pope possessed a dominium altum,
or extraordinary power, whereby in extreme cases
of emergency, he could set the canons aside. The
Blanchardists replied, that they cared not for
the interpretations of Bossuet, but looked only to
the plain letter of the Declaration of 1682. So
if in 1791, that Declaration *indirectly* gave force
to the schism *called Constitutional*,* it was the
immediate and direct source of the schism of *the
Petite Eglise*. That schism endures to the present
day; but long ago abandoned by the bishops and
by many ecclesiastics, its adherents have now
dwindled down to an insignificant number. Let
us hope and pray that in these auspicious days
of mercy, these schismatics may be reconciled to
the Church!

Scarcely had the First Consul signed the Concordat with the Pope, when he sought to elude
some of its most important provisions. The "Organic Articles," which were now published, excited
the surprise and the indignation of the Pontiff and
his Cardinals. The "Organic Articles," said the
late venerable Archbishop of Lyons, Cardinal de
Bonald, "are nought else but an abridgment of the
'Civil Constitution of the clergy,' with its schismatical spirit and its errors."†

The twenty-fourth of these Articles prescribed
the teaching of the Declaration of 1682 in all the
clerical seminaries. The Placitum Regium, which
was first introduced after the Pragmatic Sanction
of the 15th century, and became more general in
France from the time of Louis XIV., was revived

---

* See Note C.

† Mandement de 1844, apud Gérin. Recherches Historiques
sur l'Assemblée de 1682, p. v., Paris, 1869.

by the "Organic Articles," in respect to all disciplinary, and (what was before unknown) in respect to all dogmatic, bulls of the sovereign Pontiff. Again, processions and other mere external functions of the Church were by these laws subjected to the arbitrary control of the French police. These "Organic Articles" were immediately condemned by the Holy See; and from that time to the present day, the bishops of France, even those who were partizans of the Gallican Declaration, have ever protested against them.

The First Napoleon, it cannot be denied, rendered the greatest services to religion and to civil society. He re-opened, as we have seen, the long-closed churches, replaced the desecrated altars, and called back to the sanctuary the ministers of religion who had so long languished in exile and in penury. He, at the same time, with a strong hand, curbed impious and anarchic factions, re-established order, re-organized the administration, compiled, out of the old legislation of France, with modifications and supplements, a new code of laws, and threw open to the long-suffering adherents of the throne the portals of their country. This work of religious and social reconstruction was doubtless very imperfect, was marred by many glaring defects, yet, under the awful circumstances of the times, it was a most meritorious undertaking.

Both during the consulate and the empire, Napoleon issued many edicts most favourable to religion. He permitted the re-establishment of many female communities devoted to education and to various works of mercy, spiritual and corporal, and sanctioned the order of the brothers of the Christian schools, the restoration of the Lazarists, the Saint-Sulpicians, the priests of the Holy Spirit, the house for foreign missions, and allotted funds for the support of many clerical seminaries. Some of these excellent edicts were passed just as he was on the point of coming to a rupture with the sovereign Pontiff, Pius VII., to whom he was under so many obligations. Throughout his reign, he played fast and loose with the most sacred principles, at one time favouring Catholics, at another infidels and Jacobins. Hence, it is difficult to believe that this remarkable man, though never totally devoid of faith, was yet animated by other than mere political motives in the measures he adopted for the restoration of religion.

His ascent to the imperial throne, Napoleon had stained with the innocent blood of a young and illustrious prince, shed without any provocation. Soon, in his career of rapid conquest, he grasps one kingdom after another. The Papal principalities of Beneventum and Ponte Corvo he annexes to his Italian kingdom, and likewise Venice and the adjacent countries, by a special treaty with Austria. The King of Naples, for having received an English squadron into his ports, falls under the ban of the Corsican despot; and his throne is given away to Prince Joseph Buonaparte. The Republic of Holland is erected into a kingdom, and another prince of the new imperial line set over it. The Germanic empire is dissolved; and many of its former provinces, under the name of the Confederation of the Rhine, are put under the protection, or, more properly speaking, the absolute control of the Emperor Napoleon. The insatiable ambition of this conqueror knows no bounds. He seeks to bring the Church under the same yoke, which he has fixed on the necks of temporal potentates. On the refusal of Pope Pius VII. to adhere to the system of the Continental blockade, and to shut out English vessels from his ports, the French troops in 1809 invade the Ecclesiastical States, overthrow the temporal sovereignty of the Pontiff, and virtually make him a prisoner in his palace. The sacred college is dispersed: many of its most zealous members are sent into exile or imprisonment; the most trusted counsellors of the Pontiff are removed; and himself and his faithful minister, Cardinal Pacca, dragged into captivity.

In the treatment of the Holy Pontiff, the Imperial Government seemed bent on imitating the barbarous conduct of the Jacobin Republic of 1797 towards Pope Pius VI. While the able and faithful counsellor of Pius VII. was confined at Fenestrelle, in Piedmont, his venerable master was for a long time detained at Savona, in the same state, and thence afterwards transferred to Fontainebleau. To the unjust political demands already mentioned, Napoleon added others of an ecclesiastical kind, and far more repugnant to the conscience of the head of the Church. He required the Pontiff to permit the establishment of a patriarchate in the Church of France, and to allow the institution of bishops, as proclaimed by the Constituent Assembly in the "Civil Constitution of the Clergy," to be transferred from the Holy See to the metropolitans, and, in the case of the nomination of the latter, to the bishops of the province. These imperial demands were energetically resisted by the courageous Pontiff. But the emperor now absolutely needed the co-operation of the Pope. Numerous sees in the vast French empire had become vacant; and as long as Pius VII. was detained a captive, he refused, and justly, institution to these episcopal sees. Under these circumstances, the emperor's uncle, Cardinal Fesch, archbishop of Lyons, and Cardinal Maury, who, though in the Constituent Assembly so eloquent a defender of the Church and of the monarchy, now tarnished his fair reputation by a shameful servility,—these two cardinals advised Napoleon to convoke a National Council. In the year 1811, this ecclesiastical Assembly, composed of French, Italian, Belgian, and, in part, German bishops, met at Paris. But from the arbitrary selection of its members, and the sort of intimidation exercised over it by the emperor, this Assembly had no title to the name of Council. The main subject submitted to its deliberations was, whether, from the refusal of the Pope to give canonical institution to the priests nominated to the vacant sees, that institution could be conferred by the metropolitans. This proposition was indignantly rejected by the majority of the Council. In that majority, the eloquent Monseigneur Boulogne, bishop of Troyes, the bishops of Ghent and of Tournai, the bishop of Chambéry, and a German prelate, afterwards so great a confessor, Monseigneur Droste-Vischering, put forth energetic protests against the monstrous claims of the French Government. The Council was dissolved by the emperor; and three of the prelates just named—the bishops of Troyes, Ghent, and Tournai—were committed to prison.

Napoleon gave orders to his ministers of worship in France and Italy to practise on the fears and hopes of each bishop in private, and to use, in turn, the language of intimidation and of seduction. Assured of the sentiments of the majority, he hastened to convoke the Council anew. That majority passed a decree whereby it was declared that the emperor, by the Concordat, possessed the right of nominating to vacant bishoprics; and that in case the Pope suffered six months to elapse without giving institution to the party so nominated, the right of institution would then devolve on the metropolitan, or in the case of the nomination to an archbishopric, on the senior bishop of the province. This decree was presented for ratification to the Pope by five cardinals and nine bishops, deputed to the illustrious captive at Savona.

The venerable Pontiff, advanced in years, enfeebled by sickness, and, in his long captivity, bereft of all his faithful advisers, utterly isolated, deprived sometimes of the very instruments of writing, grieving, too, over the widowhood of so many suffering churches,—the venerable Pontiff, I say, yielded at last to the urgent entreaties and remonstrances of the courtly prelates, who had been deputed to him. He consented to the despatch of bulls to the bishops nominated by Napoleon, and, by a brief, approved and confirmed the decree of the Council of Paris.

The Pope was in the course of the year 1812 transferred from Savona to Fontainebleau; and now, on the 25th January 1813, Napoleon laid before his Holiness a new Concordat, which he said was calculated to bring about a general pacification, and whereby the Pope was called on to renew the previous concession relative to the institution of bishops nominated by the emperor, as well as to renounce the temporal sovereignty of Rome. The Pope, in that state of utter isolation and dejection I have described, appends his signature to the document presented to him. The cardinals are then released from captivity, and allowed to visit his Holiness.

Ever since the Pontiff had made to Napoleon the imprudent concessions that have been mentioned, he was distracted by anxiety and grief. When he once more saw, after a long separation, his faithful counsellor, Cardinal Pacca, he unbosomed to him his deep perplexities and sorrows. The cardinal soothed the aching heart of his master, and gave him the best advice. On the 24th March 1813, the Pontiff addressed to Napoleon an autograph letter, in which he described the bitter anguish of his own conscience, and the utter impossibility he was in of executing the Convention, that had been so reluctantly extorted from him. The emperor then burst forth into idle menaces against the cardinals true to his Holiness; but the hand of God was already laid on the oppressor of Europe, and the persecutor of His Church.

In the violent contest which he had for five years carried on with the sovereign Pontiff, Buonaparte had, either by himself or by his creatures, ever insisted on the maintenance of the four Gallican propositions, as the basis of his ecclesiastical legislation. These, as we have seen, formed part of the "Organic Articles" of 1802. "With the four Articles of 1682," Napoleon once said, "I am master of the Church of France:"—"Avec les quatre Articles, je suis à cheval." "With the second of these Articles," he used again to say, "I can do without the Pope:"—"Je peux me passer du Pape."* "Imbeciles that ye are," he said, on the 6th March 1810, to the Belgian bishops, "if I had not found, in the doctrine of Bossuet, and in the maxims of the Gallican Church, principles analogous to my own, I should have become a Protestant."† Again, the Senatûs Consultum of February 1810, which despoiled Pope Pius VII. of his states, ordained that his successor should take an oath to do nothing contrary to the four Propositions of 1682; and a decree of the same month declared them a law of the French empire.

* J. de Maistre, De l'Eglise Gallicane, liv. ii., c. 9.
† D'Haussonville, l'Eglise et le premier Empire, t. iii., p. 362.

Introduction. xxi

But "the mighty hunter before the Lord," as the illustrious Görres once called the First Napoleon, was now near the close of his career. The wail of the outraged Church, and the cries of trampled nations, had risen up to Heaven. The appalling disasters of the retreat from Moscow, almost unexampled in history—the uprising of the German races, and the battle of nations at Leipsic — the glorious victories of the British troops in Spain, seconded by the heroic efforts of her people, fearfully avenged the cause of God and of humanity. The venerable Pontiff, Pius VII., was, after his long captivity, reinstated in his dominions; and his freedom secured the liberty of the Church.

But now, before we proceed further, let us turn to examine for a moment the heretical offshoots of Gallicanism.

Van Espen, a learned canonist of the University of Louvain, by his ultra-Gallican principles, prepared the way for the system of his disciple Hontheim, suffragan to the Archbishop of Treves, and who, under the name of Justinus Febronius, renewed many of the errors of Richer respecting the hierarchy. He published in 1763 a book entitled "De Statû Ecclesiæ;" and the following summary of its contents has been given by the great German canonist, Dr Phillips:—"Our Lord Jesus Christ, according to Febronius, has conferred on the whole body of the faithful the power of the keys. This power, to use the language of the author, the community of the faithful possesses *radicaliter et principaliter*, and the bishop *usualiter et usufructualiter*. Having laid down this principle, he affirms that each bishop holds his authority immediately of God, and has received, as successor of the apostles, the unlimited right of dispensation, of judgment in matters of heresy, and of episcopal consecration. He admits, indeed, that Peter was distinguished by Jesus Christ from among the other apostles, and that he received a primacy over them; but that primacy, according to him, consists in a mere pre-eminence, like to that of the metropolitan over his suffragans. The Pope has, doubtless, the spiritual charge over all the churches; he exercises over them a right of inspection and of direction; but he cannot claim any jurisdiction. As head of Christendom, he is superior to each bishop in particular; he has over him the majoritas, but not over the whole episcopal body, which is the sole true sovereign of the Church. . . . The Pope has no power over the canons, but is only charged with their execution. It is, therefore, always allowable to appeal from the Pope to the Council; as the Sovereign Pontiff is not the judge in the ultimate instance, nor an absolute monarch, nor an infallible teacher." *

Such was the teaching of Febronius. By disturbing and displacing the centre of Catholic unity, he naturally forced the Episcopate to seek a support and refuge in the secular power. And this pretended advocate of the rights of bishops called upon civil governments frequently to convoke General Councils, to have recourse to the Placet, to the appeal as from abuse, and lastly, to the renunciation of ecclesiastical obedience. The errors of this disastrous system are fully exposed in the following work; for the principles of Janus are but a further development of those of Febronius.

The production of the latter was severely condemned by the Holy See, and refuted by many

---

* Not having the German original of Dr Philips's work at hand, I have quoted from the French translation:—Traité du droit ecclésiastique, par Dr. G. Philips, t. iii., p. 211, 12.

able and learned theologians of Germany and Italy, among whom Zaccaria, the Ballerini, and Cardinal Gerdil, were the most distinguished. Later, the author himself recanted his opinions, and submitted to the decision of the Holy See. But his fatal doctrines struck deep root in Germany, and especially in Austria.

In the year 1780, an active and talented prince ascended the Imperial throne of Germany. Deeply imbued with the principles of Jansenism, the Emperor Joseph II. had been fascinated with the ecclesiastical system of Febronius, and strove, by craft and violence, to enforce its application throughout his dominions. He introduced the Placitum Regium for all Papal bulls and briefs, as well as for episcopal pastorals; suppressed diocesan seminaries, instituting for each ecclesiastical province a general seminary, to which he was to appoint the professors; interdicted the provincials of religious orders from corresponding with their superiors at Rome; forbade all parties whatsoever to recur to the Holy See for dispensations or for any kind of favour; abolished all the contemplative orders, and the greater part of the active ones; suppressed all confraternities; prohibited religious processions; regulated, with a minuteness as puerile as it was arrogant, the celebration of the divine offices; invaded the property and political rights of the clergy; everywhere encouraged and promoted Jansenistical writings and teachers, and permitted the freest circulation to irreligious works.

At the instigation of this emperor, the Archbishops of Mayence, Treves, Cologne, and Salzburg held, in 1786, a congress at Ems, and there drew up a declaration consisting of twenty-six articles. This was a manifesto, conceived quite in the spirit of Joseph II., against the appointment of Papal nuncios in Germany, and against the pretended encroachments of the Holy See on episcopal rights. This Declaration, called the Points of Ems, was energetically resisted by the other German prelates, as well as by the Elector of Bavaria, and drew down a vigorous apostolic epistle from His Holiness, Pope Pius VI. The Archbishop of Mayence withdrew his adhesion to this Febronian document. But how severely were all those unfaithful prelates chastised by Divine Providence, when, eighteen years afterwards, their temporal principalities were torn from them, and that old German empire, which had lasted for well-nigh a thousand years, and wherein they had held so brilliant a position, was levelled with the earth!

Pope Pius VI. undertook a journey to Vienna, to point out to the infatuated emperor the abyss that was yawning at his feet; to draw him back from a course of policy, that was as opposed to the stability of his throne, and to the temporal welfare of his people, as it was to the interests of the Church herself. But all the remonstrances and exhortations of the Holy Pontiff are fruitless.* The emperor persists in his schismatical course; alienates the affections of his Austrian and Hungarian subjects; drives those of Brabant and Flanders into open revolt; and witnessing the miscarriage of all his chimerical plans, dies of a broken heart.

---

* During the abode of Pius VI. at Vienna, Dr. Eybel, a Febronian canonist, and a worthy precursor of Janus, published a pamphlet entitled "Quis est Papa"—"Who is the Pope?" To this a very learned reply was written, under the title "Quis est Petrus?" But the defence of the Papacy came also from another and an unsuspected hand. The illustrious Protestant historian, John von Müller, then a young man, published at the same time a very interesting work, entitled "Journeys of the Popes"—"Reisen der Päpste," where occurs that very remarkable passage which the reader will find translated in the Appendix.

Politics enter not into the scope of this essay; but it may not be uninteresting to observe, that this emperor's political views were strictly analogous to his ecclesiastical. In the same way as he attacked the rights of the Papacy, and of the Episcopate, religious orders, and observances of discipline; so he failed not to show his enmity to aristocracy, to local legislatures, to municipal corporations, and to provincial usages and institutions.

But in his war against the Church, Joseph II. found a worthy ally in his brother, Leopold, Grand-Duke of Tuscany. In his pretended attempt to reform the Tuscan Church, the Grand-Duke received the co-operation of Scipio Ricci, the Bishop of Pistoia and Prato. The latter was a great admirer of the French Jansenistic Appellants, and especially of Quesnel, whose works he got translated into Italian. He convoked in 1786 a synod of his clergy at Pistoia, excluding from it, however, such ecclesiastics as were strongly opposed to his Jansenistic views, and, on the other hand, inviting from other parts of Italy strangers in whom he could confide. Though, as we have seen, the Assembly was a packed one, Ricci encountered much opposition to his projects from some of its members; for thirteen ecclesiastics refused to subscribe its decrees. All the articles on Grace and Free-will, on the Constitution of the Church, on the Sacraments, on the Liturgy, and on Discipline, were conceived in the spirit of the Jansenists and the Febronians. The more important decrees shall be noticed, when I speak of the great Papal Bull, *Auctorem fidei*, which condemned them.

The Grand-Duke Leopold summoned to Florence in the year 1787 an Assembly of all the Tuscan bishops, preparatory to the convocation of a national council. This Assembly he hoped might be induced to support the religious innovations of his episcopal *protégé*, Scipio Ricci. But in that Assembly of seventeen prelates, four only shared, to any extent, the opinions of the bishop of Pistoia. Most of the propositions brought forward by the latter were rejected ; and the Jansenistic writings, that had been circulated by him in his diocese, as well as a Pastoral Instruction conceived in the same spirit by the Bishop of Chiusi, were condemned as replete with grave errors. The episcopal Assembly was dissolved by the Grand-Duke Leopold ; for its decrees had disappointed him, as well as mortified his favourite. The religious innovations of Ricci had, in the highest degree, excited the indignation of the faithful of his diocese. Twice the people burst into his palace at Prato, and carried off his heretical books and papers. They ultimately triumphed ; and in despite of their bishop, retained their confraternities for works of piety and charity, their processions, relics, images, and indulgenced altars. The prelate who had caused so much trouble and scandal, was obliged to resign his see ; and his patron, the Grand-Duke, on ascending, at the close of 1789, the Imperial throne of Germany, saw the error of his course, and retraced the insensate policy he had so long pursued. Many years afterwards, Scipio Ricci himself recanted his errors, and submitted to the various decisions of the Holy See.

In 1794, Pope Pius VI. issued the famous Bull, *Auctorem fidei*, which, from prudential motives, he had long delayed. Eighty-five propositions were extracted from the acts of the Synod of Pistoia, and condemned, under various qualifications ; such as heretical, schismatical, tending to schism and heresy, erroneous, temerarious, offensive to pious ears, and so forth. The most important points only, from want of space, can here be noticed. The proposition (a favourite one with the Jansenists, and which has been revived by Janus), that, in the latter times, a certain obscuration of important truths has prevailed in the Church, *is condemned as heretical.* The second, third, and fourth propositions, purporting that the ecclesiastical authority exercised by pastors has emanated from the community of the faithful; that the Pope has derived his powers, not from Jesus Christ, but from the Church; and that in regulating external discipline, the Church abused her power;—these propositions are all respectively condemned as heretical. Other doctrines already stigmatised in the writings of Wyckliffe, Luther, Baius, Jansenius, and Quesnel, incur grave censure also. And, lastly, to bring forward a point which more directly bears on the subject of this essay, the Sovereign Pontiff, in this bull, points out the extreme temerity of the Pistoian Synod, not only in giving its adhesion to the Declaration of 1682, so often reproved by the Holy See, but in proclaiming it as binding on the conscience of all Catholics.

Not in Tuscany only, but in other states of Italy also—in Venice, Parma, and Naples—we witness the same sort of co-operation between Jansenism on the one hand, and unbelief on the other. Spain and Portugal presented the same spectacle. In all those countries, as well as in France and Germany, ultra-Gallicanism, Jansenism, and Febronianism combined with irreligion, immorality, and civil despotism in fettering the spiritual action of the Church, assailing her political and proprietary rights, encroaching on Papal and episcopal jurisdiction, suppressing the most energetic religious orders, and thus preparing the way for that great catastrophe, which has been already briefly described. While the anti-Christian foe was thundering at the gates of the fortress, disloyal and treacherous factions within sought to cripple the power, and insult the majesty of the chief; and no weapon did they find more effectual for their purpose than the propositions of 1682.

II. I have now brought down from the reign of Louis XIV. to the Restoration of 1814, the history of Gallicanism, and of its various offshoots.

Gallicanism, which sprang up in the fifteenth century, and had its rise, partly in the very untoward circumstances of that age, partly in the erroneous writings of Pierre D'Ailly, Gerson, Almain, and other French divines of that time, touching the hierarchy, was, as we have seen, revived by Louis XIV. The immediate occasion of that revival was the desire of that monarch to extend to dioceses, that had hitherto enjoyed the right of exemption, the regalian rights of the crown to the enjoyment of the episcopal revenues, as well as to the nomination to benefices during the vacancy of a see.* This pretension was resisted by only two French prelates, who in their opposition were supported by Pope Innocent XI. This conduct of the Pontiff led to the convocation of the Assembly of 1682, and was the occasion of the

* "On appelait ainsi," says M. Gérin, "le droit que s'attribuait le roi de France de jouir des revenus d'un certain nombre d'évêchés, et de nommer aux bénéfices, qui en dépendoient pendant la vacance des siéges, jusqu'à ce que les nouveaux titulaires eussent prêté serment de fidélité, et fait enregistrer leur serment à la chambre des comptes, ce qui s'appeloit clorre la régale. C'était donc une exception au droit commun et une charge pour l'Eglise, qui s'expliquoit d'ailleurs, dans certains diocèses, par le souvenir des fondations, que les princes y avoient faites. Le deuxième concile général de Lyon (1275) avoit autorisé la Régale dans les évêchés où elle étoit établie par titre de fondation, ou par une ancienne coutume, *et défendu expressément de l'introduire dans ceux où elle n'etoit pas encore reçue.*"—Recherches Historiques, c. i., pp. 41, 42.

too famous Declaration put forth by the prelates composing it. That Declaration formally contradicted those views respecting the spiritual prerogatives of the Papacy, that, in despite of a very partial and occasional dissent, had, as we have seen, on three occasions, in the course of the seventeenth century, been solemnly proclaimed by a large portion of the assembled Episcopate of France.

It will now be my duty in this second Part, briefly to describe the anti-Gallican reaction, which began with the Restoration of the Bourbons, and during which time, as well as under the subsequent governments, the French clergy gradually returned to those principles that their predecessors had, till the period of 1682, almost universally professed.

"The Restoration," said the Abbé de la Mennais in his happier days, "was hailed by the acclamations of the people. Indeed, it might be called the festival of civilization."* Its mission was the reconstruction of the religious and the social edifice. Religion, which, since the beginning of the century, had been making steady advances, now moved with accelerated progress. That progress was due to the zeal of the clergy, as well as to the active co-operation of the devout laity, to the domestic Missions, that reconciled vast numbers to the Church, to the increase of good schools and colleges for the higher and the lower classes, to eminent preachers, like Mgr. de Boulogne, Mgr. Frayssinous, and others, who so ably combated irreligion, and to great writers, that in the same cause nobly fought by their side. Of these, the most illustrious were Chateaubriand, De Bonald, De Maistre, and the Abbé de la Mennais before his

* Le Drapeau blanc, 1823.

fall. These were the four Promethean spirits that to France, enveloped in the night of irreligion, brought down fire from heaven. The first by his eloquence kindled the fire of imagination, that materialism had well-nigh extinguished in the minds of his countrymen, and poured into their desolate hearts the balm of Christian hope. The second, bearing the torch of Revelation, explored, with wonderful sagacity the depths of metaphysical and political science. The third, from his lofty eyrie, cast an eagle glance into the most hidden places of philosophy, politics, history, and theology. And the fourth, before his sad aberrations, by his burning eloquence and iron grasp of reasoning, brought multitudes over to the Church.

But now, to confine myself to the history of Gallicanism, Chateaubriand, among the writers I have named, never studied the question, and must therefore be considered neutral. De Bonald, more, I believe, from a sagacious instinct than from learned inquiry, took the Roman view of the subject; whereas his two great contemporaries, De Maistre and the Abbé de la Mennais, were the two prime movers in the anti-Gallican reaction. But I must not anticipate.

At the Restoration a great crisis occurred in the history of the Gallican system.

The venerable clergy of France had come forth from exile and from imprisonment, bearing on their limbs the scars of confessorship, and on their brows the aureola of martyrdom. This clergy well remembered the insolent encroachments of the ancient Parliaments on ecclesiastical jurisdiction, the odious machinations of the Jansenists, the violent persecution of the Constituent Assembly, and the more recent tyranny of the first Napoleon —all perpetrated in the name of the Gallican

Introduction. xxxi

Articles. They had witnessed, also, the two schisms which, directly or indirectly, had sprung out of those deplorable opinions. They knew, too, the sympathy ever professed for them by Protestants and infidels. The ecclesiastical Revolution, too, wrought by the Emperor Joseph II., and the sad doings of the Congress of Ems, and of the Pistoian Synod, could not have escaped their attention. Hence from this time forward the bishops of France strove to keep these maxims in the background.* In the letters, which, during the first years of the Restoration, they were wont to address to the venerable Vicar Apostolic of the London district, Dr Poynter, in answer to his complaints respecting the schismatical Blanchardists, they frequently wrote as follows :—" None lament more than ourselves the abuse which is frequently made of the maxims of the Church of France." Again, when under the Restoration, the ministers of state addressed circulars to the bishops, urging the teaching of the Four Articles in the clerical seminaries, even the Gallican members of the Episcopate either disregarded the injunction, or replied that it was beyond the competence of the civil power.

Again, some Gallicans, like Bishop Frayssinous and others, sought to explain the Four Articles in an Ultramontane sense.† But a party that excuses itself, is already doomed. " Qui s'excuse, s'accuse," says the French proverb.

Thus have we seen how by its evil results, Gallicanism had been gradually losing its hold on the Church of France. Providence now raised up two extraordinary men to give to this doctrine a blow,

---

* Under the Restoration, the secretary of Cardinal Latil, confessor to Charles X., told me that the bishops of France did not like to see these questions discussed.
† See Note D.

from which it was never to recover, and which was the means of bringing about that great renovation of the Gallican Church, that is one of the most consoling religious phenomena of the age.

While Napoleon was waging war against religion, a young man, yet a layman, in the remote province of faithful Brittany, took up his pen to vindicate the rights of the oppressed Church. This was the afterwards celebrated Félicité de la Mennais. He and his elder brother, the Abbé Jean de la Mennais,* began in 1808 a joint work, entitled "Tradition de l'Église sur l'Institution des Évêques," and which, in three volumes, was published in the year 1814.

The object of this work was to prove against Napoleon and some of the servile prelates who surrounded him, that ecclesiastical jurisdiction has been imparted *immediately* to Peter *alone*, in order to be communicated to the other pastors, or, to use the words of St Optatus, bishop of Milevi, "that St Peter has alone received the keys of the kingdom of Heaven, in order to communicate them to the other pastors" (Contra Parm. l. 7, n. 3). Among other things, this book shows that the great Eastern patriarchates of Antioch and Alexandria were founded by St Peter and his disciple St Mark, and that the later patriarchal sees of Jerusalem and

* The Abbé Jean de la Mennais collected for this work various passages from Councils, Papal epistles, and from the Fathers and Doctors of the Church. The younger brother then carefully revised the passages so collected, and afterwards dictated to the older the composition. The Abbé Jean was a learned theologian and canonist, and was often employed by bishops as Grand Vicar in their dioceses. He founded a religious order for popular instruction; and at times there were not fewer than a thousand religious under his direction, scattered through Brittany and the neighbouring provinces, and spreading even to the West Indies. This apostolic man, who devoted much time to preaching and other duties of the sacred ministry, exercised, as we shall see, great influence on the ecclesiastical affairs of France. Having reached an advanced age, he died a few years ago in the odour of sanctity.

of Constantinople were established by General Councils, confirmed by the Holy See.

The whole book is a learned refutation of the errors of Antonio de Dominis, Richer, Van Espen, Ellies Dupin, Tabaraud, and Jansenists like him. This vigorous defence of the prerogatives of the Holy See was, I believe, the first of the kind, which since the time of Petit-Didier, a hundred years before, had appeared in France. It was the prelude to a great work, that, published in the same country in the year 1819, constitutes an era in the history of the French Church.

The work adverted to is the "Du Pape," by the great Count de Maistre. Its aim is to vindicate the full spiritual prerogatives of the Holy See, and the infallibility of its dogmatic decrees, as well as to point out its beneficial action in the advancement of civilization, and the great utility in the Middle Age of its political umpirage. This work was followed soon afterwards by a smaller treatise, entitled "De l'Église Gallicane," and which may be looked upon as its sequel. In the first book of this treatise, the author shows that first Calvinism, and then Jansenism, which was a sort of mitigated and disguised Calvinism, had fostered in France a spirit of opposition to the Holy See. In the second book, he analyzes and discusses the Gallican system, the Declaration of 1682, the affair of the Regalia, and the liberties of the Church of France.

These two productions of the illustrious Count by their learning, force of reasoning, depth of observation, playful wit, lively and sometimes lofty eloquence, made the deepest impression on the French mind. Among the laity, and especially among statesmen and diplomatists, their influence was most salutary.*

* The publication of the author's "Soirées de St Petersbourg; or,

The Abbé Félicité de la Mennais, who, in the meantime, by his work, " Essai sur l'Indifférence en matière de Religion," had acquired a vast reputation, gave, in 1820, in a series of able articles in the journal " Le Défenseur," a critique of the " Du Pape."* By this critique he incurred the displeasure of not a few members of the French Episcopate, who still clung to the maxims of 1682. There was, if I am not mistaken, but one individual in that Episcopal body, who then openly and frankly defended the Roman doctrine touching the hierarchy. This was the holy archbishop of Bordeaux, Mgr. D'Aviau.†

But in the French Episcopate itself, a great change of opinion was about to take place. In the year 1822, a new Concordat was completed between the Holy See and King Louis XVIII., whereby twenty new sees were to be erected, making in all eighty. The Grand-Almoner, on whom devolves the right of advising the Crown as to the nomination to bishoprics, was at that time the Cardinal Prince de Croi, and his secretary was the Abbé Jean de la Mennais already spoken of. The latter recommended to his patron the names of twenty ecclesiastics, all known for their devotion to the Holy See; and among those ecclesiastics

---

The Vindication of Providence in the Government of the World"—a posthumous work that appeared in 1821—carried his reputation to the highest pitch. Count Joseph de Maistre, in my humble opinion, as a thinker and a writer, takes his place in French literature immediately after Bossuet and Pascal.

* His own work, " Tradition de l'Eglise," had been duly appreciated by the noble Count.

† In 1815 he wrote as follows to a French prelate :—" For upwards of one hundred and thirty years, twelve consecutive Popes have never ceased to disapprove (improuver) the Declaration of 1682, and for a hundred and thirty years the Papal authority is opposed by declarations, prosecutions, and decrees." Henrion, Hist. de l'Eglise, t. 13, p. 14.

so presented was Mgr. de Bonald—the worthy son of an illustrious father—then promoted from the bishopric of Puy to the archiepiscopal see of Lyons. This excellent prelate, after having for so many years edified the Church by his great virtues and charities, and adorned it by his wisdom and learning, was this very year, just before the promulgation of that definition for which he had helped to prepare the way, summoned to his eternal reward.

In 1824, the Abbé F. de la Mennais and his distinguished disciples, the Abbés Gerbet and Salinis, both afterwards promoted to the episcopal dignity, the learned Abbé Rohrbacher, the Count O'Mahony, M. Laurentie, now the venerable chief editor of the *Union*, and others, founded a monthly journal, entitled, "*Le Mémorial Catholique.*" This journal, which exercised a great influence over the clergy, was chiefly devoted to the discussion of ecclesiastical subjects, and among other matters, carried on a warm controversy against the Gallican opinions. Though the bounds of moderation were occasionally transgressed, yet the rights of the Holy See, the freedom of the Church, and the cause of Christian education, were vigorously defended in its pages.

In 1825, and in the following year, the Abbé F. de la Mennais published the first and the second parts of a work, entitled, "De la Religion, considérée dans ses rapports avec l'ordre politique et civil." In the first part, the author describes the state of political society in France, such as the Revolution had made it, and laments the indifference of the State as such for religion. This he justly calls political atheism. This stigma, yet without trespassing on the constitutional principle of religious Toleration, the Catholic and monarchical party had long striven to remove by degrees from the legislation of the country; their leader, however, M. de Villèle, after his advent to power, but very imperfectly carried out their plans.

In the second part, the author combats the Gallican maxims with great learning and eloquence. Here occurs the celebrated passage, so characteristic of his spirit of rigid deduction: "No Pope, no Church; no Church, no Christianity; no Christianity, no religion, at least for a people that was once Christian; and, consequently, no society."

It is to be lamented, however, that the Abbé de la Mennais had not discussed the first article of the Gallican Declaration in the same manner as the illustrious Count de Maistre, in his work, "Du Pape." Not content with defending the right of the Sovereign Pontiff, and of the Church, to censure injustice in the political order of things—a right exercised at all times, and in the present age, by Pope Pius VII. in regard to the first Napoleon, and by the present illustrious Pontiff in regard to King Victor Emmanuel—the abbé sought to enforce in the present divided state of Christendom, *the political effects* of a regal excommunication. Ecclesiastics and laymen most devoted to the Holy See disapproved of this course; and among others, an illustrious German Catholic writer, who, after the highest commendations on Count de Maistre, observes, with evident allusion to the Abbé de la Mennais, that other more rhetorical defenders of religion in France, by their imprudence, sometimes injure rather than serve the cause they mean to defend.*

The ministry of M. de Villèle committed the great imprudence of prosecuting this publication,

---

* Frederick Schlegel in his "Philosophy of History," Bohn's edition, p. 464. The learned and able Baron d'Eckstein, too, in his journal, *Le Catholique*, expressed the same opinion.

and of bringing its illustrious author before the tribunal of the "Correctional Police." This prosecution, and the previous abrupt dismissal of M. de Chateaubriand from office, were the two greatest political blunders the Royalist Administration ever fell into.

On the charge of an attack on the rights of the Crown, the Abbé de la Mennais was acquitted by the court, but found guilty on the accusation of attacking the Declaration of 1682, which, in despite of the freedom of religious opinions guaranteed by the Charter of 1814, was declared to be the law of the land. The author was mulcted in a small pecuniary fine.

Thirteen bishops, in an address to the King, Charles X.,* condemned in strong terms those passages in the incriminated work, that assailed the Declaration of 1682. Other bishops endorsed the censure; some gave it but a qualified adhesion; while others again refused to subscribe it.

In the year 1828, the Abbé de la Mennais published his work, entitled, " Des Progrès de la Religion, et de la Guerre contre l'Eglise." There are in this production many very able and eloquent passages, and several remarkable predictions of events which afterwards occurred. But on the whole, there is a tone of asperity and violence, which much detracts from its merits. The prosecution the author had sustained, and his consequent alienation from the Court and the Royalist party, as well as from many of the bishops, had embittered his feelings, and produced an irritation which betrayed itself in his recent writings.† The

---

* This was the last formal act of Episcopal Gallicanism.
† In the year following the publication of this work, I took the liberty of remarking to him, " that there was a certain nervous irritation manifest in his recent writings." He replied, "Ah! c'est bien possible, c'est bien possible."

calmer, more equable dignity that had pervaded his earlier works, was now gone. And, unfortunately, the severe, and even unjust comments which some prelates employed in regard to certain anti-Gallican passages in the work in question, provoked replies, wherein he sometimes forgot the reverence due to the episcopal office.

In the times immediately preceding the Revolution of July, I perceived with pain the clouds of a false political Liberalism, by degrees, gathering over his mind. And after that catastrophe, which has proved to France the source of so many evils, the faithful Bréton, who had once uttered the cry, "Vive le Roi quand-même," now in the journal *L'Avenir*, raised the wild cry, "Dieu et la Liberté;" forgetting that if religion hallows and sustains civil liberty, that liberty must be within the limits, and under the conditions of social order;—an order that has its foundations in Nature itself. Thus did a false motto betray the political exaggerations and errors of this journal. In pure theology, the *Avenir* remained quite sound; but its politico-theological tenets, which its writers had submitted to the judgment of the Holy See, at last drew down the censures of the Sovereign Pontiff. It was repugnance to those decisions, and then revolt against that supreme authority, which, by degrees, led my once great but unfortunate friend and master into those fearful intellectual aberrations, that ended in his ruin.

But with the Revolution of July, he "had finished his course." He had, by his "Essai sur l'Indifférence en matière de Religion" reclaimed very many Protestants and Deists; and if, by his philosophy, he sometimes had unduly depressed the powers of human reason, he had, by a mass of learned testimony, illustrated the doctrines of Primitive Revelation; had helped, by his writings against Gallicanism, to introduce into France sounder views as to the Papacy; had inculcated in his "Guide du Premier Age," and in the admirable notes appended to his Translation of the "Following of Christ," a spirit of manly, fervent piety; and, lastly, in his various miscellaneous writings, had advocated with great vigour and eloquence, and sometimes with profoundness of observation, the reform of public education, the observance of the Sunday, the freedom of the Church, the union of Church and State, as well as the rights of the Crown, and the liberties of the oppressed provinces of France.

When the Revolution of 1830 broke out, a great change with respect to the maxims of 1682 had already taken place in the minds of a large portion of the clergy and of the laity in France. The democratic politics of the journal *L'Avenir*, followed later by the sad fall of its chief editor, tended, I think, rather to retard the progress of what are called the Ultramontane doctrines. But as soon as matters had been cleared up by the several Encyclicals of Pope Gregory XVI., those doctrines in France pursued their onward course. During the reign of Louis Philippe, and under the second Empire, we have seen them professed by the most distinguished Catholic writers, and the most influential organs of Catholic opinion. In most diocesan seminaries, they have been taught, and, not unfrequently, they have been proclaimed even in provincial councils. A few months back, an august prince—the last hope, perhaps, of his great but unfortunate country—declared that, though he had been brought up in the Gallican maxims, reflection had taught him now to reject them, convinced that they had not a little contributed towards the misfortunes of his Royal House.

The bulk of the Legitimist party, as has been lately evinced in no unequivocal manner, shares the convictions of the prince. Independently of religious feelings, they, doubtless, are sensible that the recent solemn affirmation of the *spiritual royalty* of Christ's vicar will ultimately tend to consolidate anew *temporal monarchy*, and all its concomitant institutions.*

Lastly, in the glorious Council this year assembled, and which, by its definition respecting the Papal prerogatives, has crowned the desires of so many of the Church's children, fifty French prelates, by their words and acts, have ratified the old traditions of the Church of Gaul. While in Italy, in Spain, in South America, in Ireland, and in Switzerland, where the dogmatic inerrancy of the Holy See has but very rarely been denied within the pale of the Church, the laity have generally deemed it more prudent to leave the final settlement of the question in the hands of the Episcopate; the case in other countries has been very different. In France, where, especially since 1682, and in Belgium, where, during the domination of the First Napoleon, Gallicanism had been made such a formidable weapon of religious tyranny; the laity, as well as the second order of clergy, have in many cases earnestly petitioned the assembled Fathers to relieve them of the moral incubus.

Simultaneous with the anti-Gallican reaction in France, was the course of religious thought in Catholic Germany. Here the evils of Febronianism and Josephism induced earnest and intellectual Catholics to cling more closely to the Rock of Peter. The great lay philosophers, historians, and publicists who, in the last generation, did so much to renovate the spirit of religion in the country

* See Note E.

Introduction. xli

adverted to, Stolberg, Frederick Schlegel,* Adam Müller, Haller, Hurter, Görres, Jarcke, and others, were known for their aversion to the Gallican doctrines. Eminent canonists, like Walter, Beidtel, and Phillips, as well as such very distinguished divines as Klee, Dieringer, and Döllinger himself in his earlier works, have more or less vigorously defended the doctrinal infallibility of the Holy See. Nay, this doctrine was openly enunciated in various provincial councils held within the last few years in Germany, Austria, and Hungary; and accordingly, the attitude observed by many prelates of those countries in the Conciliar proceedings prior to the Definition, excited no little surprise at Rome and elsewhere.

To conclude, if, on occasion of the recent solemn Definition—pregnant as it is with such beneficial results to the Church—I might be allowed to express my own sense of personal exultation; I could observe that the great regeneration of the Church of France, which has occurred in the present century, was, according to all human calculation, a necessary prelude to this momentous decision. But the parties chiefly instrumental in bringing about that spiritual renovation, were many of them my own personal friends and teachers. After the great Count de Maistre, to whom the first place is due, it was the modern Tertullian, before his fatal aberrations, it was Mgr. Gerbet and Mgr. Salinis, the Abbé Rohrbacher, the Père Lacordaire, M. Laurentie, and others, who had the chief hand in the undermining of the Gallican system. Those memories are most cheering to me at the present hour; and while, as it often happens, the ideals of youth remain unrealized, and so many earthly hopes have vanished, like the false mirage of the

* See Note F.

desert, how consoling is it to find in the highest intellectual region—in the sphere of religion—the aspirations of youth fulfilled in age!

Again, is it possible to repress a feeling of patriotic delight, when I behold those British and Irish Churches, scarcely represented at Trent, playing so important a part in the great Œcumenical Synod now assembled at Rome; when, among other things, we see on one hand the Archbishop of Westminster preluding its deliberations by so learned and eloquent an appeal in behalf of the prerogatives of the Holy See; and on the other, the Chancellor of the University, which I have the honour to belong to, and its former Vice-Rector, the Cardinal-Archbishop of Dublin, and the Archbishop of Cashel, ranking by their learning, wisdom, and eloquence among the greatest luminaries of that Council!

Let us hope and pray that the demons of war, and of anarchy, which but yesterday lay crouching at the feet of the assembled Fathers, and which, since their temporary dispersion, have by the dread flapping of their wings, filled the world with dismay and havoc, may yet be laid when those Fathers shall re-assemble!

LONDON, *1st September* 1870.

20 " 1870
Italian troops entered Rome

The works chiefly made use of in this historic sketch of Gallicanism are the following:—

1. "Récherches Historiques sur l'Assemblée du Clergé de 1682," par M. Charles Gérin. Paris, 1869.
2. "Mémoires pour Servir à l'Histoire Ecclesiastique du Dix-huitième Siécle," par M. Picot. Paris, 1815.
3. "L'Histoire de l'Eglise," par l'Abbé Rohrbacher. Paris, 1850.
4. "L'Histoire de l'Eglise," par M. Henrion. Paris, 1840.
5. "Manuel du Droit Ecclesiastique," par M. le Professeur Walter, Trad. Française. Paris, 1850.
6. "L'Histoire du Droit Ecclesiastique," par M. Philips, Trad. Française. Paris, 1858.
7. "Le Mémorial Catholique," Ouvrage Periodique de 1824 jusqu'à l'an 1830. Paris.

De statu Ecclesia by Justinus Febronius i.e. the Baron de Hontheim. Suffragan to the Archbt. of Treves: Created a great stir in France A.D. 1763: it was written in the interest of extreme Gallicanism & ; the repertory [illegible] Jansenists and [illegible] Anglican sympathisers, & [illegible] most of the [illegible]: but it is not [illegible] that [illegible] ignore ye Art. Febronius of [illegible] a most masterly work. Month. Aug. 1888

NOTES TO THE INTRODUCTION.

NOTE A.

THAT the great Bishop of Meaux had a certain courtly weakness, the following anecdote related by M. Gérin will show :—

In 1681 Bossuet proposed, in the Assembly of the Clergy, that his own metropolitan, Mgr. de Harlay, Archbishop of Paris, should, together with the Archbishop of Rheims, be induced to preside, and this because he had given so many proofs of his high capacity; and that the title President of Councils, formerly given to the great Osius, might be applied to Mgr. d'Harlay. Yet of that very same prelate Bossuet, twenty years afterwards, spoke to his secretary, the Abbé Ledieu, as follows :—" Feu M. de Paris (the Archbishop Harlay) ne faisait en tout cela (namely, the proceedings of the Assembly) que flatter la cour, écouter les ministres, *et suivre à l'aveugle leurs volontés comme un valet."—Journal de Ledieu*, t. i., p. 8.

NOTE B.

THE SCHISM OF THE PETITE EGLISE.

" Un resultat de cette opposition des trente-six evêques au Concordat, fut une espèce de secte ou de schisme, appelé les Anti-concordataires ou la Petite Eglise ; secte qui se faisoit un mérite de decrier le Pape, et son autorité; schisme dans lequel paroit être mort M. de Théminnes ancien evêque de Blois."—*Rohrbacher, Hist. de l'Eglise*, t. xxvii., p. 651.

Note C.

THE CONSTITUTIONAL SCHISM.

In a very interesting work published by the Père Theiner, entitled, "Documens Inédits Relatifs aux Affaires Religieuses de la France 1790 à 1800," and which he extracted from the archives of the Vatican, we find admirable letters addressed to Pope Pius VI. by the Abbé Emery, Superior of St Sulpice, relating (among other things) his interviews with the constitutional clergy of France. He speaks of the Bishop of Viviers, who was one of the four French prelates that embraced the schismatical constitution of 1790.

A remarkable avowal which this bishop made to the Abbé Emery, confirms the observation in the text that the Gallican maxims were at least an indirect source of that schism :—" Il m'a souvent témoigné qu'il avoit été trompé par les libertés de l'Eglise Gallicane, et que ce n'étoit qu'en les suivant et les poussant jusqu'aux dernières conséquences, qu'il avoit été mené si loin ; qu'il méditait une déclaration de ses sentimens à ce sujet, qui étonnerait beaucoup de monde, et que les théologiens qu'on appelle en France *Ultramontains* lui paroissoient les seuls conséquents."—*Documens Inedits*, t. i., p. 442. Paris, 1857.

Note D.

In the text it is stated that Bishop Frayssinous sometimes interpreted the Gallican maxims in an Ultramontane sense. In the work of Dom Guéranger, entitled "De la Monarchie Pontificale," I find a passage bearing upon this point :—" Au temps du premier empire," says he, " M. Frayssinous employait son zèle à maintenir dans la croyance et la pratique chrétiennes un certain nombre d'élèves de droit et de médecine à Paris. Durant la crise violente du Sacerdoce et de l'Empire, ces jeunes gens, dont M. Perdrau faisoit partie, lui dirent un jour:

'Monsieur l'Abbé, la controverse est fort animée, et nous avons besoin de savoir de quel côté la conscience nous oblige de nous ranger. Devons-nous être Gallicans? Devons-nous être Ultramontains?' M. Frayssinous leur répondit : 'Messieurs, vous n'êtes pas, et vous ne pouvez être théologiens ; je n'ai donc qu'un seul conseil à vous donner : soyez Ultramontains ; je le préfère. Vous conserverez plus aisément ainsi la vraie foi. Si vous vouliez être Gallicans, je craindrais que vous ne fussiez bientôt entraînés dans l'erreur.' On doit rendre justice à la loyauté qui dicta cette réponse . . . . Maintenant je le demande, quelle est la sécurité d'une doctrine que l'on ne peut exposer en public, sans avoir à craindre pour la foi des auditeurs?"—*De la Monarchie Pontificale*, p. 217.

The speech delivered by Bishop Frayssinous in 1826 at the tribune of the Legislative Chamber, recounts some of the causes which had disgusted the French with the doctrines of 1682.

NOTE E.

SPIRITUAL AND TEMPORAL MONARCHY.

The Church, it is truly said, needs not kings and emperors ; but civil society *in great states* needs them ; and this is especially true under the Christian Dispensation, which, by the abolition of slavery, has indefinitely multiplied popular suffrages, and therefore aggravated the difficulties of popular government. .

NOTE F.

Frederick Schlegel, who was usually so gentle and so guarded in all his judgments on men and things, has expressed himself in regard to the Gallican system with a severity that may be deemed excessive. " But this disguised half-schism of the Gallican Church," says he, " not less fatal in its historical effects than the open schism of the Greeks, has, down to the period of the Restoration, contributed very materially towards the decline of religion in France."—*Philosophy of History*, translated by myself, p. 426.   London, Bohn's ed., 1850.

I well remember that the eminent publicist, Ludwig von Haller, author of the great work, "The Restoration of Political Science," once wrote in the "Mémorial Catholique," that those Catholics who called the defenders of Papal Infallibility *Ultramontanes*, acted like the Greek heretics and schismatics, who gave to faithful Catholics the appellation of *Ultramarines*.

The Abbé de la Mennais, who had been instrumental in converting to the Catholic faith so many Protestants and infidels of France, Switzerland, Germany, and England, once said to me, that he scarcely ever knew a convert that was favourable to the Gallican maxims.

CHAPTER I.

THE FIVE ARTICLES OF THE "ALLGEMEINE ZEITUNG."

N the month of March 1869, the *Allgemeine Zeitung*, of Augsburg, published five articles, entitled "The Council and the Civiltà."[1] In these articles, on occasion of a French correspondence, under the date

ERRATA IN ANTI-JANUS.

At p. 159, "for the absolute will of a *singular* individual", read "for the absolute will of a *single* individual".

At p. 76, "for so we reply", dele *so*.

At p. 95, for "*so* we can only reply", read "*then* we can only reply", etc.

At p. 103, for "*so* we are led to regard", read "*we* are naturally led to regard", etc.

At p. 109, for "*so* there is for other churches", etc., read "there is *on the other hand* for other churches", etc.

At p. 234, for "*so* the prospect of honours and emoluments", read "*then* the prospect of honours and emoluments", etc.

At p. 256, for "*so* this clause is found", etc., read "*yet* this clause is found" etc.

schism of the Greeks, has, down to the period of the Restoration, contributed very materially towards the decline of religion in France."—*Philosophy of History*, translated by myself, p. 426. London, Bohn's ed., 1850.

I well remember that the eminent publicist, Ludwig von Haller, author of the great work, "The Restoration of Political Science," once wrote in the "Mémorial Catholique," that those Catholics who called the defenders of Papal Infallibility *Ultramontanes*, acted like the Greek heretics and schismatics, who gave to faithful Catholics the appellation of *Ultramarines*.

The Abbé de la Mennais, who had been instrumental in converting to the Catholic faith so many Protestants and infidels of France, Switzerland, Germany, and England, once said to me, that he scarcely ever knew a convert that was favourable to the Gallican maxims.

CHAPTER I.

THE FIVE ARTICLES OF THE "ALLGEMEINE ZEITUNG."

IN the month of March 1869, the *Allgemeine Zeitung*, of Augsburg, published five articles, entitled "The Council and the Civiltà."[1] In these articles, on occasion of a French correspondence, under the date of the 6th of February of the same year, in the Roman *Civiltà Cattolica*, a very extended controversy was opened against the impending General Council, "as one chiefly called to satisfy the darling wishes of the Jesuits, and of that portion of the *Curia*, which is led by that order." In the further course of these articles, mingled with other charges, the present development of power which the Papacy possesses is violently assailed. Scarcely had the five Articles approached their conclusion, when alarum trumpets were sounded, and loudly re-echoed from the circles of this party. It was mostly, however, from the *Augsburg Gazette* these explosions were heard. A further[2] essay eulogized

---

[1] Art. I., in Nos. 69, 70, of the 10th and 11th March; Art. II., in No. 71 of the 12th; Art. III., in No. 72 of the 13th; Art. IV., in No. 73 of the 14th (Append.); Art. V., in No. 74 of the 15th March.

[2] "One Word more on the Council," No. 94 (Append.), 4th April 1869.

A

those five excellent articles, which, it was said, "will one day form an epoch in history," but found in them only two defects. The author, it was said, should in the first place have shown, that even out of France, and in despite of the tyranny of the Roman *Curia* and of the order of Loyola, the *pure* doctrine and tradition had not, even in Italy, Spain, or Portugal, entirely died out among theologians or canonists. This is proved by such names as Tamburini, the Italian Jansenist; by Solari, Bishop of Nola (far better known by the refutation of Cardinal Gerdil, than by his own writings in defence of the Synod of Pistoja and against the bull "Auctorem fidei"); by the Florentine scholar Fontani (so hostile to the Roman court); as well as by his fellows, Natali, Palmieri, Degola; then by Clement, Bishop of Barcelona, Villaróig, and Pereira; and the writer adds, it is only in the nineteenth century all ecclesiastical light has been by degrees extinguished. Further, this author ought to have pointed out the marks of a genuine, real Œcumenical Council, and should have examined the course which, in the *worst case*, was to be followed by Catholics. Next, we are informed that the Council of Florence is not Œcumenical, and that far more doubts may be raised against the Council of Trent than against the Councils of Constance and Basle, discarded by Bishop Dupanloup; that now, and in despite of the dreadful condition of the Church, there is no legitimate ground for the convocation of a General Council; and that, besides, it will be devoid of all freedom; that the Pope is merely the *caput ministeriale* of the Church, and that a theological opinion can never be raised into a dogma.

From this last proposition it would follow that the Immaculate Conception of the Blessed Virgin, which, down to 1854, was only a pious opinion, a *pia sententia*, would, even at the present day, be no dogma; and that the Church would henceforth be incapable of giving a dogmatic definition.

After such manifestations of profound theological learning, considerations drawn from canon law and public policy come to hand. Under the title, " The Œcumenical Council and the Rights of the State," a warning cry is addressed to governments, not to be lulled asleep by the arts of the well-organised Ultramontane party, not to permit that the Catholic conscience should be misled, and new elements of discord introduced among nations.

The fact is recalled to mind, that the laity, and especially princes, belong to the Church; that the first councils were convoked by emperors, and that states have in manifold ways a power of guidance. The summoning of a general Council by Pius IX., without consulting the Catholic governments, is declared to be an assault on the privileges of the secular power.[3]

But even the assembly of Protestants summoned to Worms on the 31st of last May, could not refrain from meddling with this matter. " The *rash* views which guide the powerful *party*, from which the convocation of the General Council proceeded; the intoxicating hopes that bear it up; all this your journal has set forth in articles written from a *Catholic point of view*, and which are deserving of

---

[3] *Allgemeine Zeitung* of 8th May 1869. In direct opposition to this opinion, the *Morning Post* later described the embarrassment of the Pontifex Maximus in Rome, because no foreign Power showed itself *inclined* to take part in the Council; and therefore the project, which was designed to produce the effect of an explosion, would utterly fail.

The *Allgemeine Zeitung*, which, in its number of the 19th September 1869, reports this observation, has at the same time the satisfaction to inform its readers, that the *Standard* refers to the Articles against the Civiltà, proceeding, according to report, from a *Catholic* pen.

all consideration." So runs the announcement in the great *Gazette* of Augsburg [4] on this part of the proceedings; and this was soon followed by the summons signed by Bluntschli, Schellenberg, Zittel, and other celebrities of the same tendency.[5] This announcement stated that, seven years ago, Mr Schmidt, in Herzog's Encyclopedia, called the Council of Trent the *last* synod of the Catholic Church, and held a new one to be impossible; but he only thereby proved, that much may become possible which many of our scholars deemed impossible. The objection, that this business is a mere internal concern of the Catholic Church, which in no way regards Protestants, is met by the statement—first, that the Catholic Church is a *political* power in the world; secondly, that in 1864 she proclaimed maxims, which strike at the root of all sound political life; and thirdly, that the Papal invitation to the Council, dated the 13th September 1868, requires an answer, which hitherto has not been satisfactorily given by the ecclesiastical functionaries, and hence must be given by the Protestant people. With this corresponded the real acts of the Protestant Assembly, which led to further discussions, that the *Augsburg Gazette*, at least in its columns, brought to a rapid close. The spectacle of internal discord had been but too much exhibited before the "common foe."

After further "prospects of the Council," in regard to the modern state, had been laid open,[6] came the ingenious founder of the Congress of philosophers,[7] who expressed his admiration for

---

[4] *Allgemeine Zeitung*, 10th May 1869. No. 130.
[5] *Allgemeine Zeitung*, 11th May 1869. No. 131.
[6] *Ibid.*, 20th May 1869. No. 140.
[7] *Ibid.* (Append.), 27th May 1869. No. 147. "The solution of the religious question of the day."

the celebrated five Articles of March, and of the ulterior ones of the 4th and 14th April,[8] and designated after Baader Popery as the weak side of Catholicism.

The address of the Coblentz laity,[9] and the summons issued from Carlsruhe, served to increase the sensation. The address of Carlsruhe[10] declared, that *ecclesiastical parliamentary government*, the intellectual power of the Church, has been for the last three centuries mutilated by the Jesuits, demanded provincial and diocesan synods, which even the Council of Trent had still recognized, but which had never been held,[11] and threatened with a revolt of the popular mind of Germany against Rome.

If it was soon proved that this address came from a by no means imposing number of Baden Catholics;[12] so again a voice from Styria pointed to the " efforts of the Council, that were declaring war against all civilization."[13] Attention to the Council was continually excited, particularly since the diplomatic steps taken by the president of the Bavarian ministry,[14] and since the questions had been proposed to the theological Faculties, and

---

[8] The last Article in an extra Appendix of the *Allgemeine Zeitung* announces a translation of the Five Articles into French, denounces a couple of the German Consultors in Rome, as murderers of German science, points out the sunken authority of Kleutgen, and so forth.

[9] *Allgemeine Zeitung*, 1st June 1869. No. 152, cf. No. 197.

[10] *Ibid.*, 5th June. No. 154.

[11] And from what cause were they not held? Was it by the fault of the Jesuits, or of the Popes, who constantly prescribed the convocation of such synods? The ninth section of the ordinance of 30th January 1830, and the negotiations of the bishops with the Governments of the Upper Rhenish ecclesiastical province can throw some light on this subject.

[12] *Allgemeine Zeitung*, 13th June 1869. No. 164.

[13] *Ibid.*, 16th June. No. 167.

[14] *Ibid.*, 20th, 21st June. Nos. 171 and *seq*. " Prince Hohenlohe and the Council."

conjectures had been formed upon the opinion of the Munich Faculty.[15]

So had the "liberal Theology," as it now calls itself, enlisted allies from all quarters. Jansenistical and Febronian divines, who could discover "ecclesiastical light" only in the last century, the author of the Congress of philosophers, Protestants of the most advanced opinions, statesmen and diplomatists; all were arrayed for the struggle against the Council, summoned but not yet assembled. To these might be added the authors of several pamphlets, expressing themselves in a sense more or less similar. The Augsburg organ more especially devoted itself to the defence of State interests. In a superficial survey of the history of the relations between Church and State, the modern political ideal of the complete equality of rights among all confessions, and of the school, considered as a pure Government concern, without the smallest need of the Church's intervention, without the slightest interest for scholastic dogmas, and yet disdaining a recourse to the Placet, and other measures of that kind; this modern political ideal, I say, is highly eulogized.[16] But of a corresponding action of the State there is no question. The author is affrighted by the Bull "Unam

---

[15] The *Allgemeine Zeitung*, of the 4th September, gave insertion to the opinion of the majority of the Theological Faculty of Munich; and on the 19th, it gave notice of a criticism passed on it by some disciples of Passaglia in the kingdom of Italy. On the 22d of that month appeared, in the same journal, the theological opinion of Professor Dr Schmidt, only after it had been given by the *Post-Zeitung;* and on the 6th October, as a supplement taken from the latter paper, the introduction to the dogmatic opinion of the majority of the Munich Faculty. The opinion of the Würzburg Theological Faculty, the *Allgemeine Zeitung*, from 23d to 30th September, copied from an incorrect extract in the *Post-Zeitung;* but at the same time it inserted the correction sent to the latter journal.

[16] *Allgemeine Zeitung*, 24th, 25th July. No. 205, *seq.*

sanctam;[17] he is affrighted by "Rome's lust of rule," which, indeed, appears invincible; for the past—the ruins of the city once the mistress of the world—the very malaria itself seem to foster the sense of greatness, and to cherish the idea of universal domination.[18] This sentiment, which for every other government would be deemed excusable, is not so for Papal Rome only. The clergy, from the need of a livelihood, is cowardly; nothing is to be expected from its courage. "On the laity, possessing theological culture and religious sentiments, devolves the solution of the ecclesiastical problem of the present time."[19] Now, with or without the aid of the non-Ultramontane theologians, they will begin the work of Reformation. But, lo! all hope of the clergy is not yet destroyed! In old Catholic Münster itself an agitation has commenced against the Council.[20] New succour to the cause is promised by the revolt of Père Hyacinthe (now M. Loyson) "against the Ultramontane counter-revolution in the constitution, doctrine, and discipline of the Catholic Church."[21] Nay, the correspondents of the *Allgemeine Zeitung* have succeeded in interpreting, in the sense of a protest against the dangerous manœuvres of the Roman *Curia*, the Address of the 6th of last September made by the German bishops assembled at Fulda.[22]

Very different views were put forth by the Catholic Assembly of Düsseldorf. They expressed a sentiment of unqualified submission to the decisions of the Council, from which nothing but what was good and salutary ought to be ex-

---
[17] *Allgemeine Zeitung*, 5th August. No. 217.
[18] *Ibid.*, Letter from Rome, 11th August.
[19] *Ibid.*, No. 217, 5th August.
[20] *Ibid.*, 24th September (Append.) No. 207.
[21] *Ibid.*, September 22-25. No. 265-268.
[22] *Ibid.*, 18th September. No. 261.—25th September. No. 268.

pected. To the Catholics there assembled it seemed a contradiction to confess, on the one hand, the infallibility of Œcumenical Synods, and on the other, to dread from such a Council the sanction of gross errors. Whosoever deems himself called on to warn the Council against such dangers, evidently entertains but the slightest possible confidence in its teaching. While so many newspaper readers, who, when the question is about "enlightened people," never wish to be the last, more dazzled, perhaps, by the boldness of assertion than by the brilliant colouring and the natural truthfulness of the picture unrolled before their eyes, have, though incapable of forming an independent judgment, given their unqualified applause to the learned lucubrations of the Augsburg journal; and the less they held the Pope to be infallible, the more have they believed in the infallibility of that great organ of the enlightened. Most classes of the Catholic population have preserved a calm attitude, or evinced a distrust towards the revelations pretended to be made in their behalf. A simple Catholic observed: "These publicists are cunning folks. They may think: if what we have foretold comes to pass, then we have proved ourselves true prophets; but if our predictions are not fulfilled, then it is *we*, who, by a timely cry of alarm, have prevented the passing of such fatal decrees." We may indeed reverse this remark, and say to these publicists: if the Council does not issue the decrees announced by you; then, cunning as ye are, you have been misled by the still more crafty Italians; but if it should pronounce them, then *you* have *not* been true prophets, but the Roman Jesuits, who, wisely or unwisely, have told tales out of school.

Others took the part of the much reviled Jesuits,

who only received the blows aimed at parties occupying a much more exalted position. How can those Roman Religious, who, in order to enjoy greater literary freedom, dwell in a separate house, and hold even in regard to their superiors a privileged position, but are neither employed as consultors, nor anywise more than other publicists initiated in the transactions preparatory to the Council, and of which, moreover, secrecy is an imperious condition; how can they be, I ask, regarded as official or semi-official heralds of the See of Rome? And more especially, too, when the question is about a mere correspondence from France, which is unfairly brought forward; whereas other larger essays of the same periodical upon the Council, and upon the Apostolical Letters having reference thereto—the only authentic declarations as to the object and the task of this Synod—are passed by with scarcely any notice? How can the Papal eulogium of their labours and exertions in general be construed into an approval of every special article in their journal—articles which are only the work of private individuals, and often meet with their critics in Rome itself; while the censorship in that city, represented by the Master of the sacred palace, leaves everything untouched, which is not contrary to faith and morals? And is not "the unctuous tone" of the periodical to be referred rather to the majority of its readers, belonging as they do to the Italian clergy, rather than to the character and the position of the writers themselves? And if the latter write sometimes incautiously and inaccurately, are therefore the Pope and the whole Roman *Curia* to be made responsible for these faults? This view again was enforced by others.

It is not our calling nor our task to defend the

Roman periodical. But thus much justice bids us acknowledge, that very often the German press, entirely overlooking other important articles, misrepresents its statements, in order to stamp on the whole journal the character of a ridiculous fanaticism. Nothing less than accurate was the representation which a Roman correspondent of the Augsburg journal gave of the reply of the Civiltà ;[23] and a later reply was merely characterized by the statement,[24] that the Roman journal represented its opponents as belonging to a coterie, whose vital elements were a syncretism of Royalty (meaning Regalism), Febronianism,[25] Liberalism, and Freemasonry, and that it brought forward some Scriptural passages, such as Matthew xxviii. 19, Psalms ii. 1 ; while the leading thoughts of the article were passed over in utter silence. But, on the other hand, the *Civiltà Cattolica* was to be blamed, when, on vague notices or inaccurate newspaper statements, it brought the Theological Faculty of Bonn, the lay addresses of Coblentz and of Bonn, as well as a declaration of students in that University, into a connexion quite unjustifiable. What in this declaration was addressed to the *Allgemeine Zeitung* from the Rhine under the title of " *In defence*,[26] " may, in despite of some, perhaps, verbal exaggerations, be deemed well

[23] *Allgemeine Zeitung*, 13th April. No. 120.
[24] *Ibid.*, 6th Sept. The article of the Civiltà here meant, and which bore the date of the 21st August, No. 466, pp. 462, 466, 468, relating to the work entitled "The General Council and the State of the World," we ourselves looked into.
[25] The correspondent of the *Allgemeine Zeitung* did not know the signification of the word *regalismo*, nor what among the Canonists is the school of regalists : otherwise he would not have translated the word by "royalty." His expressions in the issue of the 21st Oct. show likewise that he is not very familiar with ecclesiastical literature.
[26] *Allgemeine Zeitung*, 26th Sept. 1869.

worthy of consideration. The exhortation to prudence and moderation made in that article is very appropriate. " We should avoid," it says, " to express ourselves on undecided questions with a precision and a warmth which is in every case unsuitable, and may eventually become very irksome. We should, while boasting of our knowledge, avoid giving way to an arrogance ill becoming our position as sons of the Church."

In general, the Catholic press of Germany has spoken much less than the Protestant on the Œcumenical Council. It saw, for the most part, that, for the hypotheses hazarded, there was no certain guarantee, and that the inferences drawn from them were yet not by any means justified. After the example of French newspapers,[27] our Catholic press expressed a decided disapproval of the Roman periodical, whose expressions have afforded the much-wished-for occasion for the famous Five Articles, which, even without them, would scarcely, however, have been long held back. It disputed the statement that the Council was to last only three weeks, and discuss only the subjects marked out in the Civiltà for deliberation.[28] The literature on the Council that proceeded from clerical circles, brought replies to various statements in those Articles;[29] but none so severe as the Historisch-Politische Blätter.[30] In what, however,

[27] For example, *Le Français*, 18th March 1869.
[28] As something new, the *Times* brought forward, even later, the same three themes for deliberation. See the *Allgemeine Zeitung*, 17th Sept. 1869.
[29] The Œcumenical Council of the year 1869. Periodical papers, vol. i., Nos. 2, 3, Ratisbonne, p. 89 *et seq.*—The Œcumenical Council. Voices from Maria Laach, No. 4, Freiburg, 1869, p. 70, 92.
[30] Historisch-Politische Blätter. Vol. lxiv., Nos. 2, 4, especially p. 316, *seq*.

is there said respecting the reputed author of the Five Articles, strongly as the external proofs weigh in the balance, I find it impossible, on internal grounds, ever to concur. It must look like an outrage to a celebrated scholar to ascribe to him so shallow a performance, marked by a tendency so ill-concealed; and to assume that the views and convictions he had once openly professed, under his own name, he should now wish to deny under the veil of the anonymous. To think this seems to me a moral impossibility; and his silence in regard to the daily press may be explained by the fact, that he has deemed it beneath his dignity to reply to such an accusation.

It was soon announced that the renowned Five Articles would appear on a larger scale as a pamphlet. At length ensued the publication of the book now lying before us;[31] and this once more furnished the *Allgemeine Zeitung* with an opportunity of recurring, for the advantage of its devout readers, to the purport of the excellent articles.[32] Recalling to mind a writing that appeared shortly after the publication of the Encyclical of the 8th December 1864, the *Allgemeine Zeitung* finds "*the fearful trial* of the Divine origin of the Roman Papacy" there announced, or rather menaced as impending, to be realized in these articles. And indeed, continues this journal, in point of fulness and solidity, this book leaves scarcely anything to be desired; and the materials, though not precisely worked up with artistic skill into an harmonious

---

[31] "The Pope and the Council," by Janus. A new edition of the Articles which appeared in the *Allgemeine Zeitung*, entitled, "The Council and the Civiltà," much enlarged, and furnished with the Original Authorities. Leipsic: 1869. Translations of it into other languages are announced by the *Allgemeine Zeitung* of the 24th October 1869 (Append.).

[32] *Allgemeine Zeitung* (Append.), 3d October. No. 276.

whole, give us clearly to understand "how unchristian and unjust is the Papal absolutism, on what a hollow basis it is founded, and by what bad means it is developed." But the philosopher who pronounced this eulogium, accepts, indeed, these results of an historical investigation (in his opinion) very solid; yet passes a judgment the more severe on the incompleteness and the inconsistency apparent through this whole work.[33]

The new production challenges, in a very decided manner, an examination on the part of Catholic theologians; and this it will scarcely fail to obtain. Now, in regard to myself, though after long and fatiguing labours, and after the completion of a large scientific work,[34] I much needed repose; yet, unhindered by external considerations,[35] I have forthwith and quickly entered into the contest—one against many; for we now learn that we have to deal with several authors, and that the plural "we" used by them is not figurative. I have entered upon the struggle to comply with a holy duty, and to satisfy the claims of conscience; while supported by abundant evidence, I protest against a theology which borrows the name only of Catholicism, in order the more securely to wound it in its vital centre, and while I subject to a free criticism the historical and theological deductions of the authors in question. Who the persons may be whom I have to contend with, is to me a matter of indifference. I will hold merely to the name of

---

[33] *Allgemeine Zeitung*, 4th October. No. 277.
[34] The author's "Life of Photius."
[35] As may be seen from the distribution of the German Consultors into the various Committees published by the daily papers, I took not the least part in the Commission for Dogmatic Questions in Rome; and what I here write I would equally have written had I not been called to that city to have a share in the labours preparatory to the Council.

Janus inscribed on the title-page, and not inquire whether he have any affinity with the Janus Quadrifrons, or whether he have only a twofold or a triple front, whether he have a double face or several faces.

Although I think with Janus, that the attention of the reader should be exclusively concentrated on the subject-matter, and that this Reply can of itself, and " without any connexion with names," exert a due effect ; yet I still prefer to appear openly with my name, before the tribunal of criticism, to which I submit the present work. In doing so, I have no just ground for fearing that, contrary to their solemn assurance, it will occur to the opponents " to transfer the dispute from the sphere of objective and scientific investigation of the weighty questions under review, conducted with dignity and calmness, into the alien region of venomous personal defamation and invective " (P. xxix.) *I am evidently much more exposed* to this danger, than the anonymous adversaries. I hope also on this account to remain free from the charge of indulging in imputations of heresy, and so forth ; even though at times, contrary to my intention, I should forget a calm and measured tone, and in the course of the discussion drop a too vivacious expression, which a competent judge would not approve. I am concerned about the cause only, and not about persons ; and the criticism to which I have subjected " Janus," I will not take ill of any scholar if he should think fit to exercise towards my "Anti-Janus." If in a work so rapidly composed as the present, an inaccurate word or any incorrectness should have escaped me, I revoke both beforehand, quite prepared to change for the better what has been done amiss.[36]

---

[36] I may here be permitted to make use of the words of St Augustine : " Ego fateor me ex eorum numero esse conari, qui profi-

CHAPTER II.

THE FIVE ARTICLES IN THE "AUGSBURG GAZETTE," AND THEIR NEW EDITION.

IT is not uninteresting to compare the original with the later edition, the Five Articles in the *Gazette* of Augsburg with the book entitled "Janus." What the former gave is mostly to be found in the latter; yet the first production and its new form are by no means identical. The new title is better chosen; for the question is not so much about the *Civiltà Cattolica* as about the Pope; as this is now roundly stated, and with a sort of proud self-satisfaction. Those who found in the Five Articles a tone of mockery and of wrath, and on the other hand missed logical order, as well as calmness and dignity, will not pronounce a more favourable judgment on the revised work entitled "Janus." Of the three principal sections, "The Syllabus made Dogmatic," "The new Dogma about Mary," and "Papal Infallibility," the last is immeasurably long,

ciendo scribunt, et scribendo proficiunt. Unde si aliquid vel incautius, vel indoctius a me positum est, quod non solum ab aliis, qui videre id possunt, merito reprehendatur, verum etiam à me ipso, quia et ego saltem postea videre debeo, si proficio, nec mirandum est nec dolendum, sed potius ignoscendum, non quia erratum est, sed quia improbatum" (*Ep.* 143, *ol.* 7, *ad Marcellinum*).

especially as a multitude of matters scarcely belonging to it are here dragged in. Even the taxes of the Roman Chancery are not forgotten.

After a Preface of nineteen pages, we find ourselves at the Introduction, which is identical with the first article of the 10th of March. The first sentence has undergone a slight change in the new edition. It now runs thus: "The veil which hung over the preparations for the great General Council *and its intended doings and decrees* (now has hitherto hung over its intentions), *begins to be lifted* (now is already lifted). The tone of confidence in its statements has considerably increased." Now follows, as formerly, the correspondence of the *Civiltà Cattolica* from France. Before the paragraph in the first article, beginning with the words, "So the Civiltà, which is as well known to all," is inserted a longer passage, containing a like correspondence, addressed to the Roman periodical from Belgium; and there, our authors declare, such articles of correspondents are more than mere "feelers" in reference to the impending "dogmatic surprises." Now follows (p. 4) what in substance had been said in the first article also upon the official character of the Civiltà, as the *Moniteur* of the Roman *Curia*, according to which this journal is characterised as the best and most trustworthy source for all that is intended with the Council in Rome.! Here we again find an insertion, wherein, quite in accordance with the hints elsewhere given by the *Augsburg Gazette*, the affirmations of Papal Infallibility by recent provincial councils are repre-

---

[1] The *Allgemeine Zeitung* even asserts that the numbers of this periodical are, prior to publication, regularly submitted to the Pope. Whoever is in any degree acquainted with the business and the occupations of his Holiness, the number of his audiences, and so forth, will know what to think of this statement.

sented as provoked by Rome[2] (p. 5); nay, "the whole plan of the campaign" is unveiled, by means of which "the new dogma, without long examination, will be settled at one sitting, as by the stroke of a magician's wand" (p. 7). Our authors *can even name the English prelate* who has undertaken to give the impulse to these proceedings.[3] But, independently of this, it is *indubitably clear* from the *Civiltà*, "that the Council is summoned chiefly for the purpose of satisfying the darling wishes of the Jesuits, and of that part of the *Curia* which is led by them" (p. 7). With the designation of these darling wishes, which are now

---

[2] The revision of the Acts of such Provincial Councils has only for object to prevent decrees against the *jus commune*, and particularly against the Council of Trent. A previous "intimation," to express their opinions on this or that point, is a pure invention. Father Schneemann has certainly not wished to say what has been sought to be deduced from his words; nor is he so "well informed" that he could vouch for the deliberations with all the Metropolitans in question. The letters of a distinguished man now no more, but who was more versed in æsthetics than in theology, and who, especially in the first period of his residence in Rome, gave heedless credit to much gossip of the city, contain more than one inaccurate statement. Much he would himself have corrected, could he have anticipated the later publication of letters addressed to friends; and he could not always think of immediately rectifying what he had written down according to hearsay.

In this respect he told me himself, in the autumn of 1857:— "All the world will hear something new from Rome; but rarely is one in a position to offer what is true;" and Pliny, vi., Ep. 16, rightly observes:—"Aliud est epistolam, aliud historiam, aliud amico, aliud omnibus scribere."

N.B.—The person alluded to is, I believe, the lamented Dr Diepenbrock, bishop of Breslau. (Tr.)

[3] The "English prelate" here alluded to it is not difficult for those to guess who have read, in Art. III. *Allgemeine Zeitung*, 13th March, these words:—"Archbishop Manning, who, with the glowing zeal of a convert, has embraced the theory of Infallibility, expressed a short time ago," etc. In the same way it is said, in Art. IV., under the date of 14th March:—"The English bishops will follow Manning; the Irish will follow Cullen, imposed and set over them by Rome."

treated of in three chapters, the introduction concludes.

The Syllabus made dogmatic, whereof the first chapter treats, appears "as an enriching of the Church with a considerable number of *new* dogmas, but which (the infallibility of the Pope once presupposed) are but the first-fruits of a far richer harvest reserved for succeeding times" (p. 8).[4] Here we have some additions to the arguments in the *Allgemeine Zeitung*, especially a very significant reference to the *anti-pope* Benedict XIII., residing at Veniscola, who saw the whole Church assembled only in his rocky castle.[5] With the Jesuit Schrader (p. 9) his fellow-religious Schneemann has been associated (p. 10), after the brilliant paragraph in the articles, commencing with the words, "when once the narrow adherence," etc., has been reserved for a later investigation. The paragraph on the co-active power of the Church has received considerable extension. The further deductions in the sixty-ninth number of the *Allgemeine Zeitung* are pretty faithfully retained till p. 18,* where No. 70 begins. At p. 17, Father Schneemann is again cited, and then Father Schrader, against the Bishop of Mayence. While the remainder of No. 70 in the *Allgemeine Zeitung* is otherwise preserved *verbatim*, further proofs of the hatred of Ultramontanes against free institutions are alleged, and, moreover, the beginning of the third article (in

---

[4] Already the *Allgemeine Zeitung* (Append.), 21st October 1869, announces, "Soon will a new cultus spring up; the adoration(!) of St Joseph. Various circumstances point to this fact. Even English correspondents *from Rome* speak of it, as well as of the *bodily* assumption of this saint."

[5] After the *expulsion* of the cultivated classes from the Church, the uneducated only will remain in it; but this true flock remaining behind, will the more pliantly submit to the "pilots of Loyola."

* According to the original (Tr).

No. 72) is assigned to a more suitable place. The first chapter concludes with a quotation from St Francis of Sales, who, we are told, "expressed his dislike for writings which deal with *political* questions, such as the indirect power of the Pope over princes; "but he is no authority for the Jesuits"[6] (p. 33).

In the following chapter on the new Marian dogma, we receive, with some changes and additions, down to the second paragraph, the beginning of the second article in No. 71.

The historical statements on the tradition, "that the body also of Mary has been taken up into heaven," are completed by a reference to two apocryphal writings from the time between the fourth and fifth century, as well as to Pseudo-Dionysius and Gregory of Tours. The Patristic expressions, that the death of Mary has been a miraculous one,[7] as well as the homilies of Modestus of Jerusalem, Andrew of Crete, Germanus of Constantinople, John Damascene,[8] who enjoyed in the Eastern Church such great authority, are passed over in silence, and no attention is paid to the arguments of Pope Benedict XIV.[9] The "glorification" of Mary inspires Janus with no sympathy; he has already had more than enough in the doctrine of the Immaculate Conception, solemnly declared by Pope Pius IX. to be part of divine revelation. Yet in contrast with the intended decrees of the Council sanctioning the Syllabus, the announced new Marian dogma appears very *harmless*. It is only worthy

---

[6] Yet the Jesuits willingly quote this saint for their side, as, for example, Father Schneemann, often mentioned by Janus, in his work entitled, " The Teaching Power of the Church," p. 125, *et seq.*

[7] For example, Epiphanius, hœr. 78, n. 11.

[8] *Migne* PP, gr. t. lxxxvi. p. 3277, *seq.;* t. xcvii. p. 1046, 1072, 1089, *seq.;* t. xcviii. p. 340, 348, 360, *seq.*

[9] Bened. XIV. de festis; ii. 8, n. 1, *seq.*

of notice, that herein, again, we find the whole character of the Jesuits,[10] who are wont to despise the tradition of the ancient church, and whose appetite, when once they have obtained the immediate object of their wishes, will certainly increase, and, in all likelihood, lead to a justification of the doctrine of Probabilism, and, in general, of the whole moral system of the Order, "that ever-gaping wound in its reputation" (p. 36).[11] Yet we wish not to dwell any longer on this subject.

The long section, entitled, "Papal Infallibility," which, moreover, contains many other things, begins (p. 37) with a citation from Gretser and Cajetan (the words of the latter are repeated at p. 375), "who express the fundamental principle of the Ultramontane doctrine, that when we speak of the Church, its rights, and its action, we always mean the Pope, and the *Pope only.*" The *Civiltà Cattolica*, it is said, sets forth the same view. We get the conclusion of the first of the Five Articles, with some additions respecting these Ultramontane views upon the circumstances of Italy,[12] and the rest, in which the Mortara case, long since appreciated by Canonists,[13] is not forgotten (p. 42).

[10] Upon this theme we find scarcely any writings of the Jesuits in modern times. Among Italian writers, we may mention the treatise of the Benedictine Aloysius Vaccari (de Corporeâ Deiparæ in Cœlum assumptione); that of the Franciscan Observantine, Luigi Buselli (La Vergine Maria vivente in corpo ed in anima in cielo); and that of Padre Caspare de Luise, of the order of the Pii Operarii (L'Assunzione di Maria).

[11] Of the numerous apologies which, even down to our times, have never yet received a scientific refutation, such as those of Riffel, Moufang, Magnus Jocham, and the Baron von Ketteler, bishop of Mayence ("Attacks against Gurey's Theology," Mayence, 1869), Janus naturally takes not the slightest notice.

[12] What Janus here (pp. 37-42) alleges, shows strong prejudices, indeed, but no knowledge of the real facts. We shall, however, not pause to dwell on secondary matters.

[13] Cf. *Katholik*, 1859, vol. i., p. 64, *seq.* "Archiv. for Catholic Can. Law," vol. iv., Nos. 5, 6. (In German.)

As great spirits ever coincide, so in respect "to the Roman lust of dominion, to which all the originality and the self-efforts of the German mind are to be sacrificed;" Janus here, as in many other things, concurs with a Catholic philosopher, who has long since given up all Romanism.[14] "The whole Ultramontane habit of mind, Janus teaches us, is rooted in the personal infallibility of the Pope." Here the passage taken from the Introduction to the first Article, and which, in the new edition, had been left out in that place, is brought in—the passage inculcating the precious doctrine, that with the triumph of these views "a new principle of *immeasurable* importance, both retrospective and prospective, will be established—a principle which, when once irrevocably fixed, will extend its dominion over men's minds more and more, till it has coerced them into subjection to *every* Papal pronouncement in matters of religion, morals, politics, and social science. For it will be idle to talk any more of the Pope's encroaching on a foreign domain; he, and *he alone*, as being infallible, will have the right of determining the limits of his teaching and action *at his own good pleasure*, and every such determination will bear the stamp of infallibility" (p. 45-6).

In the same words as in the Articles, only with some changes, the terrific consequences of the dogma of Infallibility are depicted, to which the

[14] T. Frohschammer. "The Right of Private Conviction," Leipsic, 1869, pp. 229, 230. Upon the levying of taxes compare this work, p. 216, with what Janus says, pp. 195, 236, *seq*. (Lasalle, as is well known, has far better appreciated the relations of the Middle Age, so different from those of modern times.) Upon the opposition to all science, Cf. Frohschammer, p. 220, with Janus, p. 17, *seq*. 280, and alibi; upon the Inquisition and intolerance, Frohschammer, p. 9-11, with Janus, pp. 14-18, *seq*., and pp. 254, *seq*. The paging is here according to the German edition of "Janus.") [Mr Frohschammer is a suspended priest.] (Tr.)

sequel of Article II., in No. 71 of the *Allgemeine Zeitung*, entitled, "Papal Infallibility defined by the Council as an Article of Faith," is suitably annexed. The witticism about Theology assuming more and more a "Talmudic" character finds its place here also.

What next the second Article upon "Papal Errors and Contradictions," as well as the third Article upon the genesis of the theory of Infallibility, and of the forgeries made in its behalf, had but briefly indicated, has now been spun out into a long treatise. Thenceforward between the original and the newly-edited text a radical difference prevails, and very little is found in accord. A frightful picture of the mediæval Papacy, and of the circumstances it brought about, is sketched for us. The system of legates, and the bestowal of the Pallium, appeals, exemptions, and dispensations, reservations, and the oath of obedience, the Inquisition and trials for witchcraft, in short, all possible terrors, are brought before us in motley array; while again, from the fourth and fifth Articles, various episodes belonging to the last four centuries are introduced in a somewhat modified form.

We were promised a new edition of the articles in the *Allgemeine Zeitung*, provided with proofs from original sources. But precisely in those passages, where such authoritative proofs were most needed, these are not furnished;[15] while such are found in other places, where they were scarcely necessary. Several statements and assertions in the Articles, which we had wished to see fully

---

[15] For example, for the proposition p. 181 in German: "*So often* as the Pope passed a new law, the *Curia* calculated what would be its profits arising from the dispensations now rendered necessary," &c. The proofs for this *toties-quoties* it would not be so easy to adduce.

proved, have now been entirely left out. To this belong, for example, the following passages :—

1. At the conclusion of the second article, it was asserted that Pope Paul V. had sacrificed to his claims of political power even the hope of the reunion of England with Rome held out to him by King James the First; and for this assertion reference was made to a diplomatic document, dated the 22nd July 1609, and to be found in the Imperial Library at Paris.[16] This statement appeared even to the editors of the *Allgemeine Zeitung* improbable; it was, therefore, the more necessary to publish the document. That this did not take place, but that the statement was entirely omitted in the new edition, cannot have for a reason that it was not wished to give any support to the conjecture expressed by a Catholic publicist,[17] as to the authorship of the articles.

2. In the third Article that appeared in No. 72 of the *Allgemeine Zeitung*, a declaration was ascribed to Pope Alexander III., to wit, that adultery committed by a priest is a lesser sin, for which he was not to incur deprivation, nay, not even suspension by his bishop. It was not subjoined where Alexander had said this. Some thought of Canon iv. At *si clerici*, in the Decretal, entitled De Judiciis (II. 1); but from this passage that assertion is not to be proved.[18] Others thought of the Decretal " Significasti," where, however, the question is about an accused, and not yet convicted priest, to whom the Pope prescribes canonical purgation in such a way, that in case he did not

---

[16] The treasures of the Vatican, the friends of Janus could also make use of, p. 382 (in German).
[17] This is M. Jörg, the editor of the great bi-monthly periodical entitled the *Historisch-Politische Blätter*, Munich. (Tr.)
[18] *Augsburg Ecclesiastical Journal*, No. 20, of the 15th May 1869.

clear his character, he should be suspended."[19] Here was Alexander III. grossly calumniated. Now that passage is entirely left out in "Janus," without any restitution of his good name being made to the calumniated Pope.

3. In the fifth Article it was said, "That in order to silence the German Church at the Council of Trent, Paul III. had, by a special Brief, contrary to the usage of former synods, enjoined that no right of voting should be granted to its deputies." To this it was replied:[20] "The reverse is true. Paul III. had issued a Brief, *quo episcopis Germaniæ indulgebatur uses suffragii per Procuratores;* and in this the Germans were even favoured before other nations, so that the legates, from fear of exciting jealousy, kept back the Brief."[21] Now this passage also fails in "Janus," although the general accusation of the ill-treatment of the Germans by Rome has been faithfully retained."[22]

4. The statements about Count De Maistre and the Abbé de la Mennais, which were to be read in the fourth Article, are now omitted. Perhaps the explanation of the catastrophe of the latter writer by the "dogma of Infallibility," appeared too one-sided and too rash.

5. The reference also to the Declaration of 1682, and the refutation of the hypothesis of Infallibility by Cardinal La Luzerne, which adorned the same

---

[19] *Bamberg Ecclesiastical Gazette*, No. 23 of the 5th June, upon c. 5. de adult. v. 16, Cf. Farinac. Prax. crim. p. v. qu, 40. Reiffenstuel in h. l. §§ 1. n. 14.

[20] *Ibid.*, loc. cit.

[21] Pallavicini Hist. Conc. Trid. L. vi. c. 2. n. 6, 7.

[22] Pp. 232, *seq.*, 313, 315, 323, 329, 351, 359, 360, 366 (in the original). With these passages we may compare the work entitled "Imperatorum, Imperiique, principum ac procerum totiusque nationis Germaniæ Gravamina adversus Sedem Romanam totumque ecclesiasticum ordinem eruta ex actis a Jac. Frid. Georgii. Francoforti et Lipsiæ. 1725.

article, have not been reproduced. Was it because the work of Mgr. Maret, which is shortly to appear in Germany also, furnishes a substitute?[23] Or was it because new historical researches have placed the origin of that Declaration in a less favourable light?[24]

6. Even the quotation from a work of the Oratorian Laderchi, which appeared in the fourth Article, has here been omitted. Is this because the fact is not correctly alleged, or because the work sharply attacks certain critics,[25] who without any moderation, without any respect for the Church and for her doctrines, strive after the morbid fashion of Rationalists, to drag everything into the dust; men whom we may call hyper-critics or pseudo-critics?

7. That the conclusion of the five Articles, which characterizes the impending Œcumenical Council, as a " Synod of flatterers, like the Latrocinium of Ephesus," has been omitted in the new edition, we would fain regard as a sign of improvement, and of a return to greater moderation.

I should be obliged to write a book three times as thick as that of " Janus," were I to submit all its particular statements, more especially in the second half of the work, to a critical survey. For, in general, accusation requires less space than defence; and in historical controversies it is necessary, on one hand, to reduce to their true value the testimonies cited by the opponent, and on the

---

[23] Le Concile Generale et la paix religieuse, Paris, 2 vols., advertised in the *Allgemeine Zeitung* of 20th September 1869.

[24] Charles Gérin. Recherches Historiques sur l'Assemblée de 1682. Paris, 1869.

[25] La critica d'oggidi ossia *l'abuso* della critica odierna di Giacomo Laderchi, Rome 1726, pp. 81, 88. 100. [The criticism of the present day, or the abuse of criticism in the present time. By J. Laderchi.]

other hand, accurately to bring forward the opposite authorities, which have been passed over, whether from design or from ignorance. Moreover, the attacks are systematically directed on certain special isolated points, severed from their general connexion; so that, in defence, we must constantly point to this historical connexion—a connexion which is not immediately and fully apparent to every reader of the work in question. Hence, independently of other labours incumbent upon me, I must confine myself within certain limits; appreciating some of the most important points more fully, others more briefly, leaving the rest to the work of other men. On this occasion, I think I am justified in expressing a wish, that the clergy, especially in the face of an historical school, which, though in many ways one-sided, is still intellectual, and seizes on ecclesiastical questions with the greatest eagerness; that the clergy, I say, should take up many labours formerly neglected, and which exceed the powers of individuals; and, in general, devote greater attention to the pursuit of historical studies. If it is a misfortune that so many historians should be destitute of a knowledge of dogmatic theology and Canon Law, it is a misfortune also, that so many divines perfectly familiar with dogmatic questions, are not historians withal.

CHAPTER III.

MAKING THE SYLLABUS DOGMATIC.

AN appalling thought, whose whole significance the reader can scarcely realize! " To speak seriously, the contest inaugurated by the Encyclical of 1864, will have to be carried out with the free use of every available Church weapon,—a contest against the common sentiment and moral sense of every civilized people, and against all the institutions that have grown out of them" (p. 18). That is to say, the eighty propositions condemned in the Syllabus appended to the Encyclical of the 8th December 1864, are to be defined in the form of positive enunciations and affirmative theses; or, in other words, the propositions, contrary to those proscribed assertions, will receive the stamp *of articles of faith*. As now, according to the view of Janus, those condemned theses are the expression " of the common sentiment and moral sense of every civilized people, and of all the institutions that have grown out of them," and which the Jesuits, the intellectual authors of the Encyclical and the Syllabus[1] combat to the utmost extre-

---

[1] Here Janus (p. 23) perfectly coincides with the writing, entitled, "Illustration of the Papal Encyclical." Leipzic, 1865.

mity; so new articles of faith are to be created, thoroughly reprehensible, and in the highest degree irrational and absurd, calculated to revolt every Christian soul.

Were the hypotheses here made, well-founded, so the devoutest Catholic might fear he must incur the danger of being misled by his Church. But that they are happily unfounded, is a matter easy to be proved.

In the first place, it is a false hypothesis to assert that propositions, contrary to *all* the theses condemned in the Syllabus, can ever become real articles of faith. These theses are designated *in globo* as errors, but by no means as heretical propositions. Among them are such, as in a special qualification would be characterised only as false, temerarious, and so forth;[2] a distinction that was made, for instance, in the Thirty-nine Articles drawn up by Pope Martin V., in respect of the errors of Wycliffe and Huss.[3] The twelfth article of the Syllabus, namely, "The Decrees of the Apostolic See and of the Roman Congregations impede the Free Progress of Science," may well be censured as false, rash, scandalous, offensive to the Holy See, and to the whole Church, but not as heretical; for it runs not directly against revelation, or against truths defined by the Church. It is only the contrary of a *propositio hæretica*, that can be regarded as a dogma. But of all this Janus seems never to have heard.

Secondly, it is an assumption theologically inadmissible, to make the views of the modern world the touchstone of Christian truths, and to substitute for the rule of faith, and of the eccleslastical magisterium, "the common sentiment and moral

---

[2] Denzinger Enchiridion, ed. iv. Præf. p. ix.
[3] Denzinger loc. cit. p. 194. n. 555, Interrog. 11.

sense of civilized nations." Every one, Protestant as well as Catholic, knows full well how widely the modern views of the world have departed from the standard of Christianity, and how many anti-Christian elements they take in.[4] Though these principles may contain much that is true and right, still it will be necessary to separate these elements from what is false and unjust, neither blindly to condemn everything modern, nor unrighteously to glorify it. But never can these principles in their totality be made the criterion and the touchstone of Christian truths; but, on the contrary, it is by the Christian standard they must be measured and judged, so far at least as religion (and this is the highest object of concern to the believer) is at stake. Woe, indeed, to Christianity, if it must fashion itself according to the modern civilized state; if it is to be tested sometimes by the maxims of 1789, sometimes by those of 1793.

A third false assumption is, that the Syllabus, solemnly accepted as it has been by the Episcopate, contains the monstrosities which certain parties wish to find therein, and which have thrown many, who live in a state of intellectual dependence on the daily press, into the utmost anguish. Many of the Catholic laity, indeed, wished for a more detailed and practical explanation of that document, which they saw so often misunderstood and misinterpreted,[5] more especially as but few persons

---

[4] This is evinced by the complaints as to the hostile attitude of the world towards faith, by the unchristian desecration which the State is rapidly tending to, by a legislation that utterly ignores religion, by the predominant materialistic tendency of the age, and so forth; complaints which we hear at every corner, and indeed not only in sermons, but in treatises, in pamphlets, and in newspapers.

[5] On the part of Protestants, like Guizot in his "Meditations sur l'état actuel de la Religion" (Paris, 1866), this can be more easily understood.

gave themselves the trouble of recurring to the Apostolic Letters and Allocutions, from which its several propositions are taken. To interpret the latter by the former is, according to all the laws of interpretation, not only admissible, but imperative. The civilisation, the progress, with which the Pope cannot be reconciled and cannot ally himself (Syllab. n. 80; compare "Janus," p. 20), is (as is evidently borne out by the context of the Allocution of 18th March 1861 here cited), nought else but that reprehensible system which under the mask of civilisation and progress, assails and strives to root out the Church, as has been evinced in so shocking a way in Italy, and which is not the true, but the false civilisation, meriting rather the name of barbarism.[6]

Janus, indeed, is of a different opinion. But who has said, and who has proved, that it is the intention of the Syllabus, "to exalt principles at first only applied to the condition and circumstances of a particular country into universal articles of faith!" and this without any regard to existing relations, and well-founded historical rights? Who has said or proved, that according to these propositions, all established laws and constitutions must be changed, and all bishops be bound to labour for their overthrow ("Janus," p. 29). Right principles are, indeed, everywhere the same; but principles and their practical realization are to be carefully discriminated. Here we meet with a fourth false assumption of Janus.

For the Church must, from her dogmatic point of view, reject *on principle* many things, which *in life* she cannot and will not abolish; and this on the ground that this seems the lesser evil. By her the

[6] Bishop Ketteler, "Germany after the War of 1866" (in German), p. 142.

unity of faith in a purely Catholic country is estimated as a supreme blessing,[7] and with perfect justice. But thence it only follows that this unity, where it exists, should be protected; but by no means, that in those countries where, by the power of circumstances, it has succumbed, it should be re-established without any regard to the consequences thence ensuing, or to the rights of non-Catholics — a course of proceeding which the strictest theologians have never advocated.[8] The Church changes not her maxims, as ladies of fashion change their dress, or modern scholars their views; what she once held true, is still true for her to-day. The world may change, but she remains steadfast to her principles; and to those principles the laws of universal morality pre-eminently belong. When Gregory XVI. issued the Encyclical of the 15th August 1832, scarcely a voice was lifted up against it; but when Pius IX. more precisely inculcated the maxims of his predecessor, what a loud storm rose up against him! And as to the so much detested co-active power, is it only since yesterday, since 1864, the Church has attributed it to herself? Has she not from all times asserted it?[9] But the mode of application was and is different; spiritual penalties were and are the ordinary ones, the temporal being much more rare.

If among the temporal punishments mentioned by the Jesuit Schneemann, Janus (p. 10.) lays a

---

[7] Compare Döllinger, "The Church and Churches," p. 88, in German. Walter's Canon Law, §§ 56. xi. ed. in German.

[8] Cf. Martin Beccan. Duell. de primat. reg. L. iii. c. 8. n. 14 de fide hæreticis servandâ. L. ii. c. 10. Maldonat. 'n Matth. c. 13.

[9] *Vide* the Capuchin Jeremiah a Benettis Privileg. S. Petri Rom. Pontifici collatorum Vindiciæ. p. 11. tom. vi. Romæ 1761, art. 6. p. 550. De potestate coactivâ. *Vide* Wurzb. Kath. Wochenschrift 1854, No. 49 and 50.

stress upon whippings; so he may rest assured that at the present day no bishop any longer inflicts them, though he may believe that formerly, not without justice, were such penalties adjudged by bishops and synods against offenders, and the same holds good of banishment,[10] imprisonment, and pecuniary fines.[11] The Church doth not *on principle* renounce rights which she has once exercised, and whose exercise under certain circumstances (and were it only in Africa), might in a relative manner become again necessary. Thence to infer the design of the Church to overthrow all institutions of State is in nowise admissible. A manifold fallacy is it, when (p. 13.) from the 23d proposition of the Syllabus in an affirmative form, to wit, "Popes have never exceeded the bounds of their power, or usurped rights of princes," the following inference is drawn:— "Accordingly, all Catholics must for the future acknowledge, and all teachers of constitutional law (staat's-recht), (*sic*), and of theology, must maintain, that the Popes can *still* depose kings at their will, and give away whole kingdoms and nations at *their good pleasure.* For the proposition taken in itself speaks of the past only, and not of the present or of the future; and to render possible, on

---

[10] Aug. ep. 133, n. 2, ad Marcellin. tribun. Opp. ii. 396. Venet. 1729. Tantorum scelerum confessionem . . . virgarum verberibus eruisti, qui modus coercitionis et a magistris liberalium artium, et ab ipsis parentibus et sæpe etiam *in judiciis*, solet *ab episcopis* adhiberi. Cyprian in vitâ S. Cæsarii Arelat. Surius 27 Aug. t. iv. p. 927. Colon. Agrip. 1583.—S. Greg. M. L. 18 ep. 27. ad Januar. L. ix. ep. 65 ad eundem. L. xi. ep. 71 ad Anth. Opp. 11. 707, 782, 1177, ed. Paris, 1706. Cassian. Instit. iv. 16. Pallad. Hist. Laus, c. 6. Conc. Agath., 506, c. 38, 41. Matiscon, i. 581, c. 8. Narbon, 589, c. 13. (Hefele Concil, 11. 638., 111. 33, 50, 51.)

[11] Concil. Aurel iv. anno 541, c. 29. Tolet. xii. 681, c. 11. (Hefele Conc. 11. 760. 111. 289.) Greg. M. L. xi. ep. 71. c. 23, et 63, c. 9, c. 111. 9, 4, c. 3. c. ead. qu. 5.

application to the latter, legal relations of a perfectly like kind must be presupposed. Further, it must be proved, that the pontifical acts referred to were performed *purely according to good pleasure*, without any title in law; whereas many legal titles might be cited, as, for example, from the feudal law, in reference to vassal kingdoms; and, as must be clear to every unprejudiced person, the Popes, in the Middle Ages, could enforce, with full justice, many claims which are now no longer equally valid. On the other hand, the strictest theologians of the *Curia*[12] have contested the principle that Popes could depose kings *according to their good pleasure;* and besides, they by no means intended to justify every act of every Pope.

In general, the kind and mode of reasoning pursued by our Janus, is, to use the mildest word, something more than astonishing. He brings before us the Bishop of Mayence, as corrected by the Jesuits, (p. 19), and subjoins to this fact a pathetic declaration "on the unworthy mental slavery the Roman Jesuit party threatens German* Catholics with!" The state of the case is this: A proposition, from a former writing by the celebrated prelate,[13] was, in a Viennese publication, prefaced, and, indeed, composed (?) by Father Schrader, designated as one that since the Encyclical could not bear repetition;[14] whereupon followed a more ac-

---

[12] Bianchi, Della Potestà et della polizia della Chiesa. Roma 1745. t. I. L. I. § 8. n. I; p. 78. § 5. n. I *seq.;* p. 40. *seq.*: § 14. p. 116 *seq.;* § 15, p. 122 *seq.;* § 21. n. 5. p. 187, *seq.;* L. II. § 11. p. 322.

[13] Freiheit, Autorität, und Kirche. Mainz, 1862, p. 155, [Freedom, Authority, and Church.]

[14] Der Papst und die modernen Ideen. Wien, 1865. II Heft. p. 33. [The Pope and Modern Ideas.]

* Dr Hergenröther, in the quotation, writes "*German* Catholics." The English translator of "Janus" has *foreign* Catholics (Tr.)

curate explanation on the part of the episcopal author.[15] That passage of the bishop's ran as follows: "There is no established maxim of the Church, that should prevent a Catholic from holding "that, *under certain given relations*,[16] the civil power would do best to grant full religious freedom, with the limitation that the personality of God should not be denied, nor morality endangered." So runs the passage in question. But something very different is given by Janus. He makes the bishop insist, "that the Church so thoroughly respects freedom of conscience as to repudiate all outward coercion of those beyond her pale as immoral and utterly unlawful; that nothing is further from her mind than to employ any physical force against those who, as being baptized, are her members; that she must leave it entirely to their own freest determination whether they will accept her faith; and that it is absurd for Protestants to suppose they have any need to fear a forcible conversion, &c., &c." (p. 18). These are not the propositions on which the bishop "has been instructed by the Syllabus, and its commentator, Schrader," and which he subsequently explained. How came Janus to refer to propositions utterly different? Was it an illusion? or was it a falsification? We will not determine.

What the authors say as to the condemnation of the Treaty of Westphalia by Innocent X., and as to the declaration of Pius VI. about its non-ratification (p. 31), without any regard to the remarks long since made thereupon by theologians and canonists,[17] has already received in a Catholic

---

[15] Deutschland vor und nach dem Krieg von. 1866. Mainz, 1867, p. 134, *seq*. [Germany Before and After the War of 1866.]

[16] These words ought to have merited a more accurate appreciation on the part of the critic.

[17] Dr Döllinger, in the work already cited (p. 49 and *seq*.), speaks as

periodical[18] the merited correction. The same journal has done equal justice to the account of the proceedings of Pope Innocent III. in regard to the Magna Charta of England, "the pretended noble mother of European Constitutions;" proceedings which are denounced by Janus without the slightest indication of the special legal relations of the time (p. 23).

To show the ideas of Pope Pius IX. respecting the penal power of the Church, the condemnation of the writings of the Turin professor, J. N. Nuytz, which but advocate doctrines long ago censured, is alleged; and two other special documents are adduced in proof (p. 11). Here we read: "In the Concordat made in 1863 with the Republics of South America, it is laid down in *Article* 8, that the civil authorities are *absolutely* bound to execute *every* penalty decreed by the spiritual courts." Now as there are different South American Republics, so there are different Concordats with these. We know that of Bolivia, in twenty-nine articles, dated 29th May 1851; that of Guatemala and Costa Rica, 7th October 1852; that of Nicaragua, 2d November 1861; and that of San Salvador, 22d April 1862, both published only in 1863.[19] One of

---

follows:—"The Pope, indeed, did not protest, because he desired not the establishment of a just peace between Protestants and Catholics, the whole subsequent history has proved the contrary; but because it was expedient, and, indeed, an imperious duty for him, to enter a protest against a profoundly immoral and unchristian principle, which, in respect to religious stipulations, was at the bottom of that whole Treaty of Peace—I mean the territorial system, on the principle, '*Cujus regio, ejus est religio,*' 'whoso is master of the territory is master of the religion.'"—Compare Phillips's Canon Law, III. § 141, p. 465-477; Walter's Canon Law, § 113.

[18] The Historish-politische Blätter of Munich. Vol. lxiv. No. 4, p. 320, *seq.*

[19] Acta Pii IX., vol. i. p. 452, *seq.*; 509, *seq.*; Prof. Sentis, in the Archives for Catholic Canon Law, t. xii. p. 225, *seq.* (German.)

the later Concordats seems to have been intended. But of the stipulation just cited not a trace is to be found. The *eighth* article treats of the President's Indult in the nomination of bishops ; it is only in articles 13–16 there is any question of jurisdiction,[20] which in matters spiritual belongs to the Church, which in the civil affairs of ecclesiastics is abandoned to the secular judge, as also in criminal cases, in which they may be involved, provided he be in the second and third instance assisted by two ecclesiastical judges ; while to bishops is adjudged the exercise of the full penal power against clerics who have forgotten their duty. The Convention of Guatemala subjoins in its fifteenth article a clause, that in case of any disputes between ecclesiastics, an episcopal certificate, attesting the previous attempts of the ordinary to bring about a reconciliation between the parties, must be produced before the secular functionary should be allowed to try the suit. Janus seems not to have understood the text, or at least to have had before him some inaccurate accounts of it.

2. "In a letter of Pius IX.," says Janus, "addressed to Count Duval de Beaulieu, published in the *Allgemeine Zeitung* of November 13, 1864, the power of the Church (it should be said, of the Roman *Curia*,) over the government of civil society, *and its jurisdiction in temporal matters*, is expressly guarded " (p. 12).

The passage of the letter in question, communicated only in the way of extracts by the *Allgemeine Zeitung*, and which the Secretary of the Latin correspondence by desire of the Pope addressed to the above-named count on the 22d October 1864, on occasion of his writing, entitled " The Freedom of Error in the Free State," runs, according to the

[20] Sentis, loc. cit., p. 237., *seq*.

text of the *Augsburg Journal*, as follows : " Many who admit the duty of submission to all decisions of the Church in matters of faith and morals, wish to withdraw from her competence the government of civil society, and rest herein *on their own judgment, as if civil government also were not subject to the laws of justice and of truth, and as if the best polity of nations were not also traced out in Holy Writ*, whose interpretation belongs to the Church." Now, it is one thing to say, the civil power must conform to the laws of truth and of justice announced by the Church ; for this is involved *in the very nature of the Christian State, such as it should be;*[21] but quite another thing to assert *the Church has a direct jurisdiction in affairs of State*. In their context, the words do not say what Janus makes them say. They reserve to the Church the competence of judgment and of decision, but not the competence of " direct jurisdiction." Never has the Church recognized the principle, that there are other laws of morality for the collective body, for the State, and others for the individual. Accordingly she requires of those clothed with political power, that they should conform to those laws, and, indeed, such as she proclaims them. Were she to abandon this postulate, she would then renounce her very mission. He, indeed, who is possessed with the idea that the Church or the " *Curia*," particularly since the Encyclical and the Syllabus of 1864, aims at nothing less than the annihilation of the modern State, and the restoration of the mediæval supre-

---

[21] Aug. Ep. 48 ad Vincent : "Serviant reges terræ Christo, etiam leges ferendo pro Christo." Cf. c. lit. Petil. 11, 92 ; Ep. 185., al. 50, ad Bonifac. Greg. M. L. 11, Ep. 11 ad Mauritt. Imp. Leo M. Ep. 125, al. 75 ad Leon Aug. Bossuet sermon sur l'unité de l'Eglise, œuvres compl. iv. 306.

macy of the hierarchy over it;[22] he, indeed, will strive to interpret everything in a sense corresponding to this his view.

On such feeble props is founded what, immediately after these so-called documents, Janus affirms as follows:—"*It follows* that they are greatly mistaken who suppose that the Biblical and old Christian spirit has prevailed in the Church over the mediæval notion of her being an institution with coercive power to imprison, hang, and burn. On the contrary, these doctrines are to receive fresh sanction from a General Council; and that pet theory of the Popes, that they could force kings and magistrates, by excommunication and its consequences, to carry out their sentences of confiscation, imprisonment, and death, is now to become *an infallible dogma!* It follows that not only is the old institution of the Inquisition justified, but it is recommended as an urgent necessity in view of the unbelief of the present age" (p. 12).

But with other documents, also, Janus is not a whit more successful. As before in the third article, so now at p. 31, he refers to an instruction sent by Pope Pius VII. to his nuncio at Vienna in the year 1805, without dreaming that the genuineness of this document is more than disputable.[23]

With more success, Janus rests on another public act, which is to serve as a proof "that even the Bavarian constitution, too, with its equality of religious confessions and of all citizens before the law, is looked on with an evil eye at Rome" (p. 27). The document in question[24] comprises the

---

[22] Frohschammer, loc. cit., p. vi.
[23] Gosselin Pouvoir du Pape, au moyen âge. Louvain, 1845; II. 452–455. F. Walter's Canon Law, § 343. Note 9, p. 739, xiii., ed.
[24] Fogli dottrinali (which were sent with the Papal Brief of the

complaints of the Holy See as to the religious edict of Bavaria, and its antagonism to the concordat of 1817—complaints which, for the most part, long before these Papal acts were known, had been uttered in the country by Catholic ecclesiastics. No protest is made against the first section of the Religious Edict, which secures to all the inhabitants of the country perfect freedom of conscience; nor against the second section, which forbids coercion in matters of faith. But a protest is made against the fourteenth section, touching the division according to sexes of the children of mixed marriages; against the regulations as to the religion of foundlings in the twenty-second section; in general, against looking on religion as a matter of absolute indifference; against the eighteenth section, on the different cases arising from a change of religion on the part of parents; against the prohibition of embracing another religion, before the legal age of majority has been attained, as laid down in the sixth section. Further, complaint is made as to the complete parity of religions, but not as to the equality of the followers of those religions; the complaint turns on the spirit of indifferentism which pervades the whole law. On the eightieth section, which runs as follows, "The religious communities existing in the State owe *equal respect* to each other," we must observe, that the question regards not *the members* of religious communities, but the *communities themselves;* or, in other words, *the very principles* which they profess. To prescribe *an equal respect* for another religious community (not, observe, for the *persons* of its members), is to require that the doctrines of the

13th January 1819 from Rome to Munich), in the work entitled "The Concordat and the Constitutional Oath of Catholics in Bavaria." Augsburg. 1847. Pp. 244-249.

true Church should be placed on the same level with the opinions of the other religious bodies. This interpretation, Rome, from her point of view, must needs make; but we here see the great distinction between *principles and persons*, which our opponents totally ignore. The other part of this document regards the contradiction between the second appendix of the Constitution and the Concordat in its articles 1, 17, 9–12, as well as the fifty-eighth section of the first respecting the Placet.

From the Bavarian Constitution Janus passes (p. 28) to that of Austria, as well as to the Papal Allocution, "Nunquam certe," of the 22d June 1868, on the violation of the Concordat, and on the laws issued against it. He has, however, forgotten to answer the question, why the Pope has not condemned the diploma of 20th October 1860, which secured to Protestants equality, and the patent of the 8th April 1861, which carried out the same more fully and precisely. He has entirely overlooked the way in which the convention of 1855 has been undermined, the interests of the Catholic majority sacrificed to a noisy minority, and marriage and education for the most part withdrawn from the jurisdiction of the Church. He wishes only to prove " the deep hatred which lies at the bottom of the soul of every genuine Ultramontane, of free institutions, and the whole constitutional system" (p. 22). Hence he distinguishes not between Constitutions, considered in themselves, and Constitutions which are formed with the express object of ministering to the ecclesiastical and the political Revolution, nor between particular enactments of the same Constitution.[25]

[25] That the constitutionalism which from Piedmont has been propagated throughout Italy, had such objects in view, has long been

The whole reasoning in this section labours under an incredible confusion of ideas. This is manifest, for example, in the assertion that the doctrine of the mere legal origin of ecclesiastical immunities, condemned in the thirtieth thesis of the Syllabus, is, with the sanction of the Council, to be made *heresy* (p. 17 in the original). Here, again, we have the first of those false suppositions noted above, and next we see how the doctrine of theologians and canonists respecting ecclesiastical immunities, and their different classes, has not been in the least attended to. The natural, internal foundation of the same is confounded with their outward, concrete formation and development.[26] This confusion of ideas is further manifest when, in reference to the thirty-eighth proposition of the Syllabus, it is said, " Those also will become guilty of heresy, who write or teach that the extravagant pretensions of the Popes contributed to the separation of the Eastern and Western Churches, though this may be discovered in official documents from the twelfth to the sixteenth century, and in the avowals of a number of contemporary authorities."[27] That proposition may well be characterized as false and temerarious, but by no means as heretical. Besides, already in the eleventh century, the names of the Popes had been struck

---

admitted. Pius IX. had had experiences enough with the constitution of 1848, as all the world but too well knows. Hence, when the Papal Government, shortly after its restoration in 1850, pronounced itself against the constitution in Tuscany (as alleged by our author at p. 26), this is much less astonishing than the inferences deduced therefrom by Janus.

[26] Compare on this subject the theological opinion of Professors Schmid and Thalhofer, in Munich, as well as that of the Theological Faculty of Würzburg, in reply to the third question proposed by the Bavarian Government.

[27] The Syllabus condemns proposition 38, " Divisioni Ecclesiæ in orientalem atque occidentalem Romanorum Pontificum arbitria contulerunt."

out of the dyptichs of the Greek Church, which was the surest sign and the clearest expression of a schism that had been *already* consummated—a schism which far other motive agents had brought about.[28] Against this fact, later avowals could not avail. The Papal pretensions might contribute to the spread, but not to the rise, of the schism; and if the Latins repeated what the Greeks *alleged*, these testimonies in themselves have no decisive weight, more especially as others can be opposed to them.

The strongest achievement of Janus, however, is the insinuation that, on a favourable opportunity, the bishops and clergy will deny the obligatory force of any constitutional oath they may take. But all theologians and laymen know that the Pope can do nothing against the divine law; that he cannot dispense from the observance of the fourth commandment; that all Papal laws, even if they must be regarded as irreformable, still do not cease to be human. In no wise "are falsehood, treachery, and dissimulation cherished, fostered, and propagated from one generation to the other" (p. 17). The maxims of the Church were not, and are not any mystery, and neither were nor are opposed to the observance of *sworn* constitutions, though not *every new* constitution which the dominant Liberalism may think fit to impose, can be sworn to without hesitation by Catholic bishops, priests,

---

[28] I have elsewhere* expressed myself more precisely on t his matter. Pichler's History of the ecclesiastical schism has not furnished the proof given in the text, and, moreover, contains a series of historical blunders, whereof a portion the author himself, in his second volume, saw himself called on to correct, though many others may still be pointed out. The statement referred to in the text, Catholic theologians have long ere this refuted. I may refer, for example. to "Bennetti's Vindic.," par. II, t. iii., p. 720, *seq*.

---

* In the author's life and writings of the Patriarch Photius (Tr.)

or even laymen. This was already known to all the world. In Bavaria, for example, from the year 1818 to 1821, grave negotiations were carried on respecting the Constitutional Oath ;[29] and these negotiations were later renewed. But there was ever found a possible way for setting aside serious conflicts. It is only where false suppositions without number, as in the pages of "Janus," are allowed to prevail, mistrust will be found invincible. To such hypotheses belong the following, to wit—that the Episcopate and the clergy are only watching for the opportunity to get rid of their oaths—that the Pope can abrogate the Divine law—that the duty of submission to him begins only with the definition of his infallibility—that the doctrines of the Syllabus are those of the Jesuits, and of their patrons only—that the former, like the latter, are bent on the annihilation of the civil power, where they are unable to subjugate it.

According to the representation here laid before us, "Church and State are like two parallel streams, one flowing north, the other south. The modern civil constitutions, and the efforts for civil government, and the limitation of arbitrary royal power, are in the strongest contradiction to Ultramontanism, the very kernel and ruling principle of which is the consolidation of absolutism in the Church. But State and Church are intimately connected ; they act and react on one another ; and it is inevitable that the political views and tendencies of a nation should sooner or later influence it in Church matters also" (p. 21).

Here we might enforce various considerations, and especially remind our readers that, as experience shows, this very "Ultramontanism" has

---

[29] *Vide* the already cited work, "The Concordat and the Constitutional Oath," p. 110, *seq.* (in German).

existed, and still exists, under all forms of civil polity—that religious and political matters are to be kept perfectly distinct—that an absolutism exhibiting a primitive legal title in the religious and moral sphere, showing an authority conferred by God, is far more easily borne than any other, and is very compatible with struggles for freedom in other matters; further, "that Church and State, *in modern constitutions*, are no longer so intimately connected;" rather, the separation of Church and State has been already introduced, and the dangers of national decomposition have increased, and consequently in the interest of the Church, the centre of religious unity must be more jealously guarded. But we would rather ask, How comes it that, in the Middle Ages, in the flourishing period of the Papal power, popular liberties were far greater than in the period of its decline, contemporaneous as that decline was with the revival of regal despotism?[30] How comes it that, in the primitive cantons of Catholic Switzerland, the Papal "absolutism" found its truest adherents, who were not less decided republicans than the inhabitants of North America are at the present day?[31] How comes it that the present "efforts for the limit-

---

[30] With regard to Germany, to Scandinavia, to the Netherlands, to Scotland and England, see the evidence in Döllinger's "Church and Churches," p. 96, *seq.*; p. 153, *seq.* (German ed.) With regard to Southern Europe, see Balmez's "Catholicism and Protestantism Compared," part iii., especially c. 48 and 52.

[31] Janus (p. 26) appeals to the oral expressions of an American bishop as to the situation of Catholics in the United States. By Protestants it is objected to them, "that they find their principles in Papal pronouncements (the same reproach is addressed to Ultramontanes among ourselves also), and cannot *therefore* honestly accept the common liberties and obligations of a free state, but always cherish an *arrière-pensée* that, if ever they become strong enough, they will *upset* the constitution." The same has been said

Making the Syllabus Dogmatic.

ation of arbitrary royal power" are far from exhibiting the moral and political results which so many modern coryphæi of Liberalism foretold; that in many strata of society they are regarded with mistrust, as favouring only one class—the *bourgeoisie* and the capitalists; that minorities not a few, and entitled to the highest respect, complain of oppression by fraud, violence, and forgery, and look on equality before the law, and on the parity of political rights and duties, as merely illusive, and resting only on paper? How comes it, that we must hold the condition of modern states to be so perfect, and the existing relations of the Church to be so reprehensible? How comes it, that at the present day the Catholic people, which surely has its instincts, and more than instincts, is in Germany, France, and other countries, a far more solid support of the Papal throne than its several governments?

The section inscribed with the title of this chapter (pp. 8-36), I, a poor ignorant man, have repeatedly and attentively perused, and have afterwards asked myself the question, What have I thence learned? First, I meet with the ingenious remark, "The bishops assembled at the Council have nothing to do, but to set the conciliar seal on a work which the Jesuit Schrader, with right foresight, has already prepared to their hand" (p. 9). Oh, too happy bishops! They can give festive entertainments and banquets, give themselves up to the enjoyments of art, parade in the public processions with mitre and cope, indulge in the *siesta;* for the long-sighted Jesuit father has provided for everything else, and

by Protestants in Holland, England, Germany, and the rest. The North Americans can give very tranquillizing assurances (*vide* Döllinger, *loc. cit.* p. 46-48), and *by deeds* overcome distrust.

to set the conciliar seal is no arduous labour! At most one has but to answer, "Placet," and all is settled. Less clever folks take not such high flights, have far other notions as well of bishops as of the work appointed for them at Rome, and have, besides, been favoured with other experiences, which they are not in the enviable condition to trumpet forth vaingloriously before the world. But why speak we of bishops, who have nothing to say in this matter? Nay, all the world knows beforehand the decrees of the Council. "He (the theologian Schrader of the Jesuit order), has already turned the negative statements of the Syllabus into affirmatives, and so we *now* can (naturally without waiting for the Council itself), and *without any trouble*, anticipate its decisions on this subject" (p. 9).

Yet the matter appears to us not so easy. For independently of the fact, that in *a private labour*, the criticism, as well as the use of materials, is open to every one; independently of the fact, that for an appreciation of the Syllabus, a complete theological knowledge of that document is *first of all* necessary, and this, as can be shown, is not everywhere found; yet, in case the impending Œcumenical Synod should enter on a detailed examination of its contents, an explanation of it in the form of the doctrinal chapters of Trent, in opposition to the prevalent confusion of ideas, and "to the lofty licence of free spirits," would be, as many a zealous reader of "Janus" may have perceived, no such light task. Janus, indeed, following the celebrated declaration of the three celebrated weeks, calculates with mathematical precision the day (it is exactly the festival of St Thomas à Becket, the defender of ecclesiastical freedom in England), when in the year of grace 1869, which has never realised the fears of war long entertained, the "Roman Catholic

Making the Syllabus Dogmatic. 47

world" will be the richer by five whole truths, that under pain of salvation it will have to believe. Horace's "Credat Judæus Apella, non ego," occurred to me,[32] and the investigation of Janus's documents, instituted before an inquiry into his proofs, tended to augment my unbelief. Still accustomed "to prove all things, and to hold fast that which is good" (2 Thess. v. 21), I determined, in an hour usually devoted to recreation, to form a lively representation of these five truths. They are as follows :—" First, The Church has the right of employing external coercion ; she has direct and indirect temporal power."[33] This proposition would be at least in no wise absolutely new; it rests, as Janus knows, on mediæval views. But it appears, according to him, to favour the tribunal of the Inquisition ; and in this connexion the two recent canonizations and beatifications of inquisitors, following in rapid succession, gain a new and remarkable significance" (p. 13).

Secondly, The proposition as to the right of the Popes of deposing kings at will, and of giving away kingdoms and nations at their good pleasure, we have already discussed above. It is a doctrine absolutely new, unknown even to the Middle Age. Examples from the kingdom of Naples, of which the Pope was lord paramount, and wherein he could exercise his feudal rights[34] (whether his re-

---

[32] Satir., lib. I, n. 5, v. 100–1.

[33] He who strictly follows the laws of grammar and of logic will not, "in reference to the contrary of the words 'neque potestatem *ullam* temporalem directam vel indirectam,'" will not, I say, be quite clear whether, in the second number of the work entitled "The Pope and Modern Ideas" (p. 64), the contrary has been stated with *indisputable accuracy*. The opposition to *ulla* might still be a different one.

[34] About the Papal rights of feudal suzerainty Janus cares little. Thus (p. 387) in reference to Pope Clement XI. it is briefly stated, that Rome *claimed* rights of suzerainty over Parma and Piacenza ;

course to his ecclesiastical prerogatives were herein justifiable or no), will not avail to support the general proposition in the form as conceived by Janus. We maintain that "an article of faith such as this, that the Pope can, at his caprice, and for purely political or pecuniary ends, deprive millions of innocent men of what, according to the teaching of the Church, are the necessary means of salvation"[35] (p. 15) such a doctrine, we say, will never be defined, either by a Pope or by a Council.

Thirdly, What, in the next place, appears, gives us no theological proposition, still less the embryo of a dogma. The question is only as to the corrections to be made in current works of history, and as to the necessity existing for all Catholic authors, who are preparing books on history or law, to publish their researches before the 30th December 1869 (p. 16); "for afterwards they will have the savour of heresy."

Our prophet, nevertheless, announces something else, which has at least one good side. "There will at least," he says, "be required for literary and academical work, a flexibility and elastic versatility of spirit and pen hitherto confined to journalism" (p. 16). It would be of service to many a

---

and that still later, in 1768, Clement XIII. *once again* invaded the sovereign rights of the Duke of Parma by excommunication. But the Pope's rights of suzerainty over Parma were very well founded. —Compare, for example, A. Theiner's "Histoire du Pontificat de Clement XIV.," vol. i., pp. 114, 115. "Della Storia del Dominio Temporale della sede Apostolica nel ducato di Parma. Libri tre. Roma, 1720. ["History of the Temporal Dominion of the Apostolic See in the Duchy of Parma," in three books.]

[35] The interdict, to which reference is here made, by no means deprives men of the means of salvation, nor of the exercises of religion required for eternal happiness. Baptism and penance especially are not interdicted; and it is rather a limitation in the use, than a total withdrawal of religious rites which is here ordained.—Compare Walter's "Canon Law," § 191; Phillips' "Manual of Canon Law," § 196, p. 566, *seq.*

Making the Syllabus Dogmatic. 49

scholar, if he would throw off some of his pedantry; if he would, for instance, take for his model the five Articles on the Council, that appeared in the *Allgemeine Zeitung*, and " which form an era ; " if he would imitate, at least as regards polish of style, the versatility with which, according to the expression of others, many enlightened folks know how to clothe their servility, and contrive to change their views. One condition only is requisite ;—that versatility should never lead to the disfigurement and the falsification of the truth.

Lastly, follow the fourth and the fifth pretended new dogmas, religious coercion (p. 18), the condemnation of freedom of conscience,[36] and finally the condemnation of modern civilisation, and especially of constitutionalism (p. 21, *seq.*)

We have found here nothing more than what is to be read in newspapers ;—nothing which, in addition to what we have already said, is really worth the trouble of refutation. We have found the whole effusion only calculated to recruit powerful allies against the pretended pernicious theory of Papal Infallibility, which Janus has above all things in view.

[36] *Vide* the Introduction (apparently the work of an able theologian), to the edition of the Encyclical, brought out by M. Bachem of Cologne in 1865, especially p. xxviii., *seq.;* xxxii., *seq.*

CHAPTER IV.

THE DOCTRINE OF PAPAL INFALLIBILITY.

WHEN theological opinions, held by celebrated teachers, are combated, though ever so warmly, with serious arguments and becoming respect, this is in itself not to be condemned, nor even disapproved of. But bitter invectives and gross misrepresentations, which can lay no claim to scientific controversy, are worthy of the severest censure.

In the dispute on the inerrancy of Papal Pronouncements *ex cathedrâ*, we meet with a doctrine which, according to the avowal of its adversaries, prevailed in the whole Middle Age[1],—which Pope Benedict XIV. declared,[2] was received in every country except France—which even in that country[3]

---

[1] Pichler, Ecclesiastical Schism between East and West (in German), vol. i. p. 252, 253, 255, vol. ii. p. 690. Compare Klee's "History of Dogmas," Dogmen-Geschichte, vol. i. p. 92–97, Mayence, 1837. [The celebrated Klee told me himself, he firmly believed in Papal Infallibility.—Tr.]

[2] Ep. ad. Inquis. Hispan. Anno 1748. Op. xv. p. 117, ed. Venet.

[3] For example, Duval, De suprem. Rom. Pontificis auctoritate. Paris, 1614. M. Maucler de Monarchiâ divinâ. Paris, 1622. [More eminent French theologians than Duval and Maucler defended the doctrine of Papal Infallibility in the seventeenth century. For example, at the commencement of that age, it was advocated by Cardinal Du Perron, in its middle by Cardinal Richelieu (who required Richer to subscribe a formulary of be-

itself, was never without defenders, and which is at the present day advocated by distinguished canonists and theologians, as well as by eminent prelates.[4]

Dieringer says of himself, "I belong, as is well known, to that class of theologians who deem the grounds for belief in Papal Infallibility to be preponderant, nay, nearly decisive.[5] Klee characterised the opinion of the personal infallibility of the Pope, as one in the highest degree worthy of respect."[6] And Pichler, who certainly can by no means be suspected of any undue flattery towards Rome, subjoins, "that this qualification in respect to the defenders of this opinion, must *certainly* be admitted even by *all those* who do not themselves share it."[7] By all, indeed, except by Janus, who has not words and phrases strong enough to stigmatise the doctrine, who represents its adherents as miserable flatterers, and foreseeing and announcing their ascendancy in the coming Œcumenical Council, has designated the latter a synod of flatterers, and a counterpart to the Latrocinium of Ephesus.

Yet more: he disfigures this doctrine, draws of

---

lief, not only in the supremacy, but in the infallibility of the Pope *ex cathedrâ;* and at the close of the century, the doctrine was taught by the great Fenelon.—Tr.]

[4] Here we need only name the French canonist Bouix, as well as the Abbé Christophe (author of the "History of the Papacy in the Fourteenth Century"), and who has published a work, "Le Concile et la Situation Actuelle" Lyons, 1869. p. 19, *seq*. And, again, the German canonists Phillips and Beidtel, the Bishops of Mayence and of St Pölten, and the Archbishops of Westminster and of Malines, who surely merit all respect.

[5] The Theologico-Literary Journal (Theol. Literatur-blatt), of Bonn, p. 138, 1866.

[6] Klee, Dogmatik, t. 1. p. 245, 2d ed.

[7] Pichler, "History of the Ecclesiastical Schism between East and West," vol. ii. p. 746.

it a hideous caricature, and makes it a real bugbear for the cultivated laity, for scholars, and for statesmen. The fundamental idea had been already expressed in the *Gazette of Augsburg.* "To declare the Pope infallible," it was there said, "is to announce the destruction of the world; and if the Pope were himself to make the declaration, he would thereby pronounce himself the incarnate Antichrist."[8] The destruction of the world! Antichrist! The death of all civilisation! The boundless power of the Pope! The ruin to science and to the State, in consequence of the "dogmatic creative power!" and "The inspiration" attributed to the Pope! One, indeed, would have thought, that *in case* Papal Infallibility were to be defined, it could never be represented as anything absolutely new, anything that had suddenly fallen down from the skies, but only as a thing consequent on the doctrine of eminent theologians of preceding times. To these, therefore, one should have recourse, in order to learn the bearing, the purport, and the limitations set to this opinion. But before all, the violence of prejudice left no time for such inquiries; and moreover, a monster must be exhibited in order to scare the multitude.

The defenders of the doctrine in question are far from such a monstrous conception. They distinguish,[9] namely, in the first place, between *infallibility* as the product of mere assistance,[10] and *inspiration;* while our opponent identifies

---

[8] *Allgemeine Zeitung,* 15th June 1868, in the essay on Frohschammer's work entitled, "Christianity and the Modern Natural Sciences," Vienna, 1868.

[9] Dechamps, Archbishop of Malines, L'Infaillibilité et le Concile Général, Paris, c. 3. Schneemann, on the Teaching Power of the Church. Freib. 1868, p. 41, § 29, p. 200, § 331.

[10] Denzinger, (Four Books on Religious Knowledge, vol. ii. p. 152, 153 (in German).

both, nay, speaks of "the power of dogmatic creativeness" as ascribed to the Pope (p. 46). Secondly, they by no means make the Pope the *sole* and *exclusive* organ of divine truth (p. 64), but attribute infallibility to the entire body of the episcopate also." Thirdly, they assign limits to the infallibility of the Church, and thus to that of the Pope also ;—limits which are found in their very object, the *depositum revelationis ;*[12] while Janus represents this power as utterly unbounded, as extending to all departments of life and of science (p. 40). Fourthly, this inerrancy they by no means attribute, as our author everywhere supposes, to all Papal manifestoes without distinction.[13] Not every Papal expression, still less action, can be taken to be a *definitio ex cathedrâ*. Mere mandates of the Pope for special cases, and for particular persons; judgments on individuals resting on the testimony of third persons, and in general on human evidence ; declarations and answers to the inquiries of individuals ; private expressions in learned works, and in confidential letters—even mere disciplinary decrees—belong not to this category ; and hence it follows, that most of the cases enumerated by our adversary are quite irrelevant. The infallibilists (to make use of a word much employed by Janus), are as little obliged as the fallibilists (if for the sake of brevity, as well as of contrast, I may be allowed so to designate the opposite party),—the infallibilists, I say, are as little obliged to give up the position of Melchior Canus : "qui summi Pontificis *omni de*

---

[11] Schneemann, loc. cit., P. 110, *seq.*
[12] Reinerding, Theol. Fundament., Tract i., P. 11, § 1, 5, n. 389, *seq.* ; n. 492, *seq*. Schneemann, loc. cit., p. 52, *seq*. Dechamps, loc. cit., c. 4. Ketteler, The General Council. Mayence, 1869, p. 78, *seq.*
[13] Reinerding's loc. cit., Tract ii., P. 11, § 3, a. 3, n. 455, *seq.* Dechamps, c. 11, Schneemann, p. 157, *seq.*

re qualecunque judicium temere ac sine delectû defendunt, hos sedis Apostolicæ auctoritatem labefactare, non fovere, evertere, non firmare."[14] They can reprehend real abuses with as much frankness as Janus himself; but they will still reserve to themselves the right of protesting against a mode of controversy (such as, with an utter misrepresentation of the doctrine combated, is carried on in this book), as one most frivolous and most unworthy.

It is only later on, quite at the close of his work, after he had brought into the field whole squadrons of auxiliaries raked together from all quarters, Janus, in some measure, bethinks him of the necessity of more nearly inspecting his foe, of examining more closely into the doctrine of the infallibilists. This delay is fortunate for his readers, who might otherwise perhaps have lost some of the preceding valuable pages. He observes: "The distinction between a judgment pronounced *ex cathedrâ*, and a merely occasional and casual utterance, is, indeed, a perfectly reasonable one, not only in the case of the Pope, but of any bishop or professor. In other words, every one whose office it is to teach can and will at times speak off-hand and loosely on dogmatic and ethical questions; whereas in his capacity of a public and official teacher, he pronounces deliberately, and with serious regard to the consequences of his teaching. No reasonable man will pretend that the remarks made by a Pope in conversation [15] are definitions of faith. But beyond this nothing more is conceded; for the mere fact that the Pope has given a public written declaration, constitutes it an *ex cathedrâ* pronouncement;" and the

---

[14] De loc. Theol. v., 5 ad 4. Cf. Bianchi Op. cit. l. i., § 21, n. 1, p. 183.

[15] Such, for example, as the expressions of Pope Innocent X., cited by Janus (p. 414), from the works of Arnauld.

expression, *privatus doctor*, when used of a Pope, is like talking of wooden iron" (p. 404-5). Against this view, the infallibilists will certainly protest. They will show that a Pope can very well be conceived to be a private teacher, when he expresses in a private way, though even by writing, his opinion; as he is certainly a public teacher, when he proclaims in the face of the whole world any doctrine;[16] and again, that a Pope, in the composition of scientific works, may very well be classed with ordinary writers. Benedict XIV. as Pope completed his work, "De Synodo Dioecesanâ," which he had previously commenced. Herein he expressly adhered to the words of Melchior Canus, as well as to the example of his predecessor Innocent IV., who, in like manner, after his elevation to the Pontifical throne, composed his Commentary on the Decretals (p. 161); and as he had put forth his views only as a private scholar, he abandoned these to the full liberty of discussion."[17]

Against further objections, the infallibilists will argue, that the divergence of theologians on minor points does not do away with their consent on the chief matter; and that in all essential things the most eminent divines are in perfect accord.[18] If the theological conceptions of the last

[16] Bennettis' Privileg. S. Petri vindic., P. 11, t. v., Romæ, 1759. App. p. 402. Bifariam in Pontifice distingui oportere personam vice plus simplici admonui, quâ nempe *doctoris publici* aliquando personam gerit, quamque tum gerere reputandus est quum *Ecclesiæ universæ* edicit, quâ *doctoris* aliquando *privati* dumtaxat personam induit, quum ad particulares quorumdam expostulationes respondet, sive privatas quasdam suas opiniones depromit. In the latter case, quando agitur de factis mere personalibus, sive de factis ad forum contentiosum pertinentibus, sive de factis pure criminalibus, tum falli et fallere Pontificem posse, nihilque non humani pati non inficiamur.

[17] Benedict XIV., Praef. in op. de Syn. Diœc. fin.

[18] *Vide* the *Augsburg Pastoral Journal* of 9th October 1869. No. 41, *seq.*, p. 323, *seq.*

three centuries have become more precise than those of the earlier schoolmen, this has arisen from the opposition the doctrine in question has experienced; but even among the schoolmen, equivalent definitions were not wanting.[19] The distinction between official or *ex cathedrâ* infallibility, and the possibility of a personal denial of the faith, Janus himself believes to have found, with some degree of probability at least, even earlier; namely, among the Gregorians of the eleventh century. (P. 115.) If some theologians require that the Pope, before pronouncing his decision, should inform himself well on the matter, should carefully examine the subject in all its bearings, should consult his cardinals and theologians, further, should invoke the Holy Spirit, and institute prayers;—so other divines are only in so far opposed to these conditions, as they herein recognise no tokens of a dogmatic decree, but only pre-suppositions, which are in a certain degree self-evident. They suggest that even general Councils must have recourse to all human means; and that the adoption of such precautions on their part must ever be presumed; but that if we must first certify, whether such have really taken place, then every decision of the Church can be questioned and rejected by misbelievers.[20] In this most theologians

---

[19] Of more ancient authors, compare Rustic. Diac. adv. Acephalos. (Bennettis, p. 1, t. 1, p. 3). What Bonaventura (in his Summ. q. 1, a.3, d. 3) states as preliminary conditions of Papal inerrancy, signifies as much as the modern "*ex cathedrâ.*"

[20] Melchior Canus de loc. theol. v. 5: Quæ res, ut de conciliis quoque dicatur, subsunt omnino causæ eædem: Sive Pontificum, sive Conciliorum diligentiam in fidei causâ finiendâ in dubium vocant, eos necesse est omnia Pontificum judicia ac Conciliorum infirmare. . . . Si semel hæreticis hanc licentiam permittimus, ut in quæstionem vocent, num Ecclesiæ judices eam diligentiam et curam exhibuerint, quâ opus erat, ut quæstio viâ et ratione finiretur: ecquis adeo cæcus est, qui non videat, mox omnia Pontificum Con-

The Doctrine of Papal Infallibility. 57

agree, that a definition *ex cathedrâ* has then been pronounced, when the Pope, in the full enjoyment of his freedom, has, in a decree addressed to the whole Church, declared an opinion to be heretical, and laid its defenders under an anathema, or as Janus says, "cursed," or proposed any proposition as an article of faith. Nor is this the only case, where such a definition is admissible; but wherever the Pope unmistakably announces that he, as supreme shepherd, teacher, and judge, "as the father and doctor of all Christians (to use the words of the Council of Florence), wishes to decide a question, and to bind the conscience of all believers."[21] Hence definitions may be recognized by the customary expressions, without this or that formula being absolutely needful.[22] Herein it is only the main decision which is characterized as binding; but the reasonings and the rhetorical ornaments of a Papal Decree constitute no standard of belief.[23]

The infallibilists on their side urge the close intercommunion between the Pope and the Church, which they assert can never be severed.[24] While the Gallicans regard the Papal decisions as final and irreformable, when, and in so far as they ex-

ciliorumque judicia labefactari? Cf. Thomassin Dissert. in Conalia, Diss. xviii. n. 99.

[21] Bellarmin. de Rom. Pontif. iv. 3. Suarez de fide Disp. v., § 8. Card. Sfondat. Gall. vindic. Diss. iv. § 4, n. 1. Bianchi Op. cit. L. i., § 21, p. 184. Petrus Ballerini de vi ac ratione Primatûs, c. 15, n. 24, p. 288, 289. ed. Veronæ. Maur. Capellari (afterwards Gregory XVI). Triumph of the Holy See, German Trans., Augsburg 1833, c. 24, § 5, p. 458, *seq.* So also the ex-Jesuit Passaglia in his polemical writing against the Encyclical of 1864, (sopra l'enciclica promulgata il giorno 21 Decemb. 1864, et sopra le 80 proposizioni. Domande riverenti. Torino 1865 (p. 56, 57). For other authors, see Phillips's Canon Law, vol. ii. p. 340.

[22] Deschamps, l. c. c. 11, p. 136.
[23] Bennettis, loc. cit. p. 409.
[24] Schneemann, loc. cit., p. 201, *seq.*, § 333, *seq.*

press the belief of the Church;[25] the former teach, that by virtue of the promises of Christ, this is *always* the case; for Christ bound all the faithful in general, and without exception, to pay obedience to Peter and his successors. But never can an obligation to accept error be regarded as sanctioned by our Lord. God, they contend, can never permit, that believers should be obliged to submit to an untruth;[26] the *silentium obsequiosum* of the Jansenists leads to hypocrisy;[27] a tribunal, from which lies no appeal, yet withal fallible, would be an engine of tyrannical coercion.[28] But as the obligation to accept error is inconsistent with the will and the character of Christ, so where a Papal sentence is binding on belief, there the gift of infallibility follows as a matter of course. In matters, wherein a submission of faith is required, the obligation cannot be incumbent on one believer, without attaching to all other members of the Church. Hence it is not so absurd as some would wish us to believe, (p. 407) when Bellarmine, and after him so many others, speak of a decree addressed to the *whole Church* as an infallible decision. Moreover, such a privilege belongs to the Pope, only in so far as he is the teacher of the *whole Church*. That in earlier times the Popes issued decrees of faith in Synods, alters nothing in the case. This form of procedure they could adopt even at the present day, if they chose. The judi-

---

[25] Declar. Cler. Gallic. 1682, art. iv., Febron. de statû Eccl., c. vi., § 4, n. 3.

[26] Veith de primatû et infallibilitate § 11, § 31, *seq*. Ballerini Op. cit. c. 15. Devoti Jus, canon. univ. t. 1, p. 90 *seq*.

[27] Phillip's Can. Law, 11, § 89, p. 326.

[28] On the prohibition of an Appeal from the Pope to another Judge, and even to a Council, compare Bennettis, P. 11, t. iii., art. 5. § 3. p. 571, *seq*. Pignattelli Consultat. Canon., t. ix. Cons. 92, p. 240, *seq*.

cial decision was assigned to the Cathedra Petri,[29] to the Prince of the Apostles, to whom the promise was given, and who lives and judges in every Pope for the time being.[30]

But the promise of Christ alleged by the infallibilists, their opponents will not admit, at least not in an equal degree. The passage in Luke xxii. 32, *seq.*, applies, according to Janus (p. 96), to Peter personally, to his denial and his conversion. This, however, Catholic theologians deny. However, the word $\epsilon\pi\iota\sigma\tau\rho\acute{\epsilon}\psi\alpha\varsigma$[31] (converted) may be explained, "still the essential unity between the special occasion, and the significance of Christ's word of promise, embracing, as it does, all times, may easily be established."[32] "The see of Peter," observes Professor Döllinger, "was to remain a place of truth, a citadel of firm faith, conducing to the strength of all; for the words, as well as the prayers, of our Lord were addressed not merely to the individual person, and for the immediate moment, but they were meant to lay an enduring foundation; their significance was, above all, for the Church, and for her future needs beheld by Christ in spirit."[33]

When Janus further observes, that not a single doctor of the Church, down to the end of the

[29] Cf. Felix III. (Syn. Rom.) ep. 12.
[30] Bennettis, P. 1, vol. 1, § 4. Denzinger's "Criticism on the Lectures of Thiersch," 1, p. 100 (in German).
[31] Bede, Maldonatus, Grotius, Bengel, and Ewald interpret the word as a circumlocution of the adverb rursum, vicissim; and with them agrees Schneemann, loc. cit., p. 173. On the other hand, his former *confrère*, C. Passaglia, while referring to other passages in Scripture, explains *conversus* simply as the participle, yet, unlike most others, understands it not as having reference to contrition and to penance. De prærogativis B. Petri. Ratisbon, 1850, L. ii. c. 13, n. 198, *seq.*, p. 560.
[32] P. Schegg, Comment. on the Gospel of St Luke. Munich, 1865, vol. iii. p. 253-254 (in German).
[33] Christianity and the Church, p. 32, § 56, 1st ed. (in German).

seventh century, has given the interpretation of this text disputed by him, are, therefore, the passages of later Popes, and of Western teachers;[34] are, therefore, the splendid testimonies of the later Greeks, such as the patriarch John VI. of Constantinople (anno 715),[35] St Theodore the Studite (anno 826),[36] and the exegetist Theophylact of Achrida,[37] robbed of their weight? But it is not even true, as our opponent repeatedly states (p. 93), that the first to give this interpretation was Pope Agatho, in 680, "when trying to avert the threatened condemnation of his predecessor, Honorius." The same interpretation had, on the 8th October 649, been put forward in Rome by Bishop Stephen of Dora, the envoy of St Sophronius, Bishop of Jerusalem,[38] and before him by the Popes Gelasius, Pelagius II., and Gregory the Great;[39] and before these again, by the great Leo.[40] So exceedingly trustworthy are the statements of our Janus!

But even of the texts in Matt. xvi. 18, and

---

[34] For example, John viii. ep. 76, ad Petrum Com. (Mansi. xvii. 65); Leo IX. ep. ad Mich. Cærul. c. 7 (Will Acta., p. 68); S. Bernard, ep. 190, ad Innoc. II., Albertus M. (cited by Janus, p. 284).

[35] Ep. ad Constantin. Pap. ap. Combefis. Auctar. Bibl. P.P. Græc. ii. 211, *seq*. He calls "the Pope the Head of the Christian Priesthood, whom, in Peter, the Lord commanded to confirm his brethren."

[36] Lib. ii. ep. 12, p. 1153, ed. Migne. He says openly to Pope Paschal II., "'To thee Christ hath spoken the words, 'Confirm thy brethren.'"

[37] Com. in Evangel. Luc. xxii. (Migne P.P. Græc. cxxiii. 1073). "This (to confirm thy brethren) becometh thee, who, after me, art the Rock and the foundation of the Church. We may suppose that this has not been said of the apostles alone, that they were to be confirmed by Peter, but of all the faithful, even to the end of the world:" ὡς ἂν ὑποστηριχθῶσιν ὑπὸ τοῦ Πέτρου, ἀλλὰ καὶ περὶ πάντων τῶν ἄχρι τῆς συντελείας τοῦ αἰῶνος πιστῶν.

[38] Mansi. Conc. x. 849. Hard. III, 711-713. Apud Pichler, loc. cit., p. 135.

[39] Apud Schneemann, loc. cit., p. 174, § 288.

[40] Leo. M. Serm. iv. c. 3, 4. Cf. serm. 83.

John xx. 18, our opponent observes as follows :—
"Of all the fathers of that time (the first six centuries of our era), who have exegetically explained these passages in the Gospels, in respect to the power conferred on Peter, *not a single one applies them to the Roman bishops as Peter's successors*" (p. 91). But what does Janus understand by exegetical explanations? If pure exegesis be the question, so even at the present day, it were quite sufficient if the Catholic exegetist in the interpretation of Matthew and John confined his observations to Peter, and explained the import of our Lord's words merely in respect to him. But that the prerogatives bestowed on Peter were transmitted to his successors, and that those successors are the Roman pontiffs, is a truth so clearly proclaimed by tradition, that even the Gallicans have never called it in question.[41] But when in the interpretation of these texts, the Fathers inquire into the primacy of Peter, then they characterize it as a *permanent* institution. Further, when they speak of the Roman Bishop for the time being, they say of him he occupies the see of Peter—he sits in the chair of Peter—Peter lives and works in him—in him he feedeth all the Lord's sheep."[42] Have they not then herein given sufficient evidence of their convictions?

As Christ said to his disciples, " He that heareth you, heareth me ;" so the Fathers exclaim, " Whoso heareth the Bishop of Rome, heareth Peter."[43] Bishop Possessor writes to Pope Hormisdas as

---

[41] Cf. Bossuet's Discourse at the Assembly of 1682, and with this, Bennettis' Op. cit. P. I., t. i., p. 205.

[42] In Cyprian the locus Petri is the same with the locus Fabiani (ep. 52, al. 55, Coustant. p. 165). The other modes of speech see in Siric., ep. i. ad Himer. n. i., Bonif. I. ep. 4, exord. ep. 5, n. 1. p. 1021. Leo M., serm. 2, c. ii., serm. 3, c. 4.

[43] Cf. Bennettis' Op. cit. P. I, t. i., p. 95, *seq*.

follows: "From whom is the strengthening of vacillating faith more to be looked for than from the bishop of that see, whose first occupant heard from Christ those words, "Thou art Peter, and on this rock I will build my Church?"⁴⁴ Leo the Great says: "The firmness of that faith, which was praised in the Prince of the Apostles, is always enduring; and in the same way as what Peter believed in Christ, to wit, His divinity, lasts for ever; so that which Christ ordained in Peter, namely, his primacy and its invincible power, is ever abiding. Thus ever lasts the ordinance of truth: Peter perseveres in the rock-like strength conferred on him, and always holds the helm of the Church entrusted to his care." This, says Leo further, is even at present the case; and even in an unworthy heir this dignity has not ceased to exist. So even now the flock (according to John xxi. 17, 18) is still led by Peter, who confirmeth his successor, and prayeth for him.⁴⁵ What Peter has received, says Leo's predecessor, Sixtus III., that he has transmitted to his successors.⁴⁶ In the same way, Gelasius derives the pre-eminence of the Roman Church directly from the words of Christ addressed to Peter.⁴⁷ Theodore the Studite calls the Roman See the See of the Coryphæus, the See in which

---

[44] Possessor ep. Migne., lxiii, p. 489.

[45] Leo. M., serm. 3, c. 2–4; serm. 4, c. 4, cf. ep. 16, init.

[46] Sixt. III., ep. 6, ad. John Ant., c. 5, p. 120, ed. Coustant. In the same way Pope Julius I., ep. ad Euseb. n. 22, ibid. p. 388: ἃ παρειλήφαμεν παρὰ τοῦ μακαρίου Πέτρου τοῦ ἀποστόλου, ταῦτα καὶ ὑμῖν δηλῶ. Cf. Liber. ep. 8, p. 432. ["The things we have received from blessed Peter the Apostle, these I manifest unto you also."]

[47] Gelas. ep. 33, n. 5. Quamvis universa per orbem ecclesia catholica unus thalamus Christi sit, sancta tamen Romana ecclesia nullis synodicis constitutis cæteris ecclesiis prælata est, sed evangelicā voce Domini et Salvatoris nostri primatum obtinuit: Tu es Petrus et super hanc petram," etc.

Christ has deposited the keys of faith,[48] and from which we are to receive the certainty of faith.[49] And already before him, Sergius, the Metropolitan of Cyprus, addressed Pope Theodore: "O holy Head, Christ our God hath destined thy Apostolic See to be an immovable foundation, and a pillar of the faith. For thou art, as the divine Word truly saith, Peter, and on thee as a foundation-stone have the pillars of the Church been fixed.[50] The writings of the Fathers, whenever they speak of the Pope, are full of echoes and allusions to those Scriptural words,[51] and what is said of Peter, the Popes claim decidedly for themselves.[52] The Church, as well as the *petra* or rock on which it is founded, passed for invincible.[53] If some Fathers call faith the foundation of the Church, so this they take not in an absolute and abstract sense; but by it understand the living faith of Peter, which was the reason wherefore he was chosen to be the foundation-stone of the Church. Hence theologians say, the faith of Peter is *causaliter*, his person *formaliter*, the basis of the Church.[54] Not *on* his confession, says Döllinger, but *on account* of his confession, must the Church be founded on him

[48] Theod. Stud., l. ii., ep. 63, ad Naucrat. Migne. xcix., 1281, a.
[49] L. ii., ep. 129, ad Leon., p. 1420 : κἀκεῖθεν (ἀπὸ τῆς 'Ρώμης) τὸ ἀσφαλὲς δεχέσθω τῆς πίστεως. [Thence (from Rome) receive the certainty of faith].
[50] Ep. ad Theod. lecta in Sess. ii., Concil. Lat., anno 649.
[51] For example, S. Ambros. ep. ad. Siric. (Coustant, epist. Rom. Pontif. p. 669, ep. n. 1). Qui diligenter commissam tibi *januam* serves et pia sollicitudine *Christi ovile* custodias, dignus, quem oves Domini audiant, et sequantur.
[52] Simplic. Pap. ep. 4 ad Zenon. Imp. Perstat in successoribus suis hæc eadem apostolicae norma doctrinae, cui Dominus totius curam ovilis injunxit, cui se usque ad finem sæculi minime defuturum, cui portas inferi nunquam prævalituras esse promisit, etc.
[53] Origen, tom. xii. in Matt. n. 11.
[54] Philips's Canon Law, I. § 13, p. 91, et *seq.* Denzinger's "Criticism on the Lectures of Thiersch," I, p. 53.

—the man with a rock-like firmness of character; for the Church, as it consists of persons, of living beings, then also needed, and always needs, a living, personal foundation. As the edifice of the Church is one destined to endure for all times; so this pre-eminence of Peter, which with him as the foundation must hold the Church together, necessarily after him passes to others by way of transmission.[55] The power of binding and of loosing was indeed imparted to all the Apostles (Matt. xviii. 18), but only after Peter, and on the pre-supposition of his primacy. Next, it was bestowed upon them altogether, but first of all granted to Peter alone.[56] The keys of the kingdom of heaven, too, were given to him only.[57] Janus, indeed, asserts in contradiction to Döllinger, that it is against all the Patristic interpretations and the exegetical tradition of the Church, to explain the power of the keys as something differing from that of binding and of loosing. But independently of the fact, that this exegetical tradition is by no means constant and universal, one prerogative of Peter above the other Apostles lies in the extent of his power, and in its degree.

[55] Loc cit. p. 31, § 55.
[56] Bennettis, P. 1, t. i., p. 48.
[57] Tertull. de praescr. c. 22 : Latuit aliquid Petrum aedificandae ecclesiae petram dictum, claves regni coelorum consecutum? De pud, c. 21 : super te, inquit, aedificabo ecclesiam meam, et tibi dabo claves, non ecclesiae. Scorp. c. 10. Si adhuc clausum putas coelum, memento claves ejus hic Dominum Petro, et per eum ecclesiae reliquisse. Origen on Matt. tom. xiii., p. 31, points out here the pre-eminence of Peter above the other apostles. Eulogius of Alexandria (in Phot. Bibl. cod. 280, l. ii., c. nov.), remarks, that it was not to John or to any another apostle, but to Peter, Christ gave the keys (whatever Photius might contend). Optatus of Milevi de Schism. Donat. L. vii. 3 : Petrus . . . claves regni coelorum communicandas ceteris *solus* accepit. Stephen of Dora, loc. cit. says : " Claves regni coelorum creditae sunt Petro, ac ipse unus magnus secundum veritatem et princeps apostolorum ad claudendum aperiendumque illas promeruit. Cf. Ambros. in Luc., L. x. n. 67. Nyss. de castigat. op. iii., p. 314. *Morelli*. Basil de judicio Dei, n. 7.

The Doctrine of Papal Infallibility. 65

The keys of the kingdom of heaven denote the highest spiritual authority.[58] Yet this question does not specially concern the infallibilists;—it belongs to the general doctrine of the Papal supremacy, which Janus enters on without a careful discrimination of the particular matters in dispute.

Further, it is asserted by our opponent; "Up to the time of the Pseudo-Isidorian Decretals, no serious attempt was made anywhere to introduce the neo-Roman theory of infallibility. The Popes did not dream of laying claim to such a privilege" (p. 76). It seems to us, however, that independently of the liturgical formulas used at Rome in the fifth century,[59] a very serious step was in the year 517 taken in this direction by Pope Hormisdas, when he allayed the Acacian schism, and prescribed to the Oriental prelates a formulary, to wit, that all bishops were bound to submit to the decisions of the Roman See,[60] a formulary which, signed in the reigns of the Emperors Justin I. and Justinian, was often afterwards used, which in 867 was communicated to his legates by Pope Nicholas I., and in 869 again subscribed by the bishops in the eighth Œcumenical Council. The copy, signed by the Byzantine patriarch Mennas, runs as follows:[61]

[58] Passaglia speaks fully de Prærogativis B. Petri. L. ii., c. 8. *seq.*; p. 485, *seq.* Phillips's Canon Law, § 14, p. 98, *et seq.*
[59] Liber. Sacram. Leonis, p. 40, 41, ed. *Baller.* Qui secundum promissionis tuae ineffabile constitutum apostolicae confessioni superna dispensatione largiris, ut in veritatis tuæ fundamine solidata nulla mortiferae falsitatis jura prævaleant . . . ipsaque sit sacri corporis ubique vera compago, quae te dispensante, devota obsequitur, *quidquid Sedes illa censuerit, quam tenere voluisti totius ecclesiae principatum.*
[60] Mansi. viii. 451, xvi. 316. Bennettis, P. ii., t. v., p. 198, *et seq.* The Defensio declar. Cleri Gall. P. iii. L. x. c. vii. recognises the long-prevailing use of the formulary, which is still found in many manuscripts.—Card. Pitra Jur. eccl. Græc. hist. et monum., t. i., p. xl., *seq.*, t. ii., p. iv., *seq.*
[61] Pitra, t. ii., p. 217, *seq.*

—"The first principle of salvation is to preserve the rule of true faith, and in nowise to deviate from the tradition of the Fathers. For the sentence of the Lord cannot be disregarded, who hath said, " *Thou art Peter, and on this rock will I build my Church.*" This sentence has been proved by facts, for in the Apostolic See the Catholic religion is *ever preserved inviolate.*[62] After the mention of Œcumenical Councils, of all the dogmatic letters of Leo the Great, and after a short statement of the doctrine of the Incarnation, as well as an enumeration of the heretics condemned, this formulary goes on further to declare: "*In all things following the Apostolic See*, we announce what has been ordained by it." In many copies it is even said: " I hope to be worthy to be in that one communion with you, which the Apostolic See enjoins, in which is the perfect and true solidity of the Christian religion; promising also that the names of those who are separated from the communion of the Catholic Church, that is, those who are not united in mind with the Apostolic See, shall not be recited in the Holy Mysteries."

The Emperor Justinian, who had already said to Pope Hormisdas, " We hold that to be truly Catholic which has been made known to us by your venerable response,"[63] who solicited of Pope John II., a confirmation of his own theological decree,[64] renewed before Pope Agapetus the

---

[62] Compare with this Iren. adv. haer. iii. 3, 2 : In quo semper ab his, qui sunt undique, conservata est ea, quae est ab apostolis traditio ; as well as Cyprian's expressions upon the Roman Church, as ecclesiæ catholicæ radix et matrix (ep. 48, al. 45, Coustant., p. 132,) as Petri cathedra, ecclesia principalis, unde unitas sacerdotalis exorta est. . . ad quos (Romanos) perfidia non possit habere accessum (ep. 59, al. 55 Coust., p. 184, 185.)
[63] Mansi. viii. 484.
[64] L. 7, 8, cod. i., 1 de summa Trinitate.

The Doctrine of Papal Infallibility. 67

above-mentioned Formulary, with the addition, "that he would bind all to the like obedience." [65] The judgment of Rome was so decidedly held up as final, that already Augustine declared "Rome hath spoken ; the cause is ended "—" Roma locuta est ; causa finita est." [66] Even the learned Greek exegetist, Theodoret, wrote to the Roman priest Renatus, as follows : " This most holy See has preserved the supremacy over all Churches on the earth, for one especial reason among many others ; to wit, that it has remained intact from the defilement of heresy. No one has ever sat on that Chair, who has taught heretical doctrine ; rather that See has ever preserved unstained the Apostolic grace."[67] The supervision and the *magisterium* in matters of faith, the Emperor Marcian also attributed to the Pope.[68] And St Peter Chrysologus wrote to Euty-

---

[65] Pitra, t. ii., p. 219.
[66] These celebrated words Janus (p. 70, *seq.*) vainly strives to distort. The question was not whether the heretics had completely submitted,—a submission which they did not evince even to the General Council ; but whether Augustine, in the Papal Confirmation of the African synodal decrees, found the final judgment on the Pelagian heresy. He expressed the wish : " Utinam aliquando finiatur error ;" it was not the former thing, but the latter, which was the object of his desire. With the words in the serm. 131, al. 2 de verb. apost., others are to be compared :—
Op. imperf. c. ful. L. II., resp. ad q. 103 : quid adhuc quaeris examen, quod jam factum est apud Apostolicam Sedem ? Damnata ergo hæresis non adhuc Episcopis Examinanda, sed coercenda est a potestatibus christianis. L. II. ad Bonif. c. 3 : Literis b. m. Papæ Innocentii de hac re tota dubitatio sublata est. Ep. 157 ad Optat : In verbis Apostolicæ Sedis tam antiqua atque fundata, certa ac clara est fides catholica, ut nefas sit dubitare catholicis Christianis. The usual objections are refuted by Bennettis, P. i., t. ii., p. 309, *seq.*
[67] Theodoret ep. 116. p. 1324, *seq.*
[68] Ep. 73 inter ep. P. Leonis : sanctitatem tuam principatum in episcopatu divinæ fidei possidentem. In Greek : τὴν σὴν ἁγιωσύνην ἐπισκοπεύουσαν καὶ ἄρχουσαν τῆς θείας πίστεως. Cf. Leo ep. 5 c. 2.; Qui Dominus beatissimo apostolo Petro primatum fidei sua remuneratione commisit.

ches: "The blessed Peter liveth on his Chair, and there presides, and giveth to those who seek it the truth of faith."⁶⁹ And in despite of such testimonies, to which many others might be annexed, we are told it was the Pseudo-Isidore, who first prepared the soil for the growth of the doctrine of Papal Infallibility!!

Pope Pelagius I., indeed (p. 73), asserted his orthodoxy, without appealing to the fact, that the Bishops of Rome had the privilege of inerrancy. But the reason was that, personally suspected of favouring false doctrines, he was obliged to make before others a personal justification, and indeed in reference to his conduct *before* his accession to the Papacy, which had been the immediate occasion of these attacks.⁷⁰ "But often and earnestly as the Popes exhorted separated bishops and churches to return to communion with Rome, they never appealed to any peculiar authority, or exemption from error in the Roman See" (p. 73). Surely such an appeal to heretics and schismatics would have been unfitting and idle; however necessary, on the other hand, to prove the nullity of their grounds of separation. But often, especially when without the guilt of heresy ecclesiastical obedience was withheld, have the Popes appealed to the pre-eminent authority of St Peter, as occurred particularly in the Acacian controversy. For such an appeal, the epistles of Pope Gelasius and the formulary of Hormisdas are sufficient proofs."⁷¹ Pelagius I. says of the western bishops who resisted the fifth General Council, that they ought to have

---

⁶⁹ Ep. ad Eutych. inter Leon. Epp. n. 25.
⁷⁰ Bennettis, P. xi., t. v., art. xi., p. 237. Cf. Hefele Conc. II, p. 887, *et seq.*
⁷¹ Gelas. ep. 8, ad Anast. Imp.; ep. 13, ad Episc. Dard.; Commonit. ad Faust.

referred their doubts to the Apostolic See; that they would be separated from the communion of the whole world, if they omitted in the Mass the commemoration of the Pope, in whom now rests the solidity of the Holy See.[72] As Pope Agatho, in respect to the Monothelites; so Gregory II., against the eastern Iconoclasts, appealed to the mediatorial position of the Pope between East and West, as well as to Peter, the prince of the Apostles.[73] But we shall elsewhere have occasion to adduce on this matter proofs more numerous still.

As to the further grounds against the doctrine of Papal Infallibility, Janus ever proceeds on the same false assumptions, which have been already sufficiently appreciated. While in his opinion, the hypothesis of infallibility seems to recommend itself by its convenience, by the facility of its use, and renders Councils, as well as all scientific inquiry, superfluous; it makes on the one hand a systematic falsification of Church history absolutely requisite, and raises up on the other a wall of separation between Catholics and the separated religious communities, and "indeed a wall the strongest and the most impenetrable of all" (p. xxvii.) What Protestant must not be deterred by the prospect "of incurring excommunication in this world, and everlasting damnation in the next, when after infallibility has been made into a dogma, he should venture to question the full weight and value of any new article of faith coined in the Vatican mint!" (p. 47). How must he be deterred, "when the Pope encroaches on a quite foreign domain," when he makes decisions "according to the will of the Jesuits, and of the bishops acting under their guidance!" (p. 16). Yet the very

---

[72] Pelag. I., ep. 2, ad Narset. Patric. Op. 6, ad Episc. Tusc.
[73] Greg. II., ep. 1, ad Leon. Mansi. xii. 959, *seq*.

monstrosity of the hypothesis we have stated, seems to spare the advocates of Papal Infallibility the trouble of a serious refutation, for occasionally even the organs of their opponents cite theological expressions, which are calculated in some degree to diminish in their eyes the terrors of this bugbear.[74]

That the matter should be contemplated from every point of view, Janus now proceeds to moral, ascetic, and psychological reflections. Under the influence of the idea of their infallibility, the popes themselves, in our author's opinion, become corrupt, are involved in the clouds and fumes of self-conceit and arrogance, as even several pontiffs who had been earlier excellent cardinals, became, after their elevation to the Papal throne, totally changed (p. 416). We question very much whether the assumption of infallibility (which can be regarded only as a privilege imparted *for the benefit of the faithful*,[75] and not for the private advantage of the Pope for the time being, which exempts the Pope as little as a General Council from the obligation of prayer for divine assistance, as well as from the careful

---

[74] The *Allgemeine Zeitung*, of the 14th of October 1869 (No. 287), cites, among other things as especially worthy of notice, the following words from a pastoral letter of the Prince-Bishop of Seckau:— "The infallibility of the Pope by no means signifies that in those things, which refer not to divine revelation, his opinions are unerring; for, in reference to things which lie out of the sphere of divine Revelation, Christ has not appointed him as His vicegerent," &c. This may sound new to the readers of the "Five Articles" in the *Allgemeine Zeitung*; but to those conversant with theological literature, this doctrine is tolerably old.

[75] This is expressed by Dante, who is so highly honoured by Janus also, in the following words of his "Comedia Divina:"

"Be ye more staid,
O Christians! Not like feather by each wind
Removable; nor think to cleanse yourselves
In every water. Either Testament,
The Old and New, is yours; and *for your guide*,
The Shepherd of the Church. Let this suffice
To save you."—*Paradise, Canto V., Cary's Trans.*

The Doctrine of Papal Infallibility. 71

examination of all necessary data), leads in itself more easily to pride, than the other prerogatives involved in the Papacy, which, though by no means completely unlimited,[76] are still very extensive, and, for practical matters, far more serviceable. We question whether the arrogance possibly arising out of the possession of such exalted power, especially of a power that imposes the heaviest burden, and involves a fearful responsibility before the Supreme Judge, can ever equal the pride evinced in the intellectual conceit of so many modern scholars. We question whether, amid the constant difficulties, embarrassments, and struggles which the Holy See, especially for the last centuries down to our times, has had on all sides to endure, an old man seated on the chair of Peter, much tried in his previous life, and now mostly near the brink of the grave, should, amid the manifestations of homage paid to him, and amid the "fumes of incense," lose, *as a rule*, all sobriety of mind. "An individual Pope, we are told, is always exposed to the danger of falling under the influence of sycophants and intriguers, and thus being forced into giving dogmatic decisions. Advantage is taken of his predilection for some theological opinion, or for some religious order and its favourite doctrines, or of his ignorance of the history of dogma, or of his vanity and ambition for signalising his pontificate by a memorable decision, and one supposed to be in the interest of the Roman See, and thus associating his name with a great dogmatic event, which may constitute an epoch in the Church. Nor is anything easier for a Pope than to keep all contradiction at arm's length: as a rule, no one who is not expressly consulted,

---

[76] *Vide* thereupon Döllinger, "Church and Churches," pp. 38-44. Bennettis, P. i., t. iii., p. 255, *seq.*

ventures even to make any representation, or suggest any doubts to him" (p. 412, 413).

Here, indeed, is the Pope conceived after the type of a Louis XIV., or of a Napoleon I. But the history of the popes furnishes numerous examples, how many well-grounded remonstrances have been brought before them, and how many have found a favourable hearing. The instruction for the framing of the ordinary [77] *relationes statûs* has a special section for the Postulata and Desiderata of bishops. In the granting of audiences, the popes are far more obliging than other princes, far more condescending than many worldly grandees, who are not princes. But the sovereign Pontiff is in the very greatest danger!! "The flattering conviction, so welcome *to the old Adam*, grows up easily within his soul, that his wishes and thoughts are *divine inspirations*, that he is under the special grace and guidance of heaven, and that, by virtue of his office, the fulness of truth and knowledge, as of power, is his *without effort of his own*" (p. 413).

Happy, indeed, would the Pope now be! He could dismiss most of his functionaries, totally abolish the "*Curia*," so odious to many, save much money, and withal keep more soldiers. Excellent arrangement! Nay, we are told, "he will the more believe, and *the more quickly catch* at this idea, the smaller is his information, and the less suspicion or knowledge he has of the doubts and difficulties, which restrain *learned theologians* (like Janus, for example) from adopting a particular doctrinal opinion. And thus even a well-meaning Pope (how kind!) *may come to imagine* that he is far removed from all self-exaltation, and is simply the

---

[77] Issued by Benedict XIII., and explained by Benedict XIV. in his work " De Synodo Diœcesanâ." L. xiii., c. 7, *et seq.*, especially c. 13, *seq.*

humble *organ of the Holy Ghost, who speaks through him*" (p. 413). No Pope has ever attributed to himself *inspiration*, but divine assistance only ; but we see how Janus *imagines* he has searched the hearts, and tried the reins of popes. " Their likeness unto God " (p. 48) will not make them shudder so much as it does Janus.

Yet the latter has still other weapons in store ; for history proves to him, with noon-day evidence, the very reverse of the inerrancy of the popes.

CHAPTER V.

ALLEGED ERRORS AND CONTRADICTIONS OF THE POPES.

T is no small undertaking to pronounce upon questions treated in many hundreds of learned works, a fixed judgment within the compass of a few lines. But for this task, Janus has mustered sufficient courage; he arrays, even from the fourth century, his arguments against Papal Infallibility. Happy are the popes of the first three centuries, of whom we possess but few documents; for, from the less precise and definite terminology, which has already exposed to sharp criticism many of the ante-Nicene Fathers, these pontiffs would have hardly escaped the severest censures. Let us now briefly examine what, on the part of the advocates of Papal Infallibility, may possibly be alleged against the examples adduced.

1. "Pope Julius I. pronounced Marcellus, of Ancyra, an avowed Sabellian, orthodox at his Roman synod" (p. 68). Not only Pope Julius had done this, but the Council of Sardica also. Marcellus had waited in Rome for his accusers a year and three months.[1] When these did not appear, and his confession of faith appeared satisfactory, Pope Julius acquitted him. On the doctrine of Mar-

---
[1] Ep. ad Jul., p. 392, Coustant.

Alleged Errors, etc.

cellus, opinions still differ. Natalis Alexander, Montfaucon, and Möhler have defended his orthodoxy; and Hefele remarks, that it is difficult to pronounce a decisive judgment upon him.[2] Yet it must be admitted that recent research seems less favourable to his orthodoxy.[3] But no infallibilist has ever asserted, nor any fallibilist proved, that the sentence of Julius was a doctrinal decision, or that this Pope sanctioned any dogma. In a judgment upon the *sentiments of an individual*, the Pope, no less than a General Council, can, according to the most rigid upholders of infallibility, fall into an error of fact (*error facti*).

2. "Liberius purchased his return from exile from the emperor by condemning Athanasius, and subscribing an Arian creed" (p. 68).

The advocate of infallibility can reply, the fall of this Pope into Arianism is by no means certain, nay, subject to grave doubts, and, if certain, so not the result of full free-will; for the fear of the Emperor Constantius was the motive; and still less in this fall was a definition of faith involved.[4] Many authors, like Socrates, Theodoret, and Sulpicius Severus testify in favour of Liberius. Of the testimonies brought against him, several are evidently spurious,[5] and even if they were genuine,

---

[2] "Concil. Geschichte," vol. i., p. 456.—["*Hist. of Councils.*"]

[3] According to the investigations of Dorner, Döllinger, Hefele, and Th. Zahn. See the latter's *Marcellus of Ancyra*, Gotha, 1867.

[4] Liberii lapsus non certus, nec si certus, voluntarius, nec in definitione fidei. P. Ballerini de vi ac ratione primatûs, c. 15, § 13, n. 30, p. 297, 299, 300.

[5] The fifth Fragment of Hilary is, according to Hefele, spurious; (Concil., vol. 1, p. 605, *et seq.*), but, according to Reinkens, it is genuine (Hilarius, p. 216, *seq.*) Even Mr Renouf sees himself forced to give up a portion at least of the Fragment; for the maintenance of it would have involved him in the most flagrant self-contradiction. (*Vide* "The Condemnation of Pope Honorius," London, 1868, p. 41, *seq.* note.)

they would show only a semi-Arian Catholicizing formula, but not "an Arian creed." Liberius can be accused, not of what he did, but of what he omitted to do ; he can, from a moral point of view, be blamed for his silence, for his weakness, while the dogmatic purity of his faith remains intact.[6] If now we are further told, "that this apostasy of Liberius sufficed, through the whole of the Middle Ages, for a proof that popes could fall into heresy as well as other people;" so we reply, that it is perfectly well established, that in those ages the doctrine of Papal Infallibility was the prevalent one ; while in this passage, on the other hand, we find the explanation, that inerrancy is to be ascribed only to the formal dogmatic decisions of the Pope, as father and teacher of all Christians, and which are alone binding on the whole Church, and not to his other measures and acts.

3. "Innocent I. and Gelasius I. declared it to be so indispensable for infants to receive communion, that those who die without it go straight to hell. A thousand years later the Council of Trent anathematized this doctrine."[7]

On the 6th of June 1562, the question whether by the Divine Law the Blessed Eucharist was to be administered to children before the use of reason, was submitted, amongst others, to the theologians of the Council of Trent, and the Council maturely weighed the passages of the Fathers concerning it, and, in particular, the words of Pope Innocent.[8] The words of Innocent on the subject, exactly

---

[6] Hagemann in the *Journal of Theol. Literature* of Bonn, 1869, No. 3, p. 79-81.

[7] A like observation is made in a pamphlet which is in manifold accordance with Janus, "The Roman Congregation of the Index, and its Working," Munich 1863, p. 26.

[8] Pallavic Hist. Council, Trident. Lxvii. c. 1, n. 1, c. 6, n. 12, c. 12, n. 5, *seq.*

agree with the conclusion drawn by St Augustine, who argued thus against the Pelagians: "No one can attain everlasting life without being a partaker of the body and blood of Christ; but none can thus participate without baptism; therefore no one can obtain eternal life without baptism."[9] The reference to the text (vi. 54) does not necessarily imply actual communion, for St Augustine often explains this passage in a wide sense;[10] but it was fully justified with reference to the practice which obtained at that time, and far into the Middle Ages, of giving communion to infants; a practice which implied baptism as a previous condition. The words of Innocent are directed in exactly the same way against the doctrine of the Pelagians, that it is possible to obtain eternal life without baptism; and in the same way he bases his argument on John vi. 54. *Directly* he asserts only the necessity of baptism;[11] the precise proposition asserted, and not the *ratio addita*, is authoritative.[12] The same remarks apply to Gelasius[13] and others. The Council of Trent defends the Holy Fathers, who had a *probabilis causa* for acting according to the practice of their time, and is very far from condemning any one of them."[14]*

4. "That Pope Zosimus spoke on the Pelagian doctrines in a very different fashion from his immediate predecessor, Innocent" (p. 70), is utterly

---

[9] Aug. de peccat. mer. et rem., iii. 4. Cf. i. 20. Op. imperf., ii. 29. Tract. 26 in John.
[10] Noris. Vindic. Aug., § 4. Bona Liturg., ii. 19. Natal. Alex. II. E. Saec. V., cap. IV., a. 3, § 10, n. 7.
[11] Pallav. l. c., n. 9, upon Innoc., 1. ep. 26 ad PP. Milev. Aug., ep. 93.
[12] Melch. Canus de loc. theol. v., §. Nonne igitur.
[13] Gelas. ep. ad Episc. per Picenum constitutos.
[14] Sess. xxi., cap. 4, de commun. coll. can. 4.
* The translation of this passage was given in the *Tablet*, and as it was a very good one, it has been retained.—TR.

false. Innocent had decided the dogmatic question, but not the personal one relating to the orthodoxy of Cælestius. The latter represented himself to Zosimus as perfectly orthodox, and obtained from him a mild treatment; as indeed Innocent had, in the case of his repentance, held out to him the same prospect; so that though for a time he deceived the pontiff, he never at least received any sort of sanction to his errors, which were afterwards fully discovered. So even Augustine, the most decided adversary of Pelagianism, regarded the matter.[15] But it was the Tractoria of Pope Zosimus which on all points settled the controversy. That document, as a doctrinal decision, was laid before the bishops for their subscription, and spread over the whole of Christendom.[16] The eighteen prelates who did not sign it, were deposed and banished.[17]

5. As regards Pope Vigilius, he by no means contradicted himself three times in a matter of faith (p. 72). The reprehensible character of the propositions favouring Nestorianism, put forth by Theodore of Mopsuestia, as well as of the expressions of Theodoret and Ibas in reference thereto, was not denied by this pontiff, but only the opportuneness and the justice of a condemnation of their persons. The positive dogmatic purport of the judicatum, of the constitutum, and of his last decree, is not involved in contradiction.[18] The reproach

---

[15] Aug. L. ii. contra duas epist. Pelag. ad Bonif., c. 3, *seq.*; quidquid interea lenius actum est cum Coelestio, servatâ dumtaxat antiquissimæ et robustissimæ fidei firmitate, correctionis fuit clementissima suasio, non approbatio exitiosissimæ pravitatis.

[16] Marius Mercator Com., p. 138, ed. Baluz.

[17] The Dominican, B. de Rubeis, in his treatise, "De peccato originali," cap. 9, *seq.*, treats this question most solidly, and from the original sources.

[18] Döllinger, Manual of Eccles. Hist., i. p. 149.

which Vigilius incurred is that of vacillation of conduct in a position of unexampled difficulty, of which nothing is here told to the reader; and even against this charge many theologians, including Frenchmen, have not failed to defend him. The schism in the West was not his fault. The East and the West, as often happened on other occasions, were then opposed to each other; and it is precisely the history of the dispute of the three chapters, which shows how necessary was the decision of the Pope.[19]

6. Naturally the case of Honorius is not passed over in silence. This pontiff, we are told, expressed himself in dogmatic epistles quite in favour of the Monothelite heresy (p. 74); and these epistles were in the sixth Œcumenical Council committed, as heretical, to the flames (p. 74). The almost immeasurable literature respecting Honorius is here in a manner sufficiently arbitrary, compressed into a few sentences; and the present state of historical research on the subject is utterly ignored. Hereupon Mr Hagemann observes, that after the new and manifold investigations (to which Döllinger and Hefele have led the way) by the journal the *Katholik*, 1863, by Schneeman (in his " Studies on the Honorius Question," 1864), by Rump (in the German edition of Rohrbacher's " History of the Church," vol. x., p. 121-47), by Reinerding (in his " Contributions to the Question of Liberius and Honorius," 1865), *the judgment on Honorius has ever assumed a more favourable form.* The unskilful defence of Damberger has alone been prejudi-

---

[19] Ludov. Thomassin. Diss. xix. in Concil., p. 621, *seq*. Petrus de Marca Diss. de Vigilio. Cf. Card. Orsi, Storia, L. 41, n. 84. Ballerini de vi ac ratione primatûs, c. 15, n. 39. p. 313. Bennettis Privileg. Rom. Pontif. Vindic., P. II., tom. v. Append., § v., p. 625, *seq*. P. I., tom. i., art. ii., § 3, p. 189-204.

cial to the cause.[20] The same reviewer observes, "it is, above all, necessary to examine the *first epistle* of Honorius in itself, in its doctrinal purport, and quite independently of its historical connexion, just as if the Monothelite heresy had never existed. We doubt not that to a really unprejudiced mind the innocence of Honorius would be apparent, and the offensive expression, ἓν θέλημα, one will be from the context referred to the *moral unity* of the divine and the human will in Christ." In fact, the arguments of Schneemann, who compares the expressions of the Pope with passages of St Augustine, which he had before his eyes,[21] have nowhere yet been refuted; and in the import of their words, these letters, which appear as *epistolæ privatæ*, and not as *epistolæ dogmaticæ*,[22] are free from heresy.[23] Thus much only is clear, the crafty Byzantine, Sergius, put the unsuspecting Pope on a false scent, and elicited from him a letter, which he was enabled to misuse for his own purpose, and indeed in favour of a heresy advocated by himself, but then totally unknown to the pontiff. These expectations were crowned with success. The expressions of Honorius, as could not fail to happen, were set up by the Greeks in connexion with the question then so warmly agitated; and so, as the Byzantines required, to whom the condemnation of so many of their patriarchs was excessively irksome and displeasing, ensued the condemnation of Honorius, defended and praised

[20] Journal of Theological Literature. Bonn, 1st February 1869. No. 3, p. 76.
[21] In the already cited "Studies on the question of Honorius," especially p. 48, *seq.* Freiburg, 1864.
[22] Natal, Alex. H. E. Saec. vii., Diss. ii., prop. 1. Hefele Conc. ii., p. 284.
[23] Rump in Rohrbacher's Church Hist., vol. x., p. 134, *seq.* p. 146 (Germ. trans.).

as he had been by St Maximus. " That the Papal legates," continues Hagemann, " did not oppose this decree, as in the case of the interpolated epistle of Pope Vigilius, may have had its ground therein, that without the anathema laid on Honorius, the Council could scarcely have been brought to a successful termination." On the other hand, we must set by the side of the Council's sentence the *letter of confirmation of Pope Leo II.;* and however we may explain the Pontiff's words, *more we cannot extort from them,* than that the anathema punished a forgetfulness of duty, rather than a *moral* complicity in the Monothelite errors.[24] This has been the view hitherto taken by the most distinguished theologians, and among others, by many doctors of the Sorbonne, to wit, that Honorius was not a heretic, but only a favourer of heresy,[25] or that he was condemned for an error as to fact, *errore facti.*[26] That Bishop d'Argentré and Archbishop Fenelon were wrongfully alleged to have denied the orthodoxy of this Pope, has long since been shown.[27] Less known is the judgment of the Sorbonne doctor, royal counsellor, and bishop, Isaac Habert.[28] The

---

[24] *Loc. cit.,* p. 77.
[25] Petrus Ballerini *loc. cit.,* pp. 306, 307; damnatus a sexta Synodo non ob hæresin, sed quia improvida dispensatione et nonnullis minus cautis locutionibus hæresi favorem impendisse visus est., pp. 306, 307, not. Præscriptum ab eo silentium, non fuit definitio fidei. The Gallican Natalis Alexander (HE. Sæc. vii., Diss. ii., prop. 2, 3) says Honorius is acquitted of the charge of heresy *tam vere quam pie,* and appeals against his accusers to Combefis and Garnier. Cf. also Lud. Thomassin., Dissert. in Conc., Diss. xx., n. 18, *seq.* Bennettis *loc. cit.,* vol. vi., pp. 655–686.
[26] L. Cozza Hist. Polem. de Græcorum Schismate. Romæ, 1719, P. ii., c. 17, p. 339.
[27] Schneeman *loc. cit.,* pp. 31–33.[1]
[28] Ἀρχιερατικόν. Liber Pontificalis Ecclesiæ Græcæ nunc primum ex Reg. MSS. Collectus Meditatione et labore Is. Haberti Ep. Vabrensis. Paris, 1676, p. 565, *seq.*

latter observes, it is not surprising that the name of Honorius also should not be wanting in the formulary of enthronization of the Greek patriarch,[29] for even in the Roman edition of the " Acts of the Sixth General Council" (*ea fides extitit et candor*) it occurs, first in the thirteenth article, where the letter of Honorius, because misunderstood, is condemned; and again in the eighteenth article his name occurs.

Habert cites the documentary evidence for the condemnation of Honorius down to the times of Pope Hadrian II., rejects the hypothesis of the falsification of the Acts of the Sixth Council, and explains the sentence in question as arising from an error as to fact, which even an Œcumenical Synod is liable to.[30] He points out especially, first, that the letters of Honorius were private letters, and not synodical epistles, the then usual form of solemn decrees, and such as Pope Agatho afterwards issued; secondly, that those epistles contain nothing heretical; and thirdly, that Pope Agatho does not name Honorius among the heretics, and that Maximus, the most decided opponent of Monothelitism, regards him and his expressions as perfectly orthodox, knowing as he did the assertions of Pyrrhus, and of his fellow-sectaries. The defenders of this Pope may, in fact, consider it a great triumph for their cause that, in despite of all the array of learning and critical acumen brought to bear against their opinion, they have not yet been refuted; still less has the adverse sentiment been raised to the fulness of evidence; nay, that

---

[29] *Ibid.*, pp. 557–559.
[30] P. 566. Hæc omnia tamen ex errore facti orta sunt, qui certe et in synodos œcumenicas cadere potest.

deeper historical inquiries serve ever to establish their belief on a more solid basis.

7. Passing over the accusations against Gregory II. and Gregory III., which have long met with their just appreciation,[31] Janus passes to Pope Stephen II., who reigned from 752 to 757, and who, according to him, issued two untenable dogmatic answers[32] (p. 54). But in one of these the question is not about the dissolution of the marriage of a slave girl, but about the expulsion of a slave girl living in concubinage; and this decision was quite in conformity with one made by Leo the Great.[33] In the other answer the matter immediately in hand regarded *the punishment of the priest* who, in a case of necessity, had administered baptism with wine. The text, moreover, is corrupt, and the genuineness of the document is called in question.[34]

8. Nicholas I., we are told, declared baptism given in the name of Jesus to be valid. But the question proposed to him regarded the *administrator* of baptism, whether Jew or heathen, and not the *form* of the sacrament, whereof Nicholas spoke only *obiter*, incidentally, and not *ex professo*;[35] and on this account many theologians say he here expressed himself only as a private doctor (p. 405).

---

[31] The above-cited pamphlet on the Congregation of the Index treats of both these Papal responses, p. 25. Compare therewith Von Moy's Archives for Canon Law. 1864 (in German.) Vol. xi., p. 174, *seq.* Chilianeum, vol. iv., 1864, p. 254.

[32] Labbé Conc. vi., 1650, 1652. Resp. ad. q. 3, 11.

[33] Leo M. ep. ad Rusticum Narbon., ep. 167, c. 5, p. 1422. Ball., p. 1205, ed. Migne.

[34] Natal. Alex. Sæc. viii., c. 1, art. 6. This subject is copiously treated by Bennettis *loc. cit.*, pp. 691–694. Compare also Hefele, Conc., vol. iii., p. 542.

[35] Nicol. ad Consulta Bulgar., c. 104. S. Alphons. Liguori, Theol. Moral., lib. vi., n. 112.

A definitive judgment was certainly not then pronounced; and the opinion in question, which occurs in other writers also, has never been termed heretical by the many scholars, who have illustrated this passage.[36]

9. The annulling of orders, and the reordinations, which we meet with from the end of the ninth century (p. 51), prove nothing against the doctrine of the Infallibilists, because no kind of dogmatic decision is involved therein, and they do not understand their doctrine as Janus interprets it. The question was still for a long time undecided;[37] and many harsh expressions against certain orders are to be construed only in the sense of *illicitness*, not of *invalidity*; for, according to ancient discipline, absolute ordinations were forbidden, and the *irritum* (the null) was very often opposed only to the *ratum* (the approved).[38] Janus might have alleged still more ancient examples of this error, even from the times of Innocent I.; but these, theologians have long since explained and duly appreciated.[39] Passages may be cited from many Popes which seem to express the absolute nullity of orders imparted by heretics, schismatics, Simonists, and the rest; and other passages again, as one, for instance, from Gregory the Great,[40] which presuppose their validity. Stephen VI. (VII.) blindly gave way to his passion, but he passed no dogmatic decree; while John IX. forbade re-

---

[36] Bennettis *loc. cit.*, § vii. pp. 706-708. Compare my Monography upon Photius, vol. iii., p. 593, *seq*.

[37] Cf. the Augsburg Pastoral Journal, 1869, No. 42, p. 334.

[38] These and other explanations are set forth at length in my Life of Photius, vol. ii., p. 321, *seq*.

[39] Bennettis *loc. cit.*, § iv., pp. 531-600. Ballerini *loc. cit.*, p. 713.

[40] Greg. M. L. iii., ep. 15, coll. L. ii., ep. 51, ad Joh. Rav. L. xi., ep. 67.

ordinations.⁴¹ That in the eleventh century a reconciliatory rite, already known to earlier ages, existed for the reinstallation into ecclesiastical dignities illicitly obtained, is certain. It is equally certain that it was the *effectus virtutis*, and not the *forma sacramenti*, which was in many cases disputed.⁴²

10. "The Capernaite doctrine, already rejected by the whole Church, and contradicting the dogma of the impassibility of Christ's body," was in a formulary proposed to Berengarius, affirmed in 1059 by Pope Nicholas II. (p. 55). This formulary, however calculated to hold fast the dexterous and ever slippery sophist, is by no means heretical. The harsh-sounding expressions may be justified by the intimate union of the outward sign with the body of Christ, which admits of a *communicatio idiomatum*, in the same way as the union of the two natures in Christ; so that what outwardly occurs to the sign can, in a certain measure, be ascribed to the body of the Lord concealed under it. In this sense the Fathers, and among others, Chrysostom, had already spoken of a touching of the body of Christ.⁴³

11. "Celestine III. tried to loosen the marriage tie by declaring it dissolved if either party became heretical.⁴⁴ Innocent III. annulled this decision,⁴⁵ and Hadrian VI. called Celestine a heretic for giving it" (p. 54).

But Celestine addressed a mere rescript to individuals; it was a *responsum juris*, and not a decree of faith; the formula *videtur nobis* expresses but a

---

⁴¹ Mansi Conc., vol. xviii. 221, *seq.*
⁴² Bennettis *loc. cit.*, especially p. 597, *seq.*, t. iv., p. 415, *seq.*
⁴³ *Vide* Döllinger's Manual of Church Hist., vol. i., p. 376.
⁴⁴ Cap. Laudabilem (iii. 33) de Convers. Infid. Cf. Urban III., cap. 6, de illa iv. 19 de divort.
⁴⁵ Cap. 7, quanto iv., 19 de divort.

private opinion; and then this is brought forward by the Pope, not *ex proposito*, but only *obiter*, incidentally.[46] If Hadrian VI. called Celestine a heretic, this was done by the Professor of Utrecht, and not by the Pope.[47]

12. Innocent III., "this father of law," was, it seems, quite ignorant of theology, because in a decretal he declared Deuteronomy, as the second book of the law, binding on the Christian Church (p. 56).[48] But this Pope, acting according to the taste of his age, and the analogy of Gregory the Great, sought, by help of an allegorical interpretation of Deuteronomy (xvii. 8–12), to draw motives of congruity for his decision, which had nothing whatever to do with the fifth book of Moses. To accuse him of an error in this case is utterly futile.[49] In the official acts of Popes, as well as of Councils, it is only the regulative parts which are authoritative, and not the arguments, nor the rhetorical adornments.[50] As little can any error be shown

---

[46] Bennettis *loc. cit.*, t. v., § viii., p. 720, *seq.* Card. Sfondratus (Gallia Vindicata., Dissert. iv., § 4, n. 1, p. 813), therein reminds us that Innocent says, "Etsi quidam prædecessores nostri aliter *sensisse* videantur," and that *sentire* is not synonymous with *definire;* and that Innocent also did not define, as the following words show: "*Credimus* aliter respondendum:" then the Cardinal subjoins: "Sed parcendum Maimburgo solius historiæ gnaro."

[47] Cf. Pichler *loc. cit.*, vol. ii., pp. 681, 682. Bennettis *loc. cit.*, p. 243.

[48] C. 13 per venerabilem, t. iv. 17. Qui filii sint legitimi. This passage is likewise cited in the pamphlet "On the Congregation of the Index," p. 26.

[49] A full investigation of this subject is to be found in the Augsburg *Postzeitung* of the 12th October 1869, Append., No. 49, in an article entitled "A Characteristic Specimen of Janus."

[50] Berardi Comment. in jus Eccles., Dissert. ii., c. 2 : In pluribus pontificiis Rescriptis nonnulla continentur extra principalem sententiam, in qua una vis Rescripti consistit, quæ sunt aut prorsus extranea, quandoque etiam minus ad rectam rationem exacta, in quibus scil. Capellanus plurimum suo ingenio indulsit, iis præsertim temporibus, quibus aut theologiæ aut canonum aut etiam solidæ philosophiæ studia non satis exculta fuisse non ignoramus.

Contradictions of the Popes. 87

in what this Pontiff says respecting the translation of bishops (p. 55).[51]

13. Pope John XXII. stands under a twofold accusation. First, with regard to the doctrine of Christ's poverty and the rule of St Francis, he was in the most direct opposition to the decretal of Nicholas III. (pp. 57-59). Secondly, he preached at Avignon the doctrine, that before the general resurrection the blessed in heaven are deprived of the beatific vision; and on this account he was in Paris accused of heresy (p. 274).

Now, as regards the first point, the earlier Gallicans found between Nicholas III.[52] and John XXII.[53] no contradiction in the substance of their doctrine, but rather in their words.[54] The opposition between them lies, not in the sphere of dogma, but in different philosophic and juridical views. Three questions, namely, come here under consideration. The first is, whether, in the things which are consumed by use, the *usus* can be severed from the *dominium* or ownership? The next is, whether a state of poverty, which excludes every species of proprietorship, be meritorious and holy? And the last is, whether Christ our Lord, by word and example, taught such a kind of poverty.[55] The first question Nicholas answered in the affirmative,

---

[51] *Vide* Phillips's Can. Law, t. v., § 226, especially page 445, and *seq.*

[52] C. 3, Exiit de V. S., v. 12 in 6.

[53] Joh. xxii., Extravag., tit. 14, c. 3. Ad Conditorem canonum; c. 4, cum inter nonnullos; c. 5, Quia quorundam.

[54] Natal. Alex. Hist. Eccles., Sæc. xiii. et xiv., Dissert. xi., art. 1. The dissertatio prævia of the Amsterdam edition of the Defensio Declarationis Cleri Gallicani of the year 1745, has, in § 46: Ceterum neque hic sollicite quærimus, qua de re præcise ageretur et an revera Nicolaus pro cathedræ auctoritate ita decreverit, nec magis curamus hic, rectene an secus ipse ac Johannes egerint et an *summâ consentiant, verbis litigent.*

[55] Cf. Raynald, anno 1322, n. 65; Bellarm. de Rom. Pont., iv. 14.

but John in the negative; and herein each started from a different philosophic and juridical conception. The words *simplex facti usus* could not signify the use of another's property against the will of the owner, for this would have been immoral, but the moderate and permitted use, such as *durante concedentis licentiâ* was allowed to the Franciscans.[56] John went from the principle, the *simplex usus facti* without the *jus utendi is usus injustus*, and held strongly to the opposite opinion, that whoever is owner of the thing can sell, exchange, and give it away, as he will; but this, by their rule, is not permitted to the Minorites. The answer to the first question determines the reply to the second. Nicholas must give an affirmative answer, and John a negative; both herein speaking according to their peculiar views of the relation of the *usus* to the *jus*. In the same way the third question may be answered in the affirmative or in the negative, according to the point of view from which it is regarded. Christ and the apostles taught and practised at times complete poverty, but they had at other times temporal goods also; they taught the perfect and the less perfect.[57] Not more than Nicholas III.[58] did John XXII. wish to pronounce a definition in this matter. He desired to resist the fanaticism of the Spiritualists, and to oppose real facts to their false enthusiasm. Highly as the rule of St Francis is esteemed, as one sanctioned and recommended by the Church for leading to a more perfect following of Christ, it is by no means in itself, and, rightly explained, a

---

[56] Ballerini de Potest. Eccles. sum. Pont. et Concil. General., liber. Veronæ, 1768. Append. de Infall. Pont., p. 277, n. 9.

[57] Bennettis *loc. cit.*, § viii., pp. 725–730.

[58] Card. Orsi, t. ii., de Rom. Pont. auctoritate, l. iii., c. 42, p. 268.

Contradictions of the Popes. 89

subject of revelation—*of the depositum fidei*. Pontifical decrees that belong to this class, are such only as solemnly sanction rules of faith and of morals for the whole Church ; and, in the case before us, this can by no means be proved.[59]

Secondly, in respect to the doctrine of the Beatific vision, John XXII. merely expressed himself by way of disputation, without attempting to frame any definition on the matter—a definition reserved for his successor, Benedict XII. Twenty-three doctors of the Paris University testified, on the 2d January 1333, that the Pope had neither *asserendo, seu opinando*, expressed the view still advocated by the Greeks, and not yet declared heretical. Moreover, before his death the Pontiff gave a very satisfactory explanation of his views on this subject, which he had treated as a learned theologian.[60]

14. The decree of Eugenius IV. on the sacraments theologians have long been familiar with ;

---

[59] Ballerini de vi ac ratione primatûs, c. 15, p. 317 : In his et similibus decretis potissimum cavendum, ne idem esse credatur aliquid pertinere ad materiam fidei, et decreta, quæ a Pontificibus eduntur, ut respondeant interpellantibus apostolicam sententiam et auctoritatem, si quo hujus auctoritatis charactere muniantur, semper esse definitionem fidei. In re enim, quæ referri queat ad jus naturale vel divinum, respondere possunt, quod ex opinione probabilius judicant vel tutius, nisi exprimant aliquid credendum aut damnandum ex Catholica fide, idque possunt, etiamsi ad .compescendas acriores contentiones sub excommunicationis pœnâ vetent constitutis glossas addere et aliter interpretari, ut Nicolaus vetuit. Potest enim excommunicatio ferri ob præsumptionem et inobedientiam, quæ pacem turbet et scandala foveat, tametsi circa articulum nondum definitum ex Catholica fide nullum læsæ fidei periculum sit. Hoc uno principio quam multæ constitutiones Pontificum aliquem characterem auctoritatis apostolicæ præferentes a proprie dictæ definitionis fidei catalogo excluduntur.

[60] Bulæus Hist. Univ. Paris, t. iv., B. p. 236. Spondan., anno 1334. Raynald, anno 1334, nn. 27, 35. Bennettis *loc. cit*., pp. 730–734. Ballerini *loc. cit*., n. 40, pp. 313, 314. Werner's Hist. of Polemic Literature, vol. iii., p. 522, *seq*.

but it was reserved for Janus to pronounce it completely erroneous. The reader unacquainted with the text might almost be misled into the belief that the Pope, instead of seven, recognized but four sacraments of the Church. But this is not so. The decree enumerates all our seven sacraments, and the omission of three is only a conclusion drawn by Janus. The decree is really a practical instruction *pro faciliori doctrinâ*, and forms part of a great whole, to which the Nicene Creed, the Definitions of Chalcedon, and even a decree on festivals, belong. These documents have certainly not all the same authority.[61] If the tendering of the vessels is stated to be the matter of holy orders, this does not certainly exclude the imposition of hands, which was already in use among the Armenians, and was prescribed in the Roman Pontifical also, to which express reference is made. Eugenius spoke of the integral and accessory form and matter, which, for greater conformity with the Roman Church, the Armenians were yet to adopt.[62] The form of Confirmation customary among the Latins is briefly stated; but it is not enjoined as an absolute form. The form usual among the Greeks was ever acknowledged;[63] as was also the case with their form of

---

[61] This is even shown by the distinction at the close: Capitula, declarationes, præcepta, etc. Denzinger Enchiridion Definitionum, p. 201, ed. iv. It is not, as Janus asserts (n. 17), that "Denzinger has omitted the first portion regarding the doctrine of the Trinity and of the Incarnation, in order to conceal in some degree the dogmatic character of this celebrated decree," but in order not to repeat what he had elsewhere already communicated.

[62] Bened. XIV. de Syn. diœces., l. viii., c. 10, n. 8. St Alphons. Liguori Theol. Moral., l. vi., n. 749. Arcud. de Concordia, vi. 5, p. 442, *seq*.

[63] Liguori *loc. cit.*, n. 167–179. Arcud. de Concordia, ii. 7. Pignatelli Consult. Can., t. viii., Cons. 78, p. 141.

Penance.⁶⁴ As this Instruction had for its object to bring the Armenians as near as possible to the Roman rite in the administration of the sacraments, its mode of speech has nothing remarkable ; still less is it chargeable with error.

15. What Janus further says on these matters refers to mere minutiæ. The question "about the comma in the bull of Pius V. against Baius" (p. 49), may, as the most recent editor of the *Baian* controversies justly remarks, be considered as settled.⁶⁵ Like disputes frequently occur, and it argues but a want of juridical instruction to exalt difficulties of interpretation into a system of irreconcilable antagonism. Janus dwells at much length (pp. 62, 63), after the manner of some Protestants, and of Launoius, on Sixtus the Fifth's edition of the Bible—a work in which that Pontiff evinced his love for biblical studies, but about which he passed no sort of decree. He promulgated no bull on the subject; he did not even desire that his work should be received *fide divinâ*, as quite correct and perfect.⁶⁶ The errors in his edition refer not to matters of faith ; and neither himself nor his successor, Clement VIII., ever imagined, or could imagine, it was in their power to put forth a perfectly faultless edition of the Scriptures, in which posterity would find nothing to change for the better.⁶⁷ The decision of Pope Alexander VII., in the year 1687, " in favour of the newly-

---

⁶⁴ Pignatelli *op. cit.*, t. iii., Cons. 60 n. 23 ; t. vii. Cons. 50, n. 1, p. 102. Decr. Congr. S. Off., 19 Dec. 1613. Arcud. *loc. cit.*, iv. 3.

⁶⁵ Linsenmann's Michael Baius and the Foundation of Jansenism. Tübingen, 1867, p. 266.

⁶⁶ For example, upon the building-charge of Patrons in Conc. Trid., Sess. XXI. c. 7, De Ref. Cf. Schulte's System of Can. Law., § 110, p. 548, in German.

⁶⁷ Bennettis *loc. cit.*, pp. 741-744

discovered doctrine of attrition" (preface xxvii.), is nothing more than a prohibition to censure one of two opinions ventilated in the schools.⁶⁸ The bull of Clement XI. against Quesnel,⁶⁹ as well as the decisions of Benedict XIII. and of earlier Pontiffs against Jansenism, are received in the whole Church; and against this universal acceptance the protest of a handful of sectaries counts for nought. And I am at a loss to understand how a Catholic theologian can say, that by the condemnation of the Five Propositions of Jansenius, Innocent X. began a controversy "which lasted for upwards of a century, *and has never found a solution*" (p. 414). Janus, with his friends of this school, might have also represented Pope Clement XI., on account of his Easter homily in 1702, as an Eutychian. Groundless as such an imputation would have been,⁷⁰ still, it could not have failed to exercise a great influence on his readers.

I have gone through in chronological order the motley, confused mass of instances of alleged Papal contradictions and errors, to which others of equal value might easily have been annexed.⁷¹ If our scholar had solidly refuted all the exceptions of the Papal advocates, he might then have boasted of a service rendered to learning. But merely to copy down, without almost any regard to the rich treasures of ecclesiastical literature on this subject, old accusations, is not to advance in any way either the interests of science, or the interests of

⁶⁸ Denzinger *loc. cit.*, n. 93, p. 322.
⁶⁹ *Ibid.*, n. 101, p. 351, *seq.*
⁷⁰ Bennettis *loc. cit.*, pp. 744–746.
⁷¹ For example, the concession of Pope Innocent VIII. to the Norwegians to make use of water instead of wine in the sacrifice of the Mass; Pope Martin the Fifth's pretended dispensation in the first degree of consanguinity; the sale of indulgences under Pope Celestine V. and Boniface IX. *See* thereupon Benettis *loc. cit.*, pp. 722, 735, 738.

the Church. It is only dust which has been thrown in the eyes of a public totally unacquainted with theological works, either of ancient or modern times; but not a single scientific opponent has been confuted.

CHAPTER VI.

THE PRIMACY AND THE PAPACY.

IN the inquiries we have hitherto made, our object has been merely to prove that the "Infallibilists" have no reason to fear the wide deductions of the anonymous Janus. Less grounds have they for such apprehension since our authors direct, for the most part, their attacks against *the Papal supremacy itself*, quite in the same way as non-Catholic controversialists have ever done, and still do.

For this assertion, in fact, abundant proofs are to be found in the book in question. "God has gone to sleep, because in His place His ever-wakeful and infallible Vicar on earth rules as lord of the world, and dispenser of grace and of punishment. St Paul's saying, 'In Him we live, move, and are,' is transferred to the Pope." So we read at p. 39. "And many Protestants say also, Christ has ceased to govern, if He has appointed a visible vicegerent on earth."[1] When we are further told

---

[1] Cf. the expressions of a Protestant in Bishop Ketteler's work, entitled "The General Council and its Importance for our Time" (p. 122, *seq.*) Nay, it would suffice to compare with Janus quite ordinary Protestant pamphlets. Out of the vast number known to me, I will point out but one, entitled "The Papacy and Christianity; or, A Proof that the Modern Papacy within the Christian Church has no just foundation: Words for the consideration of

The Primacy and the Papacy. 95

(p. 64), "That for thirteen centuries an incomprehensible silence on this fundamental article (namely, that the Pope of the day is *the only vehicle of Christ's inspirations*, the pillar and *the exclusive organ of divine truth*) reigned throughout the whole Church and her literature; when it is added that none of the ancient confessions of faith, no catechism, none of the Patristic writings, composed *for the religious instruction of the people, contain a syllable about the Pope*, still less any hint that all certainty of faith and doctrine depends on him only:"—so we can only reply, that this outpouring of the heart, if it should prove anything against the theory of Papal infallibility, tells equally against the doctrine of the supremacy of the Roman Pontiff, as defined in the Union Decree of the Council of Florence. This becomes still more apparent when, somewhat later (p. 87), "the silence of the ancient Church," in respect to the authority of the Pope, is strongly contrasted with the doctrine of his plenitude of power "which since the time of St Thomas Aquinas has been adopted in Catholic theology" (p. 86). But this doctrine all, even the most recent dogmatic theologians of Germany, have taught, without being obliged to take the inerrancy of the doctrinal decisions of the Pope as the basis of their teaching. If in earlier dogmatic works "no special treatise or *locus*" was assigned to the article of Papal supremacy, this was formerly the case *even with the article on the Church;* as, for example, in the celebrated work of St John Damascene, "On the

---

all Christendom," by G. A. Wimper, Preacher, Bremen, 1854, p. 132. There are here points of contact enough with our Janus; but I must pass them over. Luther's writing, entitled the "Babylonish Captivity," stands doubtless as the model of all such lucubrations.

Orthodox Faith," from which so many have since derived their materials. But what conclusion are we thence to draw? This the author may tell us; but we, for our parts, have our own answer, which we shall later set forth.

To this we may add, that Janus finds but very scanty testimonies for the supremacy of the Roman See in Christian antiquity (p. 87). Works in abundance, which fill whole libraries, have collected these testimonies; but for our author, only very few are in existence. Many witnesses he entirely passes over, such as Optatus of Milevi and Prosper.[2] The testimony of others he seeks to reduce to a minimum, such as those of Augustine[3] and of Jerome;[4] even Ambrose belongs to the "silent

---

[2] See the testimonies of both in Bennettis *loc. cit.*, P. i., t. ii., p. 297, *seq.*, p. 313, *seq.*

[3] Of Augustine he knows but one passage testifying for the primacy (in Ep. 43, nn. 3, 7); but even this he deems not to carry full weight (p. 88). But we may add to this many other passages; for example, (Psalm. contra partem Donati): Numerate sacerdotes vel ab ipsa Petri sede; *ipsa est petra*, quam *non vincunt inferorum portæ*. Cf. Ep. 53, n. 1-3. De Bapt. c. Don., ii. 1: Quis nescit, illum apostolatus principatum cuilibet episcopatui præferendum? Distat cathedrarum gratia. L. i. ad Bonif. c. 1 (Coust. p. 1024): Communis est omnibus nobis qui fungimur episcopatus officio, specula pastoralis, quamvis ipse in ea *præemineas celsiore fastigio*. De util. Cred. c. 17: Romanæ ecclesiæ nolle primas dare, vel summæ profecto impietatis est vel præcipitis arrogantiæ. Cf. contra, Ep. Manich., n. 5, and our fourth chapter, n. 66.

[4] That Jerome in essentials ranked Cyril of Jerusalem (whom in his Chronicle he numbered among the Arians, and in his work De Script. Ecclesiæ, c. 112, only very briefly treated of)—"that he ranked him as high as the Pope" (p. xxv.), is by no means proved. His words to Pope Damasus are not so easily explained away. Coustant. p. 545: *Cathedram Petri* et fidem apostolico ore laudatam censui consulendam . . . Profligato sobole mala patrimonio *apud vos solos incorrupta Patrum servatur hæreditas*. P. 546. Ego nullum primum nisi Christum sequens *beatitudini tuæ* (sc. Damaso) *id est cathedræ Petri* communione consocior. *Super illam petram ædificatam ecclesiam scio* . . . Quicunque tecum non colligit, spargit, h. e. qui Christi non est, Antichristi est. P. 547, n. 4: Decernite, obsecro, si placet, et non timebo tres hypostases

ones,"⁵ as well as "the most fertile of the Greek Fathers, Chrysostom."⁶ Many say nothing of the privileges of the Roman Bishop; but for those familiar with the mode of speech in Christian antiquity, it suffices that they speak of the privileges of the Roman Church.⁷

Yet the many passages from the Fathers relating to this matter we will not here bring forward, as they can be cited in a more suitable place. Here it will suffice to remind the reader of the words of Pope Pius VI., embracing as they do almost all the testimonies of Christian antiquity, when, in the year 1786, in his condemnation of the work of Eybel, entitled, "What is the Pope?" he pronounced them, with the assent and the joyous approval of the whole Catholic world. "That on the solidity of the rock the Church was founded by Christ, and by an especial favour Peter was chosen by Him before the other Apostles, that with vicarious power he should be the prince of the apostolic choir, and that he should take upon himself the supreme supervision and authority— an authority to be transmitted to his successors in every age—for feeding the whole flock, for confirming the brethren, for binding and loosing throughout the whole world; this is a *Catholic dogma*, which the whole Church hath received from

---

dicere, p. 551. Si quis Cathedræ Petri jungitur, meus est. The Roman Faith is for him the true one (Adv. Rufin., b. i., n. 4). In like manner Cyprian (in Ep. 48, al. 45, ad Cornel, p. 132, Coust.) : Communicationem tuam, id est, Catholicæ Ecclesiæ unitatem.

⁵ Cf. Dieringer in the Theol. Journal of Bonn, 1869, p. 561.

⁶ On Chrysostom, see for example, Pichler *loc. cit.*, p. 123, *seq.*, vol. i.

⁷ So, for example, when Gregory Nazianzen (Carm. de Vitâ Suâ, p. 571, ed. Migne, xxxvii., p. 1063), calls the Roman Church, "πρόεδρος τῶν ὅλων," the president of all ; and when Ignatius (Ep. ad Rom.) calls the same Church " προκαθημένη τῆς ἀγάπης," the one who presides in the covenant of love.

the lips of Christ, which she hath handed down and defended by the continuous preaching of the Fathers, which she hath firmly held in all times with holy reverence, and often against the errors of innovators, confirmed by decrees of Popes and of Councils. In this pre-eminence of the Apostolic See, Christ wished that the bond of unity should be firmly and strongly held, whereby the Church, destined to spread over the whole world, and to be composed of members ever so remote, should, by the union of all under one head, grow into a firmly knit body; and so it should be brought about that the strength of this power should serve, not so much for the elevation of this See, as rather and most especially, for the inviolability and integrity of the whole body. Therefore it is by no means to be wondered at, that all those whom in earlier ages the ancient foe of mankind has inspired with his hatred against the Church, should have been wont to direct their attacks against this first See, in which the solidity of unity is embodied; in order that, after setting aside the foundation-stone, if possible, and after dissolving the union of the Churches with their head—a union which imparts to them a special support, vigour, and prosperity—they might rob the Church herself, mishandled in this miserable way, weakened, and torn asunder, of the freedom bestowed by Christ upon her, and give her up to an ignominious servitude."[8]

But the primacy in itself Janus will not assail. "He distinguishes between the original germ of the primacy in the apostolic age, (why not in the time of Christ, or as laid down by Christ himself?) and that colossal monarchy which, in the thirteenth and fourteenth centuries, presented itself before the deluded eyes of men as a work, that came ready-

---

[8] Pius VI., Breve super soliditate, in the exordium.

The Primacy and the Papacy.

made from the hand of God." "The primacy, we are further told (p. xxi.), rests (and of that truth every Catholic is convinced, and to that conviction the authors of this book profess their adherence); the primacy, we say, rests on a higher (why not a divine?) appointment. The Church from the first was founded upon it; and the Lord of the Church *ordained its type* in the person of Peter (but did not establish it then). It has, therefore, from the necessity of the case, developed itself *up to a certain point*." But what, then, is this point which is not to be overpassed? Has the Lord of the Church *typified* it also? Who has fixed this point? Is it the ancient councils, or the scholars of the present day? Does all ecclesiastical development cease at a certain definite point? We hear only: "That from the ninth century there occurred a *further development* —artificial and sickly rather than sound and natural—*of the primacy into the Papacy*, a transformation more than a development: *the presidency in the Church became an empire*, when, in place of the first bishop deliberating and deciding in union with his 'brethren' on the affairs of the Church, and setting an example of submission to her laws, was substituted the *despotic rule of an absolute monarch*" (p. xxii.)

Thus the expressions, not immediately intelligible to many Catholic readers, become perfectly clear. The Papacy, in contradistinction to the primacy, is the despotic rule of an absolute monarch; the *primacy* is the position of the first bishop, of the *primus inter pares*, of the guardians of the canons and of unity, of the president in the episcopal assembly.[9] Far beyond this notion of the primacy does the holy Bonaventura go when

[9] Febronius (Hontheim) de Statû Eccles., c. 2, § 4.

he writes: "One is *the Father of Fathers*, who is rightly called Pope (Papa), as the sole, first, and supreme spiritual father of all fathers, nay, of all believers, the most eminent hierarch, the sole bridegroom, the undivided head, the supreme high priest, the vicegerent of Christ, the source, the origin, and the rule of all ecclesiastical powers, from whom, as from the chief, and as his eminent dignity in the ecclesiastical hierarchy requires, descends the order of jurisdiction down to the lowest members of the Church."[10] Far beyond this notion rises, too, St Bernard, when he addresses Pope Eugenius III. thus:[11] "Who art thou? The high priest, the supreme bishop. Thou art the prince of bishops—thou art the heir of the Apostles. Thou art Abel in primacy, Noah in government, Abraham in the patriarchal rank, in order Melchisedech, in dignity Aaron, in authority Moses, Samuel in the judicial office, Peter in power, and Christ in unction. Thou art he to whom the keys of heaven are given, to whom the sheep are intrusted. There are, indeed, other door-keepers of heaven, and other shepherds of the flocks; but thou art the more glorious in proportion as thou hast also, in a different fashion, inherited before others both these names. The former have the flocks assigned to them, each one his own: to thee all are intrusted, one flock for the one. Not merely for the sheep, but for all the shepherds also thou art the one shepherd. Whence do I prove this? thou askest. *From the word of the Lord.* For to whom, I say not among the bishops, but among the apostles, have the whole flock been committed in a man-

---

[10] Bonav. Breviloquium, P. vi., c. 12, p. 250, ed. iii. Curâ Hefele Tub., 1861. Cf. in l. iv., Sent. Dist. 29, a. 3, qu. 1.
[11] S. Bernard. de Consider., l. ii., c. 8.

ner so absolute and so undistinguishing ? '*If thou lovest me, Peter, so feed my sheep.*' What sheep ? The inhabitants of this or that city or country, those of a particular kingdom ? *My sheep*, He saith. Who doth not see that He designates not some, but *all ?* Nothing is excepted where nothing is distinguished. The power of others is limited by definite bounds ; thine extends even over those who have received authority over others. Canst thou not, when a just reason occurs, shut up heaven against a bishop, depose him from his episcopal office, and deliver him over to Satan ? (1 Cor. v. 5). Thus thy privilege is immutable, as well in the keys committed to thee, as in the sheep intrusted to thy care."

Again, Hugh of St Victor writes of the Pope : " He is called *Papa*, because he is *the Father of the Fathers :* he is called *universalis*, because he presides over the whole Church : he is called *Apostolicus*, because he holds the place of the Prince of the Apostles : he is called *Summus Pontifex*, because he is the head of all bishops." [12] These are all clear enunciations of the genuine Papal system.

But many of these names and predicates of honour had been long before attributed to the Popes, and even by the Orientals. *Father of Fathers* the Pope is frequently called by the latter, from the sixth century downwards.[13] In the same way he had

[12] Lib. i., Erud. Theol. de Sacramentis, c. 43. Cf. Serm. 64, de SS.Apostolis Petro et Paulo.
[13] So he was called in the Synodical Epistle sent from Byzantium to Rome after the election of Epiphanius, in the year 520 (Mansi, viii. 504, *seq.*) ; so again by Stephen of Larissa (Thomassia *loc. cit.*, 11, nn. 3, 4) ; so, too, by Sergius of Cyprus, and other Orientals, in the year 649 (Mansi, x. 903, 913) ; and so by Theodore the Studite (L. i., ep. 33, p. 1017, *seq. ;* κορυφαιότατος πατὴρ πατέρων, " The supreme Father of Fathers." Photius (de Spiritû Sancto Mystagog., c. 81) opposes to the Latin Fathers Ambrose and Augustine, Popes Damasus and Celestine as Fathers of the Fathers.

long borne the title of Apostolic Father, and of Apostolicus.[14] But the title *Vicar of Christ* appears to many strange; and Janus (p. 159) observes that earlier, and even down to the end of the twelfth century, the Pope called himself the Vicar of Peter, *Vicarius Petri*, but that from the time of Innocent III. the title Vicar of Christ has quite superseded the ancient one. But here the fact is overlooked that the ancients used the words "vicarius and successor," vicar and successor, as synonymous;[15] a vicar could be not only the representative of a living, but also the successor in office of a deceased person;[16] that all bishops and pastors were once called vicars of Christ;[17] while the name "Vicarius Petri" designated the heir of the Apostle endowed with special prerogatives;[18] so that we can well conceive the Pope, as holding immediately the place of Peter, and mediately the place of Christ. Yet, though more rarely, the Pope, even from the fifth century, is designated also as the

[14] Theod. Stud., L. i., ep. 34, p. 1025. Anastas. Bibl. Præf. in Conc. viii. Apostolatus vester in Paschas. ep. ad Leon. I. (Leo. ep. 54). Paulin. Diac. libell. ad Zosim, p. 960. *Vide* Coustant Præf. in epist. Roman. Pontif., p. xi., n. 15. The expression, Sedes Apostolica is, in St Augustine, synonymous with the See of Rome, as also in St Athanasius (Hist. Ar. ad mon., c. 35; ed. Migne, t. xxv., 734), ὁ ἀποστολικὸς θρόνος, the Apostolic See.

[15] Pope Gregory the Great (L. i., ep. 4,) calls the newly-elected Bishop of Milan, Vicarius S. Ambrosii. Cyprian (Ep. 68, al. 67, Coustant, p. 215) writes to Stephen, "Qui vicarius et successor eorum (scilicet Cornelii et Lucii) factus es."

[16] The Legates in Councils are called Vicarii (in Greek τοποτηρηταί) Austas. Bibl. *loc. cit.* Vicarius is in general qui vices alterius gerit, who fills the place of another. Cf. Leo M., ep. 93, c. 1.

[17] Cypr. ep. 55, ad Cornel. (p. 177, Coust.): Neque aliunde hæreses obortæ sunt aut nata schismata, quam dum (inde quod) sacerdoti Dei non obtemperatur, nec unus in ecclesia ad tempus sacerdos et ad tempus judex vice Christi cogitatur. Hormisd., ep. 25, n. 2: *Christi vicarii* sacerdotes. Regula S. Bened., c. 2: (Abbas) Christi *vices agere* creditur.

[18] Coustant, *loc. cit.*, P. x., n. 14.

Vicar of Christ."[19] The faithful have no difficulty in regarding him as the one who, in Christ's place, governs Christendom. Janus thinks, indeed (p. 40), "it is but one step from this, to declare the Pope an incarnation of God." But this is surely a long step, indeed; for nowhere has been attributed to a vicegerent full equality with the head, from whom all his powers emanate. In the substitute we require, only in so far as is requisite, the qualities of him whose place he fills. When we find, how already, in the sixth century, the idea of the Pope was a most exalted one—the highest which can be conceived of man[20]—so we are led to regard the transition from the Primacy to the Papacy (in so far as such ever took place), as one of very early occurrence.

If we seek for a further explanation, we are told "that the form which this primacy took, *depended on the concessions of the particular local churches*, and was never, therefore, the same everywhere, acting within certain fixed limits prescribed by law" (p. xxiii.) We do not for the present ask, what doctrinal and historical proofs can be adduced

---

[19] In the acclamations of bishops and priests to Gelasius: *Vicarium Christi* te videmus, Apostolum Petrum te videmus (Gelas. ep. 27, n. 15). In the Roman Synod of the year 531, under Pope Boniface II.: Neque fas est, ut a culmine Apostolatûs vestri in aliquo dissentiamus, quem videlicet ipse Christus Dominus noster omnium nostrum *ad vicem suam* in terris esse voluit caput. Anastasius the Librarian says (Præf. ad vit. S. Joh. Eleem. ad Joh. viii.), Non fas est, ut absque *vicario Dei, absque clavigero cœli*, ... absque universali Pontifice . . . . aliquid consummetur aut divulgetur. Hincmar of Rheims (Præf. ad Nicol. I.) says, Pontifex Romanus *vicem* in terris possidet *Dei*, neque fas est, ut absque *Vicario Dei*, absque universali Pontifice . . . . aliquid in rebus fidei et morum consummetur aut divulgetur. Bennettis, P. 1, t. 11, p. 337. See also the words of Isidore of Seville, in note 23 below.

[20] Liberatus (in his Breviarium, c. 22) relates how, after the exile of Pope Silverius, the Bishop of Patara went to the Emperor Justinian; judicium Dei contestatus est de tantæ sedis episcopi expulsione; multos esse dicens in hoc mundo reges, et non esse unum, sicut ille Papa est super ecclesiam mundi totius a suâ sede expulsus.

for this dependence *on the concessions of particular local churches;* but we ask only if these particular churches, without contradiction, permitted, nay, gladly assented to this extension of power in the Roman see, to this growth of the primacy into the Papacy? we ask, was this extension of power unlawful, or was the growth of the primacy into the Papacy *licit?* If the question is answered in the affirmative, then must the complaints of our Janus be hushed; if in the negative, then must he show, what besides the concessions and the consensus of particular churches (which are here supposed), was still wanting to legitimize this extension of power. If the Popes were fully convinced of the lawfulness of their proceedings (p. 186); if the ancient canons of Nicæa, Chalcedon, and others, appeared to them no longer adequate; if they were supported by the consent of particular churches;—then, subjectively, their conduct was perfectly justified. If any objective rule was opposed to their proceedings, what was it? But as regards the assent of particular churches; so, certainly, from the Catholic point of view, we must understand thereby the assent of the bishops. But, taking the Episcopate as a whole, we find but very few examples of resistance to Papal ordinances;[21] the contrary instances are vastly more numerous, and extend

---

[21] We shall have occasion later to illustrate several of these examples. Here we may be permitted to remind the reader that the independent position of the ancient Spanish Church did not arise, as Janus himself confesses (p. 284), from a non-recognition of the Roman Primacy, and that it was only after the Arab invasion the latter fell more into the background. Cf. Bennettis, P. 1, t. v., p. 31, *seq.* If individual bishops, like Hincmar of Rheims in the case of Gottschalk (p. 76), sought to avoid the sentence of the see of Rome (Neander's Church History, vol. 11, p. 263, 3d ed.), (and for such a sentence a Nicholas I. was certainly not wanting in capacity); and if ten years were then spent in disputes on the doctrine of predestination, without any appeal being made to the Pope, all this proves nothing against the rights of the Papacy.

through all ages down to the present times. Janus even complains (p. 189) of the "slavish spirit" of the French bishops in the thirteenth century, as well as of the too great patience and humility of the German nation in the fifteenth (p. 307). It is still very remarkable, that of the authors well acquainted with the charges brought against the Popes and their administration, *all* rigidly adhered to the principle of right, and preached up a silent and patient obedience (p. 233). Were they not then to counsel resistance, and to renounce their obedience? The principle that we are justified in refusing by reason of their faults to superiors, whether ecclesiastical or civil, in a state of sin, the submission due to them, has never been the doctrine of the Church; nay, has been expressly condemned by her.[22] What, then, was to be done? The view current in the whole Middle Ages, that whoever submits not to the Pope, is a heretic,[23] " has disarmed the Church; has caused the neglect of *that first principle of moral* and political prudence, that an abuse should be resisted at the *beginning*, and has thus made the corruption in the Church *incurable*, and the attempted reformation *too late*, when it was at last undertaken " (p. 262).

These are, indeed, desolate prospects! Why

---

[22] Art. 15, Wicl. damnat. a Conc. Coustant, Art. Joh. Huss, Denziger Enchir., nn. 491, 550, pp. 187, 193, ed. iv.

[23] Alcuin ep. 70 : Ne schismaticus inveniatur aut non Catholicus, sequatur probatissimam Romanæ ecclesiæ auctoritaem, ut unde Catholicæ fidei initia accepimus, inde exempla salutis nostræ semper habeamus. Ne membra a Capite separentur, ne claviger regni coelestis abjiciat, quos a suis deviasse cognoverit doctrinis. S. Isid. Hispal. ep. ad Claud. ducem : Sic nos scimus praeesse Ecclesiae Christi, quatenus Romano Pontifici reverenter, humiliter et devote tamquam *Dei Vicario* prae ceteris prælatis specialius nos fateamur debitam in omnibus obedientiam exhibere. Contra quod quem cunque procaciter venientem *tamquam hæreticum* a consortio fidelium omnino decernimus alienum.

did not the men who bear the collective name of Janus, live earlier, before it was too late? Why was not the evil immediately recognized, and what was the beginning of this evil?

The Papal primacy has surely its history. Its first times are traced by Döllinger in the following sketch :—

"Like every living thing, like to the Church herself, whose crown and key-stone it is, the Papacy has passed through an historical development full of the most manifold and surprising changes.

"But in this its history—the law, which is the fundamental principle of the Church's life, is not to be mistaken—namely, the law of constant development, of evolution from within. The Papacy must share all the destinies and the vicissitudes of the Church, and must take part in her every process of formation. Its birth begins with two mighty, pregnant, and far-reaching words of the Lord. He, to whom these words are addressed, realises them in his person and in his acts, and transplants the institute to which he has been appointed into the centre of the infant Church, to the Roman capital itself. Here it grows up in silence, *occulto velut arbor ævo;* and in the earliest times it manifests itself only in particular traits, till the outlines of the ecclesiastical power and action of the Bishop of Rome become ever clearer and more definite. *Already, even in the times of the Roman empire, the Popes are the guardians of the whole Church; who in all directions put forth warnings and exhortations, who administer and judge, bind and loose.* Not rarely complaints are uttered of the use which they make of their power. Resistance is offered, because the Pope is held to be deceived, and an appeal is made to a Pontiff better informed; but never is the

The Primacy and the Papacy.

Papal authority contested. In general, the intervention in ecclesiastical concerns was the less necessary; the reins of ecclesiastical government less needed to be tightly drawn, so long as the whole Church, with a few exceptions, was contained within the limits of the Roman empire, and was so held together by the strong bonds of that political organisation, that there was neither occasion nor prospect of success for any resistance on the part of the various nationalities, broken up and down-trodden as they were by the domination of the Romans."[24]

But this development of the Papal power we must now more closely examine in detail, and furnish historic proofs of its growing activity.

[24] Döllinger's "Church and Churches," pp. 31-33.

CHAPTER VII.

THE PRIMACY AND ITS DEVELOPMENT

OF the Popes of the first ages, who were mostly martyrs, but little has been handed down to us; but even the extant documents suffice to show the power and the influence of the Roman See. In the first centuries, all the consequences, which were to be evolved from the idea of the Primacy, were naturally not yet developed; but the idea remained ever the same, and ever did the Church possess and desire in the Primacy a centre of unity.[1]

"What St Irenæus in the second century had so clearly and conclusively enunciated, that the Roman Church, among all churches of apostolic origin, is the first and the most eminent; that among these churches it has the same superiority as Peter and Paul among the apostles; and that the faith of this Church is the rule and the standard for the faith of all other churches;—this language of St Irenæus, I say, is that of all succeeding ages, with all who are truly and loyally devoted to the Church. But if this is the case, if Rome ever stood in the course of its development at the head of the

---

[1] Beidtel Canon Law, p. 108; Ratisbon, 1849. See also Ritter's Church History, t. 1, p. 149, 6th ed. (in German).

The Primacy and its Development. 109

whole Church, and in all ecclesiastical questions gave the final decision;[2] then must this Church be animated by a peculiar spirit, and be endowed with a special grace of the Holy Ghost, that guideth the Church into all truth : then on this particular Church must the essence of the whole Church be most faithfully impressed, and be most strikingly apparent. And, on the contrary, if nowhere as here, the ruling of the Holy Spirit reveals itself in such fulness and force ; if nowhere as here, ecclesiastical faith and ecclesiastical maxims find their true, full expression ; so there is for other churches, in so far as they have by the side of Rome an independent existence, and pursue a course of development, the possibility and the danger of falling, in a greater or a less degree, into a one-sided course, of either falling short of the full truth, or of stepping beyond it, and distorting it. In the many and manifold forms of ecclesiastical life, Rome appears as the general regulator, as the power at once tenacious and stirring, conservative and creative alike—the true vital centre of the Church, whereby the unity of the whole is preserved, and all the parts rescued from the danger of isolation and disrupture, and brought back and retained in general harmony."[3]

Already in the question proposed by the Corinthians to Pope Clement in the lifetime of St John the Apostle,[4] already in the efforts of the most ancient heretics to find recognition at Rome,[5] already in the journey of St Polycarp, Bishop of Smyrna and of Hegesippus to Pope Auicetus, and

[2] Adv. Hæres. iii. 3. Cf. Hagemann, The Roman Church, p. 614, *seq.* Freiburg, 1864.
[3] Hagemann, *loc. cit.*, P. 1, *seq.* For this truth the whole book furnishes copious proofs.
[4] Upon the epistle see Hagemann, especially p. 684, *seq.*
[5] Valentinus, Marcion, Cerdon, Theodotus, Praxeas, Cleomenes, &c.

in the epistle of Pope Soter,[6] held at Corinth in as much reverence as that of Clement's, we find significant data and traces of the superior power of the Bishops of Rome. Pope Victor I., in whose pontificate even Protestant authors "have found combined all the agencies of the Papacy,"[7] excluded Theodotus of Byzantium from the Church,[8] commanded Synods to be everywhere held upon the question of the paschal celebration, and menaced with excommunication the recalcitrant inhabitants of Asia Minor. His competency to enforce this last measure none disputed, not even Irenæus, who sought on very different grounds to dissuade him from it. The view supported by Victor was everywhere, except in Asia Minor, accepted, and in like manner adopted by the Nicene Council.[9] Surely the resistance of some individual bishops—a resistance which we meet with later, even down to the last centuries—cannot be adduced by the opponents of the primacy as a decisive proof in their favour.

How powerful was the intervention of Victor's successors, Zephyrinus and Callistus, in all the ecclesiastical questions of their time, especially in that of the Penitential discipline, we learn from the lips of their opponents.[10] Pope Fabian issued a decree against the guilty Bishop, Privatus.[11] His successor, Cornelius, who is known to have written nine epistles, whereof three only are extant,[12] held a

---

[6] Iren. ad Vict, Eus. Hist. Eccles. v. 24, iv. 22, 23, Hier. catal. c. 22.
[7] Schwegler, The Post-Apostolic Age, II., pp. 214, 215.
[8] Eus. H. E., v. 28.
[9] Eus. H. E., v. 22-25. Hagemann, P. 14, *seq.*; 22, *seq.*; 75, *seq.*; 561, *seq.*; 582, *seq.* Hefele Conc. I., p. 73, *seq.* Coustant in Epist. Rom. Pontif., p. 91, *seq.*
[10] Philosophoumena, L. ix. Compare Döllinger, Hippolytus, and Callistus, p. 130, *seq.* Hagemann, p. 51, *seq.*
[11] Cypr. ep. 55, p. 84. Ed. Baluz. Jaffé Reg., n. 6.
[12] Jaffé Reg., n. 7-15, pp. 7, 8.

The Primacy and its Development. 111

Synod of sixty bishops against Novatian,[13] and kept up a friendly intercourse with Cyprian, Bishop of Carthage. The latter required his successor, Stephen I., to ordain the deposition of Marcianus, Bishop of Arles, and the election of another in his place. To Stephen, the Spanish Bishop, Basilides appealed, and from him obtained restoration to his See; an act in which Cyprian disputed not the right of the Pope, but blamed only the special exercise of that right.[14] What we yet know of the expressions of Pope Stephen in the controversy on heretical baptism, shows a full consciousness of his exalted dignity, and a high sense of duty. "With energetic determination, and apostolic courage," he opposed the error of the rebaptism of heretics, and required the acceptance of the Roman practice, which at last obtained a final triumph in the Church."[15] The controversy of Cyprian and Firmilian was as passionate as it was sophistic, and on that account cannot be here taken into consideration, to say nothing of Cyprian's earlier attitude towards the Roman See. Dionysius, Bishop of Rome, received from Dionysius of Alexandria, who had been accused before him, an apology, and gave in reply an accurate dogmatic exposition of the doctrine of the Trinity.[16] This

---

[13] Eus. H. E. vi. 43. Lib. synod. ap. Voell. et Just. Bibl. II., p. 1117.
[14] Döllinger's Manual of Church History, vol. i., p. 49. Ritter, *loc. cit.*, p. 15. Cypr. ep. 67, 68.
[15] Hagemann, p. 52. Cf. Nat. Alex. Eccl. Saec. III., c. 3, a. 5, § 4. . . . Certainly Stephen also appealed to his primacy. Cyprian (Ep. 71, ad Quintum) holds up before him the example of Peter (quem primum Dominus elegit, et super quem ædificavit Ecclesiam suam) in his dispute with Paul, wherein the former did not say, se primatum tenere, et ohtemporari à novellis et posteris sibi potius oportere. Cf. Coustant in Epist. Rom. Pontif. Diss. de Stephani sententiâ, pp. 227-255. Denzinger's "Criticism on the Lectures of Thiersch," I., p. 88, *seq.*
[16] Athan de syn c. 43, Migne xxvi. 669, Jaffé n. 24, p. 11. Cou-

Janus himself acknowledges. He finds this the only exception from the rule, " that the Bishops of Rome in the first ages accomplished no dogmatic result." But he subjoins, "the writing of Dionysius, if any authoritative importance had been ascribed to it, was well fitted in itself to cut short, or rather strangle in its birth, the long Arian disturbance; but it was not known out of Alexandria, and exercised no influence whatever on the later course of the controversy" (p. 64). But how many authoritative writings of the primitive ages have been otherwise lost, or by a happy chance only have been preserved in fragments? And hereby the fact remains clear, that according to the testimony of Athanasius, his celebrated predecessor was accused before the tribunal of the Bishop of Rome, justified himself before the latter, and accordingly corrected his views by the doctrinal standard of the Roman Church.

If now, in the whole period from Dionysius to Sylvester (an. 269-335), " there is no sign of doctrinal activity" (p. 67);[17] so it by no means thence follows, that no records of such activity had been in existence. The genuine Papal Decretals, that have been preserved, begin only with the year 385. But we know in what a reverential way the Synod of Arles wrote in the year 314 to Pope Sylvester;[18] how then Pope Julius enforced against the Eusebians, what he had received from the

---

stant, p. 271, *seq.* Routh Rel., Sac. iii. 179, *seq.* Cf. Dittrich Dionysius the Great, pp. 93, 111, 115. Freiburg, 1867.

[17] We here pass over the fragment of a dogmatic epistle of Pope Felix I., who flourished from 269 to 274, and which was cited at the Council of Ephesus, in the year 431. Vide Mansi Concil. i., p. 1114; Jaffé, n. 27, p. 11, which Hagemann also speaks of, *loc. cit.*, p. 480. Cf. Coustant, *loc. cit.*, p. 295.

[18] Communi copulâ caritatis et unitate matris Ecclesiæ catholicæ inhaerentes ad Arelatensium civitatem piissimi Imperatoris voluntate

The Primacy and its Development. 113

Apostle Peter, and blamed them for not having written anything on the cause of Athanasius to Rome, whence the decision was to be obtained;[19] how, lastly, Damasus praised the Orientals for having manifested towards the Roman See the due reverence, whereby they had achieved for themselves the greatest honour.[20] But we are assured (p. 67), in the Arian disputes the Roman See for a long time remained *passive*. *No one* sought from it aid or counsel; in the transactions and commotions that occurred from the year 359, "the Pope's name is never once mentioned; and it was only some years afterwards he gave *a sign of life*, when he adopted the procedure of the Synod of Alexandria against the bishops, who had fallen at Rimini" (pp. 68, 69).

Thus the loss of many Papal epistles is used for a proof of the inactivity and the insignificance of Rome. But all in vain. Against this assumption speaks, in the first place, the sentence of Pope Julius for the restoration of Athanasius and of the other bishops deposed by the Arians, as related by the

---

adducti, inde te, *gloriosissime Papa, commerita reverentia* salutamus ... Utinam ad hoc interesse spectaculum *tanti fecisses!* Profecto credimus, quia in eos severior fuisset sententia prolata, et te pariter nobiscum judicante, coetus noster majore laetitia exultasset. Sed quoniam recedere a partibus illis minime potuisti, *in quibus et Apostoli quotidie sedent* et cruor ipsorum sine intermissione Dei gloriam testatur, &c. ... placuit etiam a te qui *majores dioeceses tenes* per te potissimum omnibus insinuari. Coustant, p. 345, *seq.* Hagemann, p. 561, *seq.*

[19] Jul. ap. Athan. Apol., c. 35, (Migne xxv. 308): ἢ ἀγνοεῖτε, ὅτι τοῦτο ἔθος (Nic. c. 6) πρότερον γράφεσθαι ἡμῖν καὶ οὕτως ἔνθεν ὁρίζεσθαι τὰ δίκαια; Are you ignorant, that this is the custom (old custom, as Nic. can. 6) first to write to us, that thence what is just may be decreed?—Tr.

[20] Dam. ep. ad Orient. Theod. HE. v. 10, Coustant, p. 517. Jaffé n. 59: ὅτι τῇ ἀποστολικῇ καθέδρᾳ τὴν ὀφειλομένην αἰδῶ ἡ ἀγάπη ὑμῶν ἀπονέμει κ. τ. λ. That your charity accords to the Holy See the due reverence, &c.—Tr.

H

Greek historians;[21] in the second place, the confession presented to the Pope by Valens and Ursacius, wherein they assert that they have received pardon from him;[22] in the third place, the efforts of the Emperor Constantius to bring over to his side the Pope Liberius, above all, who had been so long steadfast;[23] and in the fourth place, the steps taken by the semi-Arian bishops of the East to obtain the recognition of Rome;[24] fifthly, the decrees issued by Pope Damasus against various heresies,—decrees which were subscribed by the bishops of the province of Antioch, and obtained great authority in the whole Church;[25] sixthly, the request of St Basil to Athanasius to send, by reason of the calamities of the East, envoys to the West, where he was held in the greatest consideration, and from which help was more im-

---

[21] Socr. II. 17, al. xi.; ὁ δὲ, ἅτε προνόμια τῆς ἐν Ῥώμῃ ἐκκλησίας ἐχούσης, παρρησιαστικοῖς γράμμασιν ὠχύρωσεν αὐτοὺς καὶ ἐπὶ τὴν ἀνατολὴν ἀναστέλλει αὐτούς, τὸν οἰκεῖον ἑκάστῳ θρόνον ἀποδιδοὺς καί καθαπτόμενος τῶν προπετῶς καθελόντων αὐτούς. And he (the Pope), inasmuch as the Church in Rome possessed special privileges, in outspoken letters confirmed them (the bishops), and sends them back to the East, restoring to each his own see, and rebuking those who had rashly deposed them.

[22] Coust., p. 405: ἡ θεοσέβειά σου κατὰ τὴν ἔμφυτον ἑαυτῆς καλοκἀγαθίαν τῇ πλάνῃ ἡμῶν κατηξίωσε συγγνώμην δοῦναι: Thy piety, according to its innate rectitude and goodness, has deemed right to pardon our error.

[23] Athan. Hist. Arian. ad mon. c. 35, p. 734, ed. Migne. The Heathen Ammianus Marcellinus (xv. c. 7.) relates the pressure of the emperor on Liberius, Christianæ legis Antistes, and observes id enim (the expulsion of Athanasius) licet impletum sciret, tamen *auctoritate* quoque *quâ potiores æternae urbis episcopi, firmari desiderio nitebatur ardenti.*

[24] Hefele Conc. I., p. 712, *et seq.* Coustant, ep. 14, p. 453, *seq.* *Ibid.*, the Answer of Pope Liberius, ep. 14, p. 457, *seq.* The Pope wished to proclaim the just things to those seeking them: Βοηθῆσαι τοῖς δίκαια αἰτουμένοις.—*Ibid.*, n. 4., p. 464.

[25] Theod. HE. V., 11. Hefele I., 718, 719, n. 1. Merenda Admonit in Dam. ep. 4. Coustant, p. 489, *seq.* Compare Janus, pp. 73, 74.

The Primacy and its Development. 115

mediately to be expected;[26] and lastly, the testimony of the same Basil in his letter to Damasus, that the Roman Church had, in former times, ever solaced and visited the Orientals, as these now desired.[27] An epistle received thereupon, and the mission of the deacon Sabinus were in the year 372 received by Basil with great joy, and the delegation of several envoys from the West was ardently requested.[28] The priest Evagrius brought back in the year 373 the documents which had been sent by Basil to Rome, and which did not satisfy the Roman spirit of exactness, and stated the desire that they were to be worded according to the formulary there sketched, and that trustworthy men were, at the same time, to be deputed to Rome.[29] From Ascholius the papal vicar in Thessalonica, Basil moreover received letters, that gave him great pleasure;[30] but, in a letter to Evagrius he complains that he wants a competent man for the journey to the West; for the way to Rome in 375 was very unsafe.[31] Of all these earlier epistles Janus knows nothing; he knows only the later ones (p. 87, Note), wherein is expressed the displeasure of the great Cappadocian with the Westerns, who were so ill-informed of the

---

[26] Basil. ep. 66–69. (Migne xxxii., p. 424, *seq.* 432.) Cf. ep. 68, ad Melet., p. 428.

[27] Basil. ep. 70, p. 433 (Coust. p. 476): τούτων μίαν προσεδοκήσαμεν λύσιν τὴν τῆς ὑμετέρας εὐσπλαγχνίας ἐπίσκεψιν καὶ ἐψυχαγώγησεν ἡμᾶς ἀεὶ τὸ παράδοξον τῆς ὑμετέρας ἀγάπης τῷ παρελθόντι χρόνῳ. (Horum unicam solutionem exspectavimus, miserationis vestræ visitationem : ac nos semper consolata est mirabilis vestra caritas præterito tempore. Maurist Translation, Paris, 1730.

[28] Bas. ep. 90, 91, 92, p. 472, *et seq.*

[29] Ep. 138, c. 2, ad Eus., p. 580.

[30] Ep. 154, p. 609; ep. 164, 165, p. 633. The Archbishop of Thessalonica belonged certainly, in the opinion of Basil, to the Westerns (the δυτικοί).

[31] Bas. ep. 156, c. 3, p. 617 ad Evagr.—ep. 215, p, 792, ad Doroth.

circumstances of the East, who repulsed Meletius, the patriarch of Antioch, and who were arrogant withal.[32] But this displeasure may easily be accounted for by the historical circumstances of the time. Deceived in his hopes, he will expect nothing more from the West, yet he yearningly turns to it again : the Westerns are to be physicians to the sick, and teachers of those in health.[33] Later, he cherishes again more hope ;[34] and, in the year 377, he sends a letter of thanksgiving to Rome. He states that a Council of Tyana reestablished Eustathius, bishop of Sebaste, who had brought a Papal rescript; but he laments his errors, as well as those of Apollinarius and Paulinus.[35] Had the epistles of Pope Damasus been known to him (he died on the 1st January 379), they would have made him truly happy : so deeply did he grieve to see Meletius numbered among heretics by Pope Damasus, as well as by Peter, patriarch of Alexandria.[36]

The more abundantly historical sources are opened to us, the more numerous are the testimonies for the primacy of the Roman Church. From all parts of the Christian world, the popes received reports ;[37] it is universally acknowledged that all important affairs of the Church are to be referred to their see. This fact is declared not

---

[32] Ep. 214, c. 2, p. 785 ; ep. 239, c. 2, p. 893. Basil calls the Pope τον κορυφαῖον τῶν ἐκ τῆς δύσεως, "the Head of the Westerns."
[33] Ep. 242, c. 3, p. 901. Cf. ep. 243.
[34] Ep. 253, 254, 255, p. 940, *seq.*
[35] Ep. 263, p. 976.
[36] Ep. 266, p. 993, c. 2.
[37] Pope Damasus (ep. 3, pp. 481, 488, ed. Constant) mentions the ἀναφορά (report) of the Brethren in Gaul and in Venice; Pope Siricius, too (ep. 1, c. 1, p. 624), makes mention of the report (relatio) of Himerius, bishop of Tarragona, to his predecessor, Damasus.

The Primacy and its Development. 117

only by popes, like Innocent I. for example,[38] but by councils also, as by those of Sardica, Milevi, and Ephesus,[39] as well as by the most eminent bishops,[40] and even by emperors themselves.[41]

[38] Innoc. I., ep. 29, n. 1, p. 888, ed. Coustant : In requirendis Dei rebus, quas omni cum sollicitudine decet a sacerdotibus, maxime a vero justoque et catholico tractari Concilio, *antiquæ traditionis exempla servantes et ecclesiasticæ memores disciplinæ, vestræ religionis vigorem non minus nunc in consulendo quam antea, cum pronunciaretis, vera ratione firmastis,* qui ad nostrum referendum approbastis esse judicium, scientes, quid Apostolicæ Sedi. . . . debeatur. Ep. 30, n. 2, p. 896 : Diligenter ergo et congrue apostolici consulitis honoris arcana (honoris inquam illius, quem præter illa, quæ sunt extrinsecus, *sollicitudo* manet *omnium ecclesiarum*) *super anxiis rebus quæ sit tenenda sententia: antiquæ* scilicet *regulæ formam secuti, quam toto semper ab orbe mecum nostis esse servatam.* . . . . Quid id etiam *actione firmastis,* nisi *scientes quod per omnes provincias de apostolico fonte petentibus responsa semper emanent ? Præsertim quoties fidei ratio ventilatur,* arbitror omnes fratres et coëpiscopos nostros nonnisi ad Petrum, *i.e.*, sui nominis et honoris auctorem, *referre debere.*, &c. Ep. 37, n. 1, p. 910. Mirari non possumus dilectionem tuam sequi *instituta majorum,* omniaque, quæ possunt recipere aliquam dubitationem, *ad nos quasi ad caput atque ad apicem episcopatus referre,* ut consulta videlicet Sedes Apostolica ex ipsis rebus dubiis certum aliquid faciendum pronunciet.

[39] Conc. Sardic., ep. ad Jul., n. 1, p. 395, Coust. : Hoc enim optimum et valde congruentissimum esse videbitur, si *adcaput, id est, ad Petri Apostoli Sedem,* de singulis quibusque provinciis Domini referant sacerdotes. Conc. Milevit, anno 416, ad Innoc. I., ep. 27, n. 1, p. 873 : Quia te Dominus gratiæ suæ præcipuo munere in Sede Apostolicâ collocavit, talemque nostris temporibus præstitit, ut nobis potius ad culpam negligentiæ valeat, si apud tuam venerationem quæ pro ecclesiâ suggerenda sunt, tacuerimus, quam ea tu possis vel fastidiose vel negligenter accipere, magnis periculis infirmorum membrorum Christi pastoralem diligentiam adhibere digneris. Conc. Ephes. ep. ad Cœlestin. Papam. (ep. 20, n. 1, p. 1165) : ἐπειδὴ ἐχρῆν ἅπαντα εἰς γνῶσιν τῆς σῆς ὁσιότητος ἀνενεχθῆναι τὰ παρακολουθήσαντα ; since it was necessary that all the things which have ensued should be brought to the knowledge of thy Holiness.

[40] Cyril of Alexandria writes in the year 430 to Pope Celestine (Cælest. ep. 8, p. 1085, Coust.) that he would have observed silence, could he have lawfully done so, and had it not been his duty to write to the Pope upon existing controversies, especially in matters of faith ; but old ecclesiastical usage requires (τὰ μακρὰ τῶν ἐκκλησιῶν ἔθη) that he should make a report thereon to his Holiness. From the Pope he wishes to have the decision. (N. 7, p. 1093.)

The elder Protestants wished to make Gregory VII. the first real Pope; the later ones wished to make Nicholas I.; others, again, Gregory I.; while the moderns make Leo the Great. But we are ever carried back to a higher antiquity: what we find said by and in Leo, may be already shown, as far as our documents reach, to be the language of his predecessors. But we must ever keep in view, that the primacy was never as a ready-made system traced out for the constitution of the ancient Church, but was deposited in it like a fructifying germ, which developed with the life of the Church. Hence, we ought, says Ferdinand Walter, from whom we borrow this passage, not so represent the circumstances of the case as if the Roman see had clearly foreseen all for which it was destined, and did, as it were, but watch the opportunity for bringing it to a consummation. Its task was rather prescribed to it by the circumstances and by the demands of the Church; and hence, with the growth of the whole body, the primacy came out in more distinct outlines.[42] "The Divine Founder of the Church," says George Phillips, "has defined the rights of his vicegerent on earth only in general traits, and not in minute particulars. According to the will of providence, the primacy was to enter on the domain of history. Hence, it could not be circumscribed within exact and sharply-defined limits, but must be allowed such a *freedom of movement* and of development, as would enable it to enforce in every sphere its

---

Avitus of Vienne writes (ep. 36): Scitis Synodalium legum esse, ut in rebus, quæ ad Ecclesiæ statum pertinent, si quid dubitationis fuerit exortum, ad Romanæ ecclesiæ maximum sacerdotem quasi ad caput nostrum membra sequentia recurramus.

[41] Justinian. I., ad Joh. II., ep. 3, n. 3, L. 7, Cod. I., 1. Marcian Imp. in ep. 76, 100, 110, Leon. M.

[42] *Walter*, Canon Law, § 19.

divine power, according to the various circumstances, and the special needs of different ages. With this predetermination, Christ made Peter the Apostle the foundation-stone of His Church, and endowed him with the three prerogatives of royalty, the teaching office, and the high-priesthood. He has hereby conferred on him the plenary, the supreme, and the regular power, immediately relating to the whole Church."[43]

It is a thoroughly false view to concede to the Church the principle of development, and, on the other hand, to prescribe to the Papal primacy a point of development beyond which it must not go; and this without any regard to the historical expansion of the Eastern Patriarchates, which extended their power even over countries for whose subjection no more ancient title existed; while the Bishop of Rome, as patriarch of the West, had converted to Christianity almost the whole South, West, and North of Europe, and founded countless filial churches.[44] And these were brought into no greater state of dependence than that in which the Eastern churches had, from a very early period, stood in relation to the patriarchs. If we had to deal with another opponent than Janus, we should

---

[43] Phillips's Canon Law, vol. v., § 201, p. 6. The copious treatment of the subject in this work may be strongly recommended to the reader.

[44] Innoc. I., ep. 25, ad Decent., n. 2, p. 856, ed. Coust.: cum sit manifestum in omnem Italiam, Gallias, Hispanias, Africam atque Siciliam et insulas interjacentes nullum instituisse ecclesias, nisi eos, quos venerabilis Apostolus Petrus aut ejus successores constituerint sacerdotes. Aut legant, si in his provinciis alius Apostolorum invenitur, aut legitur docuisse. Qui si non legunt, quia nusquam inveniunt, oportet eos hoc sequi, quod ecclesia Romana custodit, a quâ eos principium accepisse non dubium est. Of Ireland, Germany, Scandinavia, as well as of the Anglo-Saxons in England, it is besides known that they received the gospel from Rome.

have endeavoured to distinguish between the primatial and the patriarchal rights of the Church of Rome. Here we confine ourselves to that which must needs be stated in reply to our opponent. The latter, "in order to show the enormous difference in the position and action of the primacy, as it was in the Roman empire, and as it became in the later Middle Ages" (p. 77), points out to his readers *ten facts*, which require our minute examination.

(1.) "The Popes took no part in convoking councils. All great councils, to which bishops came from different countries, were convoked by the Emperors, nor were the Popes ever consulted about it beforehand" (p. 77). Doubtless, the first eight Œcumenical Councils were convoked by the emperors.[45] This was rendered necessary for ensuring the safety, under the circumstances of the times, and for facilitating the journeys of the bishops, who made use of the imperial posts.[46] Then again this intervention was unavoidable on account of the territorial power of the emperors and of their general influence;[47] so even Pope Liberius was obliged to request the convocation of a synod from the Emperor Constantius.[48] That, however, in the convocation of such Councils the popes took no part, is utterly untrue. Many of the acts relating to these Councils have been lost; but of the fourth Council we still possess numerous documents,

---

[45] Hefele Conc. I., p 7. Phillips's Canon Law, II., § 84, p. 238, *et seq.*

[46] In reference to the Synods so frequent under Constantius, Ammianus Marcellinus (xxi. 16) complains that the vehicles (res vehicularia) were almost ruined; and Hilary (Fragm. iii., op. hist., n. 25) says, Currus ipse publicus attritus ad nihilum perducitur.

[47] Cf. Bellarm. de Concil. I., 13. Bennettis, P. II., t. III., p. 154.

[48] Liber., ep. 4, pp. 423-427, ed. Coust.

The Primacy and its Development. 121

which prove the negotiations carried on on this subject by the Emperor Marcian with Pope Leo I., and the share of the latter in this business.[49] Not long after the holding of this Council, the bishops of Mœsia wrote, "that it had been by the command of Pope Leo, who was truly the head of bishops, convened."[50] The sixth General Council expressly asserts of the first, that it was assembled by the Emperor Constantine and by Pope Sylvester; and data from other sources coincide in this statement.[51] That Innocent I., in the affairs of Chrysostom, and Leo I., after the Latrocinum of Ephesus, applied to the court of Constantinople for the convocation of Synods, is easily explained from the indispensable need of imperial co-operation. In some cases the popes took the initiative, in others the emperors, who then assured themselves of the papal sanction, as occurred in the sixth, seventh, and eighth General Councils; and, as may be proved, was the case with the third also. The second Œcumenical Synod of the year 381, was originally but a General Council of the Greek Church. Respecting the summoning of the fifth General Council, the Emperor Justinian negotiated with Pope Vigilius.[52] But soon after this Synod, Pope Pelagius II. could claim the convocation of Œcumenical Councils as a privilege of his see.[53]

(2.) " The popes also were not always allowed to preside personally, or by deputy, at the great Councils, though no one denied them the first

---

[49] Hefele, loc. cit., p. 10, *et seq.*
[50] Hard., Conc. II., 710.
[51] Hard. III. 1417. Hefele, loc. cit., p. 256, *seq.*
[52] Hefele, I., p. 9, 11-13.
[53] Pelag. II., ep. 6, ad Orient.: cum generalium synodorum convocandi auctoritas Apostolicæ Sedi B. Petri singulari privilegio sit tradita, et nulla unquam synodus rata legatur, quæ apostolicâ auctoritate non fuerit fulta.

rank [the rank merely?] in the Church. Only at Chalcedon, in the year 451, and at Constantinople in 680, did the papal legates preside" (pp. 77, 78).

But the papal privilege appears an undisputed one, and the two Synods referred to too clearly show the importance of that privilege—a privilege which Janus quickly passes over. In the second General Council, there could not be, from the reason already alleged, any question of the exercise of this right. At the fifth Council, Pope Vigilius, though most respectfully invited by a brilliant deputation, headed by the Oriental patriarchs, refused, by reason of the non-fulfilment of the stipulated conditions, to take part in its proceedings.[54] Even before this Synod, this papal privilege was undisputed. Macedonius II., patriarch of Constantinople (who flourished from the year 496 to 511), declared, when desired by the Emperor Anastasius to condemn the Council of Chalcedon, that such a step, without an Œcumenical Synod presided over by the Pope, was impossible; and this emperor, though strongly inclined towards the heretics, very well knew that the presidency of the Pope was necessary, when he promised to let a General Council be held at Heraclea, but which afterwards failed.[55] At Ephesus, Cyril, patriarch of Alexandria, to whom Celestine had previously delegated his authority, presided with the papal legates afterwards sent.[56] Here, too, the power of the

---

[54] Hefele, p. 8, II. 43.
[55] Theophan. Chronogr., pp. 234, 242, 346, *seq.* Theod., Lect. II. 24. Cedren. I., 632. Malal. L. xvi. p. 596. Marcellin. Chron., a. 514, 515.
[56] Cœlestin., ep. 11, ad Cyrill., n. 4, p. 1105. Coust.: συναφθείσης σοι τῆς αὐθεντίας τοῦ ἡμετέρου θρόνου ... ταύτην ἐκβιβάσεις ἀκριβεῖ στερρότητι τὴν ἀπόφασιν. Cf. ep. 14, n. 8, p. 1145. "The

The Primacy and its Development. 123

Roman See was brilliantly displayed. Its legates were appointed to execute its decrees, and charged to show themselves, not as contending parties, but as judges.[57] Bishop Firmus characterized the epistle of the Pope as the rule of the Assembly;[58] and that Assembly itself declared that it was bound by this epistle, as well as by the Canons, to proceed to the deposition of Nestorius.[59] Of the first Nicene Council, we know that Bishop Hosius and two Roman priests, in their quality of papal representatives, first subscribed the decisions; and this fact is confirmed by the testimony of Gelasius of Cyzicus, as well as by that of other witnesses.[60] Even by Eusebius the Emperor Constantine is distinguished from the presidents of the Council.[61] The fact that in the year 449, at the Latrocinium of Ephesus, Dioscorus, patriarch of Alexandria, setting aside the papal legates, assumed the presidency, was afterwards, in the Council of Chalcedon, imputed to him as a crime.[62] The Emperor Theodosius II., in his embarrassment, had indeed committed to that patriarch the conduct of the deliberations; but from the fact that Leo still sent his deputies to Ephesus, it by no means follows that he renounced the presidency of the Council; for in his epistle to the Synod, convoked for Ephesus, he emphatically points out the primacy of his See.[63] The new Council was, according to the

whole authority of our see having been committed to thee, . . . thou wilt enforce this decision with a firm exactitude."—Tr.

[57] Cœlestin., ep. 17, p. 1152. Coust. Mansi. IV. 556. Cf. Eph. Conc., act. ii., ibidem. p. 1287.
[58] Conc. Ephes., act. ii. Mansi, loc. cit., p. 1287-1290.
[59] Ibid., Act. iii., p. 1295.
[60] Hefele I., p. 32-38.
[61] Eus. Vita. Const. III. 13.
[62] Hefele I. p. 6, seq. 38. Mansi VI. 581. Hard. II. 68.
[63] Leo M., ep. 33, ad Synod Ephes., c. 1.

express words of the Emperor Marcian, to be held under the direct guidance of the Pope.⁶⁴ The presidency of his representatives Leo several times mentions ; ⁶⁵ and the Council of Chalcedon writes to him, that, by his vicars, he presided over all, as the head over the members.⁶⁶

(3.) " Neither the dogmatic nor the disciplinary decisions of these Councils required papal confirmation, for their force and authority depended on the consent of the Church as expressed in the Synod, and afterwards on the fact of their being generally received " (p. 78).

To this assertion many facts are opposed: first, the letter of the Synod of Chalcedon to Pope Leo, with the request for confirmation, followed by another from the Emperor Marcian, which solicited a document of approval to be made known to all the churches ; ⁶⁷ secondly, the request of the Synod of 680 to the Pope, wherein it is said : " The brilliant light of the true Faith we have clearly announced with thee ; and we, therefore, earnestly request thy paternal Holiness to confirm this anew by thy venerable decrees ;" and to this request Leo II. responded ; ⁶⁸ thirdly, the efforts of the Emperor Justinian to procure from Pope Vigilius the confirmation of the fifth Council, and this was at last granted by the Pope ; fourthly, the repeated attempts of the Emperor Justinian II. to obtain

---

⁶⁴ σου αὐθεντοῦντος. Leo, ep. 73.

⁶⁵ Ep. 89, Marcian Im., prædictum patrem et coepiscopum vice meâ Synodo convenit præsidere. Ep. 93, ad Synod. c. 1. In his fratribus . . . me Synodo vestra fraternitas æstimet præsidere.

⁶⁶ Leo, ep. 98, c. i. p. 1089, 1090, ed. Ball.

⁶⁷ Ep. cit. c. 4, p. 1099, ep. 110, Marc. p. 1183, *seq*. Tua pietas literas mittere dignabitur per quas omnibus populis et ecclesiis manifestum fiat in sancta Synodo peracta a tuâ Beatitudine rata haberi.

⁶⁸ Hard. III. 1632–1469. Hefele, Conc. p. 43.

⁶⁹ Hefele, Conc. ii., p. 881, *seq.;* iii. p. 315, *seq.*

The Primacy and its Development. 125

from Rome the approval of the Council in Trullo, held in 692, but which found there no recognition, and which, therefore, no theologian will designate, with Janus (p. 157), an Œcumenical Synod. When the forged confirmation of the first Nicene Council by Pope Sylvester is alleged, we must still remember that, independently of our false records, which, in all probability, owed their origin only to the generally known fact; that fact itself is attested by forty Italian bishops, at a Synod in the year 485, as well as by the very sober and prudent Dionysius Exiguus.[70] A synodical letter of Pope Damasus had already declared that the Council of Rimini, with all its number of bishops, could have no weight, when neither the Roman Bishop, whose sentence was above all to be waited for,[71] nor Vincentius of Capua, and other bishops had given in their adhesion. This right of confirmation is expressed by Pope Gelasius in a very definite manner.[72] And even the Greeks recognize as a rule, that without the Romans no synodical decree has legal force;[73] that on the Pope depends the

[70] *Ibid.*, I., p. 40, 41, 421, *seq.;* 425, *seq.*
[71] οὗ τὴν γνώμην πρὸ πάντων ἔδει ἐκδέξασθαι. Theodoret, H. E., L. ii. c. 17, al 22. Coustant, p. 485. Compare the words of Pope Julius in note 19 above.
[72] Gelas, I. ep. ad Episc. Dard. : Quæ (sedes prima) et unamquamque synodum suâ auctoritate confirmat, et continuatâ moderatione custodit. Tom. de anathem. vinculo. Totum in sedis Apostolicæ positum est potestate : ita quod firmavit in synodo sedes Apostolica, hoc robur obtinuit, quod refutavit, habere non potuit firmitatem.
[73] Niceph. Cpl. pro. s. imag.c. 25 (Mai N. Bibl. pp. ii. 30. Migne C., p. 597); ὧν (the Romans presiding in the seventh Council), ἄνευ δόγμα κατὰ τὴν ἐκκλησίαν κινούμενον θεσμοῖς κανονικοῖς καὶ ἱερατικοῖς ἔθεσιν νενομισμένον ἄνωθεν τὴν δοκιμασίαν οὐ σχοίη ἡ δέξαιτ' ἄν ποτε τὴν περαίωσιν, ὡς δὴ λαχόντων κατὰ τὴν ἱερωσύνην ἐξάρχειν καὶ τῶν κορυφαίων ἐν ἀποστόλοις ἐγκεχειρισμένων τὸ ἀξίωμα. Without whom (the Romans presiding in the seventh Council) a doctrine brought forward in the Church could not, even though confirmed by canonical decrees and by ecclesiastical usage, ever obtain full approval

validity of Œcumenical Synods;[74] and that it is no detriment to a General Council, if the Oriental patriarchs be absent, provided that the apostolic Pope in Rome concur in its decisions, and be there represented by his legates.[75]

(4.) "For the first thousand years no Pope ever issued a doctrinal decision, intended for, and addressed to the whole Church" (p. 78). The reverse of this we have already seen. Leo's letter to Flavian is (p. 69) called only the first dogmatic document of a Pope; but this letter was published throughout the whole Church, and already, before the Council of Chalcedon, was subscribed by the bishops of the East and West.[76] Such decisions we have, further, from Popes Damasus, Innocent, and Zosimus, which we have already adduced, as well as from Siricius against Jovinian (p. 72). When Pope Siricius did not wish to issue a decision respecting Bishop Bonosus, for which the Illyrian prelates subject to his patriarchate had "*vel pro veritate vel pro modestia*" requested him; he by no means absolutely said that "he had no right to take such a step," but he wished to preserve in the first place the jurisdiction in the first instance of the neighbouring bishops, as established by the Synod of Capua.[77] The second Synod of Orange,

---

or currency. For it is they (the Roman Pontiffs) who have had assigned to them the rule in sacred things, and who have received into their hands the dignity of headship among the Apostles.

[74] Theod. Stud .L. II., ep. 129, p. 1420 : ᾧ (τῷ ἐκ δύσεως) καὶ τὸ κράτος ἀναφέρεται τῆς οἰκουμενικῆς συνόδου, "cui (Episcopo Romano) et potestas summa defertur Synodi Œcumenicæ " (tr. Jac. Sismondi.)

[75] Conc. vii., ap. Mansi. xii., 1134. Cf. Thomassin. de vet. et nova Eccl. disciplinâ. P. I., L. 1, c. 13, n. 6; c. 14, n. 8.

[76] Hefele II., Pp. 374, 378, *seq.*, 385, 388.

[77] Let us attend to the addition in Siricius, ep. 9, p. 680, ed. Coustant . . . . : Nam si integra esset hodie synodus, recte . . . . decerneremus; and Coustant's note d. Cf. Bennettis, op. cit., P. II., tom. iii., p. 175.

in the affair of the Massillians in 529, found general recognition only by the confirmation of Pope Boniface II. in the year 531, although its decrees were for the most part made up of judgments sent by Pope Felix IV.[78] They passed for a general standard of doctrine; and it is by no means true that Papal decisions then only obtained that character, "when they had been read, examined, and approved at an Œcumenical Council" (p. 78). This refers particularly "to the careful examination" of the above-mentioned dogmatic letter of Leo I. to Flavian (p. 47). But it is right to observe that this letter was immediately, on its first reading in the second session of Chalcedon, greeted amid joyful acclamations, as the rule of faith ("Peter hath spoken by the mouth of Leo," and so forth); and it was only afterwards, when some less informed bishops expressed certain doubts, which were completely set aside even in the fourth session, a more minute inquiry took place.[79] Accordingly, theologians regard this as a mere *examen elucidationis*, and not as an *examen revisionis*, in the same way as the Council of Basle examined the decree of Constance relative to the use of the chalice.[80] That Leo the Great himself acknowledged, his decree first needed a confirmation by the bishops, before it could become a fixed rule of faith, is certainly not to be inferred from his correspondence with the prelates of Gaul.[81] The signatures of bishops were required

---

[78] Mansi. VIII., 735. Hefele II., 705, 716.

[79] Hefele II., 422, *seq.*; 435, *seq.*

[80] Bennettis, P. I., t. i., p. 173, *seq.* Card. Gerdil Esame dell' opposizione alla Bolla *Auctorem fidei* (Examination of the motives of opposition to the Bull Auctorem Fidei), P. II., § ii. Op. xiv., pp. 191-210. *Card. Litta* Lettere, 23. Zaccaria Antifebronio, P. II., p. 336, *seq.*

[81] Leo (ep. 67, p. 1001, Ball., p. 886, ed. Migne) gave the

for a full security against the further spread of the heresy which had sprung up in the East, but not for a confirmation of the dogma itself; for the consent of all to the decree issued is demanded by every Œcumenical Council. " But Pope Celestine's condemnation of Nestorius was superseded" (in the eye of the Church?) "by the emperor's convoking a General Council at Ephesus" (p. 71). The fathers of Ephesus, however, did not think so, when, as we saw above, they declared themselves forced by the letter of Pope Celestine to pronounce an identical sentence; and when they deemed the matter decreed by the Pope as by no means invalid. The reading of other dogmatic testimonies also, by no means proves that a confirmation was enunciated only after a formal revision.

Against the Papal power it is further alleged: "Never, during the first *nine* centuries, had the Popes ever *once made even the attempt* to gather about them a great synod of bishops from different countries" (p. 190). But yet such *an attempt* Agatho made, who summoned to his Roman synod even the Frankish, English, and other prelates; Stephen III., who in the year 769 held his Lateran synod with fifty-three bishops, among whom were twelve Frankish prelates; and, lastly, Nicholas I., who in 867 had entertained the idea of assembling all the bishops of the West in order to deliberate on the charges preferred by the

notice, the Bishops (ep. 68) thanked the Pope for his paternal care, and uttered praises on the letter, c. 1, p. 888. Magna et ineffabili quâdam nos peculiares tui gratulatione succrescimus, quod illa specialis doctrinæ vestræ pagina ita per omnium Ecclesiarum conventicula celebratur, ut vere consona omnium sententia declaretur, merito illic principatum sedis apostolicæ constitutum, unde adhuc apostolici spiritus oracula (" the odious oracles," Janus, p. 45), reserentur. Cf. ep. 99, c. 2, ep. 102, 103. Upon the letter to Theodoret, *vide* Bennettis, *loc. cit.*, p. 178, *seq.*

The Primacy and its Development.

Greeks.[82] The assembling of an Œcumenical Council at Rome was not agreeable to the imperial court of Constantinople, and from regard to this court the project could scarcely be entertained. Moreover, the history of the Western Kingdoms points to the many difficulties which opposed the convocation of the greater synods.

From the relation of Popes to Councils, Janus turns to the definition of their other rights and powers.

"The Popes possessed none of the three powers which are the proper attributes of sovereignty—neither the legislative, the administrative, nor the judicial" (p. 78). Hitherto we have believed that these three powers were already comprised in the office of Peter, involved in the very idea of the Papal supremacy, and exercised long before the times of pseudo-Isidore. We must now, so it appears, correct not only the manuals of canon law,[83] but those of Church history also.[84] But what we have hitherto discovered in Janus bids us look beforehand somewhat more carefully into this matter.

1. As regards more immediately the supreme judicial power, Janus well knows (p. 79) that the Council of Sardica can be opposed to him ; but to this he is prepared to offer several objections. In the first place, the judgment on bishops, in the second and third instance, was committed only to the person of the then Pope, Julius ; and, secondly, neither the Eastern Church nor the African ever received this regulation. The first objection is, however, solved, if we compare with the third

---

[82] Hefele Conc. III., 227, *seq.*, 403 ; IV. 349. *Vide* Bennettis, L. i., p. 250, *seq.*
[83] Phillips's Canon Law, I., § 11, *seq.* ; v. § 201, *seq.*
[84] Döllinger's Manual of Church History, I., p. 177, *seq.*, § 40.

canon of Sardica—where Julius is named—the two following ones, having material connexion therewith, but which are passed over by Janus, and that make express mention of the Bishop of Rome.[85] The second objection, as to the non-acceptance of the regulation on the part of the Orientals, was long ago refuted by Pope Nicholas I. John Scholasticus admitted these canons into his collection of ecclesiastical laws; the Council in Trullo, in the year 692, names the two canons expressly; Photius inserted them in his Nomocanon, and many Greeks have appealed to them.[86] The African Church took offence at these canons being designated from Rome as Nicene; and to this mistake the arrangement of the more ancient collections of ecclesiastical law (p. 122) had led. It opposed, on weighty practical grounds, the appeal of a mere priest, like Apiarius, but by no means assailed the Pope's judicial power in general;[87] a power which Augustine, particularly in his letter on Bishop Anthony of Fuscala, while alleging even earlier examples, decidedly recognized.[88] Numerous precedents of appeals[89] refute the assertion, that before pseudo-Isidore the ordinance of Sardica did not come into force. Chrysostom

---

[85] Hefele, i. 549, 550. Phillips's Can. Law, v. § 216, p. 262, *seq.*
[86] Nicol. I. ep. 6. Mansi xv. p. 174, *seq.* In regard to collections of Canon Law, see *Joh. Schol.*, tit. 16. *Voell. et Justell. Bibl.*, Jur. Can., ii., p. 537, *seq. Pitra* Juris Gr. eccl. monum., ii. 377, 380. *Ballerini* de Ant. Can. Collect., P. i. c. 6. Phillips, p. 272, *seq.*
[87] Phillips, § 217, p. 274, *seq.* Hefele, ii. 107, 120, *seq.* Döllinger, *loc. cit.*, p. 186, *seq.* The English writers, Mr Allies and Bishop Ullathorne, also concur in the results obtained from recent researches. Vide *Journal of Theol. Literature*, p. 522, *seq.*, 1866.
[88] Aug. ep. 209, *seq.* Cœlestini I. ep. 1., p. 1051, *seq.* Here it is said, n. 8, p. 1056, Existunt exempla, *ipsâ sede Apostolica judicante, vel aliorum judicata firmante*, quosdam pro culpis quibusdam nec episcopali spoliatos honore, nec relictos omnimodis impunitos.
[89] Phillips, § 218, p. 292, *seq.*

The Primacy and its Development. 131

sent epistles and deputies to Pope Innocent I., to obtain from him speedy correction of the acts done against him,[90] and the annulling of his condemnation,[91] as well as the chastisement of those who had violated all canonical law. Pope Celestine not only passed a penal sentence against Nestorius, but quashed even the judgments pronounced by that heresiarch.[92] Boniface I. assumes to himself (according to 1 Corinthians iv. 21) full penal jurisdiction.[93]

2. When, in respect to *legislative* power, it is said that the popes in those early times made no attempt to exercise it, we must first be permitted to observe, that the non-exercise of a right proves nothing against its existence; that in general the primitive Church had but few and simple laws; that the Papacy, for the most part, intervened only in cases absolutely necessary; and further, that the *forms* of legislation were different at different times. First of all, the laws were discussed with the Roman Presbytery, issued at Synods, or set forth in epistles to the bishops of different provinces and countries.[94] In the Papal answers, too, to consultations from *all parts of the world*,[95] the exercise of legislative power is unmis-

---

[90] ταχίστην παρασκευάσαι γενέσθαι τὴν διόρθωσιν. Innoc. in ep. 4, n. 1, p. 773, ed Coust. Bennettis, P. ii. t. 3, p. 399, *seq.*
[91] The Pope is to declare, μηδεμίαν ἔχειν ἰσχύν (τα ὄυτω παρανόμως γεγενημένα) that the acts thus done contrary to law have no force. *Ib.* n. 7, p. 785. Cf. Phillips *loc. cit.*, pp. 296–301.
[92] Cœlestin., ep. 13, n. 5, p. 1121; n. 11, p. 1129; ep. 14, n. 7, p. 1145, ed. cit.
[93] Bonifac. I., ep. 14, n. 3, p. 1038; scitis, B. Petro utrumque possibile, id est in mansuetudine mites, in virga superbos arguere.
[94] Phillips, iii. § 152, p. 613, *seq.*, § 253, p. 626, *seq.*
[95] Jerome (ep. 123, ad Agerruch., c. 10) speaks of the consultationes synodicæ Orientis atque Occidentis, answered by direction of Pope Damasus. Pope Celestine I. (ep. 3, p. 1063) speaks of the diversa negotia, quæ ad nos ex cunctis veniunt ecclesiis. Cf. Leo

takable. Already Pope Siricius makes mention of the *generalia decreta*,[96] which his mediate predecessor, Liberius, after the rejection of the Council of Rimini, dispatched into the provinces; and he charges Himerius, bishop of Tarragona, to bring his decrees to the knowledge of the neighbouring provinces. His words,—" What by a general sentence we decide should be observed by all the Churches, and what avoided," [97] are truly, indeed, the words of a legislator. In like manner, Innocent I. requires Victricius, bishop of Rouen, to communicate to the neighbouring bishops the disciplinary regulations that had been sent to him; and the same commission he gives to the patriarch of Antioch. And in the same way Pope Zosimus, in 417, acts towards Patroclus, bishop of Arles: he expresses his surprise to Hesychius, bishop of Salona, that the statutes of the Apostolic See on the question proposed, and which had been forwarded to Gaul and to Spain, had not yet reached him.[98] Leo the Great often " sets forth the *statuta* of the Apostolic See," and declares that a transgression of the *decretalia constituta* of Innocent I., as well as of all his other predecessors, should be punished without mercy.[99] The same had been already decreed by Zosimus.[100] Hence the Roman synod, held under Gelasius I., declared nothing new when it decided "that the decretal epistles which the blessed popes had at different times, on the consultations of the different fathers, put forth," were to be received with all

---

I., ep. 10, ad Episc. provin. Vienn., and the passages cited above in note 38.
[96] Siric. ep. 1, ad Himer., n. 2, p. 625; n. 20, p. 637, ed. Coust.
[97] *Ibid.* n. 12, p. 633.
[98] Innoc. I., ep. 2, cap. 2, p. 746, *seq.;* ep. 24, ad Alex. Antioch, c. 4, p. 854. Zosim. ep. 7, c. 2, p. 962; ep. 9, c. 1, p. 968.
[99] Leo M., ep. 12, ad Episc. Afr., c. 4, 5; ep. 4, c. 5.
[100] Zosim., ep. 9, c. 4, p. 970.

The Primacy and its Development. 133

reverence.[101] And yet the popes of those times, we are told, made *no attempt* to exercise legislative power. There was yet, it is true, no *curia*, in the later sense of the word (p. 80); but the host of functionaries surrounding the monarch do not constitute the legislator. Moreover, there was at Rome a very numerous clergy: there were ecclesiastical functionaries of various grades; and under Gregory the Great, and long before him, we find notaries, archivists, and defensors or advocates.[102] But very distinctly the popes declare that they have to bear the burdens of all, and are troubled with the solicitude of all the Churches.[103]

3. But herein is involved their administrative power also. This is especially manifest in the guidance and the confirmation of the principal bishops, in the establishment of new episcopal sees, in the treatment of the more important concerns having reference thereto.[104] Many of these rights the patriarchs and the metropolitans had earlier possessed; but these they often abused. "It was the hierarchs themselves," says Phillips, "who, by overstepping the limits assigned to them, threatened the Church even with ruin; they would have given her up as a prey to the powers of hell, had Christ, in His love and wisdom, not placed His Bride upon a rock. Hence, if in later times the popes, in order to save what was not yet lost, took into their own hands the power of erecting new bishoprics, as well

---

[101] Gelas. I., ep. 33.
[102] Thomassin., op. cit. P. i., L. ii., c. 104, n. 1, 2, 8, 10, 11; c. 98, n. 2-4, 7.
[103] Siric., ep. 1, n. 1, p. 624. Leo M., ep. 6, c. 2: per *omnes* ecclesias cura nostra distenditur. *Cælestin.*, ep. 3, p. 1064: Nosque præcipue circa *omnes* curâ Constringimur, quibus necessitatem *de omnibus* tractandi Christus in S. Petro Ap., cum illi claves aperiendi claudendique daret, indulsit.
[104] Causæ majores. *Vide* Innoc. I., ep. 2, n. 6, p. 749, 750.

as many other duties which by God's ordinance had been imposed on them, and no longer delegated them, as before, to others, this was indeed no acquisition of new rights, but nothing more than an augmentation of burden, rendered necessary by circumstances." [105] From his position as representative and guardian of ecclesiastical unity, the pope's right of superintendence over the Church necessarily followed.[106] The patriarchal rights which the popes possessed in the west gave them powers there, such as the patriarchs exercised in the east, and over which the sovereign pontiffs preserved the supreme jurisdiction.[107] In many provinces of their patriarchate, they appointed apostolic vicars, or reserved to themselves certain special affairs.[108] Other administrative rights will appear from what follows.

6. "Nobody thought of getting dispensations from Church laws from the Roman bishops" (p. 80). In the more ancient times, indeed, the dispensations, like the laws, were of more rare occurrence; but the necessity of new laws led to the need of more frequent dispensations also. But the principle of the right of dispensation is involved in the very Primacy itself; and it was no subversion of discipline, that its exercise should pass from bishops to provincial Councils, and from these to the Popes, more especially as in the first five centuries, and even in cases where the bishops could grant dispensations, recourse was had to the Roman

---

[105] Phillips, v., § 219, p. 317. Cf. E. Amort. Elem. Juris Can., t. iii. Diss. v., n. 9.

[106] *Ibid.* § 203, p. 34, *seq.*

[107] Boniface I. (ep. 15, n. 6, p. 1042, *seq.*) cites examples, such as the recognition of Nectarius, patriarch of Constantinople, at the urgent request of the Emperor, Theodosius I. Pope Agapetus, in the year 536, deposed Anthimus and other metropolitans.

[108] Coustant, Præf. in Epist. Rom. Pontif., n. 22, *seq.*, p. xvii. *seq.*

Sec.[109] But we have numerous examples of Papal dispensations in the most ancient decretals extant.[110] Pope Siricius granted a dispensation to retain their orders to those in Spain, who, though public penitents and bigamists, had been irregularly ordained. Like dispensations were granted by Innocent I. to those ordained by Bonosus; by Boniface I. in respect to the translation of Bishop Perigenes to Corinth, after he had been rejected by Patras; by Sixtus III., with regard to the adherents of Nestorius; by Leo I., for the consecration of Anatolius, patriarch of Constantinople, and of Maximus, patriarch of Antioch; and, lastly, by Gelasius, in respect of those baptized and ordained by Acacius.[111] It was also by no means universally held, "that the power of the keys, or of binding and loosing, belonged to the other bishops just as much as to the Bishop of Rome" (p. 81). If this were the general view, how could Cœlestius, by gaining over the Pope, hope for his absolution from the anathema pronounced upon him in Africa?[112] how could the Abbot Eutyches, deposed by his patriarch Flavian, expect from Pope Leo restitution?[113] how could Leo, in an

---

[109] Phillips, v., § 210, p. 147, *seq*.

[110] Thomassin op. cit., P. II, L. III, c. 24. Phillips, § 211, p. 158, *seq*.

[111] Siric., ep. 1, ad Himer. n. 19, p. 636. Innoc., ep. 17, ad Ruf. n. 9, p. 835. Bonifac. I., ep. 4, ad Ruf. p. 1019. Sixt. III., ep. 2, n. 2, p. 1238, *seq.*; ep. 1, n. 5, p. 1235. Leo M., ep. 104, 105. Ballerini Admonit. in Leon. M., ep. 1, 2, § 4, t. i., p. 578. Gelas. ep. ad Euph. Mansi. viii. 5.

[112] *Marius* Mercator Commonit., c. 2. Zosim., ep. 2, n. 2, p. 944. Facund. Herm. vii. 3. *Natal. Alex.* HE. Sæc. v., Dissert. ii.

[113] Hefele II., 315, *seq.* 329. Eutych. ep. ad Leon (ep. 21). Cf. Leo, ep. 23, ad Flav., c. 1. Eutyches said, "Libellum appellationis se obtulisse nec tamen fuisse susceptum." Leo desires further information, "Quoniam nihil possumus incognitis rebus in cujusquam partis præjudicium definire." Cf. Bennettis, t. ii., P. iii., p. 404, *seq*.

epistle to the patriarch Anatolius, reserve to himself judgment on the heads of the Eutychian heresy?[114] and Theodoret request of the same Pope his restoration, and, in virtue of the Papal sentence, obtain his seat among the Bishops of Chalcedon?[115] Moreover, the correspondence carried on during the Acacian controversy, clearly shows, in despite of Byzantine resistance, the higher power of the keys possessed by the Bishop of Rome. Hereby we may explain what is further said :—

(7.) "The Bishops of Rome could exclude neither individuals nor churches from the Communion of the Church Universal. They could withdraw their own Church from communion with particular bishops or churches, and they often did so ; but this in nowise affected their relation to other bishops or churches, as was shown, among other instances, by the long Antiochene Schism from 361 to 413. And, on the other hand, if they admitted into their own Communion one excommunicated by other churches, this did not bring him into communion with any other church" (p. 81).

As regards Meletius of Antioch, who long passed for an Arian, the Orientals, who were devoted to him, regarded the Westerns as ill-informed in the matter,[116] and exerted their utmost endeavours to procure for him the recognition of Rome. But Meletius, as well as his rivals, uniformly asserted that they were ever in the communion of Pope Damasus ;[117] and afterwards the orthodoxy of Meletius,[118] as well as of Paulinus, was acknow-

[114] Leo, ep. 85, c. 2.
[115] Hefele II., 371, 406, *seq.* ; 423, 459, *seq.* Natal. Alex. Sæc. v., dissert. xiv.
[116] Basil., ep. 214, ad Terent. Com. c. 2. Migne xxxii. 785.
[117] Hier, ep. ad Damas., p. 551 ; *Meletius*, Vitalis atque Paulinus tibi hærere se dicunt.
[118] Meletius, in the year 378, subscribed the tome of Pope Dama-

The Primacy and its Development. 137

ledged. The patriarch Flavian, raised to the place of the former in the year 381, and whom, after the death of Paulinus, Evagrius opposed, obtained even the communion of Rome and of Alexandria long before 415, and about the year 398.[119] This schism, a consequence of the Arian commotions, is rather a proof for the reverse of what our opponents assert; and in nowise can a rightful claim be deduced from it.

(8.) "For a long time nothing was known in Rome of definite rights bequeathed by Peter to his successors. Nothing but a care for the weal of the Church and the duty of watching over the observance of the canons was ascribed to them" (p. 81). But *every duty* establishes definite rights also, and the object of the primacy, which is the preservation of ecclesiastical unity, requires corresponding means. It was, therefore, not even necessary that the special definite rights of the successors of Peter should be determined. What the Papal legate, Philip, declared at Ephesus in the year 431,[120] met with no contradiction, and expressed but the firm conviction of the Roman Church. If the Popes appealed to synods, this they did without wishing to call in question the derivation of their power from Peter, which, on the contrary, these same Popes prominently brought forward. But Leo I., we are told, did not venture to contradict

sus of 369. Coustant, p. 500. Hefele I. 718, not. in Nat. Alex. HE. Sæc. v., diss. xxxiv.

[119] Vales. not. in Theod. HE. Sæc· v. 23. Soz. viii. 3. *Döllinger's* Manual of Church History, i. 91.

[120] "It is a matter of doubt to none, nay, it is known to all ages, that the holy and blessed Peter, the President and the Head of the Apostles, the pillar of faith, and the foundation of the Catholic Church, received from our Lord Jesus Christ the keys of the Kingdom of Heaven.... His successor and vicar, the holy and most blessed Pope Celestine, has, in order to supply his presence, sent us to this holy Synod." Conc. Ephes. act. iii. Mansi., t. iv., p. 1295.

the Council of Chalcedon in its twenty-eighth canon, which asserted that it was the fathers who had adjudged the primacy to Rome, and that on account of the political pre-eminence of the city (p. 82). But if Leo more immediately opposed the exaltation of the see of Constantinople above those of Alexandria and of Antioch, (for the Roman primacy was not disputed,[121] but only inaccurately explained); so he still protests against this last declaration also; for he shows that secular pre-eminence could establish no ecclesiastical one; that Constantinople is indeed an imperial city, but not *an apostolical see;*[122] and he makes use of his high prerogative, as "by the authority of Peter" he rejects and annuls this canon.[123] The edict of Valentinian III., under the date of the 8th July of the year 445,[124] states, as the legal titles of the Roman primacy, in the first place the merits of St Peter, next the dignity of the city, and the authority of the synod, and characterizes the conduct of Hilarius of Arles as an act of disobedience and rash usurpation. The sentence of Leo,[125] which, moreover, was thoroughly justifiable, would be fully valid without, as is said, the imperial sanction; but this had been rendered necessary by the continued armed resistance. This edict, according to Janus, if it had obtained full force, would have transformed the whole constitution of the Western Church as it then stood; and *would thus have rendered a pseudo-Isidore superfluous.*

[121] πρὸ πάντων τὰ πρωτεῖα καὶ τὴν ἐξαίρετον τιμήν, "pre-eminence above all, and exalted dignity," is what even the imperial commissioners in this transaction adjudged to the Pope. Cf. Hefele II., 524.
[122] Leo, ep. 104, c. 3, p. 993.
[123] Ibid., ep. 105, c. 3.
[124] Ibid., ep. 11, p. 636, *seq.*
[125] Ibid., ep. 10, ad. Episc. Gall., p. 628, *seq.*

The Primacy and its Development. 139

But that this edict did not come into force, so far as regards submission to the authority of the Roman see; that it was an innovation, and had not for its object, as it declares, the protection of old ecclesiastical usage, is by no means proved. That Leo, in dealing with the Orientals, appealed, in the first place, to the sixth canon of the Nicene Council (p. 83), was grounded on the fact, that he conceived himself bound to protect chiefly the rights of the sees of Alexandria and of Antioch, while his own primacy, not directly assailed, remained unshaken. That the opposition he and his successors offered to the innovation made at the Council of Chalcedon remained fruitless, is utterly false. Anatolius himself acknowledged that the confirmation was reserved to the Papal power;[126] the Emperor Marcian sought to curb the ambition of his patriarch;[127] the collections of canons down to John Scholasticus, who, like Theodore the Lector, knows only twenty-seven canons, did not receive the twenty-eighth canon.[128] It was only much later that any one ventured to appeal again to this canon.

(9.) "What was afterwards called the Papal system, when first proclaimed in words only, was repudiated with horror by that best and greatest of popes, Gregory the Great" (p. 83). But this distinguished Pontiff, who in opposition to the Byzantine patriarch of his time, did not wish to be called "Œcumenical," [129] and who ever displayed

---

[126] Anatol., ep. 142 Leon. c. 4 : cum et sic gestorum vis omnis et confirmatio auctoritati vestræ Beatitudinis fuerit reservata.

[127] Leon, ep. 128-134, ad. Marc.

[128] Theod., Lect. L. I. p. 168, ed. *Migne*. *Ballerin.* de antiqu. canon. collect. P. i., c. 2, n. 2, *seq.* Diss. i. Quesnell. a. 451, n. 14, p. 269. *Pitra* Monum. i., p. 534.

[129] Cf. Thomassin. *op. cit.*, P. i., L. i., c. 11, n. 10. *seq.* *Maur* in edit. Opp. Greg. M. Vita S. Gr., L. iii., c. 1.

the greatest personal humility, was very conscious of his own rights and dignity. He knew well, indeed, that all bishops, even that of Constantinople, are subject to the Apostolic see;[130] he knew that to Peter, the prince of the Apostles, was committed, by the mouth of our Lord, the care of the whole Church;[131] like many of his predecessors, he puts Peter and the Pope exactly on the same footing; for to come to the Apostolic see, signifies with him to come to Peter.[132] He firmly adhered to his right of receiving appeals from the whole Church;[133] rebuked the rigid excesses of bishops, as in the case of the Iconaclast, Serenus of Marseilles;[134] like former Pontiffs, appointed Vicars Apostolic;[135] examined into the conduct of bishops;[136] and so forth. The substantial power of the Primacy is found in the acts of Gregory also; and many rights were exercised by him which Janus denies to the earlier popes.

10. "There are many National Churches which were never under Rome, and never even had any intercourse by letter with Rome, without this being considered a defect, or causing any difficulty about Church communion" (p. 84). With such Churches

---

[130] L. ix., ep. 12, p. 941, ed. Paris 1705.
[131] L. v., ep, 20, p. 748.
[132] L. ii. ep. 53, p. 619, *Bennettis*, P. i., t. i., p. 111. Cf. Pichler i., p. 128, who (in note 2) at the same time observes, that although Pope Gregory I. has so zealously sought to protect the rights of his fellow-bishops, that he many times seems to sacrifice his own, yet the writing of the abbé Guettée (La Papauté moderne condamnée par le Pape S. Gregoire le grand, Paris, 1861) goes much too far.
[133] L. iii., ep. 53; L. iv., ep. 132; L. v., ep. 18; L. vi., ep. 14, 17, 66, ; L. vii., ep. 5-34; L. vi., ep. 24, ad ep. Ravenn.; Causa, quæ a Johanne presbytero contra Johannem Constantin. . . . orta est, secundum canones ad Sedem Apostolicam recurrit, et nostrâ est sententiâ definita.
[134] L. ix., ep. 105; L. xi., ep. 13.
[135] L. ii., ep. 22, 23; L. v., ep. 53-55, &c.
[136] L. i., ep. 77; L. ii., 24; L. iii., ep. 40; L. iv., ep. 10, &c.

The Primacy and its Development. 141

is classed, in the first place, the Armenian Church. We will not here adduce what Armenian writers have observed respecting the earlier connexion of that Church with Rome.[137] We only assert, that before Armenia, for the most part, fell into the Monophysite errors, and thus its Church became heretical (and so cannot here come under consideration), it was under the jurisdiction of the See of Cæsarea,[138] and thereby mediately united with Rome. A more active intercourse was prevented by intestine wars, and by the Persian conquest. In the second instance alleged, that of the Persian Church, so grievously persecuted, and at last utterly extirpated, this was still more the case. The suspicions of the rulers, the religious fanaticism of the fire-worshippers, and the magnitude of the persecution, must here be taken into account. Who could regard the present severance of the Polish Catholics from Rome, as a fact proving the proposition, that an union with the Papal See is not necessary to Catholicity? Thirdly, with respect to the Ethiopian Church, it stood through the See of Alexandria (until it embraced the Monophysite heresy), in a mediate connexion with Rome. Fourthly, that the old Irish Church was for centuries separated from Rome, has been disproved by Dr Greith, bishop of St Gall.[139] And lastly, with respect to the ancient British Church, which had very much degenerated in the times of Pope Gregory the Great, the answer is likewise given in historical data.[140]

---

[137] Samueljan's "Conversion of Armenia," Vienna, 1844. *Theological Quarterly Review*, t. v., p. 546. Tübingen, 1846.
[138] *Le Quien* Oriens Christianus, i., 1355, Neander's Ch. Hist., i., 469.
[139] History of the Old Irish Church. By Charles John Greith, Bishop of St Gall, vol. i., especially p. 453, *seq.*, Freiburg, 1867 (in German).
[140] Döllinger's "Manual of Church History," i., p. 62, *seq.*

Janus continues: "If we put into a positive form this negative account of the position of the ancient Popes, we get the following picture of the organization of the ancient Church:—Without prejudice to its agreement with the Church Universal in all its essential points" [but in these matters the five National Churches did not seem to care much about the Church Universal], "*every Church manages its own affairs with perfect freedom and independence*" [just as in the fifteenth section of the Prussian Constitution of the 31st January 1850, which thereby receives an antique stamp, as the old Constitution of the Church looks so very modern], "and maintains its own traditional usages" [with regard to rites there was later also perfect freedom allowed] "and discipline; all questions not concerning *the whole Church*, or of *primary importance*" [these two exceptions, as our previous investigation shows, are well and prudently put], "being settled on the spot. The Church is organized in dioceses, provinces, and patriarchates; National Churches were added afterwards in the West" (p. 85).

Certainly the organization in patriarchates is not *primitive*, nor does it belong to the first ages of Christianity; and if the later development of the Papacy could establish no right, can such a claim on behalf of the patriarchates be yet set up? Would it not be here necessary to assign a *terminus fixus*, which for both should be uniformly maintained as a *terminus normalis*? Do we not expose ourselves to the suspicion of arbitrary caprice, when, according to pleasure, we recognize even in the fifth, sixth, seventh, eighth, and ninth centuries the validity of historical claims?

But this is said only in passing. Our historian of those happy old times teaches us further: "The bishop of Rome stands at the head as *first patri-*

arch" [he stood at the head before the name of patriarch had even been heard of], "as the centre and representative of unity" [how fared it then with the five National Churches, who knew nothing about him?], "as the bond uniting east and west, the Churches of the Greek and Latin tongue, the chief watcher and guardian of the, as yet very few, common laws of the Church—for a long time only the Nicene;—*but he does not encroach* on the rights of patriarchs, metropolitans, and bishops. Laws and articles of faith, of universal obligation, are issued only by the whole Church, concentrated and represented at an Œcumenical Council" (p. 85-6). How the Church could have been served by a head and a *centre* of unity "*not encroaching*," that were yet a matter of inquiry; but we have, on the contrary, found a head manywise encroaching, while the paragraphs of the Ecclesiastical Constitution respecting Œcumenical Councils, as alleged by Janus, are to be found in no ancient canon, but are simply to be deduced from practice. But why should not practice be decisive in the case of the Popes also?

CHAPTER VIII.

ROMAN FORGERIES.

HITHERTO we have adduced in favour of the Papal Primacy, only documents acknowledged to be genuine; and the inference to be drawn from these must be apparent to every reader. But as the full account of the forgeries made in favour of the bishops of Rome has been characterized as one of the chief services of Janus,[1] it is worth while to cast an inquiring glance into this matter.

We do not regret that the *naïve* poesy of the old Christian times has long disappeared, and that the severest historical criticism has been arrayed against it. But since the extinction of the school of the Romanticists, one-sided, doubtless, but still full of feeling and of intellect, the understanding for that poetry has by degrees disappeared, and men are no more satisfied with eliminating the spurious and the interpolated, nor with investigating times, places, authors, and circumstances; but even entire ages are recklessly stigmatized as epochs of barbarism and darkness, of conscious fraud, and intentional falsification; while they are measured exclusively by the standard of the present, and no grounds of palliation are in anywise admitted.

[1] *Allgemeine Zeitung*, 3d October, App., n. 276.

Even pseudo-Isidore once found an apology, in so far as his compilation was calculated to furnish the proof, " that there are times in the history of the Church, wherein supposititious books contained far more Christian sense and spirit, than in our days the greater part of genuine works."[2]

Independently of the apocryphal gospels and histories of the apostles, the Sibylline, Orphic, and other verses, the pseudo-apostolic and pseudo-Clementine literature; Christian antiquity had many sagas and legends, which certainly did not all spring from heretics, attaching, as they did, to the apostles, to celebrated martyrs, and their adversaries. Already, in the period of the Christian persecutions, the narrative of the contest of the apostle Peter with Simon the magician in Rome, had been worked up, and was widely diffused. Must all these legends have been wicked inventions and conscious forgeries? This our historians appear to assume, when (p. 123) they speak of the compilation of spurious acts of Roman martyrs, begun towards the end of the fifth century, and continued for some centuries, and " which modern criticism, even at Rome, has been obliged to give up;" after they had previously spoken of the process of forgeries and fictions, " carried on *in the interests of Rome.*" Was then Rome, pre-eminently the city of martyrs, to be still more glorified by these inventions? This she certainly needed not. Historic documents, and the Catacombs, sufficed to insure to her this glory. Edifying and entertaining legends sprang up everywhere, and in the countries of the East also.

We can examine those forgeries only which can be stated as, in some degree, invented for the

[2] Möhler on the Pseudo-Isidore. Miscellaneous Writings, edited by Döllinger, vol. i. p. 284.

exaltation of the Papal power. Strictly considered, the saga of the conversion and the baptism of the Emperor Constantine by Pope Sylvester, with the legends connected therewith,[3] and which was afterwards adopted by the Greeks also, does not belong to this class of fictions. It responded to the religious feelings better than the record furnished by Eusebius; it could serve for the glorification of the emperor, as well as of the Roman Church, but not for the extension of the Pontifical power. The Gesta Liberii followed, with the object of confirming the fable of the Roman baptism of Constantine, and of representing Liberius as a Pontiff purified by penance, and favoured by a divine miracle (p. 124).[4] But we must look for forgeries of a weightier purport.

For a right treatment of the subject, it were imperiously necessary to have followed a strict chronological order, especially as Janus (p. 117) asserts: " Like the successive strata of the earth covering one another, so layer after layer of forgeries and fabrications was piled up in the Church." Instead of this method, Janus proceeds without any regard to the order of time, springing arbitrarily from one statement to another. At p. 94, he speaks of pseudo-Isidore; then old and new are brought together in a motley group; no reader not perfectly familiar with the subject can find his way; everything is piled together; misrepresentations of genuine texts, substitution of spurious ones, various readings, and erroneous interpretations. Even the form of exposition shows that the whole object of the work is a purely polemical one, and that the position of the author, or rather

---

[3] Cf. Döllinger, Papstfabeln, p. 52, *seq.*
[4] *Ibid.*, p. 112, *seq.*

authors, is that of party men. Everything, whether suitably or unsuitably, is brought against the hated theory of Infallibility, as in pages 96–100, seq.

Yet the separate stones are to be shown us, out of which the whole papal system of universal monarchy was erected. " For a long time all that was done was to interpret the canon of Sardica,[5] so as to extend the appellant jurisdiction of the Pope to whatever could be brought under the general and elastic term of 'greater causes.' But from the end of the fifth century the Papal pretensions had advanced to a point beyond this, in consequence of the attitude assumed by Leo and Gelasius ; and from that time began a course of systematic fabrications, sometimes manufactured in Rome, sometimes originating elsewhere ; but adopted and utilized there " (p. 122).

Above all, our historian alleges that the Roman legates at Chalcedon, in the year 451, appealed to the sixth Nicene canon, with an additional clause about the Roman Church ; but that the deceit, *to their confusion*, was discovered by the reading of the genuine text (p. 123). But such a "confusion" of the legates is, as Hefele has shown,[6] not to be proved from the acts ; it is certain that the Emperor Valentinian III., in the year 445, knew of that clause, and several ancient Latin codices have the reading ;[7] then it can be shown that the main views in that Canon, in regard to the power of the Eastern patriarchs, have for their basis the recognition of the Roman primacy.[8] But that a forgery of the

---

[5] The matter hereto belonging was commented on in the preceding chapter, where also is to be found an appreciation of the other assertions.

[6] Concil. i., p. 384, *seq*. ii., p. 522 *seq*.

[7] Valent. ed. s. ep. 11. Leon. M. Prisca ap. Mansi. vi. 1127.

[8] Hagemann, *loc. cit*, p. 596–598.

sixth Nicene Canon did not proceed from the Popes, and that they knew of no Nicene Canon touching the primacy, the assurances given by them *before* and *after* the year 451 show that the first General Council contained nothing upon the Papal supremacy, founded as it had been by the word of Christ himself.[9] The spurious Arabic Canons of this Council only prove that, even among the Orientals, the recognition of the Roman primacy was not utterly extinct. They were certainly not fabricated by Rome.[10]

Towards the end of the sixth century there was a fabrication of Cyprian's book on the Unity of the Church—a fabrication made in Rome, and, indeed, in a letter of Pope Pelagius II. to the Istrian bishops, because his words on the equality of the apostles were in too glaring a contradiction to the theory set up since the time of Gelasius (p. 127). But why were the latter words not rather expunged here as well as in other writings? Why were merely some words here inserted, which, moreover, contain nothing but what has been elsewhere, and even more distinctly, expressed by Cyprian?[11] The genuine text says enough with these words: tamen ut unitatem manifestaret, unitatem ab uno incipientem suâ auctoritate disposuit. . . . Exordium ab unitate proficiscitur.[12] The inserted words

---

[9] Bonif. I., ep. 14, n. 1, p. 1037. Nicænæ Synodi non aliud præcepta testantur, adeo ut non aliquid super eum ausa sit constituere, cum videret, nihil supra meritum suum ei posse conferri; omnia denique huic noverat Domini sermone concessa. Gelas. ep. 33. (See above, chap. iv., note 47.)

[10] Hereto belong Can. 39 Turr.; Can. 44 Labbé. t. ii. Cf. Bennettis, P. I., t. i., p. 145, 146. Respecting the discovery of these canons, see Hefele Conc., vol. i., p. 345, *seq*.

[11] Möhler's "Patrology," p. 862, note. Lumper Hist., crit. xi., p. 413-418.

[12] Corp. Script. Eccles. Lat. editum consilio et impensis acad. lit. Cœs. Vindob., vol. iii., P. i. Cypriani Opp. rec. *Gulielmus Hartel*.

are, indeed, nothing more than the marginal note of a copyist or reader, which afterwards crept into the text,[13] whereof we have many hundred examples. Such a Codex Pelagius II. might have had before him; and *nothing* justifies us in here assuming an intentional forgery. That Cyprian, in despite of his controversy with Pope Stephen I., can not be regarded as an opponent of the Roman primacy, has long been proved.[14] It is also not true, that the equality of all the apostles can in no way be reconciled with "the theory set up since the time of Gelasius."[15] Lastly, it is a most arbitrary assumption to speak like Janus (p. 127-8), on the relation of the fourth and of the fifth division of the catalogue of Gelasius, in reference to the judgment on Cyprian's writings.[16]

"But already, at the beginning of the sixth century, some very effectual and gradually acknowledged fictions were put forward in Rome, which were to establish the maxim, that the Pope, as the highest authority in the Church, can be judged by no one" (p. 103 G.) For this purpose, and in order to keep off secular judges, the pretended Synod of Sinuessa, the Constitutum Sylvestri, the

Vindob. 1868, p. 212, de Cath. Eccl. unitate, c. 4. The Munich Codex (p. 208, sec. ix., x.) has the interpolated words. Cf. also Coustant, Præf. in ep. Rom. Pont., P. i., note, 7, 8, p. 4-6.

[13] Cf. Alzog Patrology, second ed., p. 170 (in German.)

[14] *Prudent. Maran.* Præfat. in Opp. Cypr., § 3, Card. *Gerdil* Confutazione di due libelli contro il Breve: Super Soliditate, P. i. (Opp. ed. Rom. xii. pp. 69-77.) Schwane's "History of Dogmas in the Ante-Nicene Period," Münster, 1862, p. 724, *seq.*

[15] The unlimited and universal jurisdiction of the apostles appears as an extraordinary legatine power not to be transmitted; while in Peter it formed an ordinary and transmissible power. So thinks the Gallican Natalis Alexander (Hist. Eccl. Sæc., § 1; Dissert iv., § 4), together with many theologians. Very copiously has Passaglia treated this matter (De Eccl. Christi., vol. ii. Ratisb., 1856. Lib. iii., c. 9, *seq.*) Cf. Coustant, *loc. cit.*

[16] Cf. Hefele Conc. ii., § 217, p. 597, *seq.*; 601, *seq.*

Gesta Xysti III., and of Polychronius, were fabricated during the pontificate of Pope Symmachus, who flourished from 498 to 514; and these fabrications had reference to the attitude of Rome towards the Church of Constantinople (p. 124). These documents are indeed spurious;[17] but do they justify the conclusion that the maxim " prima Sedes a nemine judicatur" was first introduced by them? If the maxim were so new, it would be a matter of astonishment that so many Italian bishops, and among them those of Milan and Ravenna, should, in the year 501, have affirmed it in a Roman synod; and likewise, that the Church of France, under Avitus of Vienne, should have sanctioned it.[18] Janus even says, "that Pope Gelasius, about 495, for the first time insulted the Greeks, and their 28th Canon of Chalcedon, by affirming that every Council must be confirmed, and every Church judged by Rome; but she can be judged by none. It was not by canons, as the Council of Chalcedon affirmed, but by the word of Christ, that she received the primacy" (p. 125).[19] The holy Pope Gelasius yet belongs to the witnesses of the first six centuries, who alone possess any credit with our author; but he is rejected, for in this he went beyond all the claims of his predecessors. We might, indeed, modestly reply, that like claims were put forth by earlier Pontiffs; that Zosimus, in particular, who reigned from 417

---

[17] *Vide* Döllinger Papstfabeln, p. 48, *seq.*

[18] Hefele, Conc. ii. 624. Thomassin Diss. in Conc. Diss. xv. n. 5, 6.

[19] We trust that the last proposition, also, will not be designated as an assertion put forth *for the first time;* for this would be utterly unhistorical, and in contradiction with the more ancient testimonies already adduced by us. The framing of the 28th Canon of Chalcedon was merely selected, in order to justify for the new imperial city the next rank after Rome.

to 418, had claimed for the Papal see the privilege, that its judgment should be the ultimate and decisive one. But this Janus has already obviated, as he remarks (p. 82); "By Zosimus it was still said, *the Fathers* it was who imparted this privilege to the Roman see." To this we may venture to reply; first, that the difference is not as to *the right itself*, but as to *the source of right;* whether, according to Gelasius, it is derived from Christ, or, according to Zosimus, from the Fathers. Now, not the popes only, but other prelates, metropolitans, and patriarchs, also, deduced their prerogatives from various titles, and often name one, without thereby excluding the other; for the proximate title excludes not the remoter one. Accordingly, the right established by the Fathers has its own force; the see of Constantinople could not at all claim any other; why, then, should this right be valid for the latter, and not for Rome? (Cpl. c. 3; Chalc. c. 28.) Secondly, Zosimus has, for one of the privileges involved in the primacy, alleged the tradition of the Fathers, and most appropriately, indeed; for, in respect to that privilege, this tradition was pre-eminently decisive; but he has immediately pointed out the foundation of that primacy, lying as it does in the promise of Christ, and proclaimed that the Roman Church is founded *on divine as well as on human right;* and at the close of the introduction he repeats, that none can reverse the Papal sentence.[20] Our appeal to Zosimus, with refer-

---

[20] Zosim., ep. 12, ad Aurel., p. 974, ed. Coust. : Quamvis *patrum traditio* apostolicæ Sedi auctoritatem tantam tribuerit, *ut de ejus judicio disceptare nullus auderet*, idque per canones *semper* regulasque (eadem Sedes) servaverit, et currens adhuc suis legibus ecclesiastica disciplina, *Petri nomini a quo ipsa quoque descendit*, reverentiam quam debet exsolvat; tantam enim huic Apostolo canonica antiquitas *per sententias omnium* voluit esse potentiam *ex ipsa quoque Christi Dei*

ence to the first three words of his letter, is fully sustained by the whole context. Like Zosimus, Boniface I., who flourished from 418 to 422, puts in the claim also, that from his tribunal there is no appeal, and that it has never been lawful to reform a Papal judgment.[21] Here the proposition is enunciated without the appeal to the "Fathers." So we again find the proof, that what some wished to make pass for a novelty, shows itself to be much older; and that it was not by a forgery the privilege in question of the Roman see was first established.[22] Under Symmachus, the chief object was to prevent the intervention of the Arian King Theodoric in the affairs of the Church of Rome.[23]

nostri promissione, ut et ligata solveret et soluta vinciret; par potestatis conditio data in eos, qui sedis hæreditatem ipso annuente meruissent. . . . Cum ergo tantæ auctoritatis *Petrus* caput sit et sequentia omnium majorum studia firmaverit, *ut tam humanis quam divinis legibus* et diciplinis omnibus firmetur, Romana Ecclesia, cujus locum nos regere et ipsius quoque potestatem nominis obtinere non latet vos, sed nostis, fratres carissimi et, quemadmodum sacerdotes, scire debetis, tamen cum tantum nobis esset auctoritatis, ut *nullus de nostra possit retractare sententia, &c.*

[21] Bonif. I., ep. 13, ad Ruf. n. 2; ep. 15, ad eumd. n. 5, p. 1035, 1042. In the first passage the Pope says he has written to the bishops who had unlawfully assembled that they ought not by any means to have met without thy privity, namely, of the Vicar Apostolic; in the next place, that our sentence was not to be rediscussed; Primo se citra tuam conscientiam convenire minime debuisse, deinde de nostro non esse judicio retractandum. In the latter passage, the Pope says no one has ever daringly raised up his hands against the Apostolic power, whose judgment it is not lawful to question; nemo unquam Apostolico culmini, de cujus judicio non licet retractari, manus obvias audacter intulit.

[22] If the history of Polychronius was invented in order to bring forward the Pope, even in the year 435, as judge of an Oriental patriarch (Janus, p. 125); so this invention was certainly foolish and unnecessary; for already, in 430, Pope Celestine had judged an Oriental patriarch, namely, Nestorius, not to make mention of other cases.

[23] Even many not unimportant historical notices have been preserved to us in the Apocrypha of Sylvester. See Döllinger's "Hippolytus and Callistus," p. 246, seq.

"While this tendency to forging documents was too strong in Rome, it appears very remarkable to Janus (p. 126), that for a thousand years no attempt was made there to form a collection of canons of her own, such as the Easterns had as early as the fifth century." To such a collection, the tendency to fictions ought to have chiefly impelled. For this Janus soon finds the reason; the share of Rome in ecclesiastical legislation was for a long time extremely limited. Still he remembers at the right time the abbot, Dionysius Exiguus, whose importance indeed he but very superficially appreciates. This abbot compiled several collections of canon law; he collected even Papal decretals, but this others also had done before him.[24] The collection made by the order of Hormisdas,[25] had for its object by a strictly literal translation, and by the juxtaposition of both texts, the Greek and the Latin, to meet the objections of those who, under the pretext that they better understood Greek, blamed the former translation, as well as to oppose the objections of those who wished to uphold other standards of law, in order to violate the Nicene Canons; and lastly, to furnish the Pope with an insight into the canons common to the Greeks and Latins. The canons of Sardica which were not before him in the Greek text, the African, and the so-called Apostolical Canons, which were inserted in his former collection, he now left out, because they were not uniformly recognized by all. This latter collection, compiled for a definite purpose, and which is now

---

[24] Ballerini de antiqu. collect. canon. P. III., c. I., § 2., n. 6. (Gall. Syll. i., p. 477.)
[25] The text of the preface cited by Janus (note 94) is in Phillips's Can. Law, vol. iv., p. 39, n. 17, and in Pitra Monum., vol. i., p. 41, *seq*. It is in many passages obscure.

lost, could not obtain the authority of the former one, which was used in the Roman Church, and afterwards enlarged, was widely diffused, even out of Italy.[26] But that long before Dionysius, Papal decrees were in use in the West, as standards of ecclesiastical law, by the side of canons of Councils, is established beyond all doubt.[27] To this class certainly belonged the later Roman codices down to the time of Pope Adrian I.[28] This collection is precisely calculated to show how far removed were the popes from all intentional forgeries. This is attested, too, by the Liber Diurnus, that book of Roman formulas, which had had no hesitation in admitting the condemnation of Honorius.[29]

But the Liber Pontificalis is opposed to us.[30] The compilation of this Papal book, made about the year 530, and which contains the biographies of the popes, appears to Janus as a fiction designed for a fourfold purpose—first, to attest the mass of spurious acts of Roman martyrs; secondly, to confirm the existing legends about the Emperor Constantine, and the Popes Sylvester, Felix, Liberius, Sixtus III., and others; thirdly, to assign a greater antiquity to some later liturgical rites; and, fourthly, to exhibit the popes as legislators for the whole Church (p. 129).

But here, indeed,

"The mountain labours, and a mouse is born."

[26] Phillips, *loc. cit.*, p. 40, *seq.*
[27] Siric. ep. 1, ad Himer., n. 20, p. 637 : Fraternitatis tuæ animum ad servandos canones et tenenda decretalia constituta magis ac magis incitamus. . . . Quamquam statuta Sedis apostolicæ vel canonum venerabilia definita nulli sacerdotum Domini ignorare sit liberum, etc. Cf. note 98, *seq.*, in our preceding chapter.
[28] Ballerini. *loc. cit.*, c. 2 (p. 484-488, ed Gall.) Walter's Can. Law, § 85. Phillips, *loc. cit.*, p. 43.
[29] Ed Garnerii, Paris, 1680, p. 41.
[30] Cf. herewith Döllinger Papstfabeln, especially p. 119.

The first and the third of these four "intentions" must, indeed, even from Janus's point of view, appear as "harmless," and of no importance for the question under discussion. As regards the second, the confirmation of more ancient legends may, as the continuation of a previous labour, and the union of various stories, be recognized as a matter of little signification.

It is only the fourth "purpose" which is really of importance. But as nowhere is a definite law alleged which Damasus, Gelasius, and other popes had issued, so the forger ill understood his craft; it would be rather the pious simplicity of the compiler, than a craftily-designed fraud; rather an endeavour to fill up, as well as possible, the gaps in the catalogues of popes, in which little heed was given to the contradictions that might arise, than any set purpose to represent the Pope as in possession of a universal monarchy. But if the popes, from the year 440 to 530, are represented as judges and teachers of faith in regard to the Orientals (p. 130), so in this belief men were most fully justified by the Papal epistles, and by the other genuine documents of those times.[31]

The famous Deed of Donation of Constantine must, we are told, have been composed in Rome, and by a cleric of the Lateran Church (p. 132). Although no strong proof is adduced for this assertion, especially as many documents still conflict with it;[32] although nowhere is it attested that

---

[31] The notices of the Liber Pontificalis might very well furnish the occasion to pseudo-Isidore to forge special Papal briefs; they could further his deceit (Janus, p. 130). But of themselves these notices could certainly not make any change in ecclesiastical discipline, and in nowise has the demon, who filled the breast of Isidore Mercator or Peccator, for any length of time before inspired a Roman compiler.

[32] So Pope Adrian I. (Cenni, vol. i., p. 353) says, that the pro-

Pope Stephen III. pressed this document on the attention of king Pepin, we shall not enter into a discussion on this subject. But when it is further asserted, that not only the Donation of Constantine was made use of in 754, to urge on the Frankish king Pepin to continue his policy towards Rome, and to make new donations, but that twenty years later a document equally spurious was presented to his son, Charlemagne, and which the latter renewed (p. 136); so this, indeed, exceeds all belief. But that in 774 Charlemagne, more than thirty years of age, and well-educated, too, should have been deceived by a false instrument of donation which, it was pretended, had proceeded from his own father; how can any one accept such a statement without the most decisive proofs? A donation Pepin had, at all events, made; and even in the lifetime of that king, the Pope, in letters addressed to him, had appealed to the fact.[33] That the the Roman Church possessed many and rich patrimonies in Italy, which had been wrested from it, and were subsequently restored, is likewise beyond all doubt. Judicious scholars have fully recognized the reality and the

perty of the Roman Church has been granted it by various emperors, patricians, and godly persons, and that records thereof have been preserved in Sacro Scrinio Lateranensi, in the sacred archives of the Lateran Church. Why need he have appealed to these particular documents, if he had before him the extraordinary, extensive, and long-published Donation of Constantine? The Pope says, indeed, Constantine's munificence has exalted the Roman Church; but we know from Eusebius, Athanasius, and others, how many gifts this emperor made to the more celebrated Churches. The expression "restituere" (restore), which Janus (p. 133) refers to, it is not difficult to explain. Many patrimonies the Roman Church previously possessed, and, in fact, in the general abandonment of Italy, she had exercised the rights of sovereignty. Gosselin, *loc. cit.*, vol. i., p. 230, *seq.;* 236, 242, *seq.*, vol. ii., p. 421.

[33] Donationem manu vestrâ firmatam. *Steph.* ep. ad. Pipin. 7. *Cenni*. Mon. I., p. 81.

genuineness of the donation of Pepin.[34] This donation was enlarged by Charlemagne, particularly in regard to territories, which were not in his power, and to which he had no right. But they belonged to those who, under Gregory II., had given themselves up to the Holy See, in order, in their state of abandonment, to obtain from it protection. These territories Charles promised to restore, although this promise remained for the most part unfulfilled.[35] It would have done little credit to the state of diplomacy under Lewis I., Otho I., and Henry II., if it had blindly given confirmation to spurious documents.[36]

The epistle to the Franks, written in the name of St Peter (p. 134), belongs not certainly to the class of "fictions." It is a document written in a rhetorical style, and easily explicable from the state of severe oppression under which Rome was then labouring, and from the general circumstances of the time.[37] In Holy Writ not merely lifeless things are personified, but even the dead are introduced as speaking;[38] and long had the Popes been in the habit of speaking in the name of

---

[34] Hefele III., 541 *seq.* Gosselin, *loc. cit.* I., 241 *seq.* Cf. Guizot, Hist. de la Civilization en France. Leçon. 27, p. 316. Pappencordt. Hist. of the City of Rome in the Middle Ages. Münster, 1857, p. 88, 137.

[35] Gosselin, *loc. cit.*, p. 251, *seq.* Pappencordt, p. 99. Döllinger's Manual of Church History, I., p. 409.

[36] Phillips's Can. Law, v., § 244, p. 697, *seq.* III., § 119. Th. D. Mock (de Donatione a Carolo M. Sedi Apostolicæ oblatâ. Monasterii Brunn. p. 102) accepts the confirmation of Pepin's donation by Charlemagne, yet so that this received an extension from the latter. The new researches on this subject have, as Janus admits (p. 147), led to no result, entirely overthrowing these donations.

[37] Gosselin I., p. 237–240.

[38] Cf. Jerem. xxxi. 15, coll. Matth. ii. 18; Isa. xiv. 10; Ezech. xxxii. 21, *seq.*

Peter, and referring to him their acts;[39] nay, for every Church the saint, who happened to be its patron, spoke in its behalf. This letter, therefore, is not so strange, and Janus himself believes that it exerted an influence in the Frankish kingdom. Yet all this is for us a matter of less importance; we must hasten to things of more weight.

Of the Pseudo-Isidorian-Decretals, it is asserted by Janus, after the fashion of Febronius,[40] that they gradually brought about a complete change in the constitution and government of the Church (p. 97). But at the same time it is admitted, that in all history there is scarcely a second example to be found of a so completely successful, and withal so clumsily an arranged fiction. Most inquirers, however, in recent times have called in question such a total revolution in ecclesiastical discipline, and have shown that the spread of the spurious collection was of such easy accomplishment, only because it corresponded to the prevailing views and circumstances of the times, as well as that the immediate and real design of the author was not the exaltation of the See of Rome, nor the extension of its power.[41] The last-named fact, indeed, but this only, is admitted by our opponent; but the increase and extension of the Papal power was, in his opinion, the means at least for the attainment of his immediate design (p. 97).

But what were the destructive principles in consequence whereof the Church at last "was necessarily to assume the form of a monarchy, subject to the

---

[39] Defens. declar., L. iv. c. 10.
[40] De Statû Ecclesiæ, c. 8, § 7, especially n. 6. Cf. c. v., § 3.
[41] Walter's Can. Law, § 98. Phillips's Can. Law, iv., § 174, p. 74, *seq.* Schulte's Can. Law, i., p. 302. Cf. Hinschius Decretal. Ps.-Isidori, Lips. 1863. Praef. p. ccxvii., *seq.* Döllinger (II. 41–46), as the learned Janus says (n. 43), "has assigned reasons, which seem to betray an inadequate knowledge of the Decretals."

absolute will of a singular individual?" They were these: Firstly, every synod needs the approval or confirmation of its decrees by the Pope. Secondly, the fulness of power (thus in matters of faith also) resides in the Pope alone. Thirdly, the bishops are but ministering assistants to the Pope; but he is the bishop of the whole Universal Church (p. 96). Behind these dangerous propositions lurks the ghost of infallibility, as even the popes of pseudo-Isidore assure us—(but, as we have seen, they were neither the first, nor the solitary witnesses of that fact)—that the Roman Church remains intact from every stain of error. Let us now more closely examine these three propositions. Rightly understood, the first proposition involves a perfectly true principle, namely, that no council is valid which the Pope has not either tacitly or expressly approved,[42] and that synods rejected by him, possess no authority in the Church. With regard to General Councils, we have already proved the Papal right of confirmation; and many provincial councils, too, were confirmed by the popes,[43] as, for example, by Boniface II., Leo I., Gelasius, and Hormisdas; yet in regard to them the principle had not passed into universal practice, nor was this even after pseudo-Isidore the case. Yet the source for this, we are told, was the Latin translation of the historian Socrates, in which the Italian Epiphanius, with a new distortion of the words of Pope Julius, already distorted by that Greek historian, who "welcomed an opportunity of pointing out the ambition of the Roman Church,"

---

[42] Phillips's *loc. cit.*, p. 77, 79, 80. Cf. II., §§ 85, 86, p. 244, 286.
[43] Thus also wrote, in 416, the Fathers of Carthage to Pope Innocent I. (Inn. ep. 26, n. 1, p. 869): Hoc intimandum duximus, ut statutis nostræ mediocritatis etiam Apostolicæ Sedis adhibeatur auctoritas.

had made that Pope declare "that no council could be held without his consent" (pp. 177, 118). But in this reasoning many false assumptions are combined; Socrates, as well as Sozomen, lay before Epiphanius, not the former only; and he has not distorted, as alleged, the words of Pope Julius.[44]

[44] Compare Hist. tripart. iv. 9 : quum itaque regula ecclesiastica jubeat, non oportere *præter sententiam Romani Pontificis* Concilia celebrari with Sozom. H.E., iii. 10 : εἶναι γὰρ ἱερατικὸν νόμον ὡς ἄκυρα ἀποφαίνειν τὰ παρὰ γνώμην πραττόμενα τοῦ 'Ρωμαίων ἐπισκόπου (for there is a sacerdotal canon which declares that, whatsoever is decreed without the sanction of the Bishop of Rome, is null and void). Oxford, trans. London, Bagster, 1846. We here find that Sozomen is not less used by Epiphanius than Socrates. We are also reminded of him by the 71st Arabic Nicene canon, edited by Abraham Echellensis : " Nec debere *præter assensum Romani Episcopi* concilia celebrari." In Socrates (ii. 17), we read as follows :—ἐπεμέμψατο (Julius) παρὰ κανόνας ποιοῦντας, διότι εἰς σύνοδον αὐτὸν οὐκ ἐκάλεσαν, τοῦ ἐκκλησιαστικοῦ κανόνος κελεύοντος, μὴ δεῖν παρὰ γνώμην τοῦ ἐπισκόπου τῆς 'Ρώμης κανονίζειν τὰς ἐκκλησίας. (The last words are to be found in c. viii. also.) Per literas respondit. . . . . eos contra Ecclesiæ canones egisse, quod illum ad concilium non vocassent quippe cum canon ecclesiasticus vetet, ne decreta *præter sententiam episcopi Romani* Ecclesiis sanciantur. "Julius replied by letters, that they had acted contrary to the canons of the Church, in not having invited him to the Council, since the ecclesiastical canon forbids that decrees should be enacted by the Churches, without the sanction of the Bishop of Rome."
Hefele (Conc. i., p. 7) remarks on this passage, "that, if we consider the matter impartially, there can be no doubt that by the word Κανονίζειν is signified the setting forth of general decrees by and at synods." The words, "because they have not invited him to the synod," determine the sense more closely. Peter de Marca (Concord. Sac. et Imp. v., 12, 1) thought the words of the Greek historians are too much amplified ; but Gieseler observes (Church Hist., ii., § 94, p. 207), that the then practice must have furnished a basis for this amplification. Socrates (L. viii., c. 11) censures the bishops of Rome for their severity towards the Novatians, and speaks on that occasion of their δυναστεία (their spirit of domination), quite like that of the Alexandrine bishops ; but this does not justify us in assuming, in other passages of his writings, an intentional distortion of words and acts.
As regards the words of Pope Julius, it is, indeed, said : " It was necessary to have written to us all," ἔδει γραφῆναι πᾶσιν ἡμῖν, where the question regarded the sentence on so many deposed bishops ; but in the subsequent words in reference to the Church of Alex-

Roman Forgeries. 161

The ecclesiastical practice described by us shows that in the fifth century the interpretation given by these historians was perfectly justifiable. The second of the cited propositions has likewise been enunciated elsewhere, and is quite conformable to the more ancient decretals.[45] But the third proposition, that the bishops are mere ministering assistants or delegates of the Pope, does not agree with many declarations elsewhere found, in which the pseudo-Isidore derives the episcopal power immediately from Christ and His apostles;[46] and it in no way belongs to this ecclesiastical system. These three propositions in themselves have been unable to accomplish any revolution in the constitution of the Church.

As the true point in the controversy between more ancient and more modern scholars respecting the influence of these decretals, we have an indica-

---

andria (see chapter vii. above, note 19), the word πᾶσί (to all) fails. Hence Coustant (p. 385, note c.) inferred, that it was only over the Bishop of Alexandria the Pope alone reserved judgment to himself. This statement, however, is with good reason contested by Bennettis (P. II., t. iii., pp. 174, 175), who for his part declares : Itaque S. Julius, ut insinuaret rite ad tribunal suum trahi denuo debere, quæ inscio se et inconsulto in synodo orientali de episcoporum causis actitata erant, suo dumtaxat usus est nomine *Nobis*, cui paullo ante pronomen *omnibus* adjecerat, ideo ut indicaret, juxta morem Romano Pontifici receptum, ejusmodi causas præsertim a veritate facti pendentes finiri in concilio consuevisse. The passages of Julius are to be found in pseudo-Isidore also (p. 459-465, ed. Hinschii).

[45] Vigil. (P. II., c. 7, p. 712, ed. Hinsch.) is taken from the decretals of Innocent I. and of Leo I., ep. 14. Cf. Gregor, iv., c. 11, 9, 6. The sollicitudo omnium ecclesiarum Pope Innocent I. (in ep. 30, n. 1, 2) attributes to himself, and Pope Siricius also (in ep. 6, n. i., p. 659) the cura omnium ecclesiarum. The fourth Lateran Council adjudges to the Roman Church the ordinariæ potestatis principatum. The confession of the Emperor Michael Palæologus, which he addressed to Pope Gregory X. (Conc. Lugd. ii., Hard. vii., p. 696, *seq.*) assigns to the Pontiff the plenitudo potestatis. Phillips' Can. Law, vol. v., § 201, p. 9, *seq.*

[46] Anaclet., ep. ii., 2 (xx.), p. 77, ep. iii., 3 (xxix.), p. 82. Jul. I., ep. 9, p. 461. Phillips 18, § 174, p. 75.

L

tion as to the earlier forgeries made in Rome, of which many were received into the collection of Isidore, and so obtained a wider diffusion; but these in the question before us prove nothing.

Secondly, we find a remark upon "the contradiction" which the Isidorian doctrine involved, as it aimed at two mutually incompatible things, to wit, the perfect independence and impunity of bishops on the one hand,[47] and the advancement of the Papal power on the other. "The first point it sought to effect by such strange and unpractical rules, that they never attained any real vitality, while, on the contrary, the principles about the power of the Roman See worked their way, and became dominant *under favourable circumstances*, but with a result opposed to the views of Isidore, by bringing the bishops into complete subjection to Rome" (p. 97).

But how was all this realized? Now the forged decretals of the earliest popes were "eagerly seized upon by Pope Nicholas I. at Rome, to be used as genuine documents, in support of the *new* claims put forward by himself and his successors" (p. 95). But while the Synod of Kiersy in 857, and Hincmar, archbishop of Rheims, made use of them,[48] Pope Nicholas I. was not yet acquainted with them even in the year 858,[49] nay, not even in 863. It was only in 864 these decretals became known to him through Rothad, bishop of Soissons;[50] and in this statement Janus also concurs (p. 98).

---

[47] Here it has been forgotten to add, *of whom* the bishops should be independent, and in what quarter they should be inviolable. An absolute and universal inviolability would be a nonentity; but independence of the secular power, and dependence on a higher spiritual authority, would not be "two things inwardly incompatible."

[48] Mansi. xv., 126. Hard. v., 115. Hefele iv., 192.

[49] Jaffé Reg., n. 2016, 2051.

[50] Weizsäcker in Sybel's Historical Periodical. iii. 84. Dümmler's Hist. of Franconia, vol. i., p. 538, *seq.* (in German).

Nicholas, "who," we are told "exceeded all his predecessors in the audacity of his designs" (p. 98), must be classed among the greatest popes, even though he did not rightly interpret the seventeenth canon of Chalcedon (p. 98).[51] But it is precisely the interpretation which he gives of the designation, "Exarch" (in Latin "Primas"), of the diocese, that agrees not with the one given by pseudo-Isidore, who distinguishes the primate from the Pope,[52] while Nicholas identifies both. The charge of the "most daring, though little noticed, torturing of a single word against the sense of a whole code of law," is purely imaginary. For the proposition that recurrence must be had to a higher judge, and that for bishops the Papal See is the ultimate tribunal, Nicholas I. adduced historical precedents and genuine decretals ; the mere title of " Primas " gave to the Pope nothing which he had not long possessed. Nor is it anywhere clearly proved that Nicholas, although he used spurious writings of an earlier date, which had long been current, ever made use of pseudo-Isidore.[53] Nicholas, indeed, disputed the view advocated by Hincmar,[54] that those decretals, which were not in the received Codex of Adrian, had no legal force, and this with perfect justice; for thus the later decrees would have been excluded; and to reject a decretal merely on that ground was certainly inadmissible.[55]

Nicholas had mostly before him decretals and testimonies decidedly genuine.[56] The propositions

[51] And Canon 9. Cf. Hefele ii., 494-496. Papæ Nicol., ep. 8, ad Mich. Imp.

[52] Anicet., ep. 1, c. 3, p. 121; Victor, ep. 1, c. 6, p. 128, ed. Hinschius.

[53] Blasco de Coll. Isid., c. 4. Ballerini, *loc. cit.*, P. III., c. 6, § 1. Opp. Leon. iii., p. ccxv.

[54] Hincm., ep. ad Hincm. Laud. Opp., ii., 543.

[55] Nicol., ep. 42, ad Episc. Gall. Mansi. xv., 695. Cf. Phillips iv., p. 45 (in Gratian, c. 1, § 1, d. 19).

[56] In the Epistle to Charles the Bald (Mansi. i. 688, Hard. v.

—that without the previous knowledge of the See of Rome, no national synod was to be held;[57] that every accused bishop had the right to appeal to the Pope, especially from suspected and hostile judges; that the *causæ majores* belonged to the jurisdiction of the Roman See:[58]—these propositions are all more ancient than pseudo-Isidore; and Pope Nicholas had no need of him.[59] "If, indeed, all Papal utterances, as is said, were a rule for the whole Church, and all decrees of Councils depended on the Pope's good pleasure, as Nicholas asserted on the strength of the Isidorian forgery,—then there would be but *one* step farther, to the promulgation of Papal Infallibility" (p. 99). Hence the danger of those utterances. But in secular affairs decisions of the emperor can constitute the rule, and decrees of the diet have no force against his veto; must we then assume an Imperial Infallibility? But Rome's tradition,[60] Rome's decrees,[61]

---

585) the pseudo-Isidorian Julius is said to have been cited; but here the Pope had the genuine letter of Julius and Theodoret's History of the Church (II., c. 4) before his eyes, as clearly appears from another passage in Hardouin (v. 167). The second canon (C. xv., q. 6) belongs to Pope Nicholas II.

[57] Sermo de causa Rothadi. Hard., *loc. cit.*, 585.

[58] Here has pseudo-Isidore, Pelag. II. (ep., p. 124, H.): Majores vero et difficiles quæstiones, ut S. Synodus statuit et beata consuetudo exigit, ad Sedem Apostolicam semper referantur. This says no more than Innocent I. (ep. 2, n. 6, p. 749, 750 Coust.): Si majores causæ in medium fuerint devolutæ, ad Sedem Apostolicam, sicut synodus (according to Coustant Sardic. in ep. ad. Jul., cap. vii., n. 39) statuit et beata consuetudo exigit, post judicium episcopale referantur. Elsewhere we find antiqua traditio (Innoc. ep. xxix., n. 1) or antiqua regula (ep. xxx., n. 2).

[59] Phillips iv., § 174, pp. 78-84, 85, *seq.*

[60] Innoc. I., ep. 25, ad Decent., n. 2, p. 856; Quis enim nesciat aut non advertat, id quod a principe Ap. Petro Romanæ ecclesiæ traditum est ac nunc usque custoditur, *ab omnibus debere servari?*

[61] Siric., ep. 1, n. 3, p. 627, *seq.*: Nunc præfatam regulam teneant *omnes sacerdotes*, que nolunt ab apostolicæ petræ, super quam Christus universalem construxit Ecclesiam, soliditate divelli.

were even from an early period the standard of doctrine ; the Roman Church was the head of the whole body ;⁶² the synods rejected by her never found recognition. Where is, then, the frightful innovation? Even in 1085, the false Decretals had yet little weight in Rome, as is apparent from the synod of Gerstungen.⁶³ If now *French* and *German* bishops, whether in their individual capacity, or at synods, from the ninth to the eleventh century, appealed to these decretals ;⁶⁴ so certainly the new maxims of ecclesiastical legislation had not been imposed on them by Rome, least of all at a time when Rome was in so lamentable a condition ; *rather, they had laid the yoke on themselves* (p. 100). When, then, the Popes in the eleventh century cited likewise those decretals, whose authenticity among their contemporaries, and even for two centuries, had remained indisputed, what blame can they incur? Is it that in historical criticism they were not far in advance of their age? If, as our authors pretend, the want of historical perception was constantly, and from of old, the defect of Rome ;⁶⁵ how can they then allege, as an imputation against that very Rome, that it gave credit to fictions, which had found general acceptance, and which corresponded to the existing state of the Church?

But new fictions were ever piled up. On a bad foundation a bad building only can spring up. This Janus teaches us more by what he has really achieved himself, than by what he pretends to prove. Springing over several intermediate links,

---

⁶² Siric., ep. ad Him., n. 20, p. 637 ; Romana Ecclesia caput corporis. Cf. Bonif. I., 1 ep. 14, n. 1, p. 1037.

⁶³ Kunstmann in the "Theological Journal of Freiburg" (iv., p. 116, *seq*). Phillips's, *loc. cit.*., p. 86.

⁶⁴ Hefele, Conc. IV., pp. 317, 365, 473, 483, 533, 548, 609.

⁶⁵ Nay, we are told (Janus, p. 204) there were kinds of historical information unattainable in those times (namely, the Middle Ages).

the collection of canon laws dedicated to the Milanese Anselm, that of Regino of Prüm, that of Burkard of Worms, who is first named at p. 143, our new historian of ecclesiastical law (p. 102), passes to Anselm of Lucca, who died in the year 1086, and who appears to him as the founder of the "New Gregorian Canon Law." This canonist, we are told, "through a tissue of fresh inventions and interpolations, altered the law of the Church in accordance with the requirements of *his party*,— and the point of view of Gregory" (p. 102). Thus not even pseudo-Isidore was enough for the insatiable party; after 200 years it needed again a new transformation. It was only mediately Anselm of Lucca made use of pseudo-Isidore; his first six books he took from the collection dedicated to Anselm of Milan; and the following books he took from Burkard of Worms.[66] To the latter a greater importance ought to have been adjudged; and Anselm, the nephew of Alexander II., whose work, like those of Cardinals Deusdedit and Gregory, had little circulation (p. 143), had thus not the importance of a "founder of the new Gregorian Canon Law;" his work was not the most important (p. 103). Moreover, in competition with him, there were Bonizo, Deusdedit, and Gregory of Pavia (p. 103), nay, Gregory VII. himself in his thesis called the "Dictatus" (p. 107).

Although it is very doubtful whether the brief remarks of Giesebrecht[67] have fully settled the question as to the authorship of this work,[68] yet for Janus the matter is decisively established. Gregory

---

[66] Phillips, *loc. cit.*, § 177, pp. 128, 129. Moreover he, like Deusdedit, drew a part of his materials from the Roman Archives. *Ibid.* 129, 130.

[67] The "Munich Historical Annals," 1866, p. 149.

[68] Janssen in the "Journal of Theological Literature," 1867, p. 821 (in German). Cf. Hefele v. 67.

VII., who inaugurated a new epoch, exercised his pontifical power in a way corresponding with his ideas. "Little familiar as he was with theological questions, we are told, he must have held the prerogative of infallibility to be the most precious jewel of his crown" (p. 111). "That Papal Infallibility might be more firmly believed, personal sanctity was also ascribed to every Pope: a sanctity which Gregory made the foundation of his claim to universal dominion,[69] and in furtherance of this claim, asserted the sinful origin of royalty" (p. 113).[70] If Gregory appealed to documents and to narratives,[71] which cannot stand the test of criticism (p. 107); so the circumstance is overlooked, that he did not fabricate those documents and narratives, but found them already in existence; that his contemporaries held them to be genuine; and even that not all which is declared interpolated, is really so.[72] Every inaccurate citation is imputed to him as a crime. He unduly extended, we are told, the effects of excommunication (p. 120); whereas before him, and before pseudo-Isidore, the discipline in this matter was much severer.[73] Nay, it was precisely Gregory who in so far mitigated it, that members of a household, women, children, all, in fact, who were incapable of confirming the sinner in his bad sentiments, were allowed to hold inter-

---

[69] Bianchi (*op. cit.*, t. i., L. ii., § 10, n. 3, p. 280, *seq.*), has accurately examined this charge.

[70] *Vide* Bianchi, *loc. cit.*, n. 2, p. 275, *seq.*: where it is shown that other expressions also of Gregory VII. are opposed to these; and hence the latter are to be explained in a limited sense, according to the analogy of the words of Augustine and of Gregory the Great.

[71] Particularly the 8th book, ep. 21, ad Herm. Metens.

[72] Against Launoius (Janus, p. 114, n. 53), see Anthony Charlas, Tract de Libertatibus Eccles. Gallicanæ, II., B. vii. c. 6, 10, 3d ed. Romæ, 1720. Bianchi, *loc. cit.*, § 11, p. 287, *seq.*

[73] *Vide* proofs in Gosselin, *loc. cit.*, p. ii., c. 1, a. 3, p. 77, *seq.*

course with the excommunicated.[74] That princes, no less than the rest of the faithful, were liable to excommunication, was never doubted in the Church.[75] As to the claims of the Popes over Spain, Hungary, Russia, Saxony, and Provence, the expressions relative thereto have long been duly appreciated [76] (p. 285).

But let us return to the collections of Canon Law. Whatever we know respecting these from the times of Anselm, bishop of Lucca, down to those of Gratian, in no way justifies us to assume an intentional fraud (p. 105), or a new forgery. In the age of Gregory VII. the testimonies for the plenitude of the Papal power were so numerous, that a forgery in these would have been quite superfluous, and have answered no end. If Deusdedit (p. 103) and so many others derived all ecclesiastical jurisdiction from Peter, they said no more than what the most ancient Popes six hundred years before had affirmed.[77] If they taught that all decrees of the Apostolic See were so to be received, as if they were confirmed by the very voice of Peter (p. 104);[78] they said no more

---

[74] Greg. Syn. Rom. iv., c. 4. Mansi. xx., 504, *seq.* Hefele v. 108. Gosselin, *loc. cit.*, p. 100.

[75] Cf. Conc. Rom. Greg., v. 998, 999, c. 1. Mansi. xix, 223. Baron., a. 998, n. 3. Defensio Declar. Cleri. Gallic. t. i., P. ii., L. vi., c. 27.

[76] Bianchi, t. i., L. ii., § 14, *seq.*, p. 352, *seq.*

[77] Siric., ep. 5, n. 1, p. 651, Coustant: per quem (Petrum) et apostolatus et episcopatus in Christo cepit exordium. Innoc. I., ep. 2, ad Victric., n. 2, p. 747: Adjuvante S. Ap. Petro, per quem et apostolatus et episcopatus in Christo cepit exordium. Ep. 29, ad PP. Carthag., n. 1, p. 888: a quo ipse episcopatus et tota auctoritas nominis hujus emersit. Bonifac. I., ep. 4, p. 1019: B. Ap. Petrus, cui arx Sacerdotii Dominica voce concessa est. Ep. 14, n. 1, p. 1037: Institutio universalis nascentis Ecclesiæ de B. Petri sumpsit honore principium, in quo regimen ejus et summa consistit. Ex ejus enim ecclesiastica disciplina per omnes ecclesias, religionis jam crescente cultura, fonte manavit.

[78] "Consequently infallible," adds Janus, who supplies the Infallibilists with more weapons than they before used. The passage is

than what all antiquity pronounced, when it heard Peter speak by the mouth of Leo, and by the mouth of Agatho ; when it ascribed the acts of Popes to Peter, as occurs in hundreds of documents, where Peter and the Pope appear as one person.[79] The elder compilers of Canon Law, from the ninth century down to the decretals of Gratian inclusively, who, according to our Janus (p. 143), not only received in good faith the old forgeries, but even added new corruptions, sought to furnish but the greatest possible quantity of materials. They admitted even self-contradictory passages, canons rejected by the Roman Church, as well as the later Apostolic Canons, and those of the Council in Trullo, and others,[80] and evinced in this matter rather an unsystematic procedure, than premeditated fraud. Yet even this, as much as possible, is made to subserve the purposes of obstinate, tenacious prejudice. Anselm of Lucca,[81] and Gregory of Pavia, as after them Gratian,

found in Gratian, c. 2, d. 19. That also c. 12, C. xxiv., q. 1 (pseudo-Isidore, Sixtus II.) says nothing new, as shown by Phillips (II., § 89, p. 321).

[79] To the passages already cited others may still be added. Pope Bonifac. I., ep. 13. Rufo., n. 1, p. 1034 : B. Apostolus Petrus ecclesiæ Thessalonicensi cuncta commisit ; ep. 15, n. 1, p. 1039 : Manet B. Ap. Petrum per sententiam Dominicam universalis Ecclesiæ ab hoc sollicitudo suscepta, quippe quam Evangelio teste in se noverit esse fundatam, nec unquam ejus honor vacuus esse potest curarum, cum certum sit, summam rerum ex ejus delibera- tione pendere ; n. 7, p. 1044 : cujus (Perigenis Episcopi) sacer- dotium Ap. Petrus semel jam Spiritus sancti suggestione firmavit.

[80] Cf., for example, c. 4, d. 16 (Trull., c. 2) ; c. 6, d. 22 (Trull., 36) ; c. 14, d. 28 (Can. Ap., 6) ; c. 16, *ead.* (Trull., c. 26) ; c. 13, d. 31 (Trull., c. 13) ; c. 7, d. 32 (Trull., 6) ; c. 15, d. 34 (Can. Ap., 18) ; c. 1, d. 35 (App., 43, 44) ; c. 3, d. 44 (Trull., c. 9) ; c. 1, d. 47 (Can. Ap., 44) ; c. 4, d. 55 (C. Ap., 22, 23) ; c. 4, d. 77 (Trull., c. 15) ; c. 26, d. 93 (Trull., c. 7) ; c. 100, C. i., q. 1 (Trull., c. 23) ; c. 45, C. vii., q. 1 (Syn. Phot., 879, Can. ii., Ivo Carnot., P. vii., c. 149).

[81] The view of Papal Infallibility Anselm rested, not on the false decretals, but on the text of St Luke xxii. 32. Bennettis, P. I., vol. ii., p. 344.

admitted into their codes the passages from Jerome as to the small distinction between bishops and priests; and "that thereby the axe was laid at the root of the Roman Primacy, those short-sighted architects of the Papal system failed to perceive" (p. 206). They yet, however, were so crafty, so far-sighted, that they thereby aimed at a great result; "for all they wanted was to have the way for the superiority of Cardinals, and with it the domination of the Curia, and to build up the Papal system on the ruins of the ancient episcopal system" (p. 207). In consequence of this revolution, "bishops, towards the end of the thirteenth century, were brought to allow themselves to be made cardinal-presbyters, and even to regard as a promotion this degradation of the Episcopate to the Presbyterate" (p. 207). To this, indeed, a parallel might be found in the Greek Church, and even already in the eleventh century, when the office of Syncellus was an object of ambition to the metropolitans; and in the year 1029 a contest about the precedency of the Syncelli over the latter sprang up.[82] "The injurious creation of the Cardinalate" (p. 212),[83] but which, however, was nothing less than sudden, has hitherto appeared to many as commanded by the circumstances of the eleventh century; and whoever compares the Papal elections after the year 1059 with the earlier ones, will feel himself obliged to confess that that institution has rendered great services to the Church.[84]

Gratian's celebrated Decretum became the manual

---

[82] Cedren. ii., p. 486, *seq*. Thomassin., P. I., L. ii., c. 101, n. 6, *seq*.

[83] Copious details on this subject in Phillips (Can. Law, vol. vi., § 267, *seq.*, p. 63, *seq.*).

[84] Cardinal Deusdedit also (Janus, p. 111) had previously sought to glorify this institution, and to vindicate, on a vacancy in the Papal See, the government of the Church for the College of Cardinals.

and law-book of the western world, not by "the means applied by the Curia" (p. 148), but by its utility, and by its reception in *scholâ et foro*.[85] No one denies that the monk of Bologna was deficient in historical criticism; but no one, again, can prove that his work was intended to be a fraud. The genuine passages from Justinian's law-books, from Greek, Spanish, African, Frankish, and other councils; from doctors of the Church, like Augustine, Jerome, Isidore; from decretals of Popes Innocent I., Leo. I., Gelasius, Gregory the Great, Nicholas, Leo IX., and his successors,[86] in number and weight exceed the spurious ones. Of the popes of later times copious texts are given;[87] but that false documents should be taken by Gratian from his predecessors, when their authenticity was unquestioned by his contemporaries, cannot be imputed to him as a crime. What holds good of the thirteenth and fourteenth centuries, that no one then divined the true state of things, nor thought of forgeries and fictions (p. 253, G.), applies likewise, and with equal reason, to the preceding ages. Among other things,[88] Janus takes great offence

[85] Never was the decretum of Gratian regarded by canonists as a regular law-book; and criticism in regard to it could act with perfect freedom. Placid. Boeckhn Controv. Jurisprud., L. i., tit. 2, p. 1090. Berti de theol. disc., B. xx., c. 18. Bennettis, P. II., vol. iii., p. 211. Schulte, Man. of Can. Law, 2d ed., § 14, p. 39, n. 4.

[86] Against these popes in particular, it is made a charge that they declared simony to be a heresy. Cf. Janus (p. 298 G.) But the expression simoniaca hæresis is more ancient; it already occurs in an epistle of Pope John viii., in the ninth century (ep. 95, ad episc. Gall. Mansi. xvii., p. 83).

[87] Urban II. and Alexander II., c. 8, 9, C. i., q. 3; c. 4, 5, C. ix., q. 1; Paschal II., c. 1, C. xiv., q. 2; c. 47, C. xvi., q. 1; c. 5, C. xxx., q. 3; Innocent II., c. 29, C. xvii., q. 4; c. 25, C. xviii., q. 2; c. 5, C. xxi., q. 4; c. 40, C. xxvii., q. 1, *et seq.*

[88] On the passage cited at p. 161 (see xvi., C. xxv., q. 1). Cf. Merkle in the Augsburg Pastoral Journal, 2d Oct. 1869, No. 40. Besides, many various readings are used, as they are so frequently to be found in many ancient manuscripts. Cf. Coustant (note B. to

at the second part of Gratian's Decretum (Causa, xxiii., 9, 4–6). The case here supposed is as follows:—Catholic bishops, together with their people, are by threats and torments constrained to embrace heresy by bishops, who have themselves fallen into heresy. Prelates, armed by the emperor with secular jurisdiction, march into the field at the Pope's command, for the protection of Catholics, slay numbers of the enemy, take others prisoners, and bring several heretics by violence back to the Church. In this imagined case several questions arise. First, Is the waging of war sinful? Secondly, What sort of war is just? Thirdly, Is a wrong inflicted on allies to be repelled by force of arms? In all these cases reasons for and against are given. The fourth question is: Is it lawful to take vengeance? Then follow passages from Augustine and others on the toleration of the wicked. The chief passages in reference to the punishment of heretics are taken from Augustine.[89] The fifth question is, Whether a judge can allow criminals to be put to death? Here again two different views are advocated; first come passages from the above-named father of the Church, and others, that the wicked are to be punished, but not to be put to death. In the last of these passages, Janus (p. 147) discovers a falsification of Gratian's, in this sense, "that the Church should protect homicides and murderers." This charge of falsification he founds on the fact, that in Burkard and Ivo, according to the

---

Innoc. I., ep. 2, n. 5, p. 749). If Gratian (c. 7, d. 96) quoted the narrative of Rufinus, that had been long used by others, respecting the words of the Emperor Constantine as to bishops in general, and referred them to the Pope (Janus, p. 110); so there was here no falsification. Nay, among bishops the Pope also was included, and in truth he is the first bishop; and it was, moreover, in the spirit of the eleventh and twelfth century, to conclude *a minori ad majus*.

[89] C. 37, *seq.*, C. xxiii., q. 4.

Roman correctors, there is a negative which in our text of Gratian is omitted.[90]

But what purpose should such a forgery serve? In the following text of Gratian, which, from what had been previously said, will only support the view that criminals should not be punished with death and mutilation, there succeeds another authority for the opposite opinion, that capital punishment ought to be inflicted, and therewith ulterior inquiries are connected. Accordingly, Gratian has not touched the reason assigned, to wit, "lest the Church should have a share in bloodshed," a reason which perhaps appeared to him incompatible with that negative. The bloodshed could be applied as well to the murder perpetrated by the criminal, as to the massacre arising from his apprehension, when he took refuge in a Church. A misunderstanding could easily occur, or an error of the copyist ; but in any case the sequel shows that here by a forgery Gratian neither could nor wished to gain anything. He cites scriptural texts for the permission accorded to sovereigns to put criminals to death ; and these texts are followed by passages from the Fathers, and he concludes as follows : If thus the saints and the civil powers, in waging war, do not violate the prohibition against killing, although on criminals of all kinds they inflict merited death ; if the soldier, in obeying his superiors, and in slaying a wicked man, is not guilty of murder ; if the punishment of murderers and poisoners is not bloodshed, but the execution of the laws; if those who, from zeal for the Catholic Church, slay the excommunicated, are not judged

---

[90] C. 7, C. *cit.*, q. 5 : Greg. P. Reos sanguine defendat (Ivo. Burc. : non defendat) Ecclesia, ne effusione (al. effusionis) sanguinis particeps fiat.

as murderers; so it is clear that the wicked *may* not only be scourged, but executed also.[91]

From this Gratian turns to the question; whether even private individuals can, without legal authority, put others to death. Thus in these passages he treats of the public authority of the State, and not immediately of the Church; and "the general conclusion" is taken not merely from the suspicious words of Pope Urban II.,[92] as Janus (p. 147) asserts, but from the previously cited passages from Augustine, Pelagius, Nicholas, and others. Moreover, with regard to proceedings against religious dissenters, Gratian could the less seek to bring anything new forward, as on that point "he chiefly followed Ivo of Chartres" (p. 235), who "though in certain important articles he held to the old Church law" (p. 103, n. 3), yet "adopted into his Decretals a copious store of spurious pieces," and announced the most perfect submission to the Roman Church (p. 261).

Over the noble collection of Decretals instituted by Pope Gregory IX., Janus passes very quickly; he uses it only to bring forward divers charges against particular popes. For all the mediæval canonists he evinces a marked repugnance. "In the long period from 1230 to 1530, the *parasites of the Roman Curia cultivated and ruled the domain of canon law as interpreters of the new codes*" (p. 232). "The world was *poisoned by the Bolognese school of law,*[93] and by the Roman Curia" (p. 204). "To the Papal court-jurists and canonists were

---

[91] Grat. post can. 48, C. et, *op. cit.*

[92] C. 47, Excommunicatorum *loc. cit.* Here a struggle for the Church is presupposed; the preceding canon treats of war against unbelievers.

[93] The expressions of Savigny, and of the Jurists and Canonists following him, must then be corrected !!

added, after the thirteenth century, the Papal court-historiographers, like Martinus Polonus, and Tolomeo of Lucca" (p. 284). "From that century down to the fifteenth, historical knowledge became obscured by means of the Mendicant Orders, and since their rise the credulous mania for miracles became more prevalent." It was desired to mould the forgeries and fictions of pseudo-Isidore, of Gratian, and of the Decretals, into a coherent history,[94] and to supplement by the fable of the institution of the electors by Gregory V., the theory of translations invented by Alexander III. and Innocent III." (p. 282).[95] To the Papal court-jurists and court-historiographers[96] must lastly be added the court-theologians, and pre-eminently the schoolmen of the Mendicant Orders.

But here again there were "forgeries." In order to match the Greeks, recourse was had to a special expedient. "A Latin theologian, probably a Dominican, who had resided among the Greeks, composed a catena of spurious passages from the Greek Councils and Fathers, in which the novel Papal claims were to receive a dogmatic basis" (p. 264). These false testimonies were used by Thomas Aquinas; resting upon them, "he introduced the doctrine of the Pope and of his infallibility into his dogmatic work" (p. 266); and upon this foundation, as well as out of the forgeries in

---

[94] So far had men then already come. We were of opinion that this thought was but of later origin, and that the need of historical accuracy was not then felt.

[95] *Vide* thereupon Phillips' Can. Law iii., § 119, p. 53, § 129, p. 195.

[96] On the mention of Martinus Polonus, Janus points out that he with others related how Sylvester II., by a compact with the devil, had attained to the Papal dignity (p. 251). But the fable is certainly older, as the pseudo-Cardinal Benno already shows. See Döllinger, Papstfabeln, p. 156, *seq.*, Bennettis, P. ii., t. v., p. 712, *seq.*

Gratian, "he built up his Papal system" (p. 267). Thomas Aquinas, as afterwards Cajetan and Melchior Canus, rested upon fictions *exclusively* (p. 393); and Turrecremata is dependent upon these fictions, and upon Thomas Aquinas (p. 310, G.) So this, then, would be the origin of the dogmatic statements respecting the plenitude of power and inerrancy in the Holy See. But is this really the case? We open Thomas Aquinas, and we find that he relies for this dogma upon many other things, and especially on the passages of Scripture respecting Peter's primacy,[97] as well as upon internal theological grounds, upon inferences from dogmatic premisses, as, for example, from the necessary unity of faith,[98] on the authority of Pope Leo at the Synod of Chalcedon, attested as it is in genuine documents,[99] and on a genuine passage of Pope Innocent I., and of others.[100] If now, at a period in which the Latins could as yet use but few writings of the Greek fathers,[101] Thomas Aquinas cited passages from the pseudo-Cyrill, and other false texts; so this could not, and cannot even at the present day, damage his other proofs. Nay, these new fictions might have been abundantly replaced by other genuine texts. Theodore the Studite,[102] Ignatius, patriarch of Constantinople,[103] Maximus in a passage

---

[97] On Matt. xvi., Sum. Supplem. q. 25, a. 1; Com. in h. l.; on ke xxii. 2–22, q. 1, a. 10; L. iv. Sent. d. 24, q. 3, a. 2.
[98] C. Gent. L. iv., c. 76; Quodlib. ix., a. 16.
[99] De potentia q. 10, a. 4, ad 13.
[100] Sum. 2. 2. q. 11, a. 2, ad 3, can. Quoties C. xxiv., q. 1, Innocent I., ep. 30 (see above cap. vii., n. 38). The Opusculum contra Græcos bears the same relation to the Summa, as a treatise composed in the Hours of Leisure, to a great work carried on with predilection for many years.
[101] Under Eugenius III., the dogmatic work of St John Damascene was translated into Latin, badly enough, indeed, by Burgundio of Pisa; and in this form was known to St Thomas.
[102] See in the fourth chapter above the notes 36, 48, and 49.
[103] This Patriarch (ep. Ignat. Patr. ad Nicol. P. Mansi xvi. 47

already made known in the West even in the ninth century,[104] would have offered such a supply. But how very superficially Janus has studied Thomas Aquinas, is apparent from the statement of his doctrine relative to the mode of procedure against heretics.[105] No apocryphal writings were also

seq., 325 *seq.*) calls the Pope the physician, whom, by the words addressed to Peter (in Matt. xvi.), Christ instituted for all, without exception, and who everywhere heals the disorders of the Church.

[104] Maximi ep. ad Petr. Illustr. ex Collectan. Anastas. Bibl. Combef. ii. 76. Migne xci., 144: " Pyrrhus (patriarch of Constantinople) must hasten to give satisfaction to the Roman Church. If this Church be satisfied, he will then be called by all and everywhere a religious and orthodox prelate. For he will speak but in vain, if he does not have recourse to the most blessed Pope of the most holy Church of the Romans, to that Apostolic see *which received from the Incarnate Word itself, as well as from all Councils, according to the holy canons and rules, universal and supreme dominion, authority, and the power of binding and* of loosing over all the holy churches of God upon this earth. That Word, which rules all the heavenly powers, binds and looses with this See in heaven also. If he seeks to pacify others, but beseeches not the most blessed Pope of Rome, he acts like to a man who, accused of murder or of any other crime, would hasten to prove his innocence before private persons, but not before him who, according to the laws, is invested with judicial powers." This passage even Pichler* has acknowledged to be genuine, *loc. cit.*, vol. ii., p. 602. In case a member of a German Academy of Sciences should have erred in respect to the genuineness of this passage, similar errors of more ancient authors, who possessed not the present critical aids, may well, in truth, be deemed *pardonable.*

[105] Janus writes (p. 236, note 2), "that St Thomas (in his *Summa*, 11 q., art. 3, 4), tries to prove from the symbolic names given them in Scripture, that heretics should be put to death." Thus, *e.g.*, heretics, are called " thieves " and " wolves," but we hang thieves, and kill wolves. Again, he calls heretics sons of Satan, and thinks they should even on earth share the fate of their father, *i.e.*, be burnt. He observes, on the apostle's saying, that a heretic is to be avoided after two admonitions, that this avoidance is best accomplished by executing him. For the relapsed he thinks all instruction is useless, and they should be at once burnt. So far Janus. Here are not found the cited inferences from the symbolic words of Scripture; and it is untrue that to the words of the apostle (Titus iii. 10), St Thomas subjoins the remark, that the avoidance of the heretic may *best* occur by his execution. In article 3 he says, "If the heretic

* Pichler is a German schismatic.—Trans.,

necessary to induce him to assert that the Council of Chalcedon had conferred on the Pope the title of universal bishop (p. 269) ; this fact was already mentioned in the epistles of Gregory the Great and of Leo IX.[106] But groundless as is the statement, that theologians before Thomas Aquinas abstained from all treatment of the subject of the Papacy (p. 266),[107] equally erroneous is it to say, that Thomas Aquinas introduced this matter into his dogmatic system (p. 86). In his *Summa* he devotes no special section to the Pope ; he presupposes his authority, and treats but occasionally of his special prerogatives.[108]

A further forgery, Janus, with Launoy and other members of that party, finds in the Decree

after being twice admonished of his error remains obstinate, so the Church, which no longer entertains any hope of his conversion, provides for the salvation of others, as by excommunication she separates him from her body, and delivers him over to the secular tribunal to remove him by death from the world. For, according to Jerome, the foul flesh is to be cut off, and a scabby sheep to be removed, that the rest of the flock may not be tainted." In article 4, the question is about those relapsed who are admitted, indeed, to penance, but not so that they liberentur a sententiâ mortis, or as it is expressed in the first article, Ecclesia a periculo mortis eos non tuetur. Cf. art. 3, *possunt* non solum excommunicari, sed et juste occidi. That they *must* be burned, St Thomas does not say ; but he only wishes to show that they can justly suffer death. He does not declare also that all instruction is useless, but presupposes a case of failure.

[106] Greg. M., L. iv., ep. 32, 36, L. vii. 30. Leo IX., ep. ad. Caerul., c. 9, p. 70, ed. Will. Cf. Hefele, Conc. ii., § 202, p. 525, *seq.*

[107] Vid. Hugo a S. Victore (see note 12 in cap. vi. above), Rupert von Deutz (Lib. ii. in Joh., c. 3 in Apoc. Et vidi. sedes. de div. offic. ii. 22. Cf. Bennettis, P. i., t. ii., pp. 347, 348), Anselm of Havelberg (Dial iii. 9, 10), Hugo Etherianus (c. Græc. errores, iii. 10, 16, 17), Peter of Blois (ep. 99, ad Urban. iii., ep. 48, 136, 145, 146), Peter Lombard (Sent., L. iv., d. 24), Alexander of Hales (p. 3, q. 40, m. 2 ; d. 4, q. 23, m. 1).

[108] Cf. Sum. 1, q. 112, a. 2, ad. 2 (Power of Absolution) ; 2, 2, q. 68, a. 4, ad. 3 (Removal of Infamy) ; *ibid.*, q. 89, a. 9, ad. 3 (Absolution from an Oath) ; 3, q. 72, a. 11, ad. 1 (Delegation of a priest with the power of confirming after the example of Gregory the Great) ; supple., q. 25, a. 1 (Grant of an Indulgence, &c.)

of Union sanctioned by the Council of Florence [109] (p. 322). There, in the Latin text, in order to transform the restriction of the Papal power into a clause of confirmation, the particle "et" was changed into "etiam." * But "et" in Latin, like "καὶ" in Greek, signifies both *and* and *also;* further, it is the same whether I say, "*as well*

[109] Cf., on this question, Ballerini de vi ac ratione Primatûs, t. ii., pp. 59-61. Gerdil, Animadv. in Com. Febronii posit. 11. Opera xiii., II. 11. Bennettis, P. i., t. i., p. 486, *seq.* Beidtel's Can. Law, p. 395, n. f.

* The undeniably true reading is that of "*etiam.*" This has been victoriously proved by Mamachi and Zaccaria. But the editor of the *Civiltà* has found three codices in the Vatican library, all of the 15th century. Two have "etiam" in full, and one "et" with a stroke of abbreviation, such as ēt. In the Archives of the Vatican Basilica he found one of the *originals* of the Decree of Union. This codex, too, has "etiam" in full. It bears the signatures of the Pope Eugenius IV., and of the Greek emperor, John Palæologus. It is divided into two columns, Greek and Latin. Just as the "etiam" is to be read here, so is it also to be read in the other original exemplars preserved at Florence, Bologna, and Paris, as may be seen in Schelstrate, in the preface to his treatise on the Council of Constance. With respect to Florence, the Canon Cecconi wrote to the editor of the *Civiltà Cattolica,* that, in the Laurentian Library of that city is preserved the first and most precious of the five originals of the Decree of Union. This has not only the signatures of the Pope and of the Emperor, but those of all the Fathers, Greek and Latin, present at the Council. Now in this, the most authoritative of all the originals, the "Quemadmodum etiam" is written at full length. In five most ancient copies of the Decrees preserved at Florence, Canon Cecconi writes that the "etiam" is also found. In a few more recent codices, and in some printed copies "et" is to be read instead of "etiam." But this may be easily accounted for by copyists leaving out the mark of abbreviation, and writing "et" instead of "ēt." Mr Foulkes declares that in the codex in the British Museum also "etiam" is to be read. The Gallican Mgr. Maret admits that in the Greek version the "καὶ" may have the signification of "etiam," because in the second member of the sentence the particle "ἐν" has been omitted. These observations have been abridged from the translation of the article of the *Civiltà Cattolica,* well executed by the "Vatican," and inserted in the present number of the *Dublin Review,* June 1870, pp. 518-20. There had been also a good article on this subject in a previous number of the *Westminster Gazette.*—Trans.

in the acts of Œcumenical Councils, *as* in the Sacred Canons;" or, "in the acts of Councils, *and* in the Sacred Canons." Moreover, ancient manuscripts [110] and witnesses have "etiam," though Biondo and the theologians following him have "et." The words "*juxta eum modum qui*"—a reading so much desired by the Gallicans—is nowhere found; but everywhere stands "*quemadmodum*." But if the Council had wished to say, that the Primacy was to be exercised only in the way prescribed by Councils and the Canons, then the decree would have involved a self-contradiction. For the plenitude of power, which had been imparted by Christ himself, cannot be limited by any human authority; it would then be no more the full power over all Christians; and if the Pope has the full power to feed, to guide, and to govern the whole Church, then he has the power over Councils also, which form but the representation of this universal Church. Further, by such a limitation, a wide field would have been opened to controversy; Eugenius IV. would not, too, in his then position have yielded in this matter to the Greeks, any more than to the Assembly of Basle. If even it can be granted, that in the words in question the Greeks might find a restriction, it certainly was not in the intentions of Eugenius IV. and of his advisers, as well as of the Latin theologians,

---

[110] Bennettis (*loc. cit.*, p. 487) enumerates five MSS. Janus (p. 325, note 2) finds all the copies, except the British, in which the words touching the primacy over the whole Church are wanting, extremely suspicious, for no original is extant. But of how few synods do we possess still the original acts! Janus even conjectures that there was an interpolation in the Greek text. But to this supposition are opposed the arguments in Joseph Methon (Migne clix., p. 1309); Card. Bessarions's Encyclical to the Greeks (*ibid.*, clxi., p. 465, *seq.* 480), nay, the Encyclical Epistle of Mark of Ephesus (*ibid.*, clx., p. 200).

especially Turrecremata, a leading witness. We know not for certain who composed the Decree of Union; it was probably the Camaldulese Abbot, Ambrosius Traversari, who, according to Syropulos, was best versed in the Greek learning.[111]

Of the preceding transactions we know the following results. The Greeks had acknowledged that the Pope should have all those privileges which he possessed from the beginning, and before the schism. Eugenius IV. demanded a further concession that, by virtue of the plenitude of his power, the Pope had been able to annex the words "*filioque*" to the creed. To this the Greeks were unwilling to assent; several of the best Latin theologians illustrated the question by many passages, for the most part genuine, and by no means " with a mass of forged or corrupted passages, derived from pseudo-Isidore and Gratian " (p. 323). Lastly, the question, respecting the right of the Pope to make the addition, was left untouched. The Greeks wished to concede the primacy under two limitations—first, that without the emperor and the patriarchs the Pope could convoke no Œcumenical Councils; but if they did not appear, he could hold them; and, secondly, he could receive no appeals from the patriarchs, nor summon these before his tribunal, but, at most, send judges into the province, and let the question be there decided. Eugenius with great decision replied, that he wished to maintain, unabridged, all his privileges, and would subtract nothing from them ; that he possessed the full power to feed and to govern the whole Church. On the 26th June the Greeks thus formulized their views : " We confess that the Pope is the highpriest and supreme governor, vicegerent and vicar

[111] Syropul. vera hist. ed. Creyghton, 1660, p. 81. Hefele, in the *Theological Quarterly Review* of Tübingen, p. 249, 1847.

of Christ, shepherd and teacher of all Christians, in order to guide and to rule the Church of God, without prejudice to the privileges and rights of the oriental patriarchs; that the patriarch of Constantinople is the second after him, and so forth." The Pope now permitted the draft of union to be drawn up. In this the Greeks were displeased with the formula of the introduction, "Eugenius, bishop, and so forth," as well as the clause that the Pope possessed his privileges "according to the determination of Scripture and the sentences of the saints;" they wished the words, "according to the purport of the canons," to be substituted. Cardinal Julian defended the first form; the Greeks at last conceded that the Pope possessed his privileges according to the canons, the sentences of the saints, holy writ, and the acts of councils. After the Greeks in the clause, "saving the rights of the oriental patriarchs," had added the word "*omnibus*" to "juribus," the fathers of the council, on the 5th July 1439, subscribed the Decree of Union."[112]

As now in the words, "that to the Pope, in the person of St Peter, full power to feed, to rule, and to administer the whole Church was given by Christ," the reference to the Scripture texts in Matthew and John was sufficiently contained; it was not especially necessary to insert the words "the sentences of the saints," which had occurred to the Greeks as redundant; and so the Latin composers of the decree were satisfied with the additional clause, "as is *also* contained in the acts of general councils, and in the sacred canons."[113] So did the Latins understand the decree, whether they

---

[112] Cf. Natal. Alex. HE. Saec. xv. et xvi. Diss. viii., art. 4, n. 12. Diss. x., art. 2, n. 12, *seq.* Bennettis, *loc. cit.*, p. 281, *seq.* Hefele, *loc. cit.*, p. 245, *seq.*

[113] So Hefele also, *loc. cit.*, p. 254.

wrote "*et*" or "*etiam;*" so did the united Greeks also.[114]

Yet the Roman forgeries are, for Janus, by no means exhausted ; they go down, according to him, to Bellarmine [115] and Baronius, who have been hitherto looked on as princes of Catholic theology (p. 394). However, I begin to fear my readers will lose all patience in following me through the labyrinthine paths of Janus, especially as I should have to speak only of less interesting forgeries in the breviary, in the martyrology, and the like. I shall, therefore, only take the liberty of stating, that it must appear as a monstrous assumption, when our author asserts that *all* those who still, in the sixteenth and seventeenth centuries, sought to defend the spurious Decretals, wished designedly to promote fraud ; and that one of these, the Jesuit Turrianus, strove to aid the Roman system by new patristic fabrications, as he appealed to manuscripts which no human eye had ever seen (p. 401). However, if Turrianus, like many of his cotemporaries, omitted to cite his manuscripts, so several of these were afterwards discovered, and the character of the much-reviled Jesuit was in several respects vindicated. To him we are indebted, for example, for the first notices upon the canons of a so-called synod of the Apostles at Antioch. Tillemont and Natalis Alexander believed this account to be a

---

[114] Joseph Methon pro Conc. Flor., P. V., § 3 : οἱ δὲ ἅγιοι κ. τ. λ. "The saints and the Acts of Œcumenical Councils confirm this in the clearest manner," p. 316, ed. Migne.

[115] Bellarmine appears to our Janus as dishonest (p. 394). If he sometimes uses pseudo-Isidore, then again ventures not to assert the undoubted genuineness of the decretals, and expresses himself at different times in a vacillating manner, so it is no longer possible to regard him as sincere. But how many scholars have oftener changed their views, and have later brought forward as very problematical, what they had previously asserted in an affirmative and dogmatic tone?

fraud; but in our age these canons were found in valuable manuscripts at Munich, Paris, Rome, and Florence;[116] and herein the calumniated man received his complete justification. The defence of the pseudo-Areopagitic writings, which the Greek Fathers, like Maximus, so highly esteemed, can truly not be alleged against the Jesuits, who neither alone, nor as a body, stood up for their genuineness.

If all the supposititious writings and interpolations of texts current among the Greeks, who at an early period were reproached with a passion for these fabrications,[117] and, further, if all the writings forged to the prejudice of the Apostolic See, as, for example, the privilege pretended to be granted by Pope Adrian I. to Charlemagne, respecting the appointment to bishoprics and to the See of Rome, and which even Gratian admitted into his collection,[118] as well as other false documents brought out in the contest of investitures,[119] and the multitude of spurious papal bulls which were fabricated like a regular manufacture, and provoked special laws;[120] if all these fabrications, we say, and upon which alone a whole book might be written, had been attended to by our author, the chapter on

[116] Bickell's "History of Canon Law," vol. i., pp. 102, 242. Giessen, 1843. Pitra *op. cit.*, t. i., p. 89.

[117] We might here remind the reader of the false letters of Pope Vigilius, and of other supposititious documents brought forward in the sixth council, of the narrative of Anastasius the Sinaite (Hodeg. c. 10, Migne lxxxix., p. 184, *seq.*), respecting the forgeries carried on on a large scale in Alexandria after the death of Eulogius, of the words of Anastasius the librarian (Præf. in Conc. viii. Mansi xvi., p. 12), as well as of the words of Pope Nicholas I. (ep. 9): Quoniam sicut nonnullæ diversi temporis Scripturæ testantur, familiaris est ista temeritas.

[118] C. 22, dist. 63. This Gratian admitted; he did not suppress the passages respecting councils (Dist. 18).

[119] Hefele, iii., p. 579.

[120] Neander's "History of the Church," ii., p. 442, *seq.*, 3d ed.

forgeries would have been a very instructive one.
How much the popes were sinned against, and
particularly Boniface VIII., to whom a false pro-
fession of faith was ascribed :[121]—all this must be
taken into account by an impartial historical in-
quirer; and not only so, but the judgments of all
eminent contemporaries, the ideas ruling each age,
the state of general intellectual culture, must not
be left out of consideration. But by the process
adopted nothing is gained; we must advance still
much farther. In order fully to prove the theses
set forth, we must reject all the papal briefs from
the year 385 to 845, acknowledged as undoubtedly
genuine by Catholic and Protestant historians, even
of recent times; nay, we must subvert all ecclesiastical history, and make a *tabula rasa* of the
history of the first thousand years of the Church,
and institute a critical process, such as F. Baur,
Schwegler, Bruno Bauer, and others have pursued
in regard to the primitive and sacred records of
Christianity. Then when all testimonies are rejected, we can set forth any favourite system; but
history we no more can write. We can, indeed,
indulge ourselves in fictions, without, however,
being dexterous enough to fasten upon the past
forgeries, which were not long since proved by
others.

[121] Bennettis, P. ii., t. v., p. 238, *seq*.

CHAPTER IX.

A GLANCE AT COUNCILS.

WE advance a step farther. Presupposing the justness of the method followed by Janus, and treating after this model extant testimonies, we might completely annihilate the authority of Councils. It could be shown in the same way, that the records of antiquity furnish far weaker proofs for them than for the Papal supremacy. Janus says indeed (p. 421): "It is commonly taught in theological manuals, schools, and systems, that the Councils of the Church are not only useful, but even *necessary*." This necessity, however, was never understood as an absolute, but only as a relative one;[1] for, according to universal consent, the dispersed Church with its Head suffices to settle and to decide all controversies. Janus himself cannot establish the absolute necessity of Councils, for, according to his own principles, the ultimate decision rests in the consent of all the faithful (p. 411). The Church in

[1] Duval de supr. Rom. Pont. potest, P. lv., q. 1. Bellarmin. de Conc. i., 10. Kilber, Theol. Wirceb., t. i. Principia Theol. Disp. ii., c. 2, art. 1, p. 206. Phillips' Can. Law, ii., § 83, p. 226. Manual, p. 470, *seq.* Schulte, System of Can. Law, p. 347. Beidtel, Can. Law, p. 408, *seq.* Against Febronius (de statu Eccl. c. 6, 7). Augustine also (ad Bonif., L. iv., c. ult.) may be cited. On the Paris Faculty, see Bennettis, P. i., t. ii., p. 677, *seq.*; 680, *seq.*

A Glance at Councils. 187

her totality is, according to this great teacher, secured against false doctrines. At the Council the bishops attest, each for the portion of the Church known to him, that a special doctrine has there been hitherto taught and believed. Or they attest, that in the doctrines hitherto believed, a truth, though not yet expressly formulized, is with inevitable necessity there contained as a logical consequence. "Thereupon, whether this testimony hath been rightly deposed, whether freedom and truthfulness and impartiality have reigned among the bishops of the synod, thereupon the Church again, which adopts or rejects the council or its decree, *decides in the ultimate instance.*" The consent of all believers must be proved; the final decision is thus placed in the hands of individuals, or at least of the majority. But why then assemble a Council that costs so much time and money, as all entitled to a vote can never meet together in one place? Would it not be far better to vote at once in local assemblies, and to promulgate the decrees by addresses, which the newspapers could give further publicity to? And if we still will have Councils, why not establish them in every parish? Nay, the bishops are no more judges, no more chief shepherds set by the Holy Ghost to rule the Church of God, but merely deputies to be judged by the faithful, and whose authority receives its last sanction from their subordinates. Quite as well, and perhaps still better than bishops, scholars and particularly professors and *literati*, could meet to represent their particular Churches, and furnish a testimony of their faith. Nay, public opinion, which we are told gave in the fifteenth century such weight and authority to the Councils of Constance and Basle, as well as their lasting influence on the condition of the Church (p. 28), is decidedly represented to-day by *literati*, like Janus, and by political newspapers, like the *Allgemeine Zeitung* of Augsburg. Should the Church even dissolve into particles and fragments, and its whole constitution be heaved from its foundations, so much the better!

Yet we overlook all the contradictions in this theory. Against an absolute necessity of General Councils, the fact that in the first three centuries of the Church none such were held, already speaks decisively;[2] and certainly an essential and indispensable element in her constitution they are not. Of the provincial Councils of that primitive period but few traces have been preserved. The African Synods, whereof we possess the most knowledge, sanctioned, in reference to the re-baptism of heretics, an erroneous doctrine; and the first Spanish Council known to us, that of Elvira, inculcated a harsh rigorism. It was only after long and arduous struggles the first General Council of Nicæa obtained undisputed recognition. Many anti-synods were held; the imperial terrorism of a Constantius appeared in the foreground. St Gregory Nazianzen[3] expressed himself very bitterly against the synods of his time, filled as he was with indignation at the ambition of the Eastern bishops, and which afterwards displayed itself in even more glaring colours. The second General Council was for sixty years after it had been held, not yet generally received among the Greeks;[4] and among

---

[2] Did Janus forget this, when (p. 421) he writes that in former times there was *no example* "that three centuries had passed away without an earnest desire for an Œcumenical Council making itself anywhere heard?" A desire, however, might certainly exist without the possibility of its being carried into effect: but loudly expressed that desire certainly has not been.

[3] Ep. 55, ad Procop. al. 130.

[4] Hefele, Conc. ii. 30.

A Glance at Councils.

the Westerns still later: and it was only after the Canons of Ephesus and Chalcedon, its own were received into the collections of law.[5] The authority of the Council of Ephesus was for several years disputed in the Patriarchate of Antioch.[6] The bishops Eutherius of Tyana, Helladius of Tarsus, and prelates of other provinces, requested of Pope Sixtus III. to undertake a revision of its decrees, and so save the world, as Pope Damasus had once saved it from the Apollinarian error.[7] Without Pope Leo the Great, the Latrocinium of Ephesus, which the Emperor Theodosius II. had confirmed, would have obtained in the East undoubted authority; whereas the Synod of the Oak of the year 403, like to the one just named, was in fact crowned with a success to which the innocent Chrysostom fell a victim. The Synod of Chalcedon found in the Patriarchates of Alexandria and Antioch numerous and decided opponents, led to much bloodshed, and presented an image of Byzantine ambition at its close, as it had of tumult and of licence on the part of the Egyptian Prelates at its beginning.[8] The fifth Council would not have been held without the authority of the Emperor Justinian; it produced manifold divisions and new disorders: those who had risen against Pope Vigilius and his successors on account of his condemnation of the Three Chapters, rose up in

[5] Ballerini de ant. canon. collect., P. i., c. 2, n. 3.
[6] Hefele, *loc. cit.*, p. 231, *seq*.
[7] Coustant, p. 1245, *seq*.—n. 2, p. 1246, n. 8, p. 1249, n. 12, p. 1252 : Sanctis tuæ religiositatis provolvimur pedibus, ut manum porrigas salutarem et auferas mundi naufragium omnemque horum inquisitionem jubeas fieri et his illicitis cœlestem superduci correctionem, n. 14, p. 1253 : Quæsumus igitur, ut absque dilatione exsurgatis et fervido zelo magnum victoriae trophæum contra æmulorum cuneos erigatis, ante oculos habeutes boni pastoris diligentiam simul et studium circa ovem, quæ erraverat.
[8] Neander's Church History, I., 704, 709, 805, *seq*. Third Ed.

like manner against this fifth Council. How many falsified texts of the Fathers came to light in the sixth General Council; what flattery towards an unworthy emperor, what petty jealousy, too, towards all non-Byzantines was displayed in the Council in Trullo, assembled in the year 692![9] What trifling arguments did the bishops of the second Nicene Council adduce, and whose decrees Pope Adrian I. so courageously defended against the Franks! The objections which are raised against this Pope on account of the Synod of Frankfort, the Caroline Books, and the Council of Paris, held in the year 824 (p. 80, 81, in German), fall more heavily still on the seventh General Council, which the Pontiff undoubtedly defended against the Franks, misled as they were by a very bad translation of the Acts; while he still, even in the year 794, had sent into the East no formal confirmation of that Council;[10] so that the Studites, who were strongly attached to Rome, doubted of the legitimacy and of the œcumenical character of that Council.[11] If it deserves all praise that Adrian preferred the course of calm inquiry, and made no use of his authority which could not even be disputed, we can, on the other hand, scarcely bestow a like praise on the prudence and the tact of those Western Synods.[12] But as the seventh Council of 787 set aside the Iconoclast Synod of 754; so in the East itself it was again assailed after 815, and then rejected, and only in the year 842 was it restored to the honours of full recognition. The eighth General Council of 869, for a long time not accounted one in the West, was in the East after ten years completely set

---

[9] Neander's Church History, I., 722, II., 106, 117, *seq.*, 306.
[10] Hadrian, I., ep. ad Carol. Jaffé, n. 1902; Nos adhuc pro eadem synodo nullum responsum hactenus Imperatori reddidimus.
[11] Theod. Stud., L. I., ep. 38, p. 1044, *seq.*
[12] Bennettis, P. I., t. i., p. 224.

aside, nay anathematized; and all attempts to bring the Greeks back to its recognition utterly failed.[13]

With these and such like facts it were easy to reduce the importance of Councils still lower, than Janus has done in regard to the Papal Primacy. The first eight General Councils, all held in the East, stand high in the estimation of our authors. They fail to show that the participation of the patriarchs of Alexandria, Antioch, and Jerusalem, in the two last of those synods, is subject to grave doubt;[14] and that their recognition in the West is due solely and entirely to the See of Rome. This silence on the part of our authors is, from their general tendency of mind, not to be wondered at ; but it is a matter of greater surprise that these eight Œcumenical Synods of the East, including the interpolated Quinisext, should find favour in their eyes, although they were not held according to that ideal, which our doctors regard as that of a Council truly œcumenical.

A severe criticism on the subsequent Synods of the West, a malicious satirist could draw from the pages of Janus. For many centuries, namely, from the eleventh to the beginning of the fifteenth century, the history of Councils would appear in the saddest light. " Not only were Councils to be made dependent (on the Popes), but the institution itself, as it existed for 900 years, was to be abolished" (p. 118). " The Synods of particular national churches were to be put an end to" (*ibid.*) National Councils, and those of particular countries, had not indeed existed for 900 years. Provincial Synods were that form of Councils that bore most

---

[13] Neander, *op. cit.*, II., 291, *seq.*, 302, 313, 317.
[14] Neander II., 316.

decidedly a legal stamp;[15] real national Synods sprang up much later, and soon degenerated into instruments of political despotism. But Gregory VII., we are told (p. 109 German), wished that *only* popes or their legates should hold Synods; otherwise the institution should disappear from the Church. That the latter event lay in the intentions of the Pope is in no way proved; the former allegation is equally destitute of proof. If Gregory wished Synods to be held under the presidency of his legates, he was induced as well as entitled to do so from the corruption of many bishops, and from the circumstances of the times.

Of the General Councils held in the West, we first meet with the first great Lateran Synod of 1123, which confirmed the Concordat of Worms. Janus finds the fact very significant (p. 190), that twice as many abbots as bishops took part therein. But that in the Council of 787, the Greek Archimandrites played a very important part,[16] and later a still more important one, is a fact totally disregarded. Our authors assert that "*no contemporary* tells us anything of this first General Assembly of the West" (p. 191): so not even Suger, abbot of St Denis, appears to be counted among these contemporaries.[17] It appears especially revolting to Janus that the Pope made and promulgated the laws in his own name; but it was the first General Council at which a Pope presided in his own person; in the following Synods the like was observed under the like circumstances, and the Decrees were promulgated by the Pope with the formula, *sacro approbante Concilio;* and this was

---

[15] Conc., Nic. i., c. 5; Antioch., c. 20; Trull., c. 8; Nic. ii., c. 6.
[16] Hefele, Conc. iii., 428.
[17] Hefele, v., 339, *seq.*

A Glance at Councils.

partly done, even at the Council of Constance.[18] This formula by no means points to a superiority of the Council over the Pope;[19] it speaks much more for the reverse.[20] The acts of this Synod we certainly do not possess, but we cannot thence infer that no deliberations took place; but thus much we see from the Chronicle of Monte Cassino, that the disputes between the bishops and the monks led to warm discussions.[21] Even of the tenth Œcumenical Council, held in the year 1139 under Innocent II., we have only some special notices and thirty canons. The bishops, we are told, "appeared only as passive witnesses to hear the Pope's lofty commands (p. 191); nay, the Synod was an accomplice in the error of the Pope relative to Orders (p. 300, German). More serious and eventful, according to Janus (p. 191), was the eleventh Œcumenical Council of 1179, whose twenty-seven canons are, in part, of very high importance; but of this Council no deliberations are extant. The three sessions occurred between the 5th and 19th days of March 1179[22] (not even "three weeks!") The decrees were promulgated by Alexander III., *sacro approbante Concilio;* and that no one then took the slightest offence therefrom, Janus himself attests. We now come to the fourth Lateran Council of the year 1215. "A free deliberation in the presence of an Innocent III. was not to be thought of" (p. 192). Important as are the decrees of this twelfth Œcumenical Council in respect to dogma and to discipline,[23] it is yet

---

[18] Hefele's Conc. I., p. 61.
[19] Defensio declarat. Cleri. Gall. P. ii., L. xii., c. 34, L. ix. c. 31.
[20] Bennettis, t. i., P. i., p. 265, *seq.*
[21] Hefele V., p. 343, *seq.*
[22] *Ibid.*, p. 632.
[23] *Ibid.*, p. 783, *seq.*

condemned as quite unfree. "From the standpoint of the Popes of that time, the only business of bishops at a Council must be to inform the Pope of the condition of their dioceses, to give him their advice, and form a picturesque background for the solemn promulgation of his decrees" (p. 192). "Innocent had his Decrees read to them, and after listening in silence, they were allowed to give their assent" (p. 192).

Quite as the prophet had announced for 1869, so the historian recounts for 1215. On the authority of the by no means always veracious Matthew Paris, it is asserted "that the Pope when the bishops wished to return home forbade them, until they had paid him large sums of money, which they had to borrow at high interest from the brokers of the Papal Court" (p. 193). The purpose for which the Pope desired this money is passed over in total silence; the funds were for a Crusade, then considered as the common concern of Christendom, and which the Pope fitted out at great personal sacrifices. Innocent himself contributed £30,000 to this expedition; all clerics were, for three years, to contribute one-twentieth of their incomes, the Pope and the Cardinals one-tenth.[24]

The first Council of Lyons, held in the year 1245, is hated on account of its decision respecting the Emperor Frederick II., and in the opinion of Janus, it is not œcumenical (p. 193, n. 2). Pope Innocent IV., it is said, summoned only some selected prelates and the King of France; but this assertion, indeed, is far from proved.[25] Supposing that, in regard to its convocation, the Council had not been œcumenical, it could still become so by its celebration and confirmation—

---

[24] Hefele V., p. 805.   [25] *Ibid.*, p. 972.

A Glance at Councils. 195

"celebratione et confirmatione." That Innocent avoided calling it œcumenical is false; in the Decrees themselves the name "holy and general Synod" occurs;[26] it was only Frederick II. who appealed to a "Council truly œcumenical;"[27] and the Gallicans themselves recognised the œcumenicity of this Synod.[28] The second Council of Lyons, held in 1274, is somewhat more leniently treated, as well as Pope Gregory also, "who, in despite of his good will, was unable to restore the old forms of Councils" (p. 194). The Pope then was not quite so all-powerful! The Council of Vienne, celebrated about the year 1311, is also declared not to have been œcumenical; as only bishops chosen out by Pope Clement V. were admitted. But this assertion, even from the number of prelates that appeared, is quite untrue;[29] and in this case, too, the Pope could not have inflicted blame and punishment on the bishops who, without any good grounds, had not obeyed his summons.[30]

As to what Janus recounts of the third and last Session, in which Pope Clement V., before the promulgation of the sentence on the Templars, imposed complete silence on the bishops; this cannot be established after an accurate statement of the proceedings.[31] But after the great schism in the Papacy, which broke out in the year 1378, "a different spirit and different principles prevailed, at the fifteenth century Councils of Pisa, Constance, and Basle, for the preponderance of Italian bishops

---

[26] Hefele V., p. 966, c. 17.
[27] *Ibid.*, p. 1000.
[28] Bennettis, P. i., t. i., pp. 285–291. Cf. Nat. Alex. Sæc. xiii., et xiv. Dissert. V.
[29] Hefele VI., p. 460, *seq.*
[30] *Ibid.*, p. 487. Cf. I., p. 51, *seq.*
[31] *Ibid.*, p. 463, *seq.*, especially 470, n. 1.

was broken by new regulations" (p. 197). Here, indeed, *innovations* were permitted ; but they were not in favour of, but against, the Papacy. The voting by nations was utterly contrary to the spirit of the ancient Councils, and was supported by no ecclesiastical tradition ; but the advocates of the " primitive episcopal system "[32] were pleased with this innovation ; all means they considered lawful against the " gigantic power of the Papacy." Quite certain it is that this forty years' schism in the Popedom shook the Pontifical power, till then deemed invincible (p. 292) ; that the French and the Italians were here engaged in a struggle for the possession of the supreme ecclesiastical dignity, and that contemporaries wavered about the question of right (p. 295)—a question indeed on which political and national interests exerted a strong influence. The struggle of the Hohenstaufens against the Church had led the Popes to attach themselves more and more to the crown of France; the residence of the Pontiffs in Avignon essentially contributed towards the subsequent schism ; and this schism inflicted very deep injury on the Roman See in the eyes of the world, as well as greatly impeded its action. The election of Urban VI. must, especially when we consider the earlier recognition of the cardinals, be considered as valid.[33] On examination of the question of right, Clement VII. can appear only as an anti-Pope, and Urban's successor, hence also Gregory XII. must be regarded as the legitimate Pope.[34] The Council of Pisa in 1409 but aggra-

[32] On the writers of that time, *vide* Bennettis, *loc. cit.*, p. 303, *seq.*
[33] Hefele VI., p. 653, *seq.*
[34] Ballerini de potest. Eccl., p. 135, n. 4, Raynaldus, anno 1409. Phillips' Can. Law, I., § 31, p. 253.

A Glance at Councils.

vated the schism; its whole mode of proceeding was utterly unbecoming,[35] and even Janus can only boast of it, that it was "a Synod assembled from all Europe, at which men could dare to speak openly and vote freely" (p. 297). Three Popes were present at this Synod—Gregory XII., the successor of Urban VI., Benedict XIII., the successor of the anti-Pope Clement VII., and the newly-elected Pontiff, Alexander V., who was soon succeeded by Balthasar Cossa, under the name of John XXIII. The latter presided at its commencement over the Council summoned to Constance. After his flight this Council issued the celebrated Decree on the superiority of the Council over the Pope; "a decision," says Janus, "more eventful and pregnant in future consequences than had been arrived at by any previous Council, and accordant in principle with primitive antiquity—for so the Church held before the appearance of the pseudo-Isidore (p. 300);—perhaps the most extraordinary event in the whole dogmatic history of the Christian Church" (p. 302).

But this Decree never obtained legal force.[36] It had emanated from a headless Assembly, which could constitute no Œcumenical Council, without the concurrence of any one of the Popes, of whom one at least was legitimate; it was a make-shift in a state of confusion, an arbitrary act of violence. Never has it received any Papal confirmation, neither from Martin V. nor from Eugenius IV. Janus indeed asserts: "an express confirmation of this Decree by Martin V. seemed at the time not only superfluous, but objectionable. It would have

---

[35] Hefele I. 52, *seq.*, VI., 902. Phillips, *loc. cit.*, p. 254.
[36] Bennettis, P. I., t. I., p. 377. Ballerini de pot. Eccles., c. 7, p. 101. Schelstrate de sensu et auctor. decret. Conc. Constant. Romæ 1686.

been like a son wanting to attest the genuine paternity of his own father, for this Decree had made him Pope. Had he wished to assail its validity in any way, he would have been bound at once to resign, and let the deposed Pope again take his place" (p. 305). But hereby the legitimacy of the Synod of Pisa, and of the Pope elected by it, is falsely pre-supposed as undoubted. Gregory XII., the legitimate Pope, had solemnly abdicated without confirming that Decree; John XXIII. was deposed by the same authority which had elevated him, in the person of his predecessor Alexander V., and, moreover, he had completely submitted on the 26th and 31st May 1415, to the ordinances of the Council of Constance;[37] Benedict XIII., confined to a small obedience, had been deposed on the 26th July 1417, and this deposition was, with the exception of a small handful, ratified in the whole Church. Accordingly, the Papal chair was vacant, and Martin V. owed his election, which occurred on the 11th November 1417, by no means solely to "the new Decree, or to the Episcopal system." Martin V. afterwards declared that he approved what had been decreed "conciliariter in materiis Fidei, et non aliter, nec alio modo"—what had been decreed "according to the forms of a Council in matters of faith, and not otherwise, nor in any other manner." From Pierre D'Ailly we know[38] that the Decree in question had not been framed "conciliariter," because it was passed without the concurrence of the Cardinals, and merely

---

[37] Hefele VII., 137, 141.
[38] Tract de auctorit. Ecclesiæ, 1416, Gerson. opp. II. 940 : Quæ deliberatio (quatuor nationum), *exclusa* deliberatione dicti Collegii (Cardinalium), et non facta in communi sessione collatione votorum, videtur multis non esse censenda deliberatio Concilii generalis conciliariter facta. That the Cardinals did not concur in this decree is shown by Bennettis, l. c., p. 399.

A Glance at Councils.

by a majority of votes according to nations.[39] Still less can a Papal confirmation be deduced from the Decrees respecting the heresy of Wickliffe (p. 305).[40] On the other hand, Martin's constitution of the 10th March 1418, which forbade an appeal from the Apostolic See, completely overthrew, as Gerson himself very well saw, these new fundamental rights.[41]

At the Synod of Basle—an Assembly, which degenerated into a stigmatised Conciliabulum, and brought a new schism upon the Church,[42] and of which even Janus himself timidly admits, "that it had some weak points" (p. 316),—the Decrees of Constance were renewed with much ostentation, but with equal ill success. The recognition of Eugenius IV. was conditional; the clause "without prejudice to the right, the dignity, and the pre-eminence of the Apostolic See," is here decisive;[43] and, moreover, the definition of the Council of Florence on the Primacy is utterly opposed to those Decrees. The assertion, therefore, is com-

---

[39] Schwab Gerson, p. 514, 515. Hefele VII., 104. Phillips' Can. Law, p. 257, iv., § 194, p. 438, *seq*.
[40] Bennettis, P. I., t. I., p. 373, *seq*.
[41] Dialog. apolog. ii. 390. Schwab., *loc. cit.*, p. 665, 666.
[42] The philologer Poggio calls the Assembly of Basle the beginning of all the evils and schisms which we have seen arise in the Church of God. (Or in fun. Cesarini, Card. Mai Spicil. X., I., p. 378). Cf. Pogg. epist., ep. 28, 38, *ib.*, ep. 34. ed. Paris. Augustin. Patric. Summa. Concil. Basil., c. 145 (Hard. IX., 1196).
[43] Bennettis, *loc. cit.*, p. 403, 454, *seq*. Phillips IV., § 195, p. 455, § 196, p. 458. That the Bull "Tanto nos pacem," issued by Nicholas from a love of peace, was a triumph of the principle of the superiority of General Councils to the Pope (as asserted by Janus, pp. 338, 339,) is utterly untrue. The abrogation of the decrees against the Assembly of Basle is nothing less than an approval of the decrees framed by it; it is simply in regard to the parties interested, a bringing back to the *status quo ante*. Cf. Bennettis, pp. 445, 474, *seq.*, and upon the general question Hefele I., p. 54, vii., p. 372.

pletely groundless; "that the foundation of the Decrees of Basle, the dogmatic decisions on the Pope's inferiority to a Council remained untouched" (p. 339); "and that Thomas de Vio or Cajetan it was who, *for the first time*, got the authority of the decisions of Constance and of Basle on the rights of Councils, which had been so solemnly acknowledged and attested by former Popes, to be assailed by Leo X." (p. 374). Has Janus, then, never heard anything of the constitutions of Pope Pius II., dated respectively the 18th January 1459, and the 26th April 1463, as well as that of Julius II. in 1509?[44] Antoninus, Archbishop of Florence, and Cardinal Turrecremata, still energetically defended the old Papal system;[45] while the adherents of the new episcopal system, who had acted too precipitately, were in many ways undeceived. To what, in fact, did the new maxims lead? Some they brought to despair of the Church herself, so that Peter d'Ailly and Jean Courteouisse went to such lengths as to call in question the infallibility of General Councils in matters of faith;[46] and others again they brought round to a reconciliation with the Holy See. This was the case with Cardinal Julian Cesarini, the former president of the Council of Basle, with Æneas Sylvius Piccolomini, afterwards Pope Pius II.,[47] with Nicholas of

---
[44] Const. Exsecrabilis *and* In minoribus agentes. Bull Rom. ed. nov. Taurin., t. V., pp. 149, 150, 173-180. Const. Julii II., *ib.*, p. 479-481.

[45] S. Antonin. Sum., p. 3, L. XXIII., c. 3, § 3, Joh. de Turrecremata de Eccl. ii. 93. Likewise Thomas Waldensis Doctrin. fidei, L. ii., art. 3, c. 32, Joh. Ferrariens. Lib. c. gent., c. 79.

[46] Mansi XXVII. 547. Schwab., *loc. cit.*, p. 500, 747.

[47] Æneas Sylvius as Pope cites the words of Cesarini, which made so deep an impression on him: "I have returned to the sheepfold, who had so long wandered outside of it; I have heard the voice of the shepherd Eugenius; and if thou art rational, do thou the like."—(Bull of Retractation, § 5.)

A Glance at Councils.

Cusa,[48] with Francis Zabarella, who had formerly advocated, though not in an unqualified manner, the superiority of the Council over the Pope, and who at Constance had approximated more to the Papal system, and afterwards became one of its most ardent defenders.[49] Janus indeed thinks (p. 412), "that a great community has no temptation to establish some particular subjective view or opinion of its own." But the history of the Council of Basle shows the contrary.[50]

Martin V., feeling himself bound, as well by his promise as by the decree "Frequens" of the Council of Constance, accepted by him, summoned a Council first to Pavia and then to Sienna (p. 309). The participation of bishops was really, and not in pretence, a very small one; and even at Basle, that participation was, in respect to the prelates, very insignificant. The scholars and writers there assembled looked only to the humiliation of the Pope; so that, even in Italy, they excited troubles against the pacific Eugenius IV., and sought to withdraw from him all pecuniary resources. The conditions stipulated in 1433 by Eugenius IV., and which Janus (p. 313, *seq.*) passes over, had remained unfulfilled; his pliancy was met with only a greater spirit of defiance. The Council of Basle withdrew from the Pontiff the Annats,[51] and afterwards adjudged them to the anti-Pope, Felix V. Even the union with the Greeks was threatened with failure from the obstinacy of the Assembly of Basle. The deposition of Eugenius

---
[48] Cf. Dr Dux's "Life of Nicholas of Cusa," vol. i., p. 166, *seq*, Scharpff, vol. ii., p. 108.
[49] Bennettis, P. I., t. I., pp. 355, 379, 385.
[50] Döllinger's "Manual of Church History," ii., pp. 355–383.
[51] Hereupon Phillips (in his Can. Law, vol. v., § 237, 238, p. 567, *seq.*) gives some excellent explanations, which may in many ways serve for a rectification of the assertions of Janus.

IV., and the elevation of an anti-Pope, even Janus is obliged to call an act of frightful disorder and arrogance; the number of the members of the Council had melted down considerably, and there remained at last but a mass composed of impure and unauthorized elements (p. 318).

The Council of Florence,[52] consisting almost entirely of Italian bishops, finds with our author little favour.[53] Nearly more dignified and important appears the French Assembly of Bourges, which assembled in 1438, and undertook the "first comprehensive codification of what have since been called the Gallican Liberties" (p. 328); while poor Germany, even before the lapse of nine years, returned to the obedience of Eugenius (p. 331.)

The fifth Lateran Council[54] is in the eyes of our author an abomination. It is called (p. 349) a hole-and-corner Council of sixty-five Italians, as in the fifth Article it had been formerly nicknamed an Italian pocket Council.[55] "That such an assemblage is no representation of the whole Church, that it sounds like a mockery to put it on a par with the Synods of Nicæa, Chalcedon, and Constantinople, is evident to the blindest eye," (p. 197). Still the Decrees promulgated by the Pope were by no means unimportant.

"Leo the Tenth's Bull, 'Pastor Æternus,'[56] enun-

---

[52] Cf. Bennettis, *loc. cit.*, p. 477, *seq.*; Phillips' Can. Law, iii., § 137, p. 390; iv., § 196, p. 457.

[53] Still here "the forms of the ancient Councils and free discussion had to be allowed on account of the Greeks, and the mere dictation and promulgation of decrees previously prepared in the Papal *Curia* had to be abandoned."—(Janus, p. 197.)

[54] Bennettis, *loc. cit.*, p. 494. *seq.* Schmalzgrueber, Jus. eccl. Diss. proœm., § 8, n. 341. Phillips iv., § 196, p. 463.

[55] At p. 197 of Janus, there were only 53 bishops.

[56] Const. 20, also Lib. vii., Decret. c. 3, iii. 7, 19th Dec. 1516.

ciated the full authority and unlimited power of the Pope over all Councils, and proved this by fabricated, distorted, or insignificant facts and testimonies. It was a long deduction, in which every statement would be a lie, if the compiler could be credited with any knowledge of Church History.[57] It closes with the renewal of Boniface VIII.'s Bull, " Unam Sanctam," (p. 198).

A great stumbling-block has this Bull of Boniface VIII. been from of old.[58] Herein " he gave a dogmatic and biblical foundation to the doctrine of the universality of Papal dominion, and condemned the independence of the civil power in its own sphere as Manicheism" (p. 162). But, firstly, in dogmatic Bulls, it is not the premisses and the ulterior arguments, but solely what is proposed as the object of faith, which serves as a standard.[59] Boniface VIII. here only defines, it is necessary to salvation, that every man should submit to the Roman Pontiff;[60] and this is a necessary conse-

---

[57] Whoever reads these words is tempted to believe that Leo X. cited *only* forged documents ; but he cites the words of Pope Damasus on the rejection of the Synod of Rimini (see above c. vii., n. 71), the requests for confirmation made by the fourth and sixth General Councils (*ibid*, n. 67, 68) ; he appeals to the letters of Pope Leo the Great to the bishops of Sicily (ep. 16, c. 7, p. 724, ed. Baller.), where, among other things, it is said : cum coram Beatissimo Apostolo Petro id semper in commune tractandum sit, ut omnia ipsius constituta canonumque decreta apud omnes Domini sacerdotes inviolata permaneant. He appeals to the veneration manifested by the eighth General Council towards Pope Adrian II., where we have the testimony in the 21st canon, according to the Latins, and the 14th, according to the Greeks (Mansi xvi., 174, 405), as well as in the request for confirmation addressed to the Pope (*ibid*, pp. 202, 413.)

[58] C. 1. de M. et O. J. 8 in. Extravagg, com. Raynald, a. 1302. n. 13. *seq.*

[59] Bianchi, *op. cit.*, t. ii.. L. vi., § 7, n. 7, p. 518, *seq.* Gosselin, *op. cit.* ii., p. 265, 293, *seq.* Edition of Münster, Beidtel's Canon Law, p. 368, note

[60] Porro subesse Romano Pontifici omnem humanam creaturam,

quence of the dogma of the Papal Supremacy, and is acknowledged by the Gallicans themselves as perfectly true.[61] Secondly, it is not the assertion, that the secular power is independent of the spiritual *in its own sphere*, and, consequently, in temporals, against which the Bull protests; but it is the assertion of its absolute independence in regard to ecclesiastical authority, even in those cases where there is a question of sin, and where the salvation of souls and church property are in question, that the Pope here condemns.[62] This is shown not merely by the other declarations of the Pope and of the Cardinals,[63] but by the purport of the Bull itself, drawn, for the most part, from the writings of the most eminent theologians. The special occasion of this Bull was the conduct pursued by Philip the Fair, who, even in spiritual matters, refused submission to the Pontiff, and prevented the French bishops from practising their obedience; but the Bull meant also to show, in general terms, and without special reference to France, that the temporal power of Christian princes does not exempt them from obedience to the Head of the Church.[64] The train of thought is as follows :—The Church of God is essentially one, a mystical body. This body has but one head, and not

---

declaramus, dicimus, definimus et pronuntiamus omnino esse de necessitate salutis (according to Thom. Aqu. opusc. c. Graec.)

[61] Defensio declar. Cleri Gall, t. i., P. ii., L. vii. (al. iii.), c. 24, p. 290, where it is said Boniface, by general expressions, has seemed to prepare the way for the assertion that every species of power is subject to the Papal, even in secular things. Yet he has restricted the proposition to submission in general, quod verissimum est., si de spirituali potestate intelligatur.

[62] Bianchi, *loc. cit.*, p. 519. Walter's Can. Law, § 45, n. 12. Phillips' Can. Law, iii., § 130, p. 256.

[63] To this Fenelon also refers in his work, de Summi Pontificis auctorit, c. 27, t. ii., p. 333, ed. Versailles.

[64] Bianchi, *loc. cit.*, pp. 519, 520.

two, like a monster. This Head is Christ, and His vicar; Peter and his successors. All the sheep of the Lord, Peter must feed; he who separates himself from his obedience belongs not to the fold of Christ.[65] There exists now in the Church (considered as the sum-total of clergy and laity—and consequently in Christendom), two powers; the spiritual and the temporal, prefigured by the two swords of Peter. The material sword is drawn *for* the Church, the spiritual *by* the Church; the former by the hand of the king, the latter by the hand of the priest; the material sword must co-operate with the spiritual and assist it. So had already spoken St Bernard, so the Emperor Frederic II., and many others:[66] and that the secular power should be guided by the spiritual as the higher, was an old Christian idea.[67] In so far now as both powers are in the Church, they both have the same object. But as both are established by God, and God has ordained all things well, so between the two authorities there must be a well-defined subordination of rank—one sword set under the other. As now the spiritual has the pre-eminence over the material, so the temporal power is subordinated to the ecclesiastical, as to the higher. Hence the inference deduced by Hugo of St Victor,[68] that the temporal

---

[65] S. Bernard, de consid. ii. 8.

[66] Bern. l. c. iv. 3 ep. 256. Frider ii. Const. 1220, c. 7. Cf. the "Saxon Mirror," vol. i., art. 1. The "Suabian Mirror," Pref. 21, *seq.* Joh. Saresb. Polycr. iv. 3. Hildeb. Cenom. ep. ii. 18. Petr. Dam. ep. vi. 4. Gerhoch Reich. de corrupto, eccl. statu, c. 3. Innoc. III. (Janus, p. 171.)

[67] Testament xii. Patriarch. Test. iv. Jud. c. 21 (Cf. "Neander's Church History," i. 201.) Constit. Apost. ii. 34. Chrys. hom. 15 in 2 Cor. : hom. 34 in Hebr., n. 1. Isidor. Pelus L. III. ep. 244. Naz., Or 17, p. 217 ed. Bill. Stephan. vi. ep. ad Basil, Imp. (Mansi xvi. 421). Ivo Carnot, ep. 51, ad Henric., Angliæ Reg. Hugo a S. Victore de sacram fid. L. ii., P. ii., c. 4. Alex. Halens, p. 3, q. 10 membr. 2, S. Thom. sum. 2, 2, q., 60, a. 6, ad. 3.

[68] Hugo, *loc. cit.*

power, if it is not good, is judged by the spiritual, and that to ecclesiastical authority the words of the prophet Jeremiah apply: "Lo! I have set thee this day over the nations and over kingdoms, to root up and to pull down, and to waste, and to destroy, and to build, and to plant"[69] (i. 10.) But these words excite great indignation in the mind of our Janus, who says: "If Jeremiah designates, after the oriental fashion, his prophetic office, and his calling to announce the Divine judgments, as a commission to destroy and to lay waste; so, according to the Papal interpretation, the Pope must be thereby meant, to whom God has imparted the power to root up and to pull down what and whom he will" (p. 379, German). But such an interpretation Boniface VIII. was not the first to give: we find it already in Hugo of St Victor, in St Bernard, in Peter of Blois, in Peter the Venerable of Cluny, in Innocent III.;[70] nay, already in the ninth century, in Pope John VIII.[71] It is not even the Popes who were the first authors of this interpretation. To the ecclesiastical power in general the words were applied by the Council of Meaux, in 845,[72] by Theodotus of Ancyra at the Council of Ephesus,[73] as well as by the Byzantine Synod, under Mennas, in the year 536.[74] About the year 512, the Eastern bishops addressed Pope Symmachus as follows:—
"Hasten to make us free; for not merely for bind-

---

[69] This passage was used later by Pope Pius V.; Const. Romanus Pontifex, 1569; Regnans, 1570.

[70] Hugo, l. c., S. Bernard. de consid. L. iv. 3, ep. 237. Petrus Bles. ep. 144, ad Cœlestin III. Petrus Venerab. L. iii. ep. 24, ad Eugen. III. Innoc. III. c. 3, de M. et O. I. 33; c. Novit. 13 eod. Serm. I. in consecr. sui Pontif.

[71] Joh. VIII. epp. ad Basil. Imp. Baron. anno 878, n. iii.; a. 879, n. 26.

[72] Conc. Meldens. in Præfat. Hard. IV., 1478.

[73] Conc. Ephes. 431, P. iv. Hard. I., 1666.

[74] Conc. Cpl. 536, act. 4. Hard. II., 1260.

A Glance at Councils. 207

ing was the power given unto thee, but also for loosing those a long time bound; not merely for plucking up and destroying, but also for planting and building, according to holy Jeremiah, or rather according to the Redeemer of the world, Christ, whose type the former was."[75] The "rooting out and the planting" of Jeremiah was usually placed in juxtaposition with the "binding and the loosing" of Peter; as in the epistle which John of Jerusalem addressed in 518 to John II., patriarch of Constantinople.[76] As little novel are the words of Boniface, when he thus continues:[77] "If now the temporal power goes astray, it is judged by the spiritual; but if a subordinate ecclesiastical authority transgresses, it is judged by the one set over it; but the supreme ecclesiastical power can be judged, not by men, but by God alone, according to the words of the apostle, 'the spiritual man judges all things; he himself is judged by no one'" (1 Cor. ii. 15). No new doctrine is it, again, when it is further said, the ecclesiastical authority, though imparted to a man, and exercised by a man, is still divine, given by a divine sentence to Peter, and to his successors. As now Boniface, at the commencement of the Bull, laid down, as the condition of salvation, that man should belong to the one Church founded by God; so he enunciates the maxim also that, for obtaining eternal happiness, each one is required to submit to the Pope. By way of comparison, he points to the Manichean heresy, which teaches the two principles of things; and, in fact, if the divine law did not subject kings, in respect of their sins, to the Papal authority, so their

---

[75] Ep. orient. ap. Baron, a. 512, n. 50.
[76] Hard. II., 1343.
[77] On the words, "terrenam potestatem instituere habet," *vide* Bianchi, l. c., pp. 522, 523. Instituere is here not *to institute*, but *to instruct*.

power must needs then be based on a principle separate from the Church; in which case they, as sovereigns, would stand completely outside its pale.[78] Moreover, many find this Bull quite in harmony with the epistle of Gregory IX., dated 23d October 1236, and show that even secular princes and statesmen have asserted and acknowledged, in the strongest language, the supremacy of the Pope, even in temporal things.[79] The "astonishment and the mockery" of the French jurists and theologians, to which Janus alludes (p. 162), are in the then circumstances of France under Philip the Fair, and from the shameful policy pursued towards the Pope, which recoiled from no misrepresentation and no forgery,[80] easily explained.

But what Boniface VIII. here defined—namely, the necessity of obedience to the Pope—is a principle of primitive Christianity, and which Paschal II. (as we are told at p. 245) was certainly not the first to enunciate, which in nowise needed the pseudo-Ambrose, since the words of the genuine Ambrose sufficed: "Ubi Petrus, ibi Ecclesia;" "Where is Peter, there is the Church." The separation from this Apostolic See, and the arrogant revolt against it, at all times passed as a separation from the Church, as a going out of the kingdom of the Lord.[81]

Pope Symmachus wrote to the Emperor Anas-

---

[78] Phillips, *loc. cit.*, pp. 205, 206.

[79] Hefele, Conc. vi., pp. 317, 318. Here the declaration of the Flemish envoys, of the 29th December 1299, is cited. Let us consider, too, what Peter of Blois, as vice-chancellor, wrote, in the name of Queen Eleanora of England to Pope Celestine III., on the occasion of the imprisonment of her son Richard, by Leopold of Austria, ep. 145, in Baron. anno 1193: "Nonne Petro Apostolo et in eo vobis a Deo omne regnum omnisque potestas committitur? Non rex, non imperator aut dux a jugo vestræ Jurisdictionis eximitur."

[80] Döllinger, "Manual of Church History," ii., p. 240, *seq.*

[81] Bonifac. I. ep. 14, n. 1, p. 1037, ed. Coust. a quâ (Sede

tasius: " Thinkest thou, because thou art emperor, that thou canst dare to despise the judgment of God? . . . or because thou art emperor, dost thou rise against the power of Peter? . . . But let us compare the dignity of the emperor with the dignity of the high-priest; between the two there exists as wide a difference as between an administrator of human and an administrator of divine concerns. Thou, O Emperor, receivest from the priest baptism, the sacraments; thou desirest of him prayer, thou hopest from him a blessing, thou beseechest him for pardon in the sacrament of penance; in short, thou administerest human things, and he administereth divine. . . . Perhaps thou wilt say, it stands written, 'We must be subject to every power' (Rom. xiii. 1). We recognize human authorities in their proper place, till they lift up their will against God. Moreover, if every power is of God, so before all, and in a higher degree, is that power of God, which is set over divine things. Honour God in us, and we will honour God in thee. But if thou honourest not God, so thou canst not avail thyself of the privilege of Him, whose rights thou despisest."[82]

Apostolicâ) se quisquis abscidit, fit christianæ religionis extorris, ep. 15, n. 4, p. 1041: In cujus contumeliam quisquis insurgit, habitator Cœlestium non poterit esse regnorum. Tibi, inquit, dabo claves regni cœlorum, *in quæ Nullus sine gratiâ Janitoris intrabit*. Had Janus read this, he certainly would have dated the " obscuration of the Church " from the Popes of the fifth century; or he would have found the fundamental thought of this passage in the pseudo-Isidorian epistle of Julius I. (c. xi., p. 464 H.), on which Gregory VII. built his plan of dominion (p. 105 Janus). Peter Damiani also had written to the Anti-Pope Honorius (in ep. 20): " Si eos sacri canones hæreticos notant, qui cum Romanâ ecclesiâ non concordant, quâ tu judicaberis dignus esse sententiâ ?" And to the clergy and people of Milan he wrote (opusc. v.) : "Quæ provincia per omnia regna terrarum ab ejus ditione extranea reperitur, cujus arbitrio ipsum quoque Cœlum ligatur et solvitur?"

[82] Symmach. Apol. ad. Anast. Labbé IV., 1298. Cf. Defens. Decl., L. ii., c. 7.

Let us now return to Pope Leo X. Supposing that all the historical arguments in the Bull "Pastor Æternus" were alike untenable, will, therefore, the theological ones be thereby overthrown, which show that the head of the whole Church is the head of its representatives also? From the dogmatic definition of Florence, further consequences could be deduced. The reasoning might be incorrect, but still the enunciated doctrine is not therefore untrue. To attend the Council was open to all bishops; the Popes gave themselves the greatest trouble in order to promote their attendance; all were summoned; and the Council was presided over by no "Papa dubius"—no doubtful pope, but by a pontiff undoubtedly legitimate.[83] There is scarcely a theological proposition upon which there is such great unanimity, as upon the necessary concurrence of the Pope to a General Council; but not less decided is the opinion of the majority of theologians, that a Council without the Pope is not œcumenical, nay, can even err in matters of faith.[84]

But once again "Councils were perverted into mere tools of Papal domination, and reduced to a condition of undignified servitude" (p. 190). So even the Council of Trent was not free (p. 368), and this at a time when all had placed their confidence in a "Council truly free, unoppressed by Papal coercion" (p. 369). "The Italian bishops at Trent were no more than a herd of slavish sycophants of Rome, acting simply at the beck of the legates" (p. 367).[85] The Pope should, indeed, have re-

---

[83] Bennettis, P. II., t. iii., p. 196.
[84] Melchior Canus de loc. theol., v. 4; Thomassin. Diss., vi. et xiv. in concil. Cabassut. in not. Conc. Trid., n. 95. Bennettis, *loc cit.*, p. 185, *seq.* Phillips' Can. Law, II., § 88, pp. 312, 313.
[85] On the contrary, the *Avenir Catholique* (N. 2, p. 19, n. 11,

nounced all his rights; then the Council would have been "free;" but a legitimate Council it would have ceased to be. Whatever of rational freedom could be desired, was abundantly secured; but without order, without the higher jurisdiction of the presiding legates, a chaos would have sprung up, which would have only filled the Catholic world with scandal, and the adversaries with malicious scorn. We do not deny that the Council of Trent, which undeniably achieved much good,[86] did not produce all the fruits which it might have brought forth. But who is to bear the blame of all this? Is it to the Roman See solely and entirely, or even chiefly, that blame attaches? This Janus seems to believe. Of the obstacles opposed to reform by many powerful sovereigns, of the negligence of the ecclesiastical princes, and of the noble chapters of Germany, of the intermission of provincial and diocesan Synods, of the non-fulfilment

Pie IV., et le Concile de Trente) endeavours to show that Pius IV. left full liberty to the Council of Trent. But between the oppression of the bishops by the Pope on the one hand—and the abandonment of Papal prerogatives on the other, whose diminution would have rather promoted the growth of heresies than have checked them (Cf. the document in Raynaldus, anno 1563, n. 67), lies a middle course, which the parties concerned did not fail to pursue. Here, also, holds good the ancient saying, "Nihil est, quin male narrando possit depravarier" (Terent. in Phorm. iv. 4). This holds good, too, of the narration of that storm which a bishop of Cadiz excited in the Council of Trent (p. 368, Janus), and which is told quite after the manner of Sarpi. But it was the Papal legates who caused the prelate to continue his interrupted discourse, and who afterwards appeased the excited Spaniards. *Vide* Pallavicini, *op. cit.*, L. xix., c. 5, n. 5; c. 7, n. 1. In the same way the conduct of the Cardinal of Lorraine (Janus, p. 276) is quite incorrectly represented. Upon him Pallav., *loc. cit.*, c. 6, n. 1, *seq.*; c. 7, n. 3; c. 8, n. 5, 6; c. 16, n. 6, *seq.*; L. xxi. c. 5, n. 4; c. 6, n. 20, 21; c. 13, n. 5, lxxiv., c. 2, n. 1. Raynald, a. 1563, n. 4, 5, p. 99. Launoy Reg. Navarr. Gymnas, p. I., c. 6.

[86] Cf. Hefele, *Theological Quarterly Review* of Tübingen, 1846, p. 3, *seq.*, "On the Destinies of the Church since the Council of Trent."

of many of the most salutary regulations, of the ascendancy obtained by the principle of Territorialism, and of many other like things, Janus has not a word to say. He knows only how to speak of the experiences (p. 419) which the non-Italian bishops must have made at Trent, of the prohibition to write commentaries on the decrees of the Council, and of the interpretation of those decrees reserved to the Apostolic See. And yet it is precisely the "Congregation of the Council" which has rendered the most indisputable and the most eminent services to the progress of canon law.

But the soil already trembles under our feet. The last Œcumenical Council of Trent, which forms the most important source of the new ecclesiastical jurisprudence, was not free, and an un-free Council is invalid, null, or at least non-obligatory (p. 425); although the whole Church has received it,[87] it still is not binding. Of all General Councils there seem to remain, then, only the first eight, as well as those of Constance and Basle; so we have no legal foundation more.

And, moreover, we have no longer any hope, for a free Council is no longer to be expected. "The chief reason," we are told, "why nobody since the Synod of Trent any longer desired a Council, lay in the conviction, that if it met, the first and most essential condition, freedom of deliberation and voting would be wanting" (p. 421).[88] "Nay, in

---

[87] Bennettis, p. i., t. i., pp. 529–532.

[88] What Pallavicini (*op. cit.*, L. xvi., c. 10, n. 9, 10) has written upon the difficulties of holding again a General Council, from the impression of the many obstacles offered by the diverging interests of different nationalities, and by the secular courts, as well as with reference to the dangers so easily menacing ecclesiastical unity, and also with reference to those data in which he concurs with Sarpi—all this is adduced by Janus (p. 421) as an expression of the general sentiment, "that Councils as little fitted into a Church constituted

the countries subjected to the Inquisition, the mere wish for another Council would have been declared penal, and would have exposed to danger those who uttered it" (p. 420). This wish was doubtless culpable, where it coincided with an appeal to a future General Council, forbidden as such appeals were by canon law, or when it proceeded from hypotheses menacing to the peace, the dignity, and the unity of the Church, where, as in the case of the French Appellants of the last century, it served as a pretext for schismatical and heretical aims. But, we are told, bishops are not free, they are bound to the Pope by an oath (p. 445, German), and by a real vassal oath (p. 169). Precisely so spoke the German Protestants, when invited on the 28th April 1545, and 24th January 1552, to take part in the Council of Trent.[89] And yet St Boniface had bound himself to the Pope by an oath,[90] and yet this is an usage dating from many centuries, and required by the need of unity. Does this oath hinder episcopal frankness? does it prevent the bishop from speaking according to the dictates of his conscience? When the newly - consecrated bishop swears to respect, to defend, and to promote the rights and privileges of the Apostolic See; so he swears in the same formula also to observe the rules of the Holy Fathers. The one clause does not, in the sense of the Church, subvert the other. The well-being of religion and of the Church constitutes for the bishop the supreme rule of all his efforts and actions; and it is by no means merely for the advantage of the *Curia* this form of oath provides.[91]

into an absolute Papal monarchy, as the States-General fitted into the monarchy of Louis XIV."

[89] Raynald, a. 1545, n. 20; a. 1552, n. 11, *seq.*

[90] Othlon. Vita Bonifac., L. i. 144. Bonif., ep. 118. Serrar., ep. 2, ed. W.

[91] The oath of bishops since the time of Gregory VII. has been

But what, then, constitutes the necessary freedom of bishops? Let us hear on this subject the old master, Febronius.[92] He requires that the Pope or his legates should exercise no preponderating influence over the deliberations of the Council, should not forbid the bringing forward of certain matters for discussion, should make use of no threats or promises, and should not hold the Council in any place unfavourable to the freedom of deliberation. If, now, such claims were regarded as conditions necessary to the legitimacy of a Synod; so from this synodical freedom new difficulties only would spring up, and various doubts as to the real legitimacy of the Council would be fostered.[93] Surely with the right of convocation, the Pope has the right of presidency and of the initiative in a Council;[94] even in the summons he can determine the subjects for discussion; he ceases not in the least degree, when he enters into deliberation with his brethren, to be the head of the entire Church, as well as of individual local Churches.[95] To use menaces or promises were unworthy of the Pope; and the employment of such means at the present day is not conceivable. But from the very fact that the Pope assembles the bishops around him, in order to deliberate with them, it follows, of course, that he will not fetter their free expression of opinion. To the bringing forward certain special matters such little hindrance is opposed that, on the contrary, even before

copiously treated of by Bianchi (*op. cit.*, t. i., L. ii., § 12, n. 2, 3, p. 330, *seq.*), and by Bennettis, ii., t. iv., p. 351, *seq.*

[92] De Statu Eccl., c. 9, § 3.
[93] Cf. Beidtel, *loc. cit.*, p. 403.
[94] Ferraris Prompta Bibl. V. Concilium, art. 1, n. 45–49. On the formula " proponentibus legatis " in the Council of Trent, see Pallavic., p. 141; L. xx., c. 8, n. 2; c. 15, n. 7, *seq.* Raynald, a. 1563, n. 66, 87, 190, 202.
[95] Zaccaria Antifebron. Vindic. I., p. 363, *seq.*

the gathering of the Council, an opportunity is offered for such proposals. Janus says, indeed, "from Gregory the Seventh's time, the weight of Papal power has pressed *ten times more heavily* upon Councils than ever did the imperial authority" (p. 425). But never was a Synod reduced to such a position by the Papal power, as the third General Council was by the Emperor Theodosius II.;[96] and at Trent episcopal freedom was far more menaced by the secular courts, than by the Roman *Curia*.[97] But when, in the sixteenth century, the demand was made, "first, that the proposed Council should not be held in Rome, or even in Italy, and, secondly, that the bishops should be absolved from their oath of obedience" (p. 425); the demand was by no means founded in right. Compliance with the latter postulate would have violated the constitution of the Church, and destroyed all hierarchical order; the granting of the former might, indeed, have been attended with advantages, but been productive of disadvantages also, especially as Germany and France were then jealous of each other, were threatened with war, and were involved in the most fearful religious contests. Moreover, in despite of the proximity of the city of Trent to Germany, but very few bishops of that country appeared at the Council.

Freedom, in the true Christian sense, is not the removal of existing limitations—not the arbitrary will of noisy demagogues—not the domination of Liberal theorists—not the faculty of doing everything *ad libitum*. *Ethical freedom* is the voluntary self-devotion to truth and to righteousness—to the kingdom of God. And in this self-devotion

---

[96] Hefele, Conc. II., 201.
[97] Vid. Pallavic., *op. cit.*, L. xxiv., c. 14.

Pope and bishops can concur; they can, if they have any conception, however small, of their task, co-operate in their endeavours. And in despite of all human infirmities, the Spirit of God breathes over the general assembly of His Church; and "*where is the Spirit of God, there is freedom.*"

CHAPTER X.

THE POPEDOM IN HISTORY.

"EVERY one who examines the internal relations of Church history, will be constrained to acknowledge that, since the eleventh century, there has been no period of it on which a *Christian student* can dwell with *unmixed satisfaction;* and as he endeavours to get at the bottom of the causes underlying that *unmistakable decay of Church life*, constantly getting a deeper hold, and more widely spreading, he will always be brought back to the distortion and transformation of the Primacy, as the *ultimate root of the evil.*" So speaks Janus (Pref., p. xviii.)

But with *unmixed satisfaction* we can dwell on no previous period of Church history. Everywhere, with the great and the lofty mingles human baseness and viciousness; even in the apostolic age, we meet at Corinth and elsewhere with great imperfections, failings, and vices. Our satisfaction is *everywhere* but a relative one, never unqualified, never untroubled. But some subjects of satisfaction we find in *all* ages, and on which the eye can rest with pleasure.

But why should these afflicting phenomena meet us only from the *eleventh* century? Why not, in conformity with the former teaching of Janus, from the year 845? Why not from the tenth century, which exhibited so many deplorable spectacles? Why precisely from the eleventh age? In the second half of that century, we thought that it was the reform of the clergy, instituted by the Popes, which raised ecclesiastical life from the deep decay into which it had sunk, and enabled it to put forth its energy in the Crusades, and in so many new creations. "The corruption of the Church," says Neander, "which the general secularization of society threatened, had reached its culminant point, and thereby a reformatory reaction on the part of the Church had been called forth. But under given conditions, this reaction could proceed only from the Theocratic point of view, as those who displayed the greatest zeal against the abuses that had crept in, were ruled by that set of principles. Gregory VII. was animated by something higher than by self-seeking and selfish ambition; it was an idea which swayed him, and to which he sacrificed all other interests. It was the idea of the independence of the Church, and of a tribunal to exercise judgment over all other human relations; the idea of a religious and ethical sovereignty over the world to be exercised by the Papacy."[1] In favour of this great Pope, other Protestant inquirers also bear testimony that he was free from idle ambition and base passions.[2] But Janus, who calls him one of the boldest Popes, a man "whom Nicholas I. only approaches" (p. 102), who precipitated Italy and Germany into a religious and civil war, charges

---

[1] Neander's "Church History," ii. p. 375, third edition.
[2] Luden's "History of the German People," vol. viii. pp. 468–471. Leo's "Universal History," ii. 125. Cf. Rühs's "Manual of the History of the Middle Ages," vol. ii. p. 367, and the works of Voigt and Gfrörer (German).

him with unlimited credulity, and "with an eager desire for territory and dominion" (p. 141). The Popes of the Middle Age carried on a great struggle for the freedom and independence of the Church ;[3] and herein all who have a heart for this great idea admire them, as those, on the other hand, who are incapable of such feelings hold them in detestation. There, where others see how the faithful, anxious for the purity and the freedom of their Church, all the better men of those times, firmly rallied around the Papal chair, and supported the Pontiffs in their contests against the sale of ecclesiastical benefices, against clerical concubinage, against violence and licentiousness ;— there Janus, entirely absorbed in his own fictions, sees "but a large and powerful party, stronger than that which, two hundred years before, had undertaken to carry through the Isidorian forgery, and had been labouring with all its might to weld the states of Europe into a theocratic priest-kingdom, with the Pope as its head" (p. 101). Of a real reform of the Church by Gregory VII. he finds no trace. Hitherto we had thought that, in the thirteenth century, ecclesiastical life, through the great religious orders of St Dominic and St Francis, fostered, as they had been, by the protection of the Popes, received a new energy, which displayed its glorious fruits in religious missions, in science, in art, in so many lovable saints. But these orders, we are now told, were quite in the service of the *Curia;* their members were Papal-Court theologians, authors of new forgeries (p. 263), the strongest props and pillars of the Pontifical monarchy (p. 152) : all that they otherwise did is obscured by "the distortion and disfigurement" of

---

[3] Pichler, *loc. cit.*, i. pp. 32, 49, *seq.*

the Primacy. This is the black spot which Janus everywhere sees. We would almost believe that he labours under the jaundice.

To many, even non-Catholic scholars, it has appeared that the great power of the Popes worked, on the whole, advantageously, especially as regards the education of the nations of Europe, and that that power was, in the design of divine Providence, a necessary step to a higher civilization. Let us hear, for example, the historian Stäudlin. "The Papacy," says he, "was productive of many beneficial effects. Faith in a living vicegerent of Jesus, in a supreme lawgiver of Christians, in a judge on the faith and morals of the Christian world, in a subordination of secular interests to spiritual—this faith was to countless souls useful and advantageous, and promoted a reverence for Christianity. The Papacy united in one common bond the different European nations, furthered their mutual intercourse, and became a channel for the communication of the sciences and arts; and without it the fine arts, doubtless, would not have attained to so high a degree of perfection. The Papal power restrained political despotism, and from the rude multitude kept off many of the vices of barbarism."[4] Let us now turn to the French historian Michaud. "The genius of the Popes," says he, "has been the subject of very great praise; this praise was accorded chiefly with the view to bring into greater prominence their ambition. But if the Popes possessed the genius and the ambition ascribed to them, so we must believe that from their very origin they were engaged in the aggrandisement of their states, or with the growth of their temporal power; but herein they

---

[4] "Universal History of Christianity," p. 223. Hanover, 1806.

were not successful, or did not attempt the execution of such plans. Is it not more natural to think that, in all their great achievements, the Popes but followed the spirit of Christendom? In the Middle Age, which was the period of their greatest power, they were themselves rather more guided by its spirit, than they themselves guided it. Their sovereign power was the result of their position, and not of their will. . . . As the nations formed no other idea of civilization than that which they had received from the Christian religion, so the Popes were quite naturally the supreme arbiters among peoples. In the midst of the darkness, which the light of the Gospel incessantly strove to disperse, their authority must have passed as the first and the highest. The temporal power needed their sanction, kings and nations besought their aid, and asked counsel of them, and the Popes therefore held themselves authorized to exercise a general (?) dictatorship. This dictatorship was often exercised in behalf of public morality and of social order; it often protected the weak against the strong; it checked the execution of criminal designs; it restored peace among states; and preserved an infant society from the wild excesses of ambition, of licentiousness, and of barbarism."[5]

Raoul Rochette observes: "During the long duration of the Middle Ages, the influence of the Popes was in general more advantageous than pernicious to Europe; and if we weigh all things in an accurate scale, we shall find that society was indebted to the Papal power for more virtues and more blessings, than for any evils and mischief which that power might have inflicted. But in order to render this assertion more feasible to

[5] "Histoire des Croisades," 4 ed., t. iv., p. 97, t. vi., p. 230, *seq*.

those who labour under the strongest prejudices, I must add that it is precisely such a state of civilization, or, if we will, of barbarism, as existed in the Middle Age, which was necessary to make the authority of the Popes attended with such favourable results."[6]

"Whatever judgment we may form," says Leopold Ranke, "of the Popes of an earlier period, they had ever great interests at heart—the fostering of an oppressed religion, the struggle with heathenism, the propagation of Christianity among the northern nations, the foundation of an independent hierarchical power;—these efforts (and it belongs to the dignity of human nature to will and to execute great things), these efforts stamped on the actions of the Popes a lofty character."[7]

Such testimonies and judgments we might considerably augment.[*][8] But suffice it to ask, Where is there in the world's history a like institution, which (to consider it only in the light of human wisdom and policy[9]) so gloriously unites and reconciles classic antiquity and modern times, which has exercised its spiritual supremacy under the most various relations, which defended it where it was contested, and won it back again where it was almost lost? Where is there another

---

[6] "Discours sur les heureux effets de la puissance Pontificale au Moyen Age," p. 10. Paris, 1818.

[7] "The Roman Popes in the Sixteenth and Seventeenth Centuries," vol. i., p. 43. Germ. ed.

[*] See Appendix, containing testimonies of German Protestant historians to the great moral and social services of the Papacy.—*Trans.*

[8] Cf. John von Müller on the League of the German Princes (Works, ix., p. 164). Hurter Innocent III., in many passages, especially vol. i., pp. 99-166, ii., p. 712. Ancillon Tableau des Revolutions du Systeme Politique de l'Europe, t. i., Introduction, pp. 133-157. Coquerel Essai sur l'Histoire du Christianisme, p. 75.

[9] Cf. the English Historian Macaulay in his Critique of Ranke's "History of the Popes," *Edinburgh Review*, 1840.

institution which, in the worst times, standing up in opposition to the mightiest rulers, and regardless of all external considerations, has protected with such energy and dignity the sanctity of the nuptial tie, the rights of the defenceless, the purity of morals, and which has with so much tact and moderation influenced the progressive march of human society? And this, indeed, in a way that subsequently even non-Catholics could express the wish to see erected anew in Rome, under the presidency of the Pope, a supreme tribunal for the settlement of disputes among princes?[10] Where is there an institution which hath so victoriously surmounted the most violent assaults from every quarter, which hath so conquered the "gates of hell," which hath so victoriously withstood all who have predicted its downfall, and have, instead thereof, incurred their own destruction, whether they inscribed on their banner state-omnipotence, or the sovereignty of the people, or free science?

And what have we to bring against this institution? It was "forged documents" that raised it to its height. As if a piece of paper or parchment, especially in times when most people were unable to read, when the sword was in higher estimation than the pen, would have been able to erect a despotism, to which all bowed! "It was the tyranny of the Popes, the subjugation of their fellow-bishops, that brought it about." As if all bishops had been servile, cowardly, imbecile

---

[10] Leibnitz Tract. de Jure Suprematûs, P. iii., opp. iv. 330. Lettre 2, à M. Grimaret. So again, in our times, David Urquhart has published a pamphlet, that has appeared in French, entitled, "Appel d'un Protestant au Pape pour le rétablissement du droit Public des Nations. Cinq Propositions sur l'œuvre du futur Concile Œcuménique." Paris: Douniol, 1869.

betrayers, of their own and of the Church's rights, who let the yoke be laid on their necks, and became mere functionaries of the Popes; and at a time, too, when the dukes of the several races raised themselves from the condition of officials, to the rank of sovereigns, and even many bishops became powerful princes!"[11] "The jurists were the first to debase science into an instrument of flattery; and it was only after the close of the thirteenth century theologians followed them in the same course" (p. 202). We may hate and calumniate the jurists; but if their doctrines had not been based on the general convictions of their contemporaries, and had not rested on a solid legal groundwork, their science could never have achieved so much. "The Interdicts, and the ever more violent measures of the Popes" (p. 180), could have effect, only on the supposition of their well-established moral authority, and on the recognition of their justice. And as if all this does not suffice, pecuniary interests are brought forward; and we are told of the extortions whereby the Popes drained whole countries. But not a word is said as to how much those very Pontiffs achieved for works of instruction and of beneficence, for the ransom of Christian slaves, for the fitting out of Missionaries, for the Crusades, for the Union of the Greeks, for the struggle against the Turks, for the interests of Catholicism in lands in which it was endangered. Not a word is said as to the grievous afflictions of the Roman Church, especially after the acts of

---

[11] In fact, under Innocent III., bishops soon began to subscribe themselves as such "by the favour of the Papal See" (Janus, p. 171). The formula Dei et Apostolicæ Sedis gratiâ, is doubtless frequent in the thirteenth century, but already occurs in the year 1093. "Zaccaria Dissert. de Rebus ad Hist. Eccl. Pertin." Fulgin. 1781, t. ii. Dissert. xii.

violence on the part of the Emperor Frederic II., who, in his antagonism to religion, recoiled from no measure,[12] and forced the Popes to make a more extended use of their ecclesiastical right of taxation.[13] Nay, scarcely a word is to be found in the pages of our opponent respecting the countless difficulties by which Gregory VII., Urban II., Alexander III., Gregory IX., Innocent IV., and so many other Popes, down to the present day, were beset.

In fact, the Apostolic See had necessarily become the centre of a new political order of states, the representative and the protector of Christian international law. But the reaction of the secular power, and especially the efforts of the Hohenstaufen directed towards the subjugation of Italy, and more particularly of Rome, had brought about a series of arduous contests, in which the Pope was more than once obliged to lean upon France, that then obtained an ascendancy, which wounded the national susceptibilities of all other peoples, and furthered a policy for the prosecution of separate interests.[14] Even in their most afflicted condition, however, the Popes fulfilled their duties till the entanglements of Italian politics, the hostile fermenting elements of the fifteenth century, and the growing corruption of morals, rendered their task more and more difficult. Already in the sixteenth century, not merely the Papal throne, but even Catholicism itself, appeared on the brink of destruction. But then an energetic resistance arose; with renovated and newly-gathered strength, the Catholic Church confronted the Protestant world.[15]

---

[12] Döllinger's "Manual of Church History," ii. p. 220.
[13] Phillips' Can. Law, v., § 235, p. 450, *seq.*
[14] Cf. Döllinger, "Church and Churches," p. 33, *seq.* (In German.
[15] Ranke, *loc. cit.*, i., p. 377.

We see holy bishops, priests, and monks adorn the Church; we see the Popes from the times of Pius IV. and Pius V. display untiring activity for all ecclesiastical interests; we see them amid a thousand obstacles propagate religion, defend with the utmost intrepidity against powerful rulers the primitive word of truth; we see them combat, and endure, as the Sixth, the Seventh, and the Ninth Pius have proved. Nay, even the hostile world would pay their homage and respect to Pontiffs, so ardently beloved by the Faithful, if as they are now so secure, and powerful in their ecclesiastical position, they could but resolve to renounce a temporal dominion, so odious to the "spirit of the age,"[16] but which appears to the rigid Ultramontanes to be at present essentially necessary.[17]

But then are all the abuses of the Roman *Curia*, proved by so many witnesses and records, to be justified? We should think that two things are here to be distinguished, the Institute of the *Curia* itself, and the abuses that in the course of ages have crept into it. That the Popes of later times needed a greater number of functionaries than those of an earlier period, no one will be inclined to dispute. In the same way no one will assert, that the modern State should dismiss all its officials, and return to the relations of the old patriarchal Government. In the eleventh century the name of *Curia* was not yet despised; Peter Damiani says, the Roman Church should imitate the ancient *Curia* of the Romans, its senate, in order to subject all mankind

---

[16] "Only if the Pope ceases to be an Italian Sovereign, can he claim to be a universal *Pontifex*." So the *Times* expresses itself. (See the notice in the Augsburg *Allgemeine Zeitung*, 6th Nov. 1869.)

[17] The Catholic literature on this point is so extremely rich, that it is needless to refer to particular writings.

to the laws of the true Emperor, Christ.[18] At an earlier period, we already find numerous functionaries of the Pope;[19] and if the name of *Curia* gave offence to Gerhoch of Reigersberg and others (p. 217), it had still long before been used in a good sense.[20] As regards abuses, we must in an accurate statement discriminate the several functionaries, as well as the different periods, and next again, the different critics of the *Curia*. Of these some viewed it from a close proximity, others judged it at a distance; some blamed it from a momentary ill-humour, others from long-cherished animosity. The ascetic zeal of some was displeased with all profane forms and legal institutes;[21] others again found fault with the covetousness and other defects of the functionaries for the time being. Among the witnesses to the corruption of the Roman *Curia*, which had partially succumbed to the temptations of wealth and luxury,[22]

---

[18] Opusc. xxxi., c. 7, p. 540 (*Migne*, p. p. lat. t. cxlv). Romana Ecclesia, quæ sedes est Apostolorum, *antiquam debet imitari curiam* Romanorum. Sicut enim tunc terrenus ille senatus ad hoc communicabant omne consilium, in hoc dirigebant et subtiliter exercebant communis industriæ studium, ut cunctarum gentium multitudo Romano subderetur imperio, ita nunc Apostolicæ Sedis ædituï, qui *spirituales* sunt universalis Ecclesiæ *senatores*, huic soli studio debent solerter insistere, ut humanum genus veri Imperatoris Christi valeant legibus subjugare.

[19] Phillips' Can. Law. vi., § 298, *seq.*, p. 343, *seq.*, where in general much rich material is found.

[20] Tertull. Apol., c. 39.

[21] Even the name *curiales* was in the more ancient signification of the word offensive to many religious people (vid. *Thomassin.* de vet. disc., p. ii., L. i., c. 66, n. 6, *seq.*, 67 n. c. 8, *seq.*, 74, n. 9). Even Peter Damiani still identifies the *curiales* with the *aulici*. Cf. Opusc. xxii., c. 3, p. 467. Let us only think of the court clergy of the Emperor Henry IV!

[22] Erasmus Rot. Explic. in Symbol., p. 32. In nullâ autem ecclesiarum diutius viguit pietatis ardor fideique sinceritas, in nullam minus hæreseon ac tardius irrepsit malum, quam in ecclesiam Romanam. Utinam non inundassent hujus mundi lenocinia! Yet even Erasmus is not herein a quite unprejudiced witness.

as well as to that of the Italian clergy in general, there are found on the one hand benevolent men belonging to that very clergy, as well as many prelates, who attended the Fifth Lateran Council, and that of Trent (p. 363). And surely those individuals are not to be considered as quite corrupt, and incapable of all improvement, who make an open avowal of their own faults, as well as of those of others. But of these faults all are by no means to be set to the account of the *Curia*; many are far more to be ascribed to that heathen spirit aroused by the Humanists, as well as to the disorders introduced by recent wars, as also to the nomination of unworthy bishops by Sovereigns.[23] Even authorities, like Adrian VI., cited by Janus (p. 357), are at fault, of whom, moreover, Pallavicini[24] not unjustly remarks, that he had never before his Pontificate accurately known the Roman *Curia*, that in this matter he had lent but a too credulous ear to the misrepresentations of his courtiers as to the preceding Pontificate, that in the selection of able men he was not near so happy as Leo X., and that his reforming zeal sometimes transgressed the rules of prudence. On the other hand, men are brought forward as witnesses who were the notorious enemies of the Popes, such as the scurrilous Infessura,[25] and such as the too celebrated Nicholas Machiavelli, who, whatever may have been his intentions, was the teacher of the most unprincipled and profligate system of politics

---

[23] How far in this respect the abuse had gone in Naples is shown by the case that occurred under Pope Clement XI., when an ecclesiastic presented to a benefice was, on account of his total ignorance of the Latin language, necessarily rejected by Rome. *Vide* Rigant. in Regul., xx. Cancell., n. 41, t. ii., p. 292.

[24] Pallavicini, Hist. Conc. Trid., l. ii., c. 7, n. 9–14.

[25] Muratori (Rer. ital. Script. iii. ii., pp. 1109, 1175, 1189) calls him *proclivis ad maledicentiam*. Cf. also Raynaldus, a. 1490, n. 22.

ever broached in the world, as well as the historian Guicciardini, who can lay claim to the title of anything but an impartial historian (pp. 355, 356).[26] Hence we find so much that is one-sided and exaggerated, that individuals are treated with the greatest injustice, as, for example, Cardinal Cajetan, who was legate in Germany, is said to have "embittered the Lutheran business by his insolence" (p. 361), whereas Luther himself, in his letter to him, acknowledged his friendliness and his agreeable manners; and from the Conference at Augsburg, we certainly may infer anything but arrogance on the part of the legate. We are told of the corruption of the Milanese Church before the times of St Charles Borromeo, but nothing is related of the acts of that saint; the decline of morality in Rome under Leo X. is described, but nothing is said of the reform under St Pius V.[27]

This corruption of the *Curia* is a noteworthy thing—an old bye-word of parties hostile to Rome—an old subject of attempted reforms on the part of men, whether called or uncalled. The Reformation here is no small work. The duty and the need of removing abuses was constantly recognized; it was only the difficulty of the task, and the at times well-founded fear lest with the tares

---

[26] A certain predilection for authors in ill-repute at Rome is apparent in the very citations of Janus. We find among his authorities (pp. 423, 445, 473) the fanatical Spanish Jansenist Villanueva (vid. respecting him Fuster Escritores de Valencia, ii., p. 304, *seq.* Castillo Historia critica de las negociaciones con Roma. Madrid, 1859, vol. ii., c. 7, p. 147, nota), the French Jansenist Arnauld (p. 414), the Calvinstic Church historian Hottinger (p. 344), the modern adversary of the Popes Antonio Gennarelli (p. 26). Launoy is far more used than cited (329). Willingly is the authority of Matthew Paris alleged (pp. 210, 237, 343, G.), who, moreover, is full of the grossest errors. (See Döllinger Manual, ii., p. 279.) With respect to Robert of Lincoln (p. 219), his assertions are refuted by Raynaldus (anno. 1253, n. 43, anno. 1254, n. 71).

[27] Cf. Ranke, *loc. cit.*, i., p. 361.

the wheat also might be plucked up, which often delayed the work of reform.[28] The great difficulty of this task even Janus appears to feel, when he represents the Popes as dependent on the *Curia*, and incapable of bursting their fetters asunder (pp. 183, 184), and when he lays the charge of corruption more on the system, than on persons (p. 184). However, it cannot be denied that many evils formerly lamented have now been in part completely set aside, in part considerably diminished; and it is very unjust to rake together abuses from different ages, as if they had remained uniformly the same. We can now no longer say that through the *Curia* Simony is the mistress of the Church (p. 222); that the *Curia* draws all petty details to itself (p. 188); the granting of benefices by the Roman See has in most countries almost entirely ceased; the dues for the Pallia and other imposts have been considerably reduced; the purchase of places has disappeared; the procedure of many tribunals has, by the wise constitutions of Pius V., Sixtus V., Benedict XIV., and other Pontiffs, been better regulated;[29] and ameliorations have been constantly designed, and introduced slowly but surely into life.

Well worthy of consideration, in more than one respect, are the words which the Papal legate Aleander addressed on this matter, on the 13th February 1521, to the diet of Worms.[30] Passing to the charges against Rome, he rejoices to speak before men whose minds are not entangled by the

---

[28] Döllinger, "Church and Churches," xxxi., No. 16.

[29] Phillips' Can. Law, vi., § 315, p. 520, *seq.;* § 319, p. 561, *seq.;* § 320, p. 565, *seq.* Bangen, "The Roman *Curia.*" Münster, 1854. Zaccaria Antifebronio, i., p. xii., lxxxii., *seq.* For the more ancient times compare still Henric. Institor., ap. Raynald. anno. 1498, n. 25, *seq.*

[30] Pallav. Hist. Conc. Trid., l. i., c. 25, n. 13, *seq.*

prejudices of the multitude; and he declares that it enters not into his design to occupy their attention with the course of procedure of the tribunals, and with the functionaries of Rome. In the same way as royal chambers are sometimes filled with dust, from which they must from time to time be cleansed; so into the courts of princes abuses creep, which often require reform. The insight of the Emperor, and of this illustrious Diet, into the wants of Germany, is not so contracted, nor their credit with the Roman See so small, that they could not—without the tragic exclamations, and the infuriated cries of a wrangling deserter, carried away by the blindness of his rage—of themselves make to the Vicar of Christ the necessary representations, and that the latter would not be ready to meet their just demands.

But what Luther seeks to destroy is the Papal power itself. His chief reason is, that one acts at Rome otherwise than one teaches; hence men are taught not by truth, but by deception. To this we may reply, that whoso will not lend his ear to calumny, but examine the matter with his own eyes, will find in Rome much that is great and worthy of admiration—so much time, so much money employed in the service of God, such abundant alms to the poor, such abstinence from all which the senses crave, and which in other countries is taken without shame, such blamelessness of conduct in most of the members of the Apostolic Senate, and in the other leading classes of society, that one is forced to avow, here is manifested something quite extraordinary, something exalted above the powers of men. I pass over the words of Christ when He exhorts us to follow the doctrine, and not the example, of those who sit in the first chair of instruction (Matt. xxiii. 2, 3). But I say that, according to the argument of Luther, the right logical conclusion would be the very reverse. It is, I assert, a clear proof of a false religion, when its constituted guides, although ever increasing in numbers, still through the course of ages are wont exactly to practise what they teach and prescribe. It was so with the religion of the Pagan Romans, it is so with that of Mohammed. But it is not so with the religion which the Popes of Rome teach. They professed at all times that religion, although it condemns all of them as subject to defects, many of them as in certain respects guilty, some (I say it boldly) as vicious, although this religion forces them to a certain submission, which mortifies their inclinations, and subjects many of their acts that, out of the pale of this religion, would be irreproachable to public blame in their life-time, and after death to historical ignominy, and although this religion, in respect of eternal glory, concedes, even here below, to a bare-footed monk a pre-eminence over the crowned Pontiff. What earthly gratifications, what earthly interests could have led to the invention of this religion? How would it have been possible for the Popes, though at times vicious, and in other things often guided by quite opposite views, to have concurred with such steadfastness, such uniformity, and such concord in the confirmation of the same doctrine, if truth had not dictated to them this religion, and heaven itself inspired them? That in Rome, even among the prelates, faults, and even very grave ones, are committed, is not there arrogantly denied, but confessed with humility. Rome it is which not very long ago canonized the same Bernard, who in his life-time had so bitterly censured her in his writings. If Luther calls Rome the home of hypocrisy, so this is the ordinary calumny of unbridled vice against the reverence paid to virtue, and envied by vice; and were it true, who does not know that hypocrisy dwells only where genuine virtue is to be found? If genuine gold were not held in high estimation, who would give himself the trouble of forging such coin? And so no one will endeavour, at the cost of an irksome dissimulation, to appear virtuous in a community, where he sees not virtue rewarded and revered. After the legate had shown how the Popes could not have usurped the supreme power in the Church, and how necessary that authority was for all, that we should not apply the standard of earlier times to the circumstances of a later period, and that the political independence of the Holy See appears to be a necessity, he then speaks on the contributions of Christendom for the adequate endowment of the head of the Church, and for the splendour of the Church itself. "Voluntary poverty is commended in Rome; its promoters revered, its despisers condemned; but so high a virtue is not to be desired or to be expected of all. Laws are then worst when they exact the best—that is to say, when they prescribe a degree of perfection not to be hoped for from all. God will not root out from all souls the innate inclinations, nor impart to all an heroic sanctity. In the service of the Lord, therefore, human incommodities must be compensated for by human advantages; and therefore we desire for the Church peace, and not persecution. The latter state of things is doubtless more fruitful in saints; but the former, from its greater ease, is far more conducive to the salvation of souls. The recourse to a human stimulus does not, by any means, deprive a good work undertaken for the glory of God of its merit, as we may see from the many earthly rewards which God promised in the Old Testament. If the capital of the Christian world is to be filled with noble, capable, learned, and able men, who have left their homes, who have given up domestic joys, and submitted to many hardships; so the prospect of honours and emoluments must serve to compensate and facilitate their sacrifices. But it is said, things could yet be tolerated, if in Rome rewards at least were bestowed according to merit. I reply, then every state would be deprived of the means of rewarding merit; for none possess in the distribution of recompenses an unerring wisdom and spirit of justice. "Nay," as an excellent writer has observed, "mistakes in this matter are necessary, in order to preserve peace and order in the state; for were it once fixed and certain that the greater reward would ever be the lot of the greater merit, then it would be intolerable to the individual to see himself repulsed. It is a splendid solace to be able to accuse fortune as the foe to virtue." Moreover, it is shown that the benefices bestowed by the Pope out of the Ecclesiastical States are, for the most part, conferred on natives of the countries in question; and where this is not the case, a compensation is found in an interchange with other provinces; that the sums demanded for the despatch of bulls and rescripts would not suffice for the maintenance of even the smallest court;[31] that in these monies ecclesiastics of all lands have a share; that numerous institutes of beneficence for the whole of Christendom exist in Rome; and that many scholars and artists find

---

[31] Janus appeals (p. 374, *seq.*, n. 394, *seq.*) to the "Taxæ Cancellariæ Apostolicæ," printed in Rome under Julius II. and Leo X., and which cannot be distinguished from the editions put forth by Protestants. But does he not know how much was published in the sixteenth century with the false print of Rome?

support in that city, as towards these, indeed, Pope Leo X. displayed the greatest munificence.

Had Janus now, in the spirit of a St Bernard and of other saints, fairly exposed the *still existing* defects in the *Curia*, and recommended their removal, instead of condemning the whole "system," and indulging in such gross and manifold exaggeration, he would then have rendered a service to the cause of Christendom, and been entitled to our warmest thanks. Had he proposed well-grounded schemes of reform, his work would certainly not have met the fate of remaining utterly disregarded, or (like to that opinion which Paul IV., before his accession to the pontifical throne, had put forth, and afterwards, as Janus assumes, condemned,[32]) of incurring a prohibition;—an event which on no account do we desire. But it only injures the cause, when facts and legal principles are inextricably confused, and the truth, which could be suggested, is distorted and disfigured by the admixture of falsehood.[33] For the tenfold grosser abuses of secular courts and of official circles, men have no eyes; for harsher discords in other spheres, they possess no ears. But it is only when the Papal court is in question, when the organs of the head of the Church are in question, they possess Argus eyes, they hear every murmur, they gather notices from the natives of all lands,

---

[32] That Paul IV., when Pope, placed on the Index his former opinion (as asserted by Janus, p. 233, n. 1.) is by no means proved. *Vide* Bennettis, p. 11, t. v. Append., § viii., p. 739-741. Zaccaria, *loc. cit.*, p. lxxxi., *seq.*

[33] We speak not of the exemptions so much complained of, but which have been, since the Council of Trent, diminished (Janus, p. 166), and which the Oriental-patriarchs exercised also. Thomassin, *op. cit.*, P. i., L. i., c. 9, n. 15; c. 16, n. 1. L. iii., c. 30, *seq.* Bennettis, P. ii., t. iv., p. 554, *seq.* Goar Eucholog. Gr., P. 612, note. Ebedjesu Collect. Can., Tract. vii., c. 6 (Mai Nova. Coll., x. p. 133, 134).

from the members of various races and classes; they give ear to the complaints of disappointed ambition, of unmasked selfishness, of bankrupt speculation, of petty jealousy, of professional slander, and circulate all these reports against Rome, giving new strength to the no-Popery cry; while Rome herself, constantly reviled, remains in her attitude of calm dignity, and belies not the ancient saying, "Roma patiens, quia æterna."

Still the charges are not yet ended. On the Papacy still lies the curse of the Inquisition, and of Witchcraft. The Inquisition, according to Janus, "had the triple object, first, to make the Papal system irresistible; secondly, to impede any disclosure of its rotten foundations; and, thirdly, to bring the Infallibility theory into full possession" (p. 235). We shall say nothing about the rotten foundations, which we have already had occasion to examine; we shall pass over the by no means stringent arguments, as well as the inquiry into the expressions of the Ancient Fathers.[34] But yet thus much in our opinion history clearly shows, namely, that the immediate object of the Inquisition was to purge the Christian countries of Europe of the most dangerous sects, that sought to bring about not only a religious, but a social and political revolution; that assailed the principles of marriage, the family, property, and the whole organisation of state, and thereby rendered the severest measures necessary for the protection of society.[35] But it is more than one-sided to disregard all the existing relations of society, to refer everything exclusively to Papal power, and to pass over all that has been said in favour of the Popes, all that has been done

---

[34] Aug. ep. 185, ad Bonifac. Retract. ii. 5. Hier. in Gal. 5, 9 ep. ad Ripar. c. Vigil. 109 n. 3 Leo M. ep. 15 ad Turrib. Greg. M. L. I. ep. 74 Opp. ii. 558 ed. Paris. 1705. Isid. Hispal. Sent. iii. 51.
[35] Döllinger's "Church and Churches," pp. 50, 51.

The Popedom in History. 237

by them for averting harsher measures, as, for example, by Innocent III. in regard to the Waldenses.³⁶ The ecclesiastical and the civil laws were in respect to heretics in perfect harmony; and the Reformers of the sixteenth century started from the same principles. For the particulars we beg leave to refer to larger works.³⁷

But even "the whole treatment of witchcraft, as it existed from the thirteenth to the seventeenth century, was partly the direct, partly the indirect, result of the belief in the irrefragable authority of the Pope" (p. 249). But in the working out of this assertion, very many things have been left out, as, for example, that in the year 799, a German Synod ordained that enchanters and witches should be incarcerated and brought, if possible, by the archpriest to an avowal of their crime;³⁸ that Gregory VII. expressed himself against a belief in witchcraft;³⁹ that besides "an incidental expression of St Augustin, used in mere blind credulity" (p. 252), passages of other Fathers lay before the eyes of the mediæval divines.⁴⁰ Yet these are trifles. But did not a belief in magic and in witches exist among the Greeks also?⁴¹ Was not under John IV., the

---

³⁶ Innoc. iii. Lib. xi., ep. 198.; L. xii., ep. 17; L. ii., ep. 141; L. xiii., ep. 78.

³⁷ Hefele's Cardinal Ximenes, 2d Edition, p. 291, *seq.* Concil. vii., p. 214, *seq.* Beidtel's Can. Law, p. 563, *seq.* Devoti Instit. Can. L. iv. tit. 8, t. iv., p. 101, *seq.;* ed Romae 1794. That, moreover, the Inquisition was not so barbarous in Italy, may be inferred from the many very free expressions against Rome and the hierarchy, which Janus has carefully collected. He himself allows (p. 356) that it is worth showing, that in spite of the Inquisition, much could be said in Italy, and many an avowal made.

³⁸ Hefele, Conc. iii., p. 684, c. 15.

³⁹ L. vii. ep. 21. Cf. Neander ii., p. 380.

⁴⁰ Cf. in Gratian the Causa xxvi. q. 5, and the passages in Görres Mysticism (vol. iii. p. 44, *seq.*) It is unnecessary to observe that this work, in other respects, much needs a prudent criticism.

⁴¹ Psell. de dæmonum operat. c. 7-19. Phot. Nomoc. ix. 25, xii. 3, xiii. 20. Matth. Blaster. Syntagma alph. M. c. 1.

Faster, who died in 595, a certain Paulinus executed as a magician in Constantinople?[42] Were not in the East investigations carried on against such persons, especially in the fourteenth century, when, for example, the Patriarch John XIV. commissioned ecclesiastics to go round the city, seeking for wizards, and when in this quest, were they not aided by the civil functionaries?[43] Did the Popes transplant witchcraft to the schismatical Greeks also? Is it worth while to give any further refutation to such charges?

Let us revert to the Papacy, which we see is free from those appendages, that some desired to attach to it. One of our German classics says, it is a severe but just law of destiny, that as all evil, so all tyranny is sure to wear itself out.[44] Is this law to be belied in the Papacy alone, or doth this institution show itself to be not such a despotism, as many would fain make us believe. Here even Janus becomes thoughtful. "It is a psychological marvel," says he, "how this unnatural theory of a priestly domination, embracing the whole world, controlling and subjugating the whole of life, could ever have become established" (p. 182). And we add, it is the greatest enigma how such an institution ever came into life. This enigma Janus does not solve. All his explanations are too artificial, too forced; the circumstances adduced by him all appear incapable of bringing about the end proposed. But if we assume the Popedom to be a divine, beneficent institution, thoroughly monarchical indeed, but not so despotic, not

---

[42] Theophyl. Simoc. I. ii., pp. 56, 57.
[43] Acta Patriarch. Constantin. Müller,et Miklosich t. l., Doc. 85, p. 184-187. Cf. *ibid.*, Doc. 79, 80, 86, 134, 137, 153, 228, 292, 377, 331. Also Balsam. in c. 24. Ancyr. 61 Trull. Basil. Can. 83.
[44] Herder in his "Ideas on the Philosophy of the History of Mankind."

so unlimited, as it has been represented, but circumscribed by its object, by the spirit and the practice of the Church, by primitive tradition and established rules—moreover, protected and borne up by the Divine aid; then not only will the enigma of the past, but that of the present also, find for the most part its solution.

CHAPTER XI.

THE CHURCH, THE DOGMA, AND THE NEW COUNCIL.

THAT the modern opponents of the theory of Infallibility, not so much by the force of an inexorable logic, as from their own want of theological skill, have been driven to the point of assailing the Papal supremacy itself—acknowledged, as it is, throughout the whole Catholic Church, as existing *jure divino*—we have already seen. But the opposition is pushed still further: it is directed against the dogma of the Church itself, as taught not merely in every dogmatic treatise, but in every catechism.

According to Catholic doctrine, the true Church of Christ possesses at all times four essential notes by which she may be ever recognized, namely, *she is One, Holy, Catholic, Apostolical.* The Church hath for her the promise of Christ, that He would remain with her " *all days,*" even to the consummation of the world (Matt. xxviii. 20); that against her, founded on the rock (Peter), the gates of hell would never prevail (Matt. xvi. 18); that the Paraclete, the Spirit of truth, would abide with her *for ever,* and teach her all truth (John xiv. 16-18). There cannot be a single moment

The Church, the Dogma, &c.

in history at which the Church is bereft of this assistance; she can never fall away from the truth; she is not merely in the days of the apostles, not merely in the first six or seven centuries, but at all times the "pillar and ground of the truth" (1 Tim. iii. 15). She is at all times in possession of the truth;[1] she hath at all times the tradition of the apostles;"[2] never can it be said she hath experienced a falsification of the true doctrine till this or that reformer came to her aid.[3] She is inundated with the light of the Lord, and she pours forth her rays over the whole surface of the earth. She, the Bride of the Lord, can never be an adulteress; she is inviolate and pure.[4] She is unconquerable; and it were easier for the sun to become extinct, than for her to be annihilated.[5] All in the Church is guided by God.[6]

In conformity with these fundamental doctrines all theologians have rejected the opinion of the Jansenists, and of their disciples, respecting an

---

[1] Iren. adv. hær., iii. 4 : depositorium dives veritatis.

[2] Tert. adv. Marc., i. 21 : Non alia agnoscenda erit traditio Apostolorum, quam quæ *hodie* apud ipsorum ecclesias editur.

[3] *Loc. cit.*, i. 20 : O Christe, patientissime Domine, qui tot annis interversionem prædicationis tuæ sustinuisti, donec tibi scilicet Marcion subveniret! Cf. de præscript., c. 28.

[4] Cypr. de unit. Eccles., c. 5, 6, p. 214. Ed. Vendob. 1868. (Corp. script. eccl. lat. ed. impens. acad. Cæs., t. iii., p. 1.) Even the words following, which we omit for the sake of brevity, are worthy of all consideration.

[5] Chrys. hom. 4 in illud: Vidi Dominum, n. 2 (Migne lvi., pp. 121, 122): "μανθανέτω τῆς ἀληθείας τὴν ἰσχὺν, πῶς εὐκολώτερον τὸν ἥλιον σβεσθῆναι, ἢ τὴν ἐκκλησίαν ἀφανισθῆναι. Learn the force of truth, that it is easier for the sun to be extinguished, than for the Church to disappear."

[6] Cypr. ep. 59 (al. 55) ad Cornel., n. 5, p. 177 : Cum ille (Dominus Matth., 10, 29) nec minima fieri sine voluntate Dei dicat, existimat aliquis *summa et magna* aut non sciente aut non permittente Deo in *Ecclesia Dei* fieri et sacerdotes, id est dispensatores ejus, non de ejus sententia ordinari? *Hoc est fidem non habere*, qua vivimus, hoc est Deo honorem non dare, cujus nutu et arbitrio regi et gubernari omnia scimus et credimus.

overclouding and obscuration of the Church enduring for centuries, as one incompatible with Catholic principle. And they have equally repudiated the assertion, that a false doctrine could have maintained itself throughout the whole Middle Age, and even have found approval and encouragement on the part of the Apostolic See. How is the Church to be that Church of Christ depicted by the Fathers, if its central guidance has become all corrupt, its head has departed from the right way, if the Papacy, as it became after the year 845, "presents the appearance of a disfiguring, sickly, and choking excrescence on the organisation of the Church, hindering and decomposing the action of its vital powers, and bringing manifold diseases in its train?" (Pref. xix.) If when one member suffereth, all the other members suffer (1 Cor. xii. 26), how much more must the members of the Church suffer, when their head hath become diseased, or even "a disfiguring, sickly excrescence?" According to the doctrine of the Fathers, the adverse condition of the Apostolic See involves the decay of all other churches; on that central See dependeth all the weal and prosperity of the Church.[7] Nay more, if a false doctrine obtained for centuries the ascendancy, then is the infallibility of the Church herself destroyed. Passive and active infallibility are inseparably connected; and with the infallibility of the

[7] Petrus Damiani Opus. iv., p. 67, ed. *Migne:* Hac (Sede Apostolica) stante reliquæ stant; sin autem hæc, quæ omnium fundamentum est et basis, obruitur, ceterarum quoque status necesse est collabatur. So already perceived the Fathers of Aquileia in their address to the emperors, A.D. 381 (Coustant, p. 554), wherein they beseech them not to permit Ursinus to carry on any intrigues in the Roman Church, for by the perturbation of the latter the whole Church is imperilled; inde enim (from the ecclesia Romana, totius orbis Romani caput) et in omnes venerandæ communionis jura dimanant.

Church her indefectibility is lost. Whoever can conceive it as barely possible, that "Catholicism, hitherto regarded as a universal religion, would, by a notable irony of its fate, be transformed into the precise opposite of what its name and notion imports" (p. 9); such a man must call in question all providential guidance of the Church, all the Divine assistance assured to her, and all virtue in the promises given unto her; he must simply quit the ground-work of Catholic principle; he must choose another set of principles; and for him "the pretended great unity of the Roman Church would be to-day no more than a myth."[8] He has no longer any right to appeal to the Gallicans and their doctrines.[9] For the latter believe, for example, that the indefectibility of the Roman Church lies, not in the one or the other Pope, but in the series of the successors of Peter, and that never in this Church could an error obtain lasting existence.[10] But according to the theology of Janus, several errors of the most grievous kind have obtained a firm footing in the Roman Church, not only for a time, but for centuries, and even down to the present day. The Universal Church has, by the very fact that it did not correct public and widely-spread errors, given to them a formal approbation; and even the reform by the Council of Trent was, we are told, no real, but only a pretended reform (p. 366, w. 3). A Church, which honours among her saints a hierarch so stigmatised as is Gregory VII. in the pages of Janus,[11] which even in the light of

---

[8] *Allgemeine Zeitung*, 21st Oct. 1869, App. p. 4531.

[9] What Zaccaria (Antifebronio, t. i., Introd., p. lv., *seq.*) shows in opposition to Febronius, has its force in respect to our authors also.

[10] Defensio declarationis Cleri Gallic., t. i., l. iii., c. 3; l. i., c. 18; t. ii., l. xv., c. 6, *seq.*

[11] On his canonization, cf. Fessler, "Miscellaneous Writings upon Canon Law and Eccl. History," p. 39, *seq.* Freiburg, 1869.

our century has canonized bloodthirsty inquisitors, like a Peter Arbues,[12] which has hitherto oppressed, and suffered to be oppressed, all rational thought, all scientific aims, which has checked the purest and the noblest aspirations of the human mind thirsting after knowledge, which even in her solemn assemblies has achieved nothing to repair the evil—how can such a Church be the true Church of God?

More consistent, therefore, those appear to be, who contest in general the infallibility of Œcumenical Councils and of the Church. This recognition is due to the philosopher Frohschammer, who writes as follows:[13]—

"Whoso holds the Pope for fallible, can no longer assert the infallibility of the Church. The council cannot save the infallibility of the Church.[14] If it pronounces for the infallibility of the Pope, then all the proofs against the infallibility of the Pope turn to proofs against the infallibility of the Church, for the Pope has often erred, and he who asserts the contrary, is in error. Then is the Church also no longer infallible. If from embarrassment, uncertainty, or on the ground of inopportuneness, the Council pronounces no decision on this matter; then is the Pope left in fact in the exercise of that infallibility, which for centuries he has claimed *de facto*, especially by the recognition of the Immaculate Conception of the Blessed Virgin,

[12] Since May 1867, the *Allgemeine Zeitung* has published upon this inquisitor several articles, which have been duly appreciated in the *Historisch-Politische Blätter*, (vol. lx., p. 854, *seq.*), as well as in other publications.

[13] "The right of private conviction," p. 96, *seq.* Leipsic, 1869.

[14] On the part of Frohschammer, it is not to be wondered at if he calls the Definition of the 8th December, 1854, a "real alteration of the faith by a Papal Cabinet order" (*loc. cit.*, p. 218). But what shall we say when Janus (p. 34, *seq.*), after he has observed that a few years ago Pius IX. *declared* the Immaculate Conception of the Blessed Virgin a part of divine revelation (and which declaration the whole Episcopate before and after loudly approved), points out

the definition whereof by the Pope involves a practical claim and exercise of Pontifical inerrancy."[15]
And in the review of the work of our Janus, the same writer observes:[16] " The authors of this book think to help the Church when, in the place of the gross *Papal system*, the *episcopal system* has been set up. But here, in our opinion, they are under a delusion, and remain but half way in their course. In the face of *this* history of the Papacy, with all its forgeries, pretensions, errors, and immoralities, which, in conformity with the aim of the popedom, must needs apply to the whole Church and penetrate it, it is *impossible* longer to assert the infalli-

that now *again* (consequently, as at the former period) that *contempt for old ecclesiastical tradition*, so characteristic of the Jesuits, is to be pursued? He who can so speak evidently concurs not in the Papal "Declaration." And yet the Council of Basle, in its thirty-sixth session, declared, Doctrinam de Immaculata Conceptione Deiparæ Virginis tanquam piam, et consonam cultui ecclesiastico, fidei Catholicæ, rectæ rationi, et S. Scripturæ *ab omnibus Catholicis approbandam, tenendam et amplectendam S. Synodus definit et declarat.* Had the Council of Basle been really Œcumenical, there would have been scarcely any need of that much less explicit addition to the decree on original sin, which the Council of Trent, in its sess. iv., issued, and whose fathers were moreover thoroughly inclined to the pious opinion (*vide* Pallavicin. Hist. Conc. Trid. ii., 7 n., 11-23), and scarcely still should we have needed the definition of 1854. But in what contradictions are not those involved, who, on one hand, respect the Council of Basle when it takes up an attitude against the Pope ; and, on the other hand, disregard it when it proclaims a dogma sanctioned likewise by the Pope ! So already at Basle "*a contempt for the old ecclesiastical tradition*" was evinced. On the matter itself, Cf. Denzinger, "Doctrine of the Immaculate Conception of the most Blessed Virgin Mary." Second ed., especially p. 30. Würzburg, 1855.

[15] Frohschammer might even have cited the words which are found, among other things, in the Sixth Lesson in the New Office of the 8th December : "Deiparæ .... in sua conceptione de teterrimo humani generis hoste victoriam. .... Pius IX., Pontifex Maximus totius Ecclesiæ votis annuens statuit supremo suo atque *infallibili* oraculo solemniter proclamare."

[16] *Allegemeine Zeitung*, October 4, 1869. This review has also appeared in the shape of a pamphlet, under the title, "Appreciation of the Infallibility of the Pope and of the Church." Ackermann, Munich.

bility of the Church any more than the infallibility of the Pope. If the Popes, who for centuries had *de facto* deported themselves as the ' Church,' and ruled that Church, are *not infallible*, then is the Church for centuries no longer so; for the Popes arrogated to themselves this ecclesiastical inerrancy, exercised it, and even thereby abolished it, if it ever existed. From the very circumstance that this occurred, it follows that *no infallibility* was imparted to the Church; otherwise it would not have permitted a fallible organ, the Pope, to assume to himself, and even to abolish, this gift of inerrancy. What! a Church, wherein all happened and could happen, which is related to us in this book, should yet be infallible, could and must, after all this, pass as infallible! A church, in which for ages an all-pervading system of deceit and violence has prevailed, should then have still remained pure and inviolate, 'a pillar and ground of the truth!' An organism whose real vital point, whose head and heart are completely corrupted, can then still remain perfectly sound in the other members! If the extremities are attacked by disease, that disease can be cured, and be prevented from falling on the healthy organs; but if this disorder occurs in the central parts, then is all hope of the restoration of health precluded. It is thus an *inconsistent and vain endeavour* to contest the infallibility of the Pope with the utmost logical acumen, and yet to assert the infallibility of the Church herself; as this prerogative we ascribe to the Episcopate, to the bishops assembled in general council. A warm controversy must then immediately ensue, as to what councils are really œcumenical, and what not; for this is by no means fixed with certainty.[17] And if, as our pamphlet has

---

[17] We saw above (chapter ix.) that, in Janus at least, this is a matter of great uncertainty.

often pointed out, earlier councils, that passed for general, showed themselves as only the pliant instruments of Popes ruling with absolute power; where was then the infallibility of the Church, if the all-ruling Pontiff were not infallible, and the Church were obliged to obey the fallible Pope and his misused instruments, the flexible bishops. This *resting half-way*, this inconsistency, is the weak side of the work in question, and the chief obstacle to its exercising a great influence, whether in regard to the representatives of faith, or to those of science." And further on this writer urges, " If the impending Œcumenical Council really pronounces the infallibility of the Pope to be a dogma, then must the authors of Janus acknowledge that even the Church (namely, the Episcopate) can err; for it declares that to be a truth, which yet by all kinds of proof can be shown to be an error. All the facts which they have brought forward against Papal infallibility, all the assertions which they have set forth against it, then, witness against the infallibility of the Church herself; for the Church in that case pronounces dogmatically, and yet erroneously, that the Pope has never erred, never could have erred; and not merely that from henceforth he will no longer err. Then our authors must either confess that all the historical facts which they have investigated and set forth are not real, but even *fabricated;* or that they all do not signify what they yet clearly attest to every unprejudiced mind ; or in conformity with the truth and the needs of the time, they must give up the infallibility of the Church also (taking that word in the usual dogmatic sense), for whose impracticability, besides, special proofs might yet be adduced in abundance. No other alternative appears to me possible." A like conclusion another theologian likewise must submit to, who in the same way ascribes infallibility to the Episcopate united with the Pope, but apprehends, however, a catastrophe, in case this Episcopate, by virtue of its unerring decree, should adjudge to the Pope, as supreme executive organ of the Church, the prerogative of inerrancy also.[18]

It would be more consistent to carry out the historical view, and to flatter the spirit of the age, by representing the " original rights of the congregations" as having soon passed over to the priests, the rights of the priests as having been absorbed by the bishops, and those of the bishops by the Pope.[19] Here we should have a progression from Democracy to Aristocracy, and from the latter to Monarchy, and a better justification for those who wish to descend from Monarchy to Aristocracy, in order by this again to reach the Oligarchical, and then the Ochlocratic Democracy. Outside the Catholic Church, and far from the Papal system, whose antiquity reaches much beyond those modern views and hypotheses, mankind have had in this respect a very large experience. " It is a very sloping path," says Dr Döllinger, " on which religious communities have in this respect gone down. First the Byzantines cried out, ' We shall have only patriarchs, whereof each shall govern a portion of the Church; but no Pope, no head of patriarchs.' Then came the Anglican Church, and said, ' We shall have neither Pope nor patriarch, but merely bishops.' On their side the Protestants of the continent declared, ' We shall have no bishops, but merely pastors, and over them the

---

[18] *Allgemeine Zeitung*, 8th October, on the in other respects more cautious pamphlet, entitled, " Reform of the Roman Church in Head and Members. Task of the Impending Council." Dunker, Leipsic, 1869.

[19] Frohschammer, *loc. cit.*, p. 217.

princes of the land.' Later came forward the new Protestant sects in England and in other countries with the declaration, 'We need no pastors, but only preachers.' At last appeared the 'Friends' or Quakers, and several new religious bodies, who made the discovery that even preachers are an evil, and that each one must be his own prophet, preacher, and priest. How to advance a step farther below has hitherto baffled all attempts; yet in the United States, it would appear, a solution of the difficulty is already sought for."[20] Female preachers, however, have been there already established, and found hearers

Thus evermore evaporates not merely the hierarchy, but every ecclesiastical office whose establishment Protestants, who still have retained some positive belief, at present earnestly strive after. But not merely doth the hierarchy, not merely the clerical office, and every kind of spiritual *magisterium* and *ministerium* disappear, but even dogma itself, whose very name has become odious to a portion of Protestants. This party will hear nothing more of symbolical books, of rigid dogmatic systems; it recognizes no more the doctrinal, but at most only the historical Christ; it admits at most a changing, fluctuating, but no immutable and ever steadfast doctrine.[21] It still tolerates Christianity, but such a Christianity only as will accommodate itself to the "genius of the age," which will submit to all the transformations, and the arts of toilette, that the fashionable heroes of the day deem indispensable for its decorous entry into modern society.

Yet even the Catholic Church, we are told,

---

[20] "Church and Churches," p. 31.
[21] See, for example, the deliberations of the third meeting of German Protestants at Bremen. *Allgemeine Zeitung*, 11th June 1868. Append.

"*makes new dogmas*, and the old Canon of St Vincent of Lerins, '*quod semper, quod ubique, quod ab omnibus creditum est*,' is set aside, and the adherence to the ancient tradition, and to the Church of the first six centuries, is broken through" (p. 46). But against this assumption Catholic theologians protest, who unanimously assert that the Church never makes new dogmas, and that she has no inspiration.[22] The substance of Faith remains the same; but much in the lapse of ages is formally and logically developed,[23] and set forth in greater clearness, especially when any opposition has been made to a doctrine.[24] The Canon of Vincent Lerins is not merely to be understood of what is to be believed explicitly; he, like other ecclesiastical authors, expressly assumes a progress even in matters of Faith.[25] "In the simple beginnings of Christianity," says Dr Döllinger, "lie energies and germs of a civilization, which in its universal destination for all mankind, is still, after eighteen centuries, ever in a state of progress and perpetual growth; there lies a wealth of creative ideas, a fulness of new formations in Church, State, art, science, and manners, which, so far from being exhausted, will, in future times, bring forth sciences

[22] Dieringer upon Lianno's Work in the *Journal of Theological Literature*, p. 830. Bonn. 1869.
[23] S. Thom. Sum. Theol., 2. 2. q, 1. a. 7.
[24] S. Aug. Enarr. in Ps. 55, n. 22.
[25] Commonit. c. 28 : Nullusne ergo in Ecclesia Christi profectus habebitur religionis? Habeatur plane et maximus. Nam quis ille est tam invidus hominibus, tam exosus Deo, qui istud prohibere conetur? Sed ita tamen, ut vere *profectus* sit ille *fidei*, non permutatio. Siquidem ad profectum pertinet, ut in *semetipsam* unaquæque res amplificetur, ad permutationem vero, ut aliquid ex alio in aliud transvertatur. Crescat igitur oportet et multum vehementerque proficiat tam singulorum, quam omnium, tam unius hominis quam totius Ecclesiæ, ætatum ac sæculorum gradibus, intelligentia, scientia, sapientia, sed in suo dumtaxat genere, in eodem scilicet dogmate, eodem sensû eâdemque sententiâ.

and institutions, that we are yet scarcely able to dream of."[26] What applies to Christianity in general, applies more especially to dogma; and true is the word of the great Pope Gregory: "The more the world draws near to its end, the more lavishly will the stores of eternal science be opened unto us."[27] Particular dogmas must, in the course of ages, undergo no change, no mutilation, no disfigurement, but receive a more precise expression, a more suitable formulisation, a development setting forth all the consequences involved in them; they must, according to Vincent Lerins, receive evidentiam, lucem, distinctionem—evidence, light, discrimination; but they must preserve also what they intrinsically possess; plenitudinem, integritatem, proprietatem—their fulness, their integrity, their peculiarity.[28] By means of a natural process of development, a religious truth can come out at one time, or in one place, more definite, more clear, more universal, than at other times, or in other places.[29] A *new* expression of an ancient truth the Church was often necessitated to put forth; and it was only heresy, which felt itself affected thereby, that opposed this expression; whilst it otherwise indulged in the most unauthorised innovations.[30] Propositions entirely new, in former times utterly and universally unknown, can never become articles

---

[26] Döllinger's "Christianity and the Church." Preface, p. 1. (German.)

[27] Greg. M. homil. xvi. in Ezech.

[28] Commonit. c. 23.

[29] *Bossuet* Réponse à M. Leibnitz 20 Janv. 1700, n. 15 (Œuvres, t. xiv., p. 475, p. 11, n 30). Pour être constante et perpétuelle la vérité Catholique ne laisse pas d'avoir ses progrès; elle est, comme en un lieu plus que dans un autre, en un temps plus que dans un autre, plus clairement, plus distinctement, plus universellement connue.

[30] Hilar. Lib. contra Constant. n. 16: In uno novitas eligitur, in alio submovetur. Ubi impietatis occasio patet, novitas admittitur; ubi autem religionis maxima et sola cautela est, excluditur.

of faith; but such propositions may become so, as have experienced manifold contradiction from individual doctors, even though they were numerous. Before the first Council of Nicæa, there were men who did not acknowledge the consubstantiality of the Father and the Son; there were before the synods of Ephesus and Chalcedon, such as entertained very unclear notions of the Person of Christ, and had difficulties about the one Person or the two Natures; there were before the Fourth Lateran Council those who took offence at the word Transubstantiation. The Church's doctrine on Justification and on the Sacraments was not formerly set forth with that perfect lucidity, as has been the case since the Council of Trent; and even the doctrine of the Primacy of the Bishop of Rome, was more precisely formulized at the General Council of Lyons in 1274, and at that of Florence in 1439. This doctrine, especially, respecting the headship of the Supreme pastor of the Church, was, on many occasions, more definitely put forth, at other times less prominently so. We find it in different places likewise not developed with the like clearness; for where centrifugal movements more easily expanded, there the importance of the centre was in many ways undervalued. But the doctrine of the supremacy of the Bishop of Rome, as successor of St Peter, was ever firmly fixed in the Church, and no assault on that doctrine could ever prevail.[31] A growth in the knowledge of this article, also, is apparent in the history of dogmas. Here, too, we see that progress stated by Vincent of Lerins, just

---

[31] Paschalis ii. ep. 6 ad Archiep. Polon (Hard. vi. ii. p. 1770). Numquid hæc nos commodi nostri professione requirimus, et non unitatis Catholicæ statuimus firmamentum? Possunt Apostolicam sedem contemnere, possunt adversum nos calcaneum elevare; datum a Deo privilegium evertere vel auferre non possunt, quo Petro dictum est : Tu es Petrus et super hanc petram ædificabo Ecclesiam meam.

as we are able to trace it from the simple Apostolic Creed, down to the Symbols of Nicæa and Constantinople, with the addition *Filioque;* and thence again down to the Tridentine Confession of Faith, proposed by Pius IV., and which even Janus holds to be obligatory (p. 93). In this all theologians agree, that much for a long time lay more obscurely hid in the consciousness of the Church, which was afterwards more clearly enunciated, and brought to the fuller apprehension of all, and thus became the subject of the *fides explicita*.[32]

As, then, regards ancient tradition, there are two sorts of things: the tradition itself, and the written testimonies for that tradition. In the Paradosis, or Tradition, of the Church, much lived before it was committed to writing; and this fact is attested by the Fathers.[33] We must not with Febronius think that it is the first six centuries that are alone authoritative, for this is repugnant to all the principles of faith, and is tantamount to saying, that Christ has abided with His Church only down to the year 600.[34] Whoso in the fifth century would have said, "The Apostolic Fathers, and at most Justin and Irenæus, I let pass as witnesses, but not the subsequent ones," would have excited the abhorrence of the whole Church. Augustine cited as authorities Fathers of the fourth century, and even such as had been his contemporaries.[35] He who, in the sixth century, would have rejected Augustine, Ambrose, Leo; or any other of the Fathers, who were cited in' the epistle of the Emperor Justinian, read in the first session of the

---

[32] Kilber in Theol. Wirceb. Tract. iv. c. 2. a. 4. n. 102, *seq.* 111.
[33] Iren. adv. hær. iii. 1-4. Basil de Spir. S., n. 66, 75, L. ii. adv. Eunom., n. 8.
[34] De Statu Eccl., c. 2, § 1, *seq.*
[35] Aug. c. Julian, L. 1, n. 3, *seq.*

Council of 553,[36] would have been regarded as a contemner of the Church's doctrine. He who, in the thirteenth century, would not have allowed a Peter Damiani, or an Anselm of Canterbury, to stand as witnesses of the Church's teaching, would have experienced the like fate. Those, too, were regarded in the same light, who, in the sixteenth century, despised the unanimous teaching of the ecclesiastical schools.[37] It was not otherwise with the later Greeks, who looked on the patriarchs Germanus, Tarasius, Nicephorus, and Theodore the Studite, as celebrated witnesses and teachers, although belonging only to the eighth and ninth centuries, and whose Councils of the years 1156 and 1166 cited as witnesses the later as well as the earlier doctors.[38] *The question at issue is not, whether all proofs be valid, whether all documents be authentic, but as to what has been believed and publicly taught in the Church.* At all times it has been deemed rash to stigmatize doctrines not disapproved by the Church, and held by authorized doctors; and it was for this reason that the twenty-ninth proposition, among those censured by Pope Alexander VIII. on the 7th December 1690, was deemed reprehensible.[39] The consent of the Fathers was in questions of faith and of morals ever decisive; but not the opinions of individual doctors, who might easily give in to one-sided and exaggerated views, as, for example, was the case with Agostino Trionfo (p. 230). The individual teacher has authority only through the Church; a man, ever so able and learned, but whose doctrine was

---

[36] *Hefele*, Conc. ii., 841.
[37] Canus *de loc.* theol., L. viii., c. 1.
[38] *Mai* Spicil. Rom. x., p. 1–93. Script. Vet. Nova Coll. iv., p. 1–96.
[39] *Denzinger* Enchir., p. 345, n. 1186.

rejected by the Church, never could, nor ought to be, considered in the same light with others as a witness, and a doctor or teacher.[40] The Church herself was not misled by the apostasy of a Tertullian and of other great minds. The principles of the faith are so great and exalted, that a theologian who, after long years of study, explains and sets them forth, should approach his work only with a holy fear, should needs be modest and humble, and often mistrust himself whether he be capable of worthily defending those principles, or of adequately repelling the attacks of opponents, ever convinced that if *he* does not succeed, others will be enabled to execute the task in a manner better, more convincing, more scientific, especially as Providence often raises up later than men expected the right men for the right act.

We live in a period of transition to a new stage of development; we see men and times quickly and unexpectedly change. A diseased society is wont to repel the salutary remedies unsuited to its taste; the carnal man, engrossed with material objects, apprehends not the things of God; and a later generation has often looked with compassionate surprise on those that went before. In the fifth century the wonderful epistle of the great Pope Leo to Flavian was violently attacked throughout whole provinces of the Church, and in entire countries; now it beams in full lustre as a splendid dogmatic masterpiece. What if one day posterity should find in one or other proposition of the dreaded syllabus, or in a Papal bull promulgated in the new Council, a beacon of light, or an anchor of safety! The present Titanic race,

---

[40] Vincent, Lir. *loc cit.*, c. 23 : Ut omnes vere Catholici noverint, se cum Ecclesiâ doctores recipere, non cum doctoribus Ecclesiæ fidem deserere debere.

however, is unable to conceive this; it is like to the contemporaries of Noah at the building of the ark; it rejects all which it has not achieved by its own energy, and by its own act.

What! Papal bulls again! Of these we surely have had an overflow, and Janus has marred our taste for them. Let us see only what he makes out of the bull of Paul IV., " Cum ex Apostolatûs officio" (p. 382). This bull was issued at a time[41] at which, in all countries, even in those under Spanish sway, Catholicism was grievously menaced, and had to defend itself to the last extremity. Its immediate object was to renew the old ecclesiastical penalties against schismatics and heretics. It rested entirely upon that principle of public law then, still generally prevalent in Catholic countries, whereby schismatics and heretics were regarded as guilty of a most grievous crime, and were consequently incapacitated for public offices, as well as for the functions of government; and if its penal enactments affected the highest ecclesiastical as well as the highest secular functionaries, even kings and emperors themselves, so this clause is found in the decrees of the Council of Constance, which, nevertheless, is of such high authority with Janus.[42] Moreover, this bull can in no way be characterised as a dogmatic or *ex cathedrâ* one; it is a mere penal law, founded on the then prevalent principle of ecclesiastical and

---

[41] Pauli IV., Const. 19, lib. vii., c. 9, de hær. v. 3. Raynaldus (anno. 1559, n. 14) gives in full the first half of this bull. Janus (p. 383) takes everything in a strictly literal sense, as, for example, when he makes the Pope say that those converted from heresy are to be shut up in a monastery, "there to do penance for the rest of their lives *on bread and water*." But the words, in pane doloris et aquâ mœstitiæ, are figurative expressions taken from Scripture.

[42] Conc. Const. Sess. xiii., xiv., xvii., xx., xxxvii. Bianchi, t. i. l. i. § 19, p. 164, *seq*.

secular jurisprudence, which as yet was in no
Catholic country given up, and was quite analogous to the constitutions of Paul III. against
Henry VIII.,[43] of Pius V. against Elizabeth,[44] and
of Sixtus V. against Henry IV. of France.[45] The
same observation applies to the bull *In Cœnâ Domini*, depicted in such fearful colours by Janus
(p. 385), but which, since the year 1770, is no longer,
as formerly, read out on Maundy Thursday.[46] It
is an old complaint of the " Ultramontanes," that
their opponents have two weights and measures,
that they pay very accurate attention to all the
relations of time, persons, and circumstances, when
they have anything to justify or to palliate, but
not so when they are about to pronounce damna-
tory judgments ; that they then exclusively apply
to the characters and acts of earlier times, the objects of their detestation, the modern standard as
alone valid.[47] Whoever, besides, will carefully
study the Bullarium of modern times, will soon
convince himself that the Apostolic See, with all
its tenacious adherence to the principles of the
Church, knows how to take into account the ne-
cessities of the times. Wherefore have those, who
have so officiously busied themselves with the impending Council, scarcely paid any attention to
the Bull of Indiction, which certainly, however,
was the first thing to be considered ?

[43] Spondan., a. 1535, n. 15 ; a. 1538, n. 14. Bianchi, t. ii., l.
vi., § 10, n. 2, *seq*. Gosselin, t. ii., c. 3, a. 1, § 2, p. 276, *seq*.
[44] Const. 101. Spondan., a. 1570, n. 3, 4. Bianchi, l. c., n. 4.
Gosselin, l. c., p. 280, *seq*.
[45] Bianchi, l. c., n. 5. Gosselin, l. c., p. 288, *seq*.
[46] Bened. XIV., de Syn. diœc., l. ix., c. 4, n. 5, *seq*. Liguori
Theol. Moral., l. vii., n. 83. Bennettis, p. ii., t. iii., p. 524. [Dr Denzinger, in the Catholic weekly paper of Würzburg, 5th May 1855,
n. 18. Theiner Histoire du Pontificat de Clement XIV., vol. i., p.
480, *seq*.; vol. ii., pp. 52, 53, 55.
[47] The strict Roman theologians, and especially the Roman clergy

R

A movement, nay, a concussion of minds, was, under the circumstances of the times, to be expected on the announcement of a General Council. That movement may be wild and tempestuous; it is still better than a dead stagnation. We stand on the eve of a momentous event. But who could have conceived it possible that this most magnanimous act should have been treated almost as a crime? The ruling Pope, Pius IX., whom all that know him must love and revere, whose conduct has been righteous, noble, and lofty, but who, in the opinion of our Janus, is nothing more than a small, very small, successor of Innocent III. (p. 24)—an opinion which we abandon to the judgment of posterity—has, from a free impulse, and guided by the best intentions, summoned an Œcumenical Council; and for this act the numerous bishops assembled from all parts of the world at the jubilee of St Peter's martyrdom in 1867, as afterwards their colleagues not then present in Rome, tendered their solemn thanks to the Father of Christendom for his resolution, and required the faithful, in instructive, edifying, and enthusiastic addresses, to prepare themselves in spirit for the celebration of this momentous and most salutary event. Even this first act, the mere convocation of the

are (in Janus, p. 201) accused of a deficiency in theological science, of the use of spurious documents, and of ignorance in history. But with their opponents it is quite otherwise, even when they make use of spurious passages in a like degree, and are still more ignorant in theology and in history, as, for example, the Spaniard Andrew Escobar, whose "Gubernaculum Conciliorum" teems with errors. (Cf. Bennettis, p. l., t. i., p. 321, *seq.*) This Escobar (p. 380) and Alphonsus Tostatus, who from a spirit of revenge against Pope Eugenius IV., who had censured some of his propositions (see Spondanus, anno. 1447), combated the doctrine formerly defended by himself, for example, in his Com. in Matth., c. 16; these two writers are adduced as proofs, that the most distinguished Spanish theologians advocated, before the tyranny of the Inquisition, the theory patronised by Janus.

synod, is in itself, and independently of the results, a splendid achievement of the Pope. " The isolation," says the venerable Bishop of Nismes,[48] "and the state of material impotence to which events have reduced the pontiff, as well as the excitement which he foresaw he would call forth in certain social spheres, have not deterred him from this act of duty. Doubly strong, as well by internal illumination as by the warm sympathy with which the bishops concurred in his design, when he communicated it to them, he has proceeded with that calm intrepidity which, from the beginning, has characterized all the important acts of his pontificate to its realization. This unexpected manifestation of his authority has been hailed by homage of every kind. Some have honoured him by their stupefaction; others by the most singular apprehensions. Several even of those, who have never been devoted friends of Rome, have publicly offered to him the tribute of their admiration; and certainly no one can forget the words spoken on that occasion in the legislative chamber by an orator, in whom political errors have not been able to efface the feeling and the respect for all that is great and noble.[49] 'There is in this act,' says he, 'a boldness and an elevation, which fill me with respect and admiration; for I love the strong powers that confide in themselves, and fearlessly and with determination manifest and unfold the faith that animates them. This is an ennobling spectacle.'"

Joyously did the supreme pastors gather round the apostolic chair, obeying the call of their chief

---

[48] Mgr. Plantier on General Councils, xxix. German Translation, pp. 74, 75. Freiburg, 1869.
[49] Emile Ollivier, in the sitting of the 10th July 1868.

not willingly only, but with enthusiasm. Pius IX. knows full well, indeed, what his illustrious predecessor Sixtus III. once declared—" There is no body which is not governed by the head. But as every body is governed by the head, so the head itself, when not borne up and upheld by its body, loses its firmness and its power, and no longer maintains the dignity which it before possessed."[50] The present Pontiff, and those around him, know full well what Benedict XIV.,[51] together with so many theologians and canonists,[52] says, "that bishops in an Œcumenical Synod are not merely counsellors, but real judges also. The primacy and the episcopate form inseparable parts of one whole; they are most closely bound together." In no age more than in our own has this been so practically evinced; and practically many questions admit of a simple and easy solution, which theoretically, especially in consequence of the confusion into which they have been thrown by different scholars, appear very complicated. It will be, as the above-named French prelate declares, proved in a brilliant and victorious manner in the Council, nay, made evident even to the blind, that in the body of the Church head and hands have but *one* life —but one and the same thought.[53]

The respect and reverence which we owe to the Catholic Episcopate, will in no way permit us to examine the insinuations that our bishops at the approaching Council will be reduced to a position of utter servitude, and be incapable of giving expression to their own opinions. The worst and

---

[50] Ep. 10 ad Episc. Illyr. n. 4.
[51] De Syn. diœces. L. xiii., c. 2, n. 2.
[52] Many authors are cited by Zaccaria, also (Antifebronio t. I. Diss. II., c. 4, p. 140).
[53] Mgr. Plantier, § xliii., p. 113.

most insolent invectives, as they appeared in the Fourth and Fifth Articles (namely, in the 73d and 74th numbers of the *Allgemeine Zeitung*), have not been admitted into the new edition; but they are still not formally disavowed, not retracted, and are presupposed, or implicitly contained, in the effusions of our Janus. With indignation and disgust, every Catholic deserving of the name repels the outrage offered in those articles to the Episcopate, but not less so the excuse, equivalent to the severest accusation, to wit, that " we should not, and ought not, to hold these men responsible for decrees and for omissions, *which depend not upon them.*"

Our historian has here become a prophet too; he predicts the non-submission to the new Council. " The new Council can never be a really free one, and, therefore, theologians and canonists must be corrected, who have held that, without complete freedom, the decisions of a council are not binding" (p. 425). " The newly-announced Council will be held not in Italy only (and this would be already frightful enough, in despite of the Government of Victor Emmanuel working for the 'Free Church,' especially from the excessive number of Italian bishops[54]), *but also* (and this is most awful, though others know at present no freer spot in the Old World), the Council, we say, will be held in Rome itself, and it is already announced (by whom ?) that, as the *sixth Lateran Council, it will faithfully attach itself to the fifth. Thereby all is said*" (p. 369, Ger.). If all the other suppositions are as little founded as this, so little of what is true

---

[54] In Italy there are nearly seventy Episcopal sees vacant (see *Allgemeine Zeitung*, Oct. 1, 1869, No. 294); many bishops of a very advanced age; and the rights of procurators are by no means equal to those of actual bishops.

will remain in this whole book. We already know, from the space in St Peter's allotted for the Sessions of this august Assembly, that the new Council, which meets a thousand years after the eighth Œcumenical Synod, will be called not *Lateranense sextum*, but *Vaticanum primum;* and we may only trust that it will not be the last, as it is the first, in the new order of things ; and perhaps many people now regret, that instead of suspending their judgment for a time, they should with blind precipitancy have ushered it into the world.

CHAPTER XII.

THE RESULTS OF JANUS.

IF we ask what this work has achieved, the answer will not be found difficult, especially after the judgment already passed on the publication in its first form. If, as we have seen, the book was not unjustly accused "by the most advanced party" of inconsistency, and of a half-course, it is still ever welcome to the enemies of the Church, on whose children, however, it has inflicted pain and scandal. Thoughtless and lukewarm Catholics it can deceive, but the zealous as little as the well-informed, it cannot. By such a course of hostile provocation, the very opposite of what was intended is brought about; and particularly the position of those also who, in regard at least to certain wishes and many questions of opportuneness, would more or less have marched together with the impetuous assailants of the doctrine, has been seriously complicated.

"The promised investigation by the light of history (Pref. xiii.), of those questions which are to be decided at the Œcumenical Council already announced," is so one-sided and defective, so coloured by the spirit of party, that it can needs satisfy those only who here find their own ideas enunciated, who, without theological training, sit in judgment on theological subjects; a habit indeed, very common to our generation, for in these matters every one thinks himself entitled to speak, even when in other departments he rigidly holds to the Horatian maxim, *Ne sutor ultra crepidam*, and most strictly forbids all the uninitiated to meddle with his own calling.[1] But the present age, so proud of its knowledge, among so many in the educated, literary, and official circles, evinces in *theological matters* precisely a degree of unfathomable ignorance, such as no preceding age ever displayed. Even the narrowest heads and perruques of the French Parliaments of the last century, even when they gave themselves up to the most violent controversy, were far more conversant with these things, than the majority of their present colleagues under other names and robes.

"A contribution to Church history" this work undoubtedly furnishes, but in a very different way indeed from what its authors may have conceived. "For a *calm* exhibition of historical events" will never be found in the confused medley of historical data, arbitrarily grouped together; often wanting, too, in chronological order, and in arbitrarily deduced inferences, in which logic is not rarely fearfully mishandled. The reader is gratified neither with a flowing historical narrative, nor with an exposition systematically arranged, qualifying him to form his own judgment. He receives only a broth cooked out of various ingredients for mere party purposes, which, with the greatest pretension, is served up to him as the purest and most savoury dish, such as no artist in cookery has ever presented,

---

[1] Hier. ep. 53, ad Paulin, n. 7. Nulla ars sine Præceptore percipi potest; *sola Scripturarum scientia est*, quam passim sibi omnes vindicant . . . præsumant, doceant, antequam discant.

and which he, in order to find it agreeable, must regard from the same party-view. As an historian, Janus can only be classed in the category of those manufacturers of history described by a real historian,[2] "who confuse the memory of the past, who flatter the malicious demon lurking in the breast of man, as they ascribe to the most magnanimous deeds impure motives and petty causes, and delight to disfigure religion by an arbitrary misrepresentation of facts, by the complacent portraiture and prominence given to the human and impure elements accidentally mixed up with sacred things." And if all will not immediately perceive that Janus has indulged in far greater fictions, than those which he has sought to prove against the Roman Church, they will still (to continue the observations of the same historian), " by virtue of their moral instinct and love of truth, so carefully cultivated and developed, refuse to such historians precisely their confidence and their belief; they will, with a right gift of divination, even when the sources are inaccessible to them, see through these unworthy proceedings, and by approximation at least, often through the mists of ingenious misrepresentation, discern the truth.

Further, the work will contribute "to the awakening and direction of a public opinion," and, indeed, "such an opinion which, strong, unanimous, and at once positive in its faith, will resist the realization of the Ultramontane scheme"[3] (Janus, Pref. xxviii.). Here predicates are united which

---

[2] Döllinger, a discourse entitled, "Error, Doubt, Truth," p. 33. Munich, 1845.
[3] So we are only threatened with the *realization* of the "Ultramontane scheme," and it can still be checked. Elsewhere Janus supposes that it is already realized, and indeed for many centuries, and in all its hideousness!

are incompatible. Unanimity does not prevail among men who are, "some for the half and some for the whole," and where unanimity fails, there vigour fails also; and positive faith is not great where only a negation, as here that of "Ultramontanism," appears in the foreground. Hence of the two alternatives, so poetically described by Janus, as to the presumptive effects of his work, "that it may perchance produce no more permanent effect than a stone thrown into the water, which makes a momentary ripple on the surface, and then leaves all as it was before; *or yet it may act like a net* cast into the sea, which brings in a rich draught of fishes." Of these two alternatives, I say, the former has the most probability, and history will be spared the pains of transferring the narrative of the rich take of fishes by Peter to the equally rich capture by Janus. Severe and subtle dialecticians may, indeed, bring out other possibilities, and avow that the work is no stone, but a net; yet perhaps a net, which some habitants of the sea will tear to pieces, or such a one, at least, that will be drawn up without any valuable draught.

"But the principal matter is an ecclesiastico-political object: in one word, it is pleading for very life, an appeal to the thinkers among believing Christians" (pref. xiii.). It is, indeed, an appeal against non-thinkers—an appeal before judgment has been pronounced, even before any interlocutory decree—an appeal, not to the Council *beforehand* stigmatized and condemned by Janus—an appeal, not to bishops, not to theologians, but to the whole educated secular world. Was such an appeal ever before made? Singular proceeding! Where the question is to weaken and to combat Papal power, the authority of bishops is relied on; but as soon as these have done their duty in regard to the Pope, they then may go their way. If the bishops are not found to hold like sentiments with themselves, these people then turn to the educated laity. Then theological controversies are retailed in political newspapers, and inquiries, which claim an authority equal to the lucubrations of the Fathers of the Church, are printed beside theatrical and artistic notices, beside domestic and political quarrels, and the vulgar gossip of the city. As once, in the times of the Arians, when men disputed upon the "begotten and the unbegotten," upon the words "from the non-existent" and "from the Father;" as in the times of the Hesitants (διακρινόμενοι), when, under the asseveration of the most rigid orthodoxy, the celebrated tome of St Leo, and the Council of Chalcedon, the most brilliant of all the earlier Councils, were rejected with horror; now in the streets, merchants, artisans, artists of every sort, soldiers, women, and boys, and especially state-functionaries, are to discuss the doctrines about Council and Pope, the propositions of the Encyclical and of the Syllabus. The mass of the "cultivated" are to sit in judgment upon the Apostolic See, and the College of Bishops, whether dispersed or assembled in General Council; and this latter Assembly is to be made subject to conditions, on whose fulfilment the submission to its decrees will be made dependent.

Further, the work of Janus is to be a "protest, based on history (?), against a menacing future, against the programme of a powerful coalition." The future is hidden from us all; the prospects which render a conjecture possible, are solely expressed by the words, "powerful coalition." But by the side of this coalition—and who has defined it?—by the side of this coalition, we say, we find no statesmen, no powerful ones of the earth. Its supreme head has ever to struggle with menacing foes; the sword ever hangs over the heads of its most eminent defenders; and lastly, this coalition has but very small material means to dispose of, and intellectual resources it can have none; for we are told "all cultivated classes" are against it. And yet withal, this coalition is mighty! And on the other side stand science and diplomacy, and behind them numerous armies and powerful allies of every kind; for the sympathy of Protestants also has been awakened; they have been alarmed and terrified, and so converted into allies against the degenerate Papacy. For though this "serious danger threatens primarily the internal condition of the Catholic Church, yet it is, as is inevitable with what affects a Corporation including 180,000,000 of men, destined to assume vaster dimensions, and take the shape of a great social problem, which cannot be without its influence on ecclesiastical communities and nations outside the Catholic Church" (Pref., p. xiv.). Already certain classes of Protestants, hostile to all "priestcraft," have taken occasion "to conjure up the spirits of the Reformation against the Obscurantists in Rome."[4]

"The danger signalized," it is further said, "does not date from yesterday, and did not begin with the proclamation of the Council. For some twenty-four years (was it in 1845, in the time of the vertigo of Ronge? or, was it twenty-one years ago, in 1848, in the time when Germany made its first efforts for ecclesiastical freedom?) the *reactionary* movement in the Catholic Church, which is now swollen to a mighty torrent (perhaps it was a

[4] Cf. the *Literary Magazine*, entitled, "Ausland," 11th Sept. 1869, n. 37, in an article entitled, "The Roman Council," on occasion of Otho Stäeckel's translation of Hutten's Dialogue, "The Roman Trinity." Berlin.

movement reverting to its source), has been manifesting itself, and now it is preparing, like an advancing flood-tide, to take possession of the *whole* organic life of the Church by means of this Council." If the danger dates from twenty-four years back, where were then the present champions of genuine ecclesiastical life? Were they not yet born, or were they then found in another camp? Have they been sleeping and dreaming away their lives? Were they then so imbecile as not to discern the danger? Were they so servile, so cowardly, as not to signalise it, although it had already "begun to manifest itself?" We know of no answer to these questions; but that we are justified in proposing them, can scarcely be denied.

Against the " programme of a powerful coalition, in whose realization a thousand busy hands are daily and hourly at work," we should have expected a counter-programme clearly defined, which we perhaps, though with some modifications, might have accepted. But nowhere is such given, or even any satisfactory explanation afforded. For the two assertions (Janus, pref. p. xv.), the first, as to the due relation to principles of political, intellectual, and religious freedom and independence, understood in a *Christian* sense, and not in the sense of Frohschammer; and the second, as to the necessity of a reform in the Church, are infinitely wide, admit of a thousand different shades, and furnish no solid palpable groundwork.[5] In the whole work of Janus there is, amid a thousand negations, scarcely anything positive to be discerned, except it be an occasional hint that seems

---

[5] As equitable concessions, which ought to have been made in the sixteenth century (that is, before the year 1560), are mentioned by Janus (p. 370), the cup for the laity, priestly marriage, but principally the abolition of the Papal system. Like thoughts were

to point to the resuscitation of "an antediluvian Church policy" (to use the words of an ingenious Catholic writer), but which is yet not so long extinct—to the resuscitation of Gallicanism, with a small dose of Jansenism and of Febronianism, in a new historical dress. Two questions would have to be examined. In the first place, what are the existing abuses in the Church? and secondly, on what do they rest? But in nowise could it be beforehand surmised, that *all* abuses should have their foundation in the present constitution of the Papacy. For many abuses many other causes and sources might be assigned, not merely human imperfections and frailties, but many foreign influences also, such as that of the non-Catholic literature, of the encroachments of the civil power upon the Church, the materialistic tendencies of the times, and so forth; then the reaction that had become necessary against other evils, in themselves perhaps not of less magnitude; and lastly, the mildness and forbearance shown towards old, long-established institutions, and towards personal and local interests. But to achieve anything practical, we must needs have before us clearly discerned and consistently prosecuted aims; but in Janus we find nothing but inconsistency. It suffices not to boast "of *a view* of the Catholic Church and her mission, which its opponents designate by that much-abused term, so convenient in its vagueness for polemical purposes—*liberal;* a term in the worst repute with all uncompromising adherents of the Court of Rome and of the Jesuits—two powers intimately allied,[6]—and never mentioned by them without bit-

---

entertained by Febronius (Append. iv., p. 133), by George Wizel (Raynald a. 1562, n. 28), and by others. Cf. *Zaccaria* Antifebronio I., p. ix.

[6] The lord and the servant are here in our times, so much in-

The Results of Janus.

terness" (Pref. xv.); nay, with a bitterness compared with which everything said in our book against Popery and Jesuitism is but the sweetest honey. "A view in the worst repute" at Rome, yet furnishes of itself no safe remedy; this even Janus will concede, and even if one boasts of this bad repute, still one is not dispensed from the duty of alleging proofs.

The protest here brought forward really constitutes, as has been shown, a protest against the supremacy of the Apostolic See, against the authority of General Councils, against the very dogma of the Church herself. *It is a shot fired off in blind passion, reaching far beyond the mark.* Or in other words, Janus has shown all the capacity to strike out the bottom of the barrel, without turning that capacity to advantage; he has contented himself with a barrel utterly perforated. He appears like an unfortunate architect, without on that account being original and successful in the art of destroying; there remains in him too much of "the Papistical leaven," which resembles too much that of the Pharisee; while to others again he offers much too little of it.[7] If it were unavoidable to bring forward the dark sides of the Papacy (p. 21), so there was still no need of exaggerating and unduly magnifying them, and this by a misrepresentation of history. The authors, who conceal themselves under the mask of Janus, fear the reproach of an absence of piety (p. 20). But let them be

clined to democracy, suitably mentioned as allies and confederates—two great powers which are to be overturned.

[7] On the whole, Janus appears to us to have come too late. (See our 6th chapter above.) Under Pope Nicholas I., Janus would perhaps have been a Hercules, slaying the dragon pseudo-Isidore; under Louis the Bavarian, he would have been a reforming antipope; and perhaps in the flourishing times of the Congress of Ems, he might have become a German national patriarch.

tranquil on that head; where there is such an "absence of passion," there surely an absence of piety cannot be spoken of. We would fain believe that the intention of these authors was a good one; that they held it to be a duty, according to the "measure of their knowledge and their working power," to make the attempt, whether something could not be done to ward off what they deemed so fatal a catastrophe (p. xix.). But as little do we deem that the means selected were the fitting ones, as the measure of knowledge was that here required and in every respect suitable. Before any Catholic denounces to the world a "disfigurement and disturbance of the Church, and of the truth" (p. xxi.), he ought to have in hand the most valid proofs; but these have not been brought forward. Instead thereof we are furnished with materials partly old, long extant in polemical writings, fully appreciated by Catholic theologians of the last two centuries, though these have not been deemed worthy of the honour of a refutation; and again, we find materials partly new, but which signify the same thing, and lead to no other inferences. The fundamental ideas of Janus have all been earlier enunciated by Richer, Sarpi, Launoy, by the Gallicans, and the Jansenists, who well understood the stratagem of striking at the "Curia;"[8] but most completely have these thoughts been expressed by Justinus Febronius, or by John Nicholas of Hontheim. From the latter we hear the same complaints as to the abuses of the Roman monarchy[9] and of the Papal tribunals;[10] he evinces the same hatred towards the

[8] According to the Jansenists, un petit détour, qu'on use, lorsque la Cour de Rome se rend digne qu'on ait pour elle quelques ménagemens. (Notes eccles. 27, Mars 1765).

[9] C. 9, § 4, n. 4. Ep. ad. Clem XIII.

[10] C. 7, § 2, n. 1; c. 5, § 3, n. 7; c. 7, § 7, n. 6; § 8, n. 7; c. 9, § 7, seq.

The Results of Janus.

religious orders,[11] the same predilection for the writers hostile to the Popes,[12] the same aversion for canonists and jurists, the same view as to the influence of the pseduo-Isidorian decretals,[13] the same tendency to exasperate princes and bishops against the sovereign Pontiff,[14] and to further a pure episcopal system, and so to transform the constitution of the Church, according to the decrees of Constance and Basle, whose undoubted validity is likewise presupposed.[15] Not even the internal contradictions of the Febronian system, which converts bishops so highly exalted by him into mere witnesses of their communities,[16] has Janus known how to reconcile. If others think to find Janus an abriged Jansenius, we find in him but a prolonged Febronius. There is the same regard for the Protestant world ; but the reunion of Protestants with the Catholic Church is not promoted, when the unity of the latter is weakened. The ancient Bossuet could bring back many non-Catholic Christians to the bosom of the Church ; but these modern Bossuets * can only frighten them away, and rather make Protestants out of Catholics, than turn Protestants into Catholics. But we must ask ourselves, Is, then, our age really so poor in ideas, that when discontented with the present state

---

[11] C. 7, § 8, n. 7, 9 ; c. 4, § 7, n. 1.
[12] C. 5, § 3, n. 4, § 6, n. 4 ; c. 8, § 7, n. 9 ; c. 9, § 9.
[13] C. 3, § 1, *seq.*
[14] See the Addresses ad Reges et principes, ad Episcopos. In the charges against Popes Alexander V., Martin V., and Eugenius IV., for abridging or frustrating ecclesiastical reforms (Janus, p. 309, *seq.*), perfectly concurs with Febronius (c. 6, § 15, n. 2, § 20, n. 3). See the reply of Zaccaria in Antifebronio I, p. lxxxvi., *seq.*
[15] C. 6, § 1, n. 2 ; § 15, n. 3.
[16] C. 6, § 8, n. 12.

* It is needless to observe, that the great Bossuet would have looked with as much horror on a book like Janus, as Bellarmine himself.—*Trans.*

of the Church, we must have recourse to the revival of extinct theological systems, such as Gallicanism,[17] to the resuscitation of long-abandoned views, such as Febronianism, so closely allied with Josephism and Regalism ? Whom do these people hope to gain ? The strictly orthodox ? But these have often enough resisted such allurements. Is it the indifferentists and the unbelievers ? They need no resuscitated Episcopal system ; they need no decrees of Constance and Basle ; they wish, indeed, for no new article of faith set up, but would fain see all the old ones, as much as possible, abolished, and most especially those on the sacraments of penance and matrimony. We know what Febronius wrought among the Protestants ;[18] how many errors were then proved against him by German and non-German theologians ;[19] and we know, too, what from the attempted execution of his projects, ensued for the Ecclesiastical Principalities, and for the old German empire.[20] Will our age show itself more favourable to his disciples, and to those who emulate his conduct ? We may answer in the affirmative and in the negative. Affirmatively in those circles, which still live in the canon law of the courtiers and statesmen of the preceding century, and know no higher ideal than the ideal of that age. But no, and again no, in all other circles, different as they may be in their

[17] *Vide Allgemeine Zeitung*, 21st Oct. 1869. App. No. 294 (article, entitled "Catholicism in France on the Eve of the Œcumenical Council"). Here we read, "The proper Gallicanism has been so much modified, that we may say it exists no longer."

[18] New learned notices, Nova acta eruditorum. Lips. 1764, p. 1. Jablonski Instit. Hist. Chr., t. iii., p. 146. Carl Frederick Bahrdt, dissert. v., Dec. 1763, §§ vi., viii., xvi.

[19] Werner ("History of Catholic Theology in Germany," p. 212), and Phillips (Can. Law, iii., § 136, p. 372, *seq.*) specify the writings.

[20] Phillips, *loc. cit.*, p. 381 f.

principles, their position, their efforts, and their claims.

Even in the circles to which Janus belongs, its small success seems more and more to be discerned. Not in vain did a writer in the official *Moniteur* of this party,[21] the Augsburg *Allgemeine Zeitung*,[22] a "distinguished" Catholic nearly akin to Janus, and appearing under a similar signature, recently show that the *political* importance of the infallibility of the Pope and *of the Church*, is *still not sufficiently appreciated;* that on the part of liberals, Rome's power is too much undervalued; and that by a course of instruction suitable to the age, the people must be emancipated from the dogma of Infallibility. In the same article there are many other proposals and insinuations, full of benevolence towards the Catholic clergy, and pointing to an emancipation of the people from the fetters of authority.[23] It was thought that the

[21] This epithet is the more justified, as the above-named organ will give publicity to no other views, and as I perceive from the criticism of Professor Merkle (p. 2, n. 1), that I have just received, closed its columns against his refutation of the falsehood propagated about Pope Alexander III. On the other hand, the same journal in its Appendix, 21st Nov. 1869, brings up, as I am now writing, an essay signed A. W., upon the confessors of princes, and which shamefully reviles the Catholic Sacrament of Penance, and serves up the most barefaced historical falsehoods, twice only giving its authorities, one the pretended "Catechism of the Jesuits," printed at Leipsic, 1820; and the other the infamous "Monita Secreta," a work which has been long proved to be a fabrication of their enemies. Yet in despite of this fact, the same work is incessantly brought up by Protestant preachers down to II. A. Bergmann (Leipsic, 1867); but by all learned inquirers it has been cast into the literary lumber-room (see the Bonn *Journal of Theol. Lit.*, No. 9, p. 329, 1867). Such historical productions are indeed worthy of the journal, in which the good Catholic Janus has thought proper to depose the fruits of his profound researches.

[22] *Allgemeine Zeitung*, 7th Nov. 1869. Extra Append. No. 311, Nov. 8.

[23] That even in the conferences respecting the new election struggles in Bavaria, the impending deliberations of the Œcumenical

impressions already produced on the readers of the paper might, by continued efforts, be renewed; and that by a repeated dose of the medicinal powder, the success already obtained might be further promoted. To revive the courage of the party the essay, entitled "The Bishops and the Council," was particularly serviceable;[24] for in this the warnings of the bishops of Hungary, Bohemia, and Germany, in Rome, were spoken of, as well as the success they had thereby attained; inasmuch as the scheme of proclaiming the dogma of Infallibility by way of acclamation appears to be given up.

We are not informed of the proceedings in Fulda, and know nothing of the letters of the bishops of Bohemia and Hungary; we have no Roman accounts as to the views and measures of the Papal congregations in recent times; but we think that these and other notices from such a source, as the *Allgemeine Zeitung*, are to be received with more than usual caution.[25] When we are informed that all hope has vanished, that the Council could conclude its labours in three weeks, so to all those who for a time had in a single commission been engaged in the preparatory labours, this statement would, even in February and March of last year, have appeared extremely ludicrous; and in fact no one, with the exception of a French journal and its malicious echo, has seriously believed in this report. It would almost appear as if the *Augsburg Gazette*

Council were made a subject of comment, we learn from a Munich correspondent of the *Allgemeine Zeitung*, 5th Nov. 1869, No. 309.

[24] *Allgemeine Zeitung*, 19th and 20th Nov. 1869. Append. No. 323, *seq*.

[25] Moreover in Rome also there is, as in the rest of the world, a pretended mortified ambition; from Rome, too, as from other capitals, false reports can be propagated. During the sittings of the Council, this will occur in a still greater degree. For this the Catholics of Germany must hold themselves prepared.

would fain secure for itself an honourable retreat. A further step is made, when *now* in connexion with the abandonment of the mode of acclamation, it is believed that measures have been introduced, whereby the bishops *may confer and deliberate on the matters proposed to the Council;* as if from the beginning this course were not of necessity presupposed, but were originally excluded from the plan of proceedings. If in the sittings of the preparatory Commissions, the members of the minority could, even under the presidency of a cardinal, defend with the fullest energy their divergencies of opinion; if in the mere prelude to the Council, a freedom of discussion was permitted, such as is not easily found in any other well-regulated assembly; then how could the design be possibly entertained of withdrawing from *the Bishops* the right of conference and deliberation, that by a much stronger title belongs to them? The insinuation is as absurd as the scornful mockery about " *the head-clerk of all the clerks of the Council*" is frivolous; while the factious summons to the bishops, " to make an attempt to *reconquer* their old apostolic (he might have added their inalienable) rights, which the Papacy had either abridged or wrested from them," is quite in the spirit of Justinus Febronius.[26] But this article could not conclude without giving a supplement to the historical exposition of Janus, and which in a second edition of that work, must certainly be incorporated into it. I should be obliged, as I am anxious to send my manuscript to the press, to add a new chapter, were I to expose, as they merit, the new charges heaped against the Popes. Yet some will I briefly touch on. The persecution of English

---

[26] According to Febronius (c. 8, § 6, cf. c. 9, § 9), no præscriptio, cessio, possessio, consuetudo can protect the popes.

Catholics, that lasted for centuries, was, it seems, brought about by the prohibition of Pope Paul V. against their taking the oath of allegiance to their kings.[27] "Although that oath, it is said, contained nothing repugnant to the religious principles of Catholics, yet the Pope declared it to be reprehensible, because identifying the well-being of the Church with his arrogated rights, he could not endure that this oath should state, that the Pope hath no power and authority to depose kings, to absolve subjects from their allegiance, and to excite against sovereigns and the state rebellion and outrages." Paul V., indeed, in 1606 and 1607, condemned the oath demanded by King James I.,[28] because it was unlawful, and on several points was openly opposed to faith and to the welfare of souls; and as it was in itself, and was intended to be but a disguised oath of supremacy, which Catholics could not take, the Pontiff was fully justified in the course he pursued. For in the sense of the oath, even supreme ecclesiastical authority is ascribed to the King as an absolutely sovereign ruler; and at the conclusion, the Catholics were called upon to confess, that the oath wherein even questions of faith were treated of, had been lawfully imposed by a full and competent authority. Next, the oath condemned an opinion, held by many men of high authority in the Church, *as godless and heretical;* and this neither individual Catholics, nor any secular power, had the right to do; and lastly, in order to render the Roman Church odious, it falsely imputed to it the doctrine, that princes excommunicated could be *slain* by any private individual at his will. If Bel-

---

[27] *Allgemeine Zeitung.*, 20th Nov., Append. 1869. Cf. Defensio declarat. Cleri gallic., t. i., P. ii., l. viii. (al iv.), c. 23.
[28] The Formula is to be found in Rapin Thoyras Hist. de l'Angleterre, t. vii., l. xviii., anno 1606.

larmine, Suarez, and others, alleged theological arguments for the indirect power of the Church; yet neither Paul V., nor any other Pope, bound English or other Catholics to hold this opinion as an article of faith; but even quite independently of this consideration, the condemnation of this form of oath was perfectly justified.[29]

We see, indeed, in what quarter excitement, restlessness, dread, and the pain of uncertainty prevail; we see how no means are left unattempted, in order to work on the public mind to confirm more and more the historical views of the party, and to propagate various reports of the like tendency. So again it is reported from Vienna,[30] that a letter has been addressed by the Roman Curia to certain eminent prelates, which appears, indeed, very questionable; though to many, in truth, it will appear but too probable, that it is precisely the clamour raised about the Papal prerogatives, and the action of the "non-Ultramontanes," which seem calculated to necessitate the Council to pronounce upon questions which, in Germany, England, and France have been agitated with so much violence and rancour. Let us hope that this heat will cool down by degrees, and that moderation and prudence will return.

Far more decorous, cautious, and measured is a small pamphlet that has recently appeared;[31] though this, too, moves in the same circle of ideas as Janus, and in a summary way reflects much of that production. But the twenty-six theses here

---

[29] *Vide* Gosselin, l. c., pp. 282–288, where the literature on this subject is given. On the decrees of Popes Nicholas V. and Alexander VI. likewise cited, see *ibid.*, pp. 269–271. Bianchi t. xi., l. vi., § 9, p. 568, *seq.*

[30] *Allgemeine Zeitung*, 23d Nov. 1869. Append.

[31] "Considerations for the Bishops of the Council respecting the question of Papal Infallibility," p. 17. October 1869. Munich.

laid down mostly want the ulterior proofs; and if we are to seek these in Janus, we shall certainly not find a firm and solid basis for these allegations. We meet with too many apodictic judgments, that yet on a closer examination turn out to be very problematical. That here no St Bernard, no Fenelon speaks, the reader will immediately discover. How any one can assert[32] that it was *only* by coercion and violence, and by the putting down of all dissentients, the opinion of Papal Infallibility could spread, is to us utterly inexplicable. This doctrine was yet advocated in France by eminent theologians,[33] and in despite, too, of the greatest disfavour on the part of the Court, and amid much opposition; while the contrary view enjoyed every kind of official patronage, and was thereby able to spread elsewhere. From the fact that, on the 20th January 1626, Papal Infallibility was proclaimed in France with a degree of spontaneousness which certainly was wanting to the Declaration of 1682, and from the very great number of Infallibilists of all countries and ages, of all positions and callings, including men of solid learning and holy lives, it is morally impossible, as well as most offensive to the whole Church, to represent the diffusion of this doctrine as brought about by acts of tyranny. In reference to the alleged forgeries, the author of the "Considerations" completely coincides with Janus; and so, likewise, with regard to the asserted obligatory force of the decrees of Constance and Basle, which

---

[32] "Considerations for the Bishops," p. 15. 22d Thesis.
[33] Cf. the above cited work of Gérin on the Assembly of 1682, which furnishes rich materials on the subject. Also Charlas de libertat. Eccl. gallic., L. vii., c. 10, *seq.*; c. 13. Bennettis, P. I, t. i., p. 303, *seq.* Zaccaria Antifebronio, 1. Introd., c. iv., p. lix. j., *seq.*

The Results of Janus. 281

the by far greater portion of the Church has not recognized. In short, we here find a recurrence of the same theory, of the same view as to the present state of the Church, which for so long a time has experienced, borne, nay, approved of a frightful disfigurement.[34]

Independently of the suspicions cast upon the defenders of Papal Infallibility, who for the greater part are represented as members of the great Monastic orders, entirely dependent on Rome, then again, as partly Cardinals, partly candidates for the Cardinalitial dignity—yet among these are not to be included very many eminent theologians belonging to the secular clergy, who never became Cardinals, nor ever canvassed for the Roman purple;[35] independently of these imputations, we say, the writer especially insists, that with the assumption of Papal Infallibility is *indissolubly* connected the acceptance of the doctrine also, "that the Popes possess an *unlimited* power over all princes and magistrates, over all states and commonwealths; that they can *at their good pleasure* interfere with sovereign power in *all* affairs of civil government, depose princes, overthrow laws, and decide on questions of peace or war."[36] But here the theological opinion respecting the indirect power of the Church in temporal matters is misrepresented and unduly extended,[37] and the writer

---

[34] As to what position (according to Janus) the Bishops are to take with regard to their "communities," this pamphlet, which in all appearance is destined for the ecclesiastical aristocracy, says not a word. It appears almost like an editio castigata in usum Delphini.

[35] P. 15. 23d Thesis. See Merkle's Critique on this, p. 38, *seq.*

[36] P. 13. 19th Thesis.

[37] Cf. the opinion of the Theological Faculty of Würzburg of the 7th July 1869, ii., § 27, *seq.* The author of the Introduction to the Cologne edition of the Encyclical and of the Syllabus of

overlooks the fact withal, that if Bellarmine, Suarez, and others held this for a dogma, this was their private sentiment, which could bind no one, nor reduce the defenders of the opposite opinion to silence. In the same way as the doctrine of Papal inerrancy did not thereby become a *dogma*, from the fact that these theologians held it for such, so this is the case also with the doctrine of the indirect power. Not all theologians who defend the former, advocate the latter also in the same degree; very many consider it only as a *sententia certa*, which is very far from being a *dogma*. Nay, even in Rome authors of the highest authority say precisely, that the doctrine of the indirect power in temporals is *no dogma*.[38] That this is not to be inferred from the Bull of Pope

---

1864, cites, at p. 18, a passage from the Manual of Canon Law by the Jesuite Tarquini, printed in Rome with a triple approbation. The passage runs as follows:—" In temporal affairs, and with regard to temporal objects, the Church has no power in civil society. Thence it follows, that civil society, even when consisting entirely of Catholics, is not subordinated to the Church, but is completely independent of it. . . . In things in which the aim of civil society, directly or accidentally (per se vel per accidens), comes into collision with the object of the Church, that is to say, with the salvation of souls, and with eternal life, there must temporal prosperity, or the aim of civil society, be postponed to the salvation of souls, and to eternal life, that is to say, to the object of the Church." To this the author of the Introduction subjoins—" Whoso, indeed, does not believe in the value of the immortal soul, nor in hell, will find it foolish that eternal life, when it cannot be purchased otherwise than by the surrender of an earthly advantage, should require and deserve the sacrifice of the latter. But if Catholics, who are no unbelievers, hold the opinion that *the independence of each of the two powers should not be pushed to the essential detriment of ecclesiastical authority*, so no one, without offending against the laws of logic, can represent this view as a denial of the independence of the state."

[38] Bianchi, *op. cit.*, L. i., § 19, n. 6, p. 166; § 21, n. 1, p. 184. Gosselin II., p. 293, 294, with the authors cited in note 2. Cf. Card. Sfondrat. Gall. Vind. Diss. ii., § ii., *seq.* Phillips' Canon Law, ii., § 116, p. 627.

Boniface VIII. we have already seen. That the interpretation given by the ablest theologians, and supported by numerous documents, would lead to the "ruin of all scientific dogmatic theology," is an assertion, indeed, which should be first scientifically proved. If it really be the case, as the *Allgemeine Zeitung* stated in its Appendix of the 18th November 1869, that Doctor Von Döllinger has composed these "Considerations," then has he certainly, in this pamphlet at least, *not* surpassed his former works, and has not secured for himself the predicate of "the greatest theologian of the present day." Neither age, which of itself does not protect from errors, nor earlier rendered services, which furnish no charter to later times, nor the distinctions received from secular and from ecclesiastical authority, which do not always promote Christian humility, can in the learned world—with the exception of some blind admirers and flatterers, whose existence has but too clearly manifested itself in our daily press—exalt the author above the ancient saying, "tantum valet, quantum probat," *he has no further value than his proofs. The Church of God stands higher in our estimation than any personage, howsoever highly respected.*

But a Church given up to darkness and to corruption, forsaken of God in a way as is here more gently insinuated, and by Janus more rudely expressed—that is no longer the Church which the Catholic represents to himself, when he says, *I believe in One, Holy, Catholic, and Apostolic Church.*

Yet an institution, which ages have revered as the holiest and the most august in the history of the world, will certainly not, by newspaper articles and pamphlets, be robbed of this veneration; she will rise the higher in the love of her members, the more impure is the spirit that dares to assail her, the more odious the means which it has employed for that purpose, the more evident the sophistry which it has poured forth. "If a man hardeneth his will against the truth, so he hardeneth thereby his understanding also."[39] This is his affair; he may shoot forth arrows from the dark, they fall back upon his head. The Church of God remains what she was; she remains great amid the modern heathenism as she was great amid the old, in the present disrupture of nations, as in the early migration of peoples; and, unembarrassed by all these sophisms and misrepresentations, by all these calumnies and assaults, millions, after many, many years, will yet exclaim in Fenelon's last words: "O Roman Church! O holy city! O dear and common home!"[40]

Great historical antagonisms—questions which ages scarcely dared to agitate—they are to be settled, they are to be brought to a final solution in a time so convulsed, so diseased, and so tempestuous as our own. There, where the principle of authority is at stake, men have ventured to put forth criminal hands in order to debase in the eyes of the multitude that supreme power, which, whether they discern or deny the fact, is a prop for all other authorities; to represent it as built and consolidated on empty fraud; to prepare the way for those who regard all religion as nought else but priestly craft, and the Deity itself as but a "fiction," and thereby to undermine all the foundations of moral and social order. But what thrones are, beside profaned altars; and what kings are, beside outraged priests—this the history of the last centuries has shown in legible characters; this

---

[39] In malevolam animam non introibit sapientia, Sap. i. 4.
[40] Card. Bausset Vie de Fénélon, t. ii., p. 170, *seq.*

The Results of Janus. 285

is shown by the words and confessions of avowed Revolutionists, a Proudhon, a Victor Hugo, a Louis Blanc, a Mazzini. What the French Jansenists, as the outposts of the Revolution, sowed, and what they reaped, this is known to all the world. And if we would make a survey of the many congresses held under various titles in Switzerland, in Belgium, in Germany, in Italy, in Spain; and if we would submit to a closer inspection the acts of the last peace-congress of Lausanne, or of the International Association of Labourers in Basle; truly our statesmen, our scholars, and educated classes would find matter for the most serious reflections, and could trace the approach of a storm, which to them, and to their interests, would be far more noxious than even to those of the Church. In this way to render good service to the Revolution, as is done by our modern Febronians, appears still the business of short-sighted men, who see not, or would fain not see, the final result of their policy. Wilful corrupters of mankind, who push all things to the abyss, which widely gapes before a deluded generation, are happily on the whole but very rare phenomena—the number of the deluded is so much the greater.

These are the considerations which, on the reading of Janus, have pressed themselves on my mind. "The *important literary phenomenon*, from which the Ultramontane party has hitherto timidly slunk away,"[41] could not remain without a decisive answer, and this was to be given as quickly as possible. Renouncing the statement of my own thoughts and wishes in regard to the Council, and bent only on repelling the malicious assaults against the Apostolic See,—assaults which by no

---
[41] *Allgemeine Zeitung*, 24th October 1869.

exaggerations and one-sided views of particular individuals, however lamentable they may be, can in any way be justified;—I enter a solemn protest against this book of Janus in the interest of science, which has been here utterly abused, as well as in the interest of the Church, which has been shamefully outraged; while at the same time, mankind at large are but ill served by sophistries and misrepresentations. However troubled the relations of the present times may be, I faint not, I despair not, of Christian nations, to whom God's mercifulness hath not denied the cure even of grievous maladies,[42] nor do I despair of the final triumph of justice, which is everlasting and immortal.[43] I confide in the power of divine truth, which strengthens faith, which purifies knowledge, which vivifies love, which secures unity in the bond of peace. I believe in One, Holy, Catholic, and Apostolic Church.

[42] Sanabiles fecit nationes orbis terrarum. Sap. i. 14.
[43] Justitia enim perpetua est et immortalis. Sap. i. 15.

APPENDIX.

Testimonies of Distinguished German Protestant Historians, in favour of the Moral and Political Influence of the Popes and Bishops of the Middle Age, referred to at Chapter 10, p. 217 (German).

MANY years ago, I appended the present note to my Translation of Frederick Schlegel's "Philosophy of History." It was suggested by the remark of that Catholic writer, that eminent German Protestants had had the merit of dispelling many modern prejudices as to the political umpirage exercised by the Popes in mediæval times. When I made these quotations for the benefit of my Protestant countrymen, I little thought that I should have ever had occasion of using them against pseudo-Catholics, like the writers of Janus. These, by their gross misrepresentations and calumnies uttered against the Papacy, have not only outraged the feelings of all Catholics, but even run counter to the sentiments of the most learned and impartial of their own Protestant fellow-countrymen.—(*Trans.*)

To show my readers the enlarged and enlightened views taken by the Protestant writers of that country on the political influence of the Papacy in the Middle Age, and on the services which at that momentous period the hierarchy rendered to the cause of social order, liberty, and civilization, it were easy to transcribe matter more than sufficient to fill a volume. Let a few examples suffice:—

"'The northern nations,' says the celebrated historian of Switzerland, John von Müller, 'rushing in upon the most beautiful countries of Europe, trampling under foot or disturbing and convulsing all social institutions, menaced the whole western world with a barbarism similar to that which, under the Ottoman sceptre, has obliterated everything good, great, and beautiful that ancient Greece and Asia had produced. Yet the Bishops and other dignitaries (Vorsteher) of the Church, strong in their authority, contrived to impose a restraint on those giants of the north, who as regards intelligence were but children. They would not have been more successful than the Greek prelates, had they been subject to four different patriarchs. The Popes of Rome (whose primitive history is as obscure and defective as that of the ancient Roman Republic, since we know little of the first Popes, except that they devoted their lives for the faith, as Decius had done for his country);—the Popes, we say, with the same address which we admire in the ancient Senate, to render their see independent, subject to its immediate action the whole western hierarchy, and establish its sway far beyond the boundaries of the ancient Empire on the ruins of the northern religions. Thus, whoever refused to honour the Christ, trembled before the Pope; and one faith and one Church were preserved in Europe amid the breaking up and subdivision of the newly-founded kingdoms into a thousand petty principalities. We know what Pope made Charlemagne the first Emperor; *but who made the first Pope? The Pope, they say, was only a Bishop.* Yes; but at the same time the *Holy Father*, the *Sovereign Pontiff*, the great *Caliph* (as he was called by Ho-Albufreda, Prince of Hamath), of all the kingdoms and principalities, of all the lordships and cities of the west. It is he who controlled by the fear of God the stormy youth of our modern states. At present even, when his authority is no longer formidable, he is still very puissant by the benedictions which he showers; he is still an object of veneration to innumerable hearts, honoured by the kings who honour the nations, invested with a power, before which, in the long succession of ages, from the Cæsars to the House of Hapsburg, a host of nations and all their great names have vanished.'

"'We declaim against the Pope, as if it were such a misfortune that there should exist an authority to superintend the practice of Christian morality, and to say to ambition and to despotism, 'Halt! so far and no further! Bisher und nicht weiter!' So speaks the illustrious John von Müller.

"The celebrated Herder allows, 'that without the Hierarchy, Europe in all probability had become the prey of tyrants, the theatre of eternal wars, or even a desert.'

"'The Hierarchy,' says Beck, 'opposed the progress of despotism in Europe, preserved the elements of civilization, and upheld in the recollection of men, what is so easily effaced—the ties which bind earth to heaven. Those ignorant men, as we affect to call them, have settled almost all the countries of Europe. The fruits of that time are the formation of the third estate, whence dates the true existence of nations, and the establishment of cities, wherein social life and true liberty were developed.'—*Beck on the Middle Age*, p. 13. Leipzic, 1824.

"'The weak,' says Rühs, in his 'Manual of the History of the Middle Age,' 'then found in spiritual authority a better protection against the encroachments of the powerful than afterwards in the so-called balance of power—a system, which as it was a *thing purely abstract, devoid of all external guarantee*, must soon have lost all influence. The Pope was always present to terminate the wars, which had broken out among Christian princes, and to protect the people against the injustice and tyranny of their rulers. The Clergy, therefore, everywhere showed themselves opposed to the power of kings, when the latter wished to become perfectly absolute. They wished not to domineer over them, but to confine them within the legitimate bounds of their authority. The priesthood were, consequently, always for princes, when vassals attacked the rights of the sovereign. They were the natural and constant guardians of the rights and liberty of all classes.'— *Manual of the History of the Middle Age.* 1816.— *Trans.*)"

Vide Frederick Schlegel's "Philosophy of History," translated by myself, Bohn's edition, p. 361. Seventh edition, 1859. Bell & Daldy, London.

INDEX NOMINUM ET RERUM.

The Figures denote the Page.

Acacian Schism, 65, 136.
Agatho, P., 60, 128.
Alexander III., P., 23.
Alexander VII., P., 91.
Allgemeine Zeitung, 1, 70, *et passim.*
Ambrose, St, 96.
Arian Heresy, 136.
Armenian Church, 141.
Athanasius, St, 112, *seq.*
Attrition, 92.
Augustine, St, 67, 77, 96 (n. 3), 130.
Austria, 40.

Baius, 91.
Baptism, Infant, 76.
Basil, St, 114, *seq.*
Basle, Council of, 199.
Bavaria, 5, 39.
Benedict XIII., Anti-P., 18.
Benedict XIV., P., 55.
Bernard, St, 100.
Bishops, 260.
Bonaventure, St, 99, 100.
Bull, "Auctorem Fidei," 2.
Bull, "Cum ex Apostolatûs Officio," 256.
Bull, "In Cœnâ Domini," 257.
Bull, "Unam Sanctam," 7, 203, *seq.*
Bull, "Pastor Æternus," 202.

Capernaite Doctrine, 85.
Celestine III., P., 85.
Chalcedon, Council of, 124, 127, 138, 147.
Charlemagne, 156.
Chrysologus, St, 67.
Chrysostom, St, 97, 130.
Church, 3, 4, 240, *seq.*
Civiltà Cattolica, 1, *seq.*, 10, 15.
Clement, P., 109.

Concordat with S. America, 35.
Confirmation of Councils, 124, 159.
Congress of Basle, 7.
Constantine, Emp., 146.
Constantinople, See of, 138.
Constitutum, Sylvestri, 149.
Convocation of Councils, 120, *seq.*
Cullen, Card., 17 (n. 3).
Curia, 9, 72, 226, *seq.*
Cyprian, St, 111.
Cyrill, St, 117, *et n.*

Damascene, St John, 96.
Dante, 70.
Decretals of Pseudo-Isidore, 64, 158.
Decretum of Gratian, 170, *seq.*
De la Mennais, 24.
De Maistre, 24.
Dionysius, P., 112.
Dionysius Exiguus, 153.
Döllinger, 59, 106, 283.
Donation of Constantine, 155, 156.
Düsseldorf, Cath. Assembly of, 7.

Emile Ollivier, 259.
Emperors, 120.
Ephesus, Latrocinium of, 120, 123.
Eugenius, IV. P., 88 *seq.*, 181.
Eutychian Heresy, 135.

Fabian, P., 110.
Filioque, 181.
Florence, Council of, 179 & (n. 109), 202.
Forgeries, 144, *seq.*
Francis of Sales, St, 19.
Franks, Epistle to the, 157.
Frohschammer, 21 (n. 14), 244.
Fulda, Bps. assembled at, 7.

Gelasius, P., 132, 135, 150.

Index.

General Councils, 186, *seq.*
Gesta Xysti, III., 150.
Gratian, 170, *seq.*
Gregory the Great, 139.
Gregory VII. P., 167, 192, 218.

Hegesippus, 109.
Heretics, 177 (n 105).
Historisch-Politische Blätter, 11.
Honorius, P., 79.
Hormisdas, P., 65, 153.
Hugo of St Victor, 101.
Hyacinthe, Père, 7.

Immaculate Conception, 19.
Infallibility, Papal, 16, 20, *seq.*; 50. *seq.*; 281, *seq.*
Innocent I., P., 117 *et n*., 132, 135.
Innocent III., P., 87.
Innocent X., 92.
Inquisition, 236.
Irenæus, St, 108.

James I., King of England, 23, 278.
Jansenism, 92, 241.
Janus, 14, 25, 69, *et passim.*
Jerome, St, 96 (n 4).
Jesuits, 1, 5, 8, 20, 33, 69.
John XXII., P., 87.
Joseph, St, 18.
Julius, P., 74, 160 (n 44).
Justinian, II., Emp., 66, 124.

La Luzerne, Card., 24.
Lateran, First General Council of, 192.
Lateran, Second General Council of, 193.
Lateran Council, Fifth, 202.
Latrocinium of Ephesus, 189.
Leo I., P , 121, 135.
Leo X , P., 210.
Liber Pontificalis, 154.
Liberius, P., 75, 114.
Lyons, First General Council of, 193, *seq.*

Magna Charta of England, 35.
Manning, Abp., 17 (n. 3).
Marcellus of Ancyra, 74.
Martin V., P., 28, 198.
Melchior, Canus, 53.
Meletius of Antioch, 136.
Middle Ages, 44.
Monothelitism, 79.

Nicæa, General Council of, 188.

Nicholas I., P., 83, 128, 162, *seq.*
Nicholas II., P., 85.
Nicholas III., P., 87, 88.

Oaks, Synod of the, 189.
Œcumenical Councils, 2, 8, 143.

Paul III., P., 24.
Pelagius I., P., 68.
Pepin, King of France, 157.
Peter, St, 61, *seq.*; 97, 138, 140.
Phillips, 118, 132.
Pichler, 51.
Pisa, Council of, 196.
Pius IX., P., 258, *seq.*
Photius, 130.
Polycarp, St, 109.
Popes, 2, 67, 71, 94, *seq.*; 120, 131, 217, *seq.*
Presidency of Councils, 122.
Primacy, 108, *seq.*
Probabilism, 20.
Pseudo-Isidore, 130, 138, 145, 158, *seq.*

Sardica, Council of, 117 *et n*., 129.
Schneemann, 17 (n. 2), 31.
Schrader, S. J., 33.
Sinuessa, Pretended Synod of, 149.
Siricius, P., 132, 135.
Sixtus V., P , 91.
Soter, P., 110.
Stephen II., P , 83.
Stephen III., P., 128, 156.
Supremacy, Papal, 95, *seq.*
Syllabus, 15, 18, 27, *seq.*
Syncellus, Office of, 170.

Tertullian, 64.
Theodoret, P., 67.
Thomas Aquinas, St, 176.
Tradition, 253.
Tractoria of P. Zosimus, 78.
Trent, Council of, 4, 210, *seq.*
Trullo, Council in, 125–130.
Tyana, Council of, 116.

Victor, P., 110.
Vigilius, P., 78, 121.
Virgin Mary, 19.

Westphalia, Treaty of, 34.
Witchcraft, 237.

Zosimus, P., 77, 151, *et n*.

PRINTED BY W. B. KELLY, 8 GRAFTON STREET, DUBLIN.

8 Grafton Street, Dublin.
December 1, 1870.

BOOKS PUBLISHED AND OTHERS IN QUANTITY KEPT IN STOCK

BY

W. B. KELLY.

THE IRISH ECCLESIASTICAL RECORD: A Monthly Journal, conducted by a Society of Clergymen, under Episcopal Sanction. Now in its sixth year of publication. Vol. vi., 1869. Imprimatur Paulus Cardinalis Cullen, Archiepiscopus Dublinensis. Terms for Great Britain, per annum, 6s.; by post, 7s.—Payable in Advance. Single Copy, 8d.; by post, 9d.

THE DIRECTORIUM ASCETICUM; or, Guide to the Spiritual Life. By JOHN BAPTIST SCARAMELLI, S.J. Translated from the Italian, and edited at Saint Beuno's College, North Wales. With Preface by His Grace the Archbishop of Westminster. 6s., crown 8vo, cloth neat, vol. 1., or by post, 6s. 6d. To be completed in 4 vols. early in Spring 1870.

COLLECTIO OMNIUM CONCLUSIONUM ET RESOLUTIONUM, quæ in causis propositis apud sacram congregationem cardinalium S. Concilii tridentini interpretum prodierunt ab ejus institutione anno MDLXIV. ad annum MDCCCLX., distinctis titulis alphabetico ordine per materias digesta cura et studio Salvatoris Pallottini s. theologiæ doctoris et in Romana curia advocati.

Associationis conditiones.

I. Hoc Opus Quindecim Voluminibus constabit quæ Folio LXXX. seu paginas 640 in-4 duabus distinctas columnis continebunt atque in X Fasciculos distribuentur paginas LXIV complectentes.
II. Unoquoque mense unus vel duo Fasciculi prodibunt: I et II jam prodierunt.
III. Solventur pro singulis Fasciculis 2 25. Vol 1. now ready, 24s. In half ellum.

DE LUGO (JOHANIS, S.J.) DISPUTATIONES SCHOL-
ASTICÆ ET MORALES. Eight Tomes, 4to, sewed, just completed,
£6, or Cash £4, 10s. Paris, 1869.

BIBLIOTHÈQUE DES PRÉDICATEURS (la) (Réimpression
du grand et magnifique ouvrage du R. P. Vincent HOUDRY, de la Compagnie de Jésus). Environ 18 vol. grand in-8, de 700 à 800 pages. Il parait un volume tous les deux mois.—Seize volumes sont en vente. Prix de chaque volume, nett, 5s., or for cash, 4s. 6d.

Cet ouvrage est, sans contredit, le plus riche et le plus solide recueil que nous possédions sur less matières de la prédication. Aussi, la réimpression en a-t-elle été encouragée par NN. SS. évêques, et, il y a quelque temps, le R. P. Marin de Boylesve, excellent juge en pareille matière, écrivait a l'éditeur. *This work is now completed.*

A TREATISE ON THE KNOWLEDGE AND LOVE OF
JESUS CHRIST. Translated from the French by Father SAINT JURE, S.J. With an original Sketch of the Author, by a member of the Order of Mercy. Now ready, in 3 vols. 8vo, cloth, 691 pages, £1, 11s. 6d.

KUHNER'S ELEMENTARY GREEK GRAMMAR AND
EXERCISES, translated, with Greek-English and English-Greek Lexicon. By C. W. BATEMAN, LL.B., Scholar, Trinity College. 12mo, bound, 663 pages, 6s. 6d. Key to the Exercise in same, 2s. 6d.

LIVES OF THE ENGLISH SAINTS; Projected and partly
Edited by the Very Rev. JOHN HENRY NEWMAN, and others, of the Oxford School, original editions, published by Mr Toovey, of London, viz.:—

ST AUGUSTINE OF CANTERBURY, Apostle of the English,
and his companions, St Mellitus, St Lawrence, St Peter, St Justus, and St Honorius; together with some Account of the Early British Church. 2 vols. in one, cloth, elegant, 3s. 6d.

ST GERMAN, Bishop of Auxerre, in Burgundy. 2 vols. in one,
cloth, elegant, 3s. 6d.

STEPHEN LANGTON, Archbishop of Canterbury. 12mo,
cloth, elegant, 2s. 6d.

LECTURES ON SOME SUBJECTS OF MODERN HISTORY AND BIOGRAPHY; History of Spain in the Eighteenth Century. Religious and Political Institutions of Spain. Reply to Mr Buckle's Civilisation in Spain. Life, Writings, and Times of Chateaubriand. Secret Societies of Modern Times, viz.:—Freemasons, the Illuminati, the Carbonari, the Jacobins, St Simonians, Socialists, &c. Papal Legislation on Secret Societies. Delivered at the Catholic University of Ireland, 1860 to 1864. By J. B. ROBERTSON, Esq., Professor of Modern History; Translator of Schlegel's "Philosophy of History," Moehler's "Symbolism," &c. Crown 8vo, cloth extra, over 500 pages. 6s.

THE LIFE OF FATHER DE RAVIGNAN, OF THE SOCIETY OF JESUS. From the French of Father de Ponlevoy, Translated at St Beuno's College, North Wales. Crown 8vo, 710 pages, cloth, elegant, 9s.

THE INNER LIFE OF THE VERY REVEREND PÈRE LACORDAIRE, of the Order of Preachers. Translated from the French of the Rev. Père Chocarne, O.P. (with the Author's permission). By a Religious of the same Order. With Preface by the Very Rev. Father Aylward, Prior-Provincial of England. Post 8vo, gilt edges, 7s. 6d.

SERMONS ON SUBJECTS OF THE DAY (with Portrait of the Rev. Father Burke, Order of Preachers), delivered by Distinguished Prelates and Theologians, at the Second Plenary Council of Baltimore, United States, October 1866; together with the Papal Rescript and Letters of Convocation, &c. To which is added the FUNERAL ORATION ON O'CONNELL, pronounced by Father Thomas Burke, O.P., at Glasnevin Cemetery, County Dublin, in May 1869, on the occasion of the removal of the remains of Ireland's Liberator to their final resting-place; and Sermon on the SOLEMN TRIDUUM. *Second Edition.* Crown 8vo, boards, neat, 250 pages, price 2s., by post 4d. extra.

The Volume contains Sermons by

Most Rev. M. J. Spalding, D.D., Archbishop of Baltimore.
Most Rev. John M'Losky, D.D., Archbishop of New York.
Most Rev. John B. Purcell, D.D., Archbishop of Cincinnatti.
Most Rev. P. R. Kenrick, D.D., Archbishop of St Louis.
Right Rev. P. N. Lynch, D.D., Bishop of Charleston.
Right Rev. S. H. Rosecrans, D.D., Aux. Bishop of Cincinnatti.
Right Rev. James Roosevelt Bayley, D.D., Bishop of Newark.
Right Rev. Wm. H. Elder, D.D., Bishop of Natchez.
Right Rev. James Frederick Wood, D.D., Bishop of Philadelphia.
Right Rev. John M'Gill, D.D., Bishop of Richmond.
Right Rev. James Duggan, D.D., Bishop of Chicago.
Very Rev. J. T. Hecker, Superior of the Paulists.
Rev. J. L. Spalding, S.T.L., of Louisville.
Rev. P. J. Ryan, of St Louis.
Rev. Father Burke, Order of Preachers.

THE FATHERS, HISTORIANS, AND WRITERS OF THE CHURCH, Literally Translated: being Extracts from the Christian Classes. 12mo, cloth extra, 4s. 6d.

Contents.

Sulpicius Severus.	St Augustine.
Eusebius.	St Jerome.
Acts of the Apostles.	Tertullian.
Socrates.	St Eucherius.
Sozomen.	Salvian.
Theodoret.	St Bernard.
Minutius Felix.	St Chrysostom.
St Cyprian.	St Basil.
Lactantius.	St Gregory Nazianzen.
St Ambrose.	St Gregory of Nyssa.

"A useful Manual for those who would attain to a general acquaintance with the early Christian writers."—*Athenæum.*

‌‌* For recommendation of this work see *Irish Ecclesiastical Record.*

A GENERAL HISTORY OF THE CATHOLIC CHURCH,
from the commencement of the Christian Era until the present time. By M. L'ABBE DARRAS. With Introduction and Notes by the Most Rev. Dr SPALDING, D.D., Archbishop of Baltimore. 4 vols. royal 8vo, cloth, plates, £2, 8s. ; for cash, £2, 2s. nett.

CATHOLIC PRAYER BOOKS, with Epistles and Gospels, elegantly printed in 48mo. Bound in various styles, viz. :—Ivory, Morocco, Russia, Calf, Cape, and Cloth, from 6d. to £1, 1s. each.

* A large assortment of Prayer Books in English, French, German, Italian, and Spanish Languages. Various styles of binding and prices.

IRISH VARIETIES; OR, IRELAND'S HISTORY MADE INTERESTING. From Ancient and Modern Sources and Original Documents. Containing an Historical, Antiquarian, and Anecdotal Description of the South-East Coast of the Bay and Counties of Dublin and Wicklow, viz. : —Dalkey, Dunleary, Kingstown, Killiney, Shanganagh, Bullock, Bray, and the Rochestown Hills. With four Illustrations in Chromo-lithograph, drawn by B. NYE. To which is added the only complete account ever published of the Mock "Kingdom of Dalkey," its Revels and Re-Unions in the last Century. By J. J. GASKIN, Author of "A Memoir of Lord Carlisle." Crown 8vo, cloth neat, price 6s., by post, 6s. 6d.

"It would not perhaps be more difficult for a stranger with only half-a-day at his disposal to make himself acquainted with the many and striking beauties of the places in the neighbourhood of Dublin, Dalkey, Killiney, Howth, Bray, Shanganagh, and others, than it is for a reviewer with only a few lines at his disposal to discuss the very multifarious attractions of a book like Mr GASKIN's IRISH VARIETIES. It professes to deal with the Historical, Topographical, and Archæological associations of the places enumerated ; but the word association has to be taken in a very large sense, if it is to embrace, as by right, all the topics contained in these entertaining pages. We can only wish it every success, as it certainly deserves."—*The Month.*

THE SHAM SQUIRE: THE REBELLION IN IRELAND, AND INFORMERS OF 1798. By WILLIAM J. FITZPATRICK, Biographer of Bishop Doyle, Lord Cloncurry, Lady Morgan, "Ireland before the Union," &c.

* Eighth Thousand, with many additions and recent revelations, valuable hitherto unpublished documents, and illustrations from contemporary portraits. Post 8vo, boards, 2s. 6d., or by post, 2s. 10d.

DUBLIN: W. B. KELLY, 8 GRAFTON STREET.

www.ingramcontent.com/pod-product-compliance
Lightning Source LLC
Chambersburg PA
CBHW030305240426
43673CB00040B/1068